Public Intellectuals

Public Intellectuals: A Study of Decline

RICHARD A. POSNER

HARVARD UNIVERSITY PRESS

Cambridge, Massachusetts
London, England   2001

CIP data available from the Library of Congress

ISBN 0-674-00633-X (alk. paper)

Contents

Public Intellectuals

Introduction

> This made [Arthur] Koestler an uncomfortable presence, who
> brought disruption and conflict in his train. But that is
> what intellectuals are for.[1]

> The correspondence between the decline of the great public
> intellectuals and the resurrection of the professors is
> thus no mere coincidence.[2]

$\mathcal{T}$HIS BOOK reflects a long-standing interest of mine in the phenomenon of academics' writing outside their field or, what often turns out to be the same thing, writing for a general audience. But it has more immediate stimuli as well. One is the discussion, in my book on the Clinton impeachment fiasco, of the contemporaneous public commentary on that remarkable episode by philosophers, historians, and law professors.[3] The commentary was of surprisingly low quality on the whole, but I made no effort in my book to account systematically for this surprising fact. Second, a review I did for the *New York Times* of public intellectual Gertrude Himmelfarb's book on the crisis (as she sees it) of contemporary American society[4] provoked a surprising number of comments, many positive. It had struck a chord and led my longtime editor at Harvard University Press, Michael Aronson, to suggest that I attempt a fuller analysis of the deficiencies, as they seemed to me, in the treatment of political and social questions by

---

1. Tony Judt, "The Believer," *New Republic*, Feb. 14, 2000, pp. 40, 46–47.
2. Tony Judt, *Past Imperfect: French Intellectuals 1944–1956* 297 (1992).
3. Richard A. Posner, *An Affair of State: The Investigation, Impeachment, and Trial of President Clinton* 199–216, 230–245 (1999). Some of this discussion appears in revised form in Chapters 3 and 10 of this book.
4. Richard A. Posner, "The Moral Minority," *New York Times Book Review*, Dec. 19, 1999, p. 14, reviewing Gertrude Himmelfarb, *One Nation, Two Cultures* (1999).

1

"public intellectuals"—intellectuals who opine to an educated public on questions of or inflected by a political or ideological concern.

The third event that stimulated this book was my appointment in November 1999 to mediate the Microsoft antitrust case, which had drawn a raft of public commentary from economists and law professors. When I got into this extremely complex case I realized that most of the commentary by this segment of the public intellectual community, to the extent disinterested,[5] reflected only a superficial engagement with the facts; it was little better than kibitzing.

But when I first began to think about the *general* subject of the public intellectual, I found myself at sea. The subject seemed formless—the term itself, "public intellectual," undefined; the activities of public intellectuals, whoever they were exactly, too heterogeneous to be squeezed into a common analytical framework; the nature of the media's and the public's interest in public-intellectual "work" unclear; the borders between that work and other cultural domains such as journalism, politics, and scholarship hazy; problems of measurement and evaluation insoluble. The world of public intellectuals seemed, in short, random and chaotic. But as my thinking and research progressed, the subject began to assume a manageable shape. The term "public intellectual" could, I found, be defined in a way that would demarcate a coherent albeit broad body of expressive activity. Different genres of public-intellectual work so defined, some with surprisingly rigid conventions, could be described. Secular trends and demographic patterns became discernible, along with possibilities for measurement and for objective evaluation. Public-intellectual work could be seen as constituting a market and a career and could be analyzed in economic and sociological terms and compared with other markets and other careers. Reliable judgments about it—not all negative, either—began to seem possible.

The fuller study that informs this book reveals that public-intellectual work indeed has a structure, has patterns and conventions, is coherent and intelligible—yet part of that structure turns out to be an absence of the quality controls that one finds in other markets for goods and services, including the market for academic scholarship. The consequence is a striking variance in the quality of public-intellectual

5. Some of the commentators were in the pay of Microsoft or its competitors.

work, coupled with a low average quality—low, and maybe falling, though it would be more precise to say that public-intellectual work is becoming less distinctive, less interesting, and less important.

No blanket condemnation of the modern public intellectual, academic or nonacademic, is intended or would be warranted, however. Distinguished representatives of each group will be found in Chapter 5's list of the hundred most prominent public intellectuals (along with a number of the distinguished dead) as measured by frequency of mentions in the popular media, an undiscriminating measure from the standpoint of intellectual distinction but a good indicator of which public intellectuals have the public's ear. Some of these modern public intellectuals, such as Henry Kissinger, Patrick Moynihan, Robert Solow, Milton Friedman, Gary Wills, and James Q. Wilson, are distinguished ornaments of American public life.[6] Yet intellectual quality may not even be the most valuable attribute of public intellectuals. Public-intellectual goods, I shall argue, are entertainment goods and solidarity goods as well as information goods; and I am not such a killjoy as to disparage intellectuals for entertaining an audience (I am more dubious about solidarity building). "Information," moreover, must be understood broadly to include the work of public intellectuals in clarifying issues, exposing the errors of other public intellectuals, drawing attention to neglected issues, and vivifying public debate. Nor is it clear how many other markets in symbolic goods would display fewer signs of "market failure" than the public-intellectual market if subjected to the same close and critical scrutiny that this book attempts, or that "market failure" is even a correct characterization of this market. But as William Blake said, bless relaxes, damn braces, so my emphasis is critical rather than celebratory. And there is much to criticize.

There is nothing new about casting a jaundiced eye on the modern public intellectual.[7] Nor about suggesting, as I shall also do, that a major cause of justifiable disappointment with him or her is the rise of

6. See, for example, Alan Wolfe, "Not the Ordinary Kind, in Politics or at Harvard: A Flawed Social Scientist with a Political Agenda? Or a Politician Whose Insights Inform His Studies?" *New York Times* (national ed.), Sept. 9, 2000, p. A15.

7. See, for example, Russell Jacoby, *The Last Intellectuals: American Culture in the Age of Academe* (1987; reprinted in 2000 with new introduction); Jacoby, *The End of Utopia: Politics and Culture in an Age of Apathy* 117–123 (1999); Tony Judt, *The Burden of Responsibility: Blum, Camus, Aron, and the French Twentieth Century* (1998); note 2 above. For a gentler critique, old but still timely, see Richard Hofstadter, *Anti-Intellectualism in American Life*, ch. 15 (1966).

the modern university[8] and the concomitant trend to an ever greater specialization of knowledge.[9] Not that specialization is a bad thing; quite the contrary. But not all its consequences are good. As the more illuminating term "division of labor" brings out, specialization works its magic by breaking up tasks into smaller and smaller components, enabling quicker learning, sharper focus, faster completion, and so greater productivity. The modern university is the symbol and principal locus of the division of intellectual labor. Knowledge is divided into disciplines, and disciplines into fields, and fields into subfields, so that an academic might devote the whole of his or her scholarly career to the stained glass windows of the Cathedral of Chartres that depict the trades, or to the history of world's fairs, or to the theological relation between late medieval nominalism and the Reformation, or to the philosophical implications of quantum theory.[10]

The depth of knowledge that specialization enables is purchased at the expense of breadth, while the working conditions of the modern university, in particular the principle of academic freedom backed by the tenure contract, make the intellectual's career a safe, comfortable one, which can breed aloofness and complacency. These tendencies are furthest advanced in American universities. That may be why so many of the most distinguished academic public intellectuals active in the second half of the twentieth century were foreigners—such as Raymond Aron, Hannah Arendt, Michel Foucault, Jürgen Habermas,

8. And of the think tank, which I treat as a quasi-academic institution. See Chapter 1.

9. See Josef Joffe, "The Decline of the Public Intellectual and the Rise of the Pundit," in *The Public Intellectual: Theory and Practice* (Arthur M. Melzer, Jerry Weinberger, and M. Richard Zinman eds., forthcoming), for an analysis and conclusion similar to mine. Edward Said also sees specialization as incompatible with the role of the public intellectual, but for unconvincing psychological reasons, such as that "as a fully specialized literary intellectual you become tame and accepting of whatever the so-called leaders in the field will allow." Edward W. Said, *Representations of the Intellectual* 57 (1994). But the trend itself, toward ever greater specialization of knowledge, seems undeniable. See, for example, Aloysius Siow, "Tenure and Other Unusual Personnel Practices in Academia," 14 *Journal of Law, Economics, and Organization* 152 (1998).

10. Joffe, note 9 above, at 7, points out that whereas in 1960 political science was broken down into five subdisciplines, by 2000 this number had risen to 104. Robert T. Blackburn and Janet H. Lawrence, *Faculty at Work: Motivation, Expectation, Satisfaction* 294 (1995), reports that between 1978 and 1988, twenty-nine thousand new scholarly journals were launched. On the growth in specialization in university research, see also id. at 118–119, 293–294.

Friedrich Hayek, Leo Strauss, and Amartya Sen[11]—even though American universities achieved ascendancy over foreign universities during this period. But of course they did so in part by hiring refugees, such as Arendt and Strauss, and other foreigners, such as Sen.

Not all intellectuals are professors, even today, but most are. Today, then, the typical public intellectual is a safe specialist, which is not the type of person well suited to play the public intellectual's most distinctive, though not only, role, that of critical commentator addressing a nonspecialist audience on matters of broad public concern.[12] That is a niche role, perhaps little more than a walk-on part in the play of politics, culture, and society. And often the wrong things are criticized. But it is *something*, and something for which few modern academic intellectuals have the requisite perspective, temperament, character, and knowledge. Their efforts to play the role are likely to yield little more than mistaken prophecy and superficial policy advice. Nowadays, moreover, because of the information overload under which the public sweats and groans, to gain traction as a public intellectual an academic normally must have achieved, however adventitiously, a degree of public fame or notoriety. Without that it is difficult to arouse the interest of even a sliver of the nonacademic public in one's opinions on matters of concern to that public. Many public intellectuals are academics of modest distinction fortuitously thrust into the limelight, acquiring by virtue of that accident sufficient name recognition to become sought-after commentators on current events. Some of them are what the French sociologist Pierre Bourdieu calls *le Fast Talker*.[13]

11. Not always an easy classification to make. In the statistical analysis in Chapter 5, I classify Arendt as an American, since, although she came here as an adult, her academic career and most of her public-intellectual writing was done in America and was in English.

12. "Specialized scholars and specialized scientists, notwithstanding their professional achievements, are likely to become a nuisance if not a positive danger when they make grand pronouncements pertaining to public choices." Theodore W. Schultz, *The Economics of Being Poor* 222 (1993).

13. Perhaps including Bourdieu himself, though he is a distinguished scholar. His book *Acts of Resistance: Against the Tyranny of the Market* (1998), which he describes as a public-intellectual work ("public position-taking," id. at vii), and in which he identifies the defining characteristics of the intellectual as "freedom with respect to those in power, the critique of received ideas, the demolition of simplistic either-ors, respect for the complexity of problems" ("The Negative Intellectual," in id. at 91–92), is in fact a superficial left-wing rant against the market economy.

But those are not the public intellectuals mainly discussed in this book. The Camille Paglias of public intellectualdom are not my targets, although I cannot resist a glance at her extraordinary career (see Chapter 3). The public intellectuals I shall mainly discuss are distinguished academics. Their difficulty in contributing to social betterment is the failure of a market rather than of individuals. And it is not a complete failure; I shall give examples of worthwhile contributions that modern academic public intellectuals have made. Many of those contributions, however, are better regarded as modest extensions of academic work (for example, translating it into language that the lay public can understand) than as distinctive contributions of public intellectuals; they bespeak the academic moonlighting as journalist. And many of the distinctive contributions are negative in the sense of combating the fallacies and follies of other public intellectuals. I believe that it is fair to say that the position, the contribution, most precisely the social *significance* of the public intellectual is deteriorating in the United States and that the principal reasons are the growth and character of the modern university.

The book is in two parts. Part One looks at the public-intellectual enterprise as a whole. It is taxonomic, theoretical, and empirical, the emphasis and approach being social scientific, though there is a good deal of anecdotal material as well. On the theoretical side it is a study in the economics of symbolic goods, a nascent, as yet rather ill-defined branch—illustrated by Tyler Cowen's book *What Price Fame?* (2000)— of the economics of nonmarket behavior. By symbolic goods I mean goods the principal content or function of which is expressive or informational: art, propaganda, journalism, and scholarship are all examples.[14]

Part One distinguishes the public intellectual from other types of "knowledge worker," distinguishes among different types of public intellectual (for example, the commentator on current events versus the critic of social trends) and among different formats of public-intellectual work (for example, the magazine article versus the full-page paid advertisement), distinguishes among the different goods that the public

14. The term is used in a different sense by Elias L. Khalil in his article "Symbolic Products: Prestige, Pride and Identity Goods," 49 *Theory and Decision* 53 (2000), the sense denoted in his subtitle, and by the sociological literature that he cites.

intellectual peddles (entertainment goods, solidarity goods, and credence goods), and identifies the various genres of public-intellectual work and the conventions that define those genres. The genres include translating one's scholarly work into a form that the general educated public can understand (self-popularizing, we might call this), making specific policy proposals based on one's academic specialty, politically inflected literary criticism, political satire, jeremiads and other prophetic commentaries on public issues, general and specific social criticism, proposing social reform outside one's field, "real time" commentary, and, the least important, expert testimony in court. The first two genres, self-popularizing and "own field" policy proposals, are the least interesting from the standpoint of analyzing what is distinctive and problematic about public-intellectual work, and so I do not discuss them at any length.

Part One also provides an economic framework for the study of the public intellectual conceived of as following a career in a market shaped by demand and supply, and it tests the implications of the theoretical analysis with empirical data. The data are both qualitative and quantitative; the statistical study of public intellectuals in Chapter 5 is the first comprehensive such study.[15]

Among the points emphasized in Part One are the decline of the independent intellectual; the debilitating impact, to which I have already alluded, on the public intellectual of academization and specialization of knowledge; the tendency of a public intellectual's media celebrity to be inverse to his scholarly renown; the problem of quality control that afflicts this market as a result, among other things, of a failure to keep track of public intellectuals' frequently mistaken diagnoses and prognoses; and the fatuity of supposing that the "marketplace of ideas" can be relied upon to optimize the performance of the public intellectual, given the serious knowledge deficits of his audience in an age of specialized knowledge and the incentives and constraints that play upon him. At least when conceived of as someone who is attempting to make a serious contribution to the improvement of public understanding, the public intellectual lacks accountability, an essential attribute of sellers

15. There is a previous statistical study of public intellectuals, Charles Kadushin, *The American Intellectual Elite* (1974), but its scope is quite limited. I discuss it in Chapter 5.

in a well-functioning market. He lacks it in comparison not only to the academic doing academic work but also to the journalist, the politician, and the policy analyst.

Part One culminates in the statistical analysis in Chapter 5; Part Two begins with a chapter on literary criticism as a public-intellectual genre. The shift in topic and, more, in method may startle some readers. In contrast to the social scientific emphasis and approach of Part One, the dominant perspectives in Part Two are those of philosophy, literary criticism, law, and intellectual history. The book thus bridges the "two cultures" of the famous debate between public intellectuals C. P. Snow and F. R. Leavis (see Chapter 6). Like Snow, I regard the social sciences and the humanities as complementary rather than antagonistic systems of inquiry. Both are necessary for a rounded view of the public intellectual. The relation of the two systems, indeed, is ultimately one of mutual dependence. Part Two substantiates claims in Part One, goes beyond definition to an explanation of the varied genres of public-intellectual expression, and deals in depth with some of the most interesting and ambitious, and not merely the typical, public intellectuals active in the United States today. In Part Two we'll see a number of different ways in which public intellectuals can go wrong in addressing public issues. We'll see public intellectuals who try to force fields new to them into the Procrustean bed of their own discipline, or who plunge into new fields without attempting to master them, or who bend facts and law to fit their political preconceptions. Looking back we'll discover that Part One has provided the tools for explaining the fundamental deficiencies in public-intellectual work that Part Two explores.

The first genre discussed at length in Part Two, politically inflected literary criticism, is the domain of literary critics and scholars who seek a general public by hitching their political commentary to works with which the public has at least a nodding familiarity. I have in mind not those literary scholars, like Stanley Fish and Michael Warner, who leave literature behind when they talk about political or other public issues, nor those literary scholars who have turned from the literary canon to nonliterary texts that have a political character (Fish again), but rather those who use accepted works of literature as commentaries on public issues. I claim that usually when they do this they are impoverishing literature, even when they are dealing with so overtly "political" a work as *Nineteen Eighty-Four* (see Chapter 7). Orwell's novel, like Dickens's *Hard Times* and Huxley's *Brave New World*, is a political satire.[16] That is a genuine, and historically very important, public-intellectual genre as well as one distinct from politically or ideologically inflected literary criticism. Orwell was one of the twentieth century's preeminent public intellectuals, as Dickens was of the nineteenth. Orwell was not an *academic* public intellectual. He was not even a university graduate. But these deficits (which he shared with Dickens) may well have been assets in his career as a public intellectual. Yet I shall argue that the public-intellectual aspect of Orwell's greatest novel, political satire though it is, is not necessarily the most interesting. This is another clue to the limitations of literary criticism as a genre of public-intellectual work.

Next up is the ever-popular jeremiad—the identification and denunciation of decadent trends (a "dolorous tirade," as one dictionary defines "jeremiad"). This is a more popular genre of public-intellectual work than those genres that are tied to literature, because it appeals to a wider audience. Few Americans have much interest in literature, but everyone is interested in where the United States is headed. Along with the rest of the world it *seems*[17] to be headed toward ever greater freedom, both personal and economic. The first trend disturbs social conservatives, the second egalitarians. But because the collapse of Marxism and growing prosperity have demoralized and disoriented the economic Left, contemporary Jeremiahs are to be found largely on the Right. Examples are Robert Bork and Gertrude Himmelfarb. There are counterexamples, however, such as Robert Putnam and the late Christopher Lasch.

The jeremiad illustrates but does not exhaust the prophetic strain in public-intellectual discourse. The jeremiad is governed by particularly strict conventions (it must be nostalgic, pessimistic, predictive, and judgmental) and assumptions, for example that of the unity of culture; without that assumption, trends in popular culture or sexual behavior would not have political significance. Other public-intellectual prophets, such as the eco-catastrophists (see Chapter 4), while no less gloomy

16. Orwell wrote another great political satire—*Animal Farm.*

17. By putting it this way I am emphasizing the high degree of uncertainty involved in extrapolating to the future from current trends. See Chapter 4.

than the Jeremiahs, do not insist on the unity of culture and in fact display little interest in cultural trends.

Next I take up the efforts of philosophers to reclaim the fallen mantle of Socrates, for it is that martyred gadfly philosopher, rather than the religious prophet Jeremiah, who is the patron saint of public intellectuals. But his emphasis was on criticism, and to a lesser extent reform, of existing institutions rather than on predicting the worst, though this is not to deny that Jeremiah's purpose was also to criticize, gloomy prophesying being merely the vehicle. Among Socrates' present-day successors I have picked out two well-known liberal philosophers, Richard Rorty and Martha Nussbaum, to focus on, the former more critic than reformer, the latter more reformer than critic. Both are social democratic in politics; their politics, indeed, are indistinguishable. Yet Rorty believes that the central philosophical tradition of the West is a stumbling block to achieving social-democratic goals, while Nussbaum believes it indispensable to their achievement—and Allan Bloom, her political opposite, believes the tradition indispensable to *preventing* their achievement. I shall argue that the tradition, and philosophy more broadly, have little to offer social critics and social reformers—except distraction from the practical considerations that determine the success or failure of efforts at social reform.

Rorty and Nussbaum are "general" social critics in the sense of ranging over a broad menu of public topics; they differ from "own field" policy proposers in roaming well outside the conventional boundaries of their fields. By the term "special" critics I refer to those public intellectuals who confine themselves to issues of particular importance to their group—blacks writing about the problems of blacks, lesbians about the problems of lesbians, and so forth—and seek their audience primarily among the members of that group rather than among a larger public. The general and the special critics overlap. A number of "general" Jewish intellectuals have written about Jewish issues without, however, making those issues the focus of their work. And some of the work of the special-interest public intellectuals is directed as much to the general public as to the members of their group. One thinks especially of black writers such as James Baldwin and Richard Wright, and, today, such black scholars as Orlando Patterson, William Julius Wilson, Shelby Steele, Patricia Williams, and Randall Kennedy. These public-intellectual scholars write primarily about the problems of blacks but are read by whites interested in the nation's racial problems, as well as by blacks; indeed there is some resentment in the black community about the degree to which the work of public intellectuals is oriented toward a white audience.[18] Nevertheless, any worthwhile analysis of the special critics would have to delve deeply into the issues concerning their special groups. Such an inquiry would carry me too far afield, and so I largely forgo it in this book. I have discussed a little of this work elsewhere.[19]

By "real time" commentary I refer to the interventions of public intellectuals in ongoing public controversies—the activity epitomized by the participation of Zola and other intellectuals in the debate over the guilt of Captain Dreyfus. That was a legal case; and because law so pervades American life, transmuting disputes of every character into legal disputes on which academic commentary is sought, real-time commentary on legal cases is a major activity of our public intellectuals.[20] I examine this activity, but I also examine the public intellectual in the courtroom, a related but distinct role from that of commentator on a case. Expert witnesses are increasingly a fixture of litigation, and not only in cases involving scientific or other technical kinds of issue. The witness box has provided an occasional though infrequent platform for public intellectuals. I question whether it is an appropriate forum for the expression of public-intellectual views.

The Conclusion examines possible measures for improving the performance of the market for public intellectuals by encouraging fuller disclosure of academics' public-intellectual activities and earnings in order to make them accountable for their forays into the public arena. I do not wish to silence the public-intellectual voice but to help it sound a steadier note.

Table 5.1 in Chapter 5 lists 546 public intellectuals who are either American or, if foreign, have a "presence" in current American social thought; and the list is incomplete. The activities of these public intel-

---

18. See Michael Eric Dyson, *Race Rules* 60–61 (1997). Some black scholars, like Stephen Carter, are not particularly focused on race issues at all, though Carter has written some about them, and so are "general" rather than "special" social critics in my terminology.

19. See, in particular, Richard A. Posner, *Overcoming Law*, ch. 18 (1995), discussing Patricia J. Williams, *The Alchemy of Race and Rights: Diary of a Law Professor* (1991).

20. The latest such episode, the commentary on the litigation that followed in the wake of the deadlocked 2000 presidential litigation, is discussed in Chapter 3.

lectuals cover an enormous range of media, formats, genres, and subject matter, not to mention periods (though only public intellectuals active in the twentieth century are included), quality, and nations. A complete analysis within the compass of a single book by a single author is out of the question. I am not aware of another book that covers as much of the ground as this one does, however, although a cardinal omission is the situation of the public intellectual today in countries other than the United States. Intellectuals are more respected in most western European and Latin American nations than they are in the United States and are therefore more likely to be solicited by the print and electronic media for comment on public matters. In France, leading intellectuals are media stars. Exploring the reasons for the cross-cultural differences in the status of public intellectuals would be a fascinating project, but it is not the project of this book, which considers foreign intellectuals only insofar as they have a presence in the U.S. cultural scene. I will merely venture the suggestion that countries with a smaller, more homogeneous governing class (the class of leaders in government, business, education, the professions, and the news media) than the United States will tend to give a more prominent role to public intellectuals. The public intellectuals in those countries, having been drawn from the same class as the political leadership and the business and technological elite, having attended the same schools and traveled in the same social circles, and sharing the same manners and mores and general outlook with the other members of the class, will, even if their stance is oppositional, tend to have more credibility with, indeed to be a part of, the nation's establishment. But I cannot develop this point within the compass of this book. A further difficulty of attaining a global perspective on the public intellectual is that public-intellectual work, like most political work, tends to be local, focused on the political and ideological concerns of a particular society.[21]

The systematic study of the intellectual, including the public intellectual, has been the domain primarily of historians and sociologists. I do not emphasize history in this book,[22] and I take more of an eco-

21. For a good example, see Jan-Werner Müller, *Another Country: German Intellectuals, Unification and National Identity* (2000). Tony Judt's books on French intellectuals, cited in notes 2 and 7 above, are exemplary studies of foreign intellectuals.

22. On the modern history of the public intellectual, see *Intellectuals in Politics: From the Dreyfus Affair to Salman Rushdie* (Jeremy Jennings and Anthony Kemp-Welch eds., 1997). See also Richard Hofstadter, *Anti-Intellectualism in American Life* (1966).

nomic approach to the subject than is customary. But I draw on sociology as well, in particular on Max Weber, an academic public intellectual of uncanny foresight. In its Weberian aspect the book is continuous with my earlier book *The Problematics of Moral and Legal Theory* (1999), which subjects a number of moral and legal theorists to a scrutiny similar to what I subject the public intellectual to in this book. I should add that if Weber is a guide, several other sociologists, including Daniel Bell and David Riesman, and Robert Putnam, a political scientist writing as a sociologist, are among the distinguished public intellectuals whose work I criticize.

So that is the book in a nutshell, and the reader will have gleaned that it is indeed critical rather than celebratory of the academic (though not only the academic) public intellectual. But the reader may sense here the paradox of self-reference. Am I not an academic public intellectual?[23] No longer a tenured academic, but tenured, nevertheless, for a number of years (thirteen and a half, to be exact), I was a full-time academic and am still one part-time, writing out of my field, writing not only judicial opinions and scholarly books and articles but also book reviews for the *New York Times* and the *New Republic* and a book on the Clinton impeachment called "journalistic" by Ronald Dworkin[24]—and writing this book, which I hope will interest not only academics. And worse: scoffing at declinists (see Chapter 8—"The Jeremiah School") yet contending that the public intellectual is in decline. And are not people often particularly acute at spotting their own weaknesses (of which they are unaware) observed in other people?

All true. I am aware that the arrows I shoot may curve in flight and hit the archer. The reader shall judge.

23. Having been described in print as a public intellectual a number of times, I reluctantly added my name to the list of such persons in Chapter 5. By the end of the book, the reader will understand that I do not consider the term "public intellectual" an honorific, but merely the name of a (usually part-time) career.

24. See Ronald Dworkin, "Philosophy and Monica Lewinsky," *New York Review of Books*, March 9, 2000, pp. 48, 50. The book was written, moreover, while the Clinton imbroglio was unfolding, and I am particularly critical of public-intellectual commentary on current events that is delivered *in medias res*—what I call "real-time commentary." See Chapter 3.

~ I
General Theoretical and Empirical Analysis

~ 1

Setting the Stage

$\mathcal{T}$HE PUBLIC intellectual has not been studied systematically before, and so an important first step is to define the scope of my study. This will involve not only defining "public intellectual" but also describing the different genres and formats (overlapping but distinct methods of classification, as we'll see) of public-intellectual work.

What Is a Public Intellectual?

The public intellectual is not what philosophers call a "natural kind," something that exists apart from the needs and purposes of the human observer. Defining the public intellectual involves demarcating an area of social life that seems likely to repay focused attention.

The process of demarcation logically begins with the "intellectual," generally understood as someone seriously and competently interested in the things of the mind. "There is in every society a minority of persons who, more than the ordinary run of their fellow men, are inquiring, and desirous of being in frequent communion with symbols which are more general than the immediate concrete situations of everyday life and remote in their reference in both time and space."[1] "The emphasis is on a 'mindset' more than anything else. [Intellec-

1. Edward Shils, *The Intellectuals and the Powers and Other Essays* 3 (1972).

17

tuals] are usually seen as generalists, rather than specialists, having a special concern with ideas which ultimately springs from disinterested sources (although this involvement with ideas may be part of their profession), as being—to varying degrees—creative, playful, sensitive, inquisitive, and somewhat impractical."[2]

Ideas and cultivation are different, so an intellectual need not have "highbrow" tastes and a person with such tastes—someone who loves abstract art or the music of Elliott Carter or Philip Glass, for example—need not be an intellectual, just as a brilliant artist need not be an intellectual. So "intellectual" is not a synonym for cultured, cultivated, creative, or even bookish, though the last is close; perhaps every true intellectual is bookish, though not all bookish people are intellectuals.

Nor is "intellectual" a synonym for "intelligent." While intellectuals (excluding people who merely have intellectual pretensions) are above average in intelligence—often far above average—many equally intelligent people are not intellectuals. They may have no interest in ideas. Or the ideas they use either at work or at play may have so limited a scope and so applied a character as to lack the *generality* that is a defining characteristic of the intellectual's ideas. A physicist who uses abstruse mathematics to illuminate the origins of the universe is an intellectual; a physicist who uses abstruse mathematics to design a computer logic board or write software code need not be.

But it is unsatisfying to base the definition of an intellectual on the distinction between the general and the applied use of or interest in ideas; the distinction is not interesting. The difference at which the distinction gestures, which *is* interesting, is between applying ideas to matters of broad public concern on the one hand, and on the other applying them to specific tasks of making things or accreting, refining, or transmitting bodies of specialized or expert knowledge, whether commercial, professional, or academic. It is the difference between the critic and the scholar, engineer, lawyer, or other expert when they are

2. Paul Hollander, *Political Pilgrims: Travels of Western Intellectuals to the Soviet Union, China, and Cuba 1928–1978* 48 (1981). Chapter 2 of Hollander's book is an excellent review of the literature on the intellectual, as is Jeremy Jennings and Tony Kemp-Welch, "The Century of the Intellectual: From the Dreyfus Affair to Salman Rushdie," in *Intellectuals in Politics: From the Dreyfus Affair to Salman Rushdie* 1 (Jeremy Jennings and Anthony Kemp-Welch eds., 1997).

working within their area of expertise.[3] It is Foucault's distinction between the "universal" and the "specific" intellectual.[4] Or between the
reflective journalist—the columnist or "pundit"—and the scholar. Or
between the amateur and the professional. Or between the political
theorist on the one hand, and on the other the "policy wonk," the ordinary muckraking journalist, the political operative or activist, and the
reform advocate (Ralph Nader, for example), any of whom may, of
course, be highly intelligent. Some members of these groups may be
intellectuals, and this suggests a further refinement: the intellectual applies *general* ideas to matters of public concern, working from the top
down, *theorizing* about the abuses, corruptions, or injustices that he has
discovered. He is not *just* a reporter or technician. So some journalists,
some activists, some policy analysts are intellectuals, and others aren't.

But to define the intellectual as one who applies general ideas to
matters of general public concern is still too broad. The definition
would cover an art historian, or a journalist trained in art history, who
reviews art books or art exhibits for a magazine aimed at a general readership, even if there is no political or ideological dimension to any
of his reviews. Although such reviews are "intellectual" in a common
sense of the word, the reviewers would not be what is generally or
centrally thought of as "intellectuals."[5] When we think of the great
intellectuals of the twentieth century, such as John Dewey, Bertrand
Russell, Max Weber, Arthur Koestler, Edmund Wilson, and George

3. See, for example, Lloyd Kramer, "Habermas, Foucault, and the Legacy of Enlightenment Intellectuals," in *Intellectuals and Public Life: Between Radicalism and Reform* 29 (Leon
Fink, Stephen T. Leonard, and Donald M. Reid eds., 1996).

4. Michel Foucault, "Truth and Power," in *Essential Works of Foucault 1954–1984*, vol. 3:
Power, pp. 111, 126–133 (James D. Faubion ed., 2000). The "universal" intellectual is termed
the "general intellectual" in Stefan Collini, "Lament for a Lost Culture: How the Twentieth
Century Came to Mourn the Seriousness of the Nineteenth," *Times Literary Supplement*, Jan.
19, 2001, pp. 3, 5, an essay on the distinguished nonacademic intellectuals of Victorian England.

5. The qualification "centrally" may be vital. It would be strange to deny the label "intellectual" to an Arthur Danto, for example—a philosopher who writes art criticism from a
philosophical perspective—or to so learned a music and cultural critic as Charles Rosen, both
publishing in magazines (primarily the *Nation* and the *New York Review of Books*, respectively),
and books that are aimed at a general educated public. Neither of them, however, salts his
criticism with politics, or a political ideology, to any significant extent. (The last qualification
is a bow to any reader who believes that all discourse is political.)

Orwell, a common thread is that all either wrote directly about political or ideological questions or, in the case of those intellectuals who were literary critics, such as Wilson (or Lionel Trilling, or F. R. Leavis, or C. S. Lewis), wrote about literature from a broadly political or ideological (sometimes religious) perspective.[6] Some, like Orwell, and to a limited extent Wilson and Lewis, both wrote directly about political or ideological questions and wrote politically or ideologically inflected literary criticism. When Allan Bloom in his bestseller *The Closing of the American Mind* wrote about rock and roll, he was writing not as a music critic but as a social critic discerning signs of moral and political decay in the attraction that such music holds for college students.[7] The noun "intellectual" first gained widespread currency during the Dreyfus Affair, when Zola, Durkheim, Barrès, Maurras, and other writers and thinkers participated actively in public debate over a tumultuous political issue.[8]

The consequence of defining "intellectual" so narrowly is to exclude from the scope of my analysis two classes of particularly valuable intellectual work. One consists of original, and sometimes very important, intellectual writing that just happens to be accessible to the educated public because the style in which it is written is plain and free of jargon. Most literary criticism until about 1970, most philosophical writing until about 1920, and much social-scientific writing until the 1970s was of this character. All such work that has no political or ideological angle is excluded by my definition.

The second class of intellectual work that I exclude, which flourishes to this day, consists of efforts, primarily in the natural sciences, to translate technical material into a form in which educated lay people

6. Contemporary examples of cultural critics who write with a political edge and aim at a nonspecialist audience, and thus are public intellectuals by my definition, are Jacques Barzun, Joseph Epstein, Hilton Kramer, and Louis Menand. They can be distinguished from literary critics such as Stanley Fish and Edward Said who also write explicitly on political subjects, but they of course are public intellectuals too.

7. See Allan Bloom, *The Closing of the American Mind: How Higher Education Has Failed Democracy and Impoverished the Souls of Today's Students* 68–81 (1987).

8. See Venita Datta, *Birth of a National Icon: The Literary Avant-Garde and the Origins of the Intellectual in France* (1999). Zola's *J'Accuse* "pitted the man of letters against the prejudices of his society . . . After *J'Accuse* the role of the man of letters in France and eventually in Western society was irrevocably altered." David L. Lewis, *Prisoners of Honor: The Dreyfus Affair* 197 (1973).

can understand it. A scientist who writes for the general public merely to explain science is not a public intellectual in the sense in which I am using the term, even though he is writing for, and therefore endeavoring to write in a manner accessible to, the general public. But scientists such as Paul Ehrlich, Stephen Jay Gould, Richard Lewontin, and Edward Wilson, who write for a general audience about the ethical and political dimensions of science,[9] are public intellectuals.

The second class—call it explaining science—is not problematic. The first, which might be called accessible scholarship, is, and it is in decline for reasons similar to those that lie behind the displacement— with which I'll be much concerned in this book—of independent by academic public intellectuals. The disappearance of a common culture that embraces both intellectual specialists and the educated public is an important development and one that bears on the political and ideological role of intellectuals. Consider Keynes's famous book *The Economic Consequences of the Peace* (1920). It is about economics and was composed at a time when economics was not yet the specialized technical discipline that it has become. Though the most famous and probably the most influential economist of the twentieth century, Keynes had no Ph.D. In contrast to his formidable treatise *The General Theory of Employment, Interest and Money* (1935), *The Economic Consequences of the Peace* is written at a level that a general audience would have no difficulty comprehending and is as much a political, in places a journalistic, work as a work of economic scholarship. Was it first-rate readable economics (in the same way that Hume and Nietzsche are first-rate readable philosophers) or a public-intellectual work, or, as seems closest to the mark, both?

These questions are not entirely idle, because I shall be arguing that public intellectuals are for the most part neither very prescient nor very influential, and *The Economic Consequences of the Peace* was both. It foresaw the economic dislocation that the Versailles Treaty, in particular its

9. And not only science: in his essay "The Cold War and the Transformation of the Academy," in *The Cold War and the University: Toward an Intellectual History of the Postwar Years* 1 (André Schiffrin ed. 1997), Lewontin argues that without our military and related governmental spending during the Cold War, our economy would have grown more slowly, or not at all. He is not an economist and offers neither theoretical nor empirical support for this Chomskyan (see Chapter 3) endeavor to explain the Cold War as a product of U.S. economic anxieties rather than of Soviet aggressiveness.

requirement that the defeated nations pay the victors' war costs, would visit on Germany and on Europe generally; and while it did not persuade the victorious powers to revise the treaty, it may have helped to avert a repetition of the treaty's mistakes after World War II. But the very difficulty of classifying Keynes's book suggests that it is an exception to my generalization that is unlikely to recur. It belongs to a period of greater fluidity of intellectual activity than ours. A person of Keynes's ability today would not have accrued the governmental experience that Keynes had acquired by 1919 (when he wrote the book), would not have hobnobbed with the leading political figures of the day, would not possess Keynes's intellectual breadth, and would be a specialist, a technician, disinclined to address large issues of foreign and security affairs in terms intelligible to a lay audience. The minuteness of the English educated elite in Keynes's day also fostered ease of movement across its various departments. Despite living in a less propitious time and place for first-rate influential public-intellectual work, Henry Kissinger may be somewhat comparable to Keynes in the respects I have mentioned, and, with reference to domestic rather than foreign issues, and minus the governmental experience, Milton Friedman as well. Neither is a youngster, however; and we may not soon see their like again.

The reader may begin to sense a certain redundancy in the term "public intellectual." Not only is "public" of the essence of the most common understanding of what an "intellectual" is ("a thinker with a public voice"),[10] but part of that understanding is that the intellectual writes for a broader public than the scholar, the consultant, or the professional does, or even than many policy analysts do. That is why not all "knowledge workers" are intellectuals. John Rawls applies philosophical ideas to a range of important political issues, but he does not write *for* the general public.[11] Although his major work, *A Theory of Justice*, has sold some two hundred thousand copies, this is over a period of three decades and I suspect that with few exceptions the buy-

10. Colin Gordon, "Introduction," in *Essential Works of Foucault 1954–1984*, note 4 above, vol. 3: *Power*, p. xi.

11. The only public-intellectual foray of his of which I'm aware is his having signed the "philosophers' brief" supporting a constitutional right to physician-assisted suicide. See Chapter 10.

ers have been other academics, university libraries, and university students rather than members of a broader public.[12] A literary critic such as Geoffrey Hartman, who writes extensively on fascism, Judaism, and the modern university,[13] as well as on literature, is surely an intellectual writing as an intellectual and not just as a literary scholar. But Hartman's style, which like Rawls's is forbiddingly academic, is too difficult for a general even though educated audience. A number of academics who would very much *like* to communicate with the big public, doubtless including Hartman when he is writing outside his field, simply cannot or will not express themselves in simple prose.

George Steiner, whose remit is at least as broad as Hartman's, probably represents the outer limit of difficulty of apprehension consistent with attracting even a tiny slice of the nonacademic reading public. Allan Bloom, despite his bestsellerdom, was in the border region too. It is unlikely that most of the people who bought *The Closing of the American Mind* could actually get through it, since most of the book is severely academic, and even esoteric, though less so than Hartman's writings. The book was published by a commercial press rather than an academic one and I am told that Bloom got a lot of help from his editor in making the book more accessible to a general audience. His sales no doubt benefited as well from the beautifully written foreword by Saul Bellow. An earlier example is David Riesman's *The Lonely Crowd*, a dense though well written sociological tome that has become one of the all-time public-intellectual classics.

In short, and to an approximation only, the intellectual writes for the general public, or at least for a broader than merely academic or specialist audience, on "public affairs"—on *political* matters in the broadest sense of that word, a sense that includes cultural matters when they are viewed under the aspect of ideology, ethics, or politics (which may all be the same thing). The intellectual is more "applied," contemporary,

---

12. He had sketched the essential ideas in *A Theory of Justice* years earlier, in an article somewhat more accessible to a lay readership than the book. John Rawls, "Justice as Fairness," 67 *Philosophical Review* 164 (1958). But it was published in an academic journal, and while it was widely read outside philosophy, the readers were other academics, not members of the general educated public.

13. See, for example, Geoffrey Hartman, *A Critic's Journey: Literary Reflections, 1958–1998* (1999).

and "result-oriented" than the scholar, but broader than the technician. Approximate synonyms for "intellectual" in this sense are "social critic"[14] and "political intellectual."

The intellectual, so defined, *is* the public intellectual, as in: "[Hannah] Arendt was the consummate embodiment of what we now refer to as 'the public intellectual,' putting her philosophical training to good—if often controversial—use by commenting on the major political themes of her day: totalitarianism, Zionism, desegregation, the Eichmann trial, the Pentagon Papers, and so forth."[15] So why the *term* "public intellectual"? Its most sensible, nonredundant use would be to distinguish between a person of intellectual disposition who did not write or speak publicly as an intellectual (a "private intellectual," we might call him) and an intellectual who did write or speak as an intellectual. All the exemplars of this species whom I named earlier (Dewey, Zola, Steiner, and so on) would today be called public intellectuals and might even receive graduate training in that calling.[16] An interme-

14. As in Michael Walzer, *The Company of Critics: Social Criticism and Political Commitment in the Twentieth Century* (1988).

15. Richard Wolin, "The Illiberal Imagination," *New Republic*, Nov. 27, 2000, pp. 27, 28.

16. Florida Atlantic University is offering "the first interdisciplinary program to educate public intellectuals." The program, leading to a Ph.D. in "Comparative Studies," is designed "for students interested in an advanced general education and life as a public intellectual . . . The program will explore historical, conceptual, and practical relationships among such areas as public policy, mass media, literature, aesthetics, ethics, gender, culture, and rhetoric." But there is a paradox here. The stated motivation is a concern that while "the pursuit of higher education can provide the space to identify that thing or area in which one excels . . . this space is more and more restricted by the pressure of finding one's own niche in the academic market. This space is also congested, because people who would once have gone into public life no longer do: the academy now seems a more attractive choice than a public life in which persecution by the less thoughtful media is all too common." (All these quotations are from the program's Web site, http://www.publicintellectuals.fau.edu, visited July 31, 2000.) If academic specialization is what's undermining the public intellectual, and I agree that it is, it is hard to see salvation in another Ph.D. program, which will tie the student ever tighter to an academic career, forcing him to specialize in order to get a job. Somewhat more promising, although much too new to evaluate, is a Center for Public Intellectuals that has been created "to re-engage the public in vital intellectual issues and examine how, why and under what conditions public intellectuals can help to transform society." The Center plans to play host to conferences and fund research and fellowships and to maintain a database of information relating to public-intellectual activities. The quotation and description are from the Center's Web page. See http://www.publicintellectuals.org. The Center is affiliated with the University of Illinois at Chicago, which will be offering courses (but not a degree program) in the work of public intellectuals.

diate case, a kind of semipublic intellectual, is one who has a day job as a political or corporate consultant, a politician, or a judge or other government official,[17] while writing on the side for a general audience. Thomas Jefferson, Woodrow Wilson, Theodore Roosevelt, Patrick Moynihan, and Newt Gingrich are examples of the public intellectual as politician. Kissinger, William Bennett, William Kristol, Moynihan (during the Nixon administration), Lawrence Summers, and William Galston are examples of public intellectuals as government officials.[18] My interest is in the expressive dimension of public-intellectual work, that is, in communication with the public on intellectual themes by means of books, magazine articles, op-ed pieces, open letters, public lectures, and appearances on radio or television. The intellectual whose use of ideas is wholly intramural, the discrete intellectual courtier of the great and the powerful, is not a public intellectual in my sense.

Let me remind the reader of what I said at the outset of this chapter, that "public intellectual" is not a natural kind. Mine is not *the* correct definition, but merely the best for my purposes, which are not everyone's. I could not quarrel with someone who wanted to call John Rawls one of our leading public intellectuals. There is a perfectly good sense in which that is true. Only it is not my sense, because for my purposes, which centrally involve analyzing a *market* for intellectual work, the fact that Rawls does not write for a general audience is critical. I am not entirely comfortable with this exclusion, because Rawls receives some play in the popular media. The media that I sample in Chapter 5 record 374 "mentions" of him in the last five years, which is modest (the one-hundredth most frequently mentioned public intellectual in the list of 546 public intellectuals in that chapter had 1,200 mentions during this period), but exceeds the number of mentions of such unquestioned public-intellectual philosophers as Thomas Nagel, Martha Nussbaum,

17. See *Intellectuals in Politics* (Nissan Oren ed., 1984).

18. The originals of the public intellectual as official are Cicero and Seneca; with Socrates they form a trio of martyred public intellectuals of the ancient world. Seneca has been described as Nero's "ideologist and publicity expert," Miriam T. Griffin, *Seneca: A Philosopher in Politics* 128 (1976), and Cicero not only served as a consul in the Roman Republic but also played a key role in opposing Mark Antony after the assassination of Julius Caesar, exhibiting on that occasion disastrous political judgment, including fatal underestimation of history's most formidable nineteen-year-old, Octavius (later Augustus) Caesar. See Ronald Syme, *The Roman Revolution* 136–147 (1939). Cicero was executed at the behest of Antony. Seneca committed suicide on orders of Nero.

and Richard Rorty (see Table 5.1). Yet all that this really means is that the media take some interest in scholars who are not public intellectuals in my sense even though they write about the things that public intellectuals write about.

The public intellectual has been with us for a very long time, even if we ignore the ancient world. His exemplars include Machiavelli, Milton, Locke, Voltaire, and Montesquieu, and his ideologist is Kant, who linked philosophy to politics through the argument that the only morally defensible politics is one based on reason.[19] How then to explain the recency of the term? (It was coined by Russell Jacoby in a book published in 1987.)[20] Morris Dickstein ascribes it to the fact that in the 1970s and 1980s a number of U.S. academics—influenced by such Continental, mainly French, social theorists as Barthes, Lyotard, Lacan, and Derrida—adopted an esoteric, jargon-laden, obscurantist style. They were (are, in the case of Derrida) intellectuals and wrote about public affairs, but they either could not or would not write in a manner intelligible to the public beyond the university. Not for them Orwell's aspiration to write prose as clear as a window pane. Yet it would be arbitrary to deny them, Barthes and Derrida in particular, the status of public intellectuals. They have a definite though modest presence in the U.S. popular media.[21] The obscurity of their style is a source of their charisma.

The vast expansion of the electronic media, and in particular in the number of radio and television talk shows, with their insatiable demand for expert commentary on matters of public concern, has given some intellectuals a degree of publicity that has made them almost celebrities. (Kissinger *is* a celebrity, and likewise Patrick Moynihan, George Will, William Buckley, and a handful of other public intellectuals.) Perhaps then a public intellectual is a celebrity intellectual. But I prefer the definition that affixes "public" before "intellectual" merely to emphasize that an intellectual who cannot communicate with more than a coterie of specialist readers is not a public intellectual in the sense in which I wish to use the term, however interdisciplinary and politically significant his writings may be.

19. See *Kant: Political Writings* (Hans Reiss ed., 2d ed. 1991).
20. "My concern is with public intellectuals, writers and thinkers who address a general and educated audience." Russell Jacoby, *The Last Intellectuals: American Culture in the Age of Academe* 5 (1987).
21. Again see Table 5.1 in Chapter 5.

The likeliest explanation for the currency that the term has achieved is that it is a belated acknowledgment of the significance, for the intellectual's role, of the changing balance between the *independent* and the *affiliated* intellectual. Before there were universities in which serious intellectual work was done, and even later when universities were becoming important centers for the production of knowledge, no one would have thought to draw a distinction between public (with reference to audience) and nonpublic intellectual endeavors. You didn't write about public affairs for an academic audience because there was no such audience, or it was minute and accounted for only a small fraction of intellectuals, many being excluded from university positions because of religion, ethnicity, sex, or marital status. Anyway, you were in all likelihood not a professor yourself or even a university graduate. You wrote for some more general, less expert audience than an audience of academic specialists, though it might be a small audience, an audience of officials or other big shots or a tiny educated elite. Machiavelli, Hobbes, Locke, Hume, Samuel Johnson, Voltaire, Burke, Bentham, Jefferson, Paine, Mill, Carlyle, Thoreau, Emerson—the list of public intellectuals before the twentieth century who were *not* professors and did not write primarily for professors is endless.

With the flowering of the modern university, an institution that fosters scholarly research and places only limited calls on its faculty's time the better to encourage creative scholarship, it became apparent that intellectuals had a career path that would enable them to write exclusively for other knowledge workers if they wanted to. But it would also allow them time to write on the same subject for two very different audiences, one consisting of students and academics in the writer's field, the other of nonspecialists, the educated general public, itself expanding with the expansion of university education. To the extent that his academic reputation or intellectual gifts were portable, an academic might even be able to write for the educated general public on subjects outside his area of specialization.

Think of the leading twentieth-century literary critics who wrote about literature under the aspect of politics, ethics, or ideology. Some were academics writing primarily for an academic audience, like Cleanth Brooks, Northrop Frye, Kenneth Burke, F. R. Leavis, and R. P. Blackmur. Some were academics writing for both academic and nonacademic audiences, like C. S. Lewis, Lionel Trilling, Edward Said, Frank Kermode, Robert Alter, Harold Bloom, and George Steiner.

Some, like Edmund Wilson, Allen Tate, Randall Jarrell, and Walter Benjamin, were nonacademics writing for both an academic and a non-academic audience. And some were nonacademics writing primarily for a nonacademic audience though happy to be read by academics, for example T. S. Eliot, W. H. Auden, and George Orwell. Likewise in the moral and political philosophy of the twentieth century, we encounter austerely academic writers such as Renford Bambrough, Christine Korsgaard, Onora O'Neill, and Derek Parfit; crossover types such as Bertrand Russell, John Dewey, Heidegger, Sartre, Arendt, Sidney Hook, Isaiah Berlin, Richard Rorty, Thomas Nagel, Peter Singer, and Martha Nussbaum; and even a few nonacademics such as Freud, Oliver Wendell Holmes Jr., Aldous Huxley (see Chapter 6), and Camus.[22] And so in other fields as well—law, history, sociology, psychology, and political science—though in some one might have to go back to the nineteenth century to find good examples of important nonacademic contributors to public discussion, such as Bentham and Mill in economics and Maine in anthropology.

By the end of the twentieth century the balance between independent and academic public intellectuals had changed. The relative number of public intellectuals who were not academics had shrunk—dramatically so if numbers are weighted by prominence or contribution. Such nonacademic public intellectuals as Orwell, Koestler, Camus, Holmes, Brandeis, Frankfurter, Freud, Lytton Strachey, Walter Benjamin, Max Eastman, Edmund Wilson, H. G. Wells, T. S. Eliot, George Bernard Shaw, T. E. Lawrence, Thomas Mann, Herbert Croly, Lewis Mumford, Dwight Macdonald, James Baldwin (who, like Mumford and Orwell, was not college educated), and Walter Lippmann, and such quasi-academic public intellectuals as Max Weber, who had only intermittent academic employment, or Philip Rahv, who became a professor only after many years as a free-lance writer and editor, loom large in the intellectual history of the first half of the twenti-

22. Called, significantly, "a philosopher uncorrupted by the pomposity and self-consciousness of the academy." John Cottingham, Review [of a recent translation of *The Myth of Sisyphus*], *Times Literary Supplement*, Aug. 25, 2000, p. 13. "One of the things that [Camus] had come to dislike most about Parisian intellectuals was their conviction that they had something to say about everything, and that everything could be reduced to the kind of thing they liked to say. He also remarked upon the characteristically inverse relationship between firsthand knowledge and the confident expression of intellectual opinion." Tony Judt, *The Burden of Responsibility: Blum, Camus, Aron, and the French Twentieth Century* 121 (1998).

eth century. Nonacademic public intellectuals loom even larger in the intellectual history of the nineteenth century: think only of Bentham, Tocqueville, Marx, Emerson, Thoreau, Dickens, John Stuart Mill, Herbert Spencer, Matthew Arnold, Harriet Beecher Stowe, and, among those with loose academic moorings, Friedrich Nietzsche and Henry Adams. All the people I have named would almost certainly be full-time academics today, or at least (in the case of the judges and writers) have had a number of years as full-time academics under their belts. The expansion and improvement of universities, and the decline of the nonacademic public intellectual, have moved in lockstep.

A number of nonacademic public intellectuals did manage to achieve prominence in the second half of the twentieth century—among Americans one might instance Susan Sontag, Renata Adler, Tom Wolfe, William Bennett, Lewis Mumford, Ayn Rand, Mary McCarthy, Irving Howe, Jane Jacobs, Gore Vidal, Michael Harrington, Rachel Carson, James Baldwin, Charles Murray, Hilton Kramer, Norman Podhoretz, William Buckley, Irving Kristol,[23] and—probably the most influential of all—Betty Friedan.[24] But the number was fewer than in earlier periods, especially when one considers how much larger the educated population has grown and how many more outlets public intellectuals have for their writing and speaking. The independent intellectual has been giving way to the academic intellectual. The trend has been apparent since the 1950s, if not earlier.[25]

The academization of intellectual life has been noted and deplored,[26]

23. Kristol had an academic appointment for some years, but has never done academic writing. My examples, by the way, are confined to the United States. It is no accident that the most illustrious nonacademic public intellectuals of the second half of the twentieth century have been foreign, such as Havel and Solzhenitzyn; they have lived under more challenging conditions than American intellectuals.

24. *The Feminine Mystique*, first published in 1963, was, in point of influence, along with Simone de Beauvoir's *The Second Sex*, the *Communist Manifesto* of the modern women's movement. I am talking about influence, not quality. See Alan Wolfe, "The Mystique of Betty Friedan: She Helped to Change Not Only the Thinking but the Lives of Many American Women, but Recent Books Throw into Question the Intellectual and Personal Sources of Her Work," *Atlantic Monthly*, Sept. 1999, p. 98. My nominees for the most influential other post–World War II American nonacademic public intellectuals are Ayn Rand, William Buckley, and Rachel Carson.

25. See Lewis A. Coser, *Men of Ideas: A Sociologist's View*, ch. 20 (1965); also Steven Biel, *Independent Intellectuals in the United States, 1910–1945*, ch. 1 (1992).

26. See, for example, Thomas Bender, *New York Intellect: A History of Intellectual Life in New*

how justly the subsequent chapters will examine. Evaluative issues to one side, the trend is unmistakable, and here is another bit of evidence: many of the most prominent academic public intellectuals of the second half of the twentieth century, such as Daniel Bell, Nathan Glazer, Irving Howe, and David Riesman, lacked what today would be (other than in law) the essential qualification for academic tenure: none had written a Ph.D. dissertation. McGeorge Bundy, a prominent public intellectual though an academic only in the early part of his career, became dean of arts and sciences at Harvard without a Ph.D.—unthinkable today. Today such people, if they don't become lawyers, have to submit to being finely ground in the Ph.D. mill, emerging as better scholars but possibly as less interesting intellectuals. The academy, ever more academized in the sense of professionalized, bureaucratized, and rationalized in the Weberian sense, is becoming ever less congenial to the free spirit, the gadfly ("tenured gadfly" sounds like an oxymoron), the scoffer—"someone," as Edward Said puts it, "whose place it is publicly to raise embarrassing questions, to confront orthodoxy and dogma (rather than to produce them), to be someone who cannot easily be co-opted by governments or corporations."[27] If this is what a public intellectual is, the modern university bids fair to squeeze him out of intellectual life.

Said's definition, however, is too narrow. It implies that the only opposition worth putting up is to governments and corporations. That is a good description of Said's own politics, which are far to the left. But dogma is not the exclusive preserve of governments and corporations.

York City, from 1750 to the Beginnings of Our Own Time 343 (1987); Jacoby, note 20 above; Jacoby, The End of Utopia: Politics and Culture in an Age of Apathy (1999); Josef Joffe, "The Decline of the Public Intellectual and the Rise of the Pundit," in The Public Intellectual: Theory and Practice (Arthur M. Melzer, Jerry Weinberger, and M. Richard Zinman eds., forthcoming). Joseph Epstein argues that the modern "public intellectual" is the debasement of the true intellectual. Epstein, "Intellectuals—Public and Otherwise," Commentary, May 2000, p. 46. In contrast, Bruce Robbins, "Introduction: The Grounding of Intellectuals," in Intellectuals: Aesthetics, Politics, Academics ix (Bruce Robbins ed., 1990), while noting the criticisms that are made of the academic public intellectual, argues that the academic affiliations of leftist intellectuals, and the resulting loss of marginality for such intellectuals, do not fatally undermine their ability to influence the society. He repeats this argument more emphatically in his book Secular Vocations: Intellectuals, Professionalism, Culture (1993), which I discuss briefly in Chapter 4. For an intermediate view, see Ron Eyerman, Between Culture and Politics: Intellectuals in Modern Society, ch. 7 (1994).

27. Edward W. Said, Representations of the Intellectual: The 1993 Reith Lectures 11 (1994).

There is religious dogma, and social dogma (such as neoconservatism), and political dogma not limited to the governing parties. Today there are academic dogmas as well, such as those of the cultural Left, the Austrian school of economics, and the followers of Leo Strauss. Intellectuals, moreover, often flock together; in fact very few of them are truly untamable individualists in the tradition of Socrates, Thoreau, Nietzsche, Camus, and Orwell. Nor is there any necessary virtue in an oppositional stance; it depends on what one is opposing. Intellectuals' oppositional reflex has frequently led them into an unthinking, and during the communist era a disastrous, rejection of the attitudes and values of their fellow citizens.[28]

But Said is on to something. "Disputing the prevailing norms"[29] may not be part of the definition of the intellectual, or even of the public intellectual, but it is the public intellectual's characteristic stance and is perhaps what gives him a distinctive, though by no means unalloyed, social value. "The role of an intellectual is not to tell others what they have to do." It is "to question over and over again what is postulated as self-evident, to disturb people's mental habits, the way they do and think things, to dissipate what is familiar and accepted, to reexamine rules and institutions."[30] That is the stance symbolized by Socrates, who is to the public-intellectual community as Jesus is to Christianity: founder, outcast, martyr.[31]

Public intellectuals on the view being expounded here "specialize in defamiliarizing the obvious." "Disturbers of the canonical peace,"[32] they contribute to the diversity of thought and life-style that Mill argued in *On Liberty* was the precondition both for individual self-fulfillment and for social progress. The intellectual is an "ironist," "someone who thinks there is no single preferred vocabulary . . . While provisionally continuing to employ her present vocabulary, she nour-

28. See, for an excellent discussion, Michael Novak, *Unmeltable Ethnics: Politics and Culture in American Life*, pt. 2 (2d ed. 1996).

29. Said, note 27 above, at 36.

30. Michel Foucault, "The Concern for Truth," in Foucault, *Politics Philosophy Culture: Interviews and Other Writings 1977–1984* 255, 265 (Lawrence D. Kritzman ed., 1988).

31. Socrates' famous ugliness, on which see Paul Zanker, *The Mask of Socrates: The Image of the Intellectual in Antiquity* 32–39 (1995), corresponds to the physical abasement of Christ on the Cross.

32. Both quotations are from Anthony G. Amsterdam and Jerome Bruner, *Minding the Law* 237 (2000).

ishes radical and abiding doubts concerning it, and has no truck with arguments phrased in it which seek either to underwrite or to dissolve these doubts."[33]

Oppositionality must be distinguished from opposition. Opposing one dogma with another is a form of opposition. There has never been a shortage of dogmatic public intellectuals (sometimes called "organic" intellectuals). The oppositional stance is the stance of such public intellectuals as Orwell and Camus, who write from the margins of their society and are clearer about what they are against than what they are for. Their negativity and self-conscious marginality distinguish them from such social critics as Sartre, who ground their criticisms in a dogma.[34] We shall encounter a tempered version of this dichotomy in Chapter 9 when comparing Richard Rorty and Martha Nussbaum.

A related point is that the public intellectual tends to be a counterpuncher. Whether oppositional or dogmatic, he is much more likely to be reacting to some contemporary event or situation (such as the impeachment of Clinton, the "crisis" of the university, cloning, the decline of sexual morality, or the Internet's threat to privacy), or to some commentary on that event or situation, than to be pursuing a well-defined research path, which is the academic style. The public intellectual obtains an audience by engaging with some matter that has the public's attention. Because the audience's attention span is short, the public intellectual has to be quick on the trigger. And because he is purveying opinion rather than news, he is drawn to taking extreme positions (or perhaps people drawn to taking extreme positions are more likely to find the public intellectual's career an attractive one); it is difficult otherwise to get the public's attention.

The public intellectual is a social critic rather than merely a social observer. Scientific observing, or ordinary observing inflected by conventional attitudes, can be left to employed journalists, as distinct from free-lance journalists, and to the university-employed, government-

33. James Conant, "Freedom, Cruelty, and Truth: Rorty versus Orwell," in *Rorty and His Critics* 268, 277 (Robert B. Brandom ed., 2000), summarizing Rorty's view.

34. The *pose* of marginality is common among academic public intellectuals, a good example being Said, a tenured professor at Columbia University who claims outsider status on the basis of his Palestinian Arab origins. The pose is unconvincing. Nothing in Said's speech or physical appearance marks him as foreign, and anyway Americans do not treat their foreign-born citizens as outsiders, as witness the career of Henry Kissinger, or of Gerhard Casper, another German immigrant, who recently retired as president of Stanford University.

employed, or think-tank-employed social scientists. These are the institutionally connected—the affiliated—intellectuals, and there are plenty of them. Yet there should be room in social space for free-range intellectuals as well—the naysayers, the heterodox, the intellectual *Luftmenschen*. Intellectuals "are usually regarded as outsiders, yet the conscience of society, the upholders of its true values and ideals."[35] (So Jeremiah and the other Old Testament prophets are distant ancestors of the public intellectual, too.) They are at once engaged and detached. A difficult role at best, it is one especially difficult for intellectuals safely ensconced in tenured university professorships to play—insiders pretending to be outsiders.

Admittedly, any effort to appraise contemporaries risks selection bias. The untenured dare not spend time writing for popular journals, and academics in midcareer cannot be expected to have accrued reputations equal to those of the most distinguished dead. One of the chief sources of cultural pessimism is the tendency to compare the best of the past with the average of the present, because the passage of time operates to filter out the worst of the past. Nostalgia and romanticizing are dangers here too. And the problems of proof are formidable, maybe insurmountable. I don't want to fall into any of these pits. So I must be extremely careful in speaking of the decline of the public intellectual. All that is certain is that with the enormous expansion in universities in the twentieth century, and in the leisure, credentials, and financial security that a university appointment offers to anyone who wants to embark on a career as a public intellectual, few would-be public intellectuals will fail to seek such appointments. The principal alternative—journalism—is not an attractive, or even a feasible, alternative for most aspiring public intellectuals in an age of specialization; journalists are not in a good position to acquire specialized knowledge. Though even today a number of public intellectuals are journalists, such as William Buckley, Andrew Sullivan, George Will, Christopher Hitchens, Gregg Easterbrook, and Leon Wieseltier, they probably are outnumbered in the ranks of nonacademic public intellectuals just by former academics, such as Robert Bork, Patrick Moynihan, William Kristol, William Bennett, and Henry Kissinger. Even among public intellectuals who are writers, like Saul Bellow, E. L. Doctorow, Joseph Epstein, Norman

35. Hollander, note 2 above, at 48.

Mailer, Cynthia Ozick, and Gore Vidal, many have part-time or even full-time academic appointments. It seems that for the foreseeable future the dominant type of public intellectual will be the full-time, or at least nominally full-time, professor.

But we must consider the bearing on this prospect of the rise of "think tanks"—nonteaching research institutions that generally are not affiliated with universities (the Hoover Institution on War, Revolution and Peace, which is part of Stanford University, is a notable exception) and that are oriented toward applied rather than basic research and toward public policy rather than scientific, technical, or cultural issues except those that bear directly on policy.[36] Among the best-known think tanks are the Brookings Institution, the American Enterprise Institute for Public Policy Research, the Hudson Institute, the Progressive Policy Institute, the Heritage Foundation, the Cato Institute, the Urban Institute, and the Manhattan Institute.[37] The majority of these are conservative, reflecting both the hegemony of liberals in many university departments and the greater availability of corporate donations to support conservative causes. All engage in some public-intellectual work, and in some of the think tanks that work dominates. Most think-tank output, however, is oriented not toward the educated public at large but toward legislators, officials, lobbyists, and other members of the political establishment. A think tank may have former government officials (sometimes officials in waiting) on its staff along with Ph.D.'s who might easily be teaching in universities instead but who either do not like to teach or are pursuing topics or using research methods that are unfashionable in their field in the universities—or who want to function primarily rather than secondarily as public intellectuals. The borderline between the think tank and the public policy school, such as the Kennedy School at Harvard or the Woodrow Wilson School at Princeton, is indistinct.

There is no doubt that the modern American think tank is an important site of public-intellectual work. But as a quasi-academic institu-

36. See the useful discussion in David M. Ricci, *The Transformation of American Politics: The New Washington and the Rise of Think Tanks* (1993), esp. pp. 219–225; also *Think Tanks across Nations: A Comparative Approach* (Diane Stone, Andrew Denham, and Mark Garnett eds., 1998).

37. For a helpful list, see Donald E. Abelson, "Think Tanks in the United States," in *Think Tanks across Nations*, note 36 above, at 107, 116 (tab. 5.1).

tion—just as an institution, perhaps—it is not an entirely comfortable home for the *independent* public intellectual. This is not just definitional (an independent is a free lance; an employee is not). Because most think tanks have a distinct political coloration, becoming an employee of one tends to be an act of affiliation with a political position, compromising independence. And like universities, think tanks hire specialists and encourage specialization. The most prominent ones—the Brookings Institution and the American Enterprise Institute—are, in terms of the makeup and quality of their professional staffs, virtually universities, albeit without students, just as university schools of public policy verge on being think tanks with students. I am inclined, therefore, to regard the think-tank public intellectual as basically interchangeable with the academic public intellectual.

To summarize, a public intellectual expresses himself in a way that is accessible to the public, and the focus of his expression is on matters of general public concern of (or inflected by) a political or ideological cast. Public intellectuals may or may not be affiliated with universities. They may be full-time or part-time academics; they may be journalists or publishers; they may be writers or artists; they may be politicians or officials; they may work for think tanks; they may hold down "ordinary" jobs. Most often they either comment on current controversies or offer general reflections on the direction or health of society. In their reflective mode they may be utopian in the broad sense of seeking to steer the society in a new direction or denunciatory because their dissatisfaction with the existing state of the society overwhelms any effort to propose reforms. When public intellectuals comment on current affairs, their comments tend to be opinionated, judgmental, sometimes condescending, and often waspish. They are controversialists, with a tendency to take extreme positions. Academic public intellectuals often write in a tone of conscious, sometimes exasperated, intellectual superiority. Public intellectuals are often careless with facts and rash in predictions.

Genres, Formats, and Styles

I mentioned in the Introduction that there are distinct genres of public-intellectual work. I elaborate on some of them here (see Table 1.1) and also distinguish genres from formats and styles.

Table 1.1 Public-intellectual genres

Self-popularizing
Own-field policy proposing
Real-time commentary
Prophetic commentary
Jeremiad
General social criticism
Specific social criticism
Social reform
Politically inflected literary criticism
Political satire
Expert testimony

The term "genre" implies a form of *expressive* activity; one would not call consulting a genre of public-intellectual work. The concern of this book is with expressive public-intellectual work, but I am least interested in the genre that consists of translating one's scholarly work into a form that the general educated public can understand. Call this genre *self-popularizing*. An example is Amartya Sen's book *Development as Freedom*. This is a book about the political economy of economic development written for the general educated public rather than for Sen's fellow economists and philosophers. Essentially it is a summary of Sen's academic work, some of which is highly technical, for a general audience.[38] An even better example involves the National Health and Social Life Survey, a large survey of the sexual practices of modern Americans. The survey was conducted by a team of academics, and their results were published by an academic press.[39] At the same time, adding as a coauthor a *New York Times* science journalist, Gina Kolata, the team published with a trade press an abridged and simplified version of their study under the title *Sex in America*.

I pass over this genre of public-expression work without much comment because the principal question that is germane to its evaluation, apart from whether the work is written at the right level to reach a gen-

38. A book on economics for a lay readership that, unlike Sen's book, which is strongly normative, avoided all political and ideological issues in economics (were that possible) would not under my definition be a public-intellectual work at all.

39. Edward O. Laumann et al., *The Social Organization of Sexuality: Sexual Practices in the United States* (1994).

eral audience and whether the "translation" is accurate,[40] is whether the ideas in the work are good, and that is a question about *academic* ideas, not about anything special to public-intellectual work. The self-popularizer is, qua self-popularizer, more of a journalist or publicist than a public intellectual in an interesting sense; the explicit recognition of this fact by the sex-survey team in bringing a journalist on board to coauthor the popular version of the study is welcome. Sen's book is quite unlike two other well-known books written by prominent economists for a general audience with which it might easily be confused at the level of genre, Hayek's *The Road to Serfdom* and Friedman's *Capitalism and Freedom*. These books range far beyond the authors' academic specialties. Only in small part are they communicating the results of academic research to a general audience.

The next and also relatively unproblematic genre of public-intellectual work is making specific policy proposals based on one's academic specialty; I call this *own-field policy proposing*. The scholar's academic research has led him to think that public policy should be changed in a particular way, and he writes up his proposal in a form accessible to a general audience. Much of Milton Friedman's public-intellectual work is of this character, including his advocacy of a volunteer army, a negative income tax, school vouchers, and the repeal of most economic regulation. (Friedman's *Capitalism and Freedom* is a combination of this genre with *general social criticism*, discussed below.) James Q. Wilson's influential "broken windows" theory of policing is of this character as well.[41] In both cases a scholar packages reform proposals based on his academic training in a verbal form that the general public can understand. As with self-popularizing, the principal issue that own-field policy proposing raises, which is whether the academic idea behind the proposal is sound, is not the key issue for the analyst of the public-intellectual market.

I have said that these two genres of public-expression work are *relatively* unproblematic. When writing for a general audience, and therefore bypassing many or even all of the gatekeepers of academic publica-

40. Not likely to be a problem when the academic research is published at the same time, as in the case just discussed.

41. James Q. Wilson and George L. Kelling, "Broken Windows: The Police and Neighborhood Safety," *Atlantic Monthly*, March 1982, p. 29.

tion, the scholar may be tempted to exaggerate his case; we shall see an example in Chapter 3 involving the economist Paul Krugman. Cutting the other way is the fact that since the self-popularizing and own-field policy-proposing genres are parasitic on the public intellectual's academic training, the quality of work in these genres will tend to improve when the underlying academic field is improving. This is a factor in evaluating public-intellectual work in economics. The scope and rigor of economics have been growing steadily, and as a result the public-intellectual work of academic economists may today be superior on average to what it was in earlier periods, though there were, of course, outstanding public-intellectual economists then, ranging from Keynes back to Adam Smith. But an improving trend in the underlying field of learning is mainly relevant only to the first two genres. Improvements in an academic specialty are unlikely to increase the quality of an academic's commentary outside his specialty, or even within it when he is engaged in a type of activity, such as commenting on ongoing events or testifying in court, that is remote from academic activity. Physics is a constantly improving field, but it would be foolish to think that a modern physicist would do a better job than Einstein in opining on economic and foreign-policy questions merely because modern physicists know more physics than Einstein did.

It is in the other genres of public-intellectual expressive activity that the problem of quality is acute and a process of decline discernible. For the danger of exaggeration, distortion, and inaccuracy is greater the farther outside his specialty the scholar wanders in his public-intellectual work, the more current or otherwise unsuitable to the methodology of scholarship the events on which he is commenting, and the more political his take on those events. *Real-time commentary*, in which the public intellectual opines on hot ongoing controversies, such as the Clinton impeachment or the Persian Gulf campaign or the 2000 presidential election deadlock, is, as we'll see, a genre of public-intellectual work that has a particularly high failure rate.

A partial exception must be noted, however, for efforts to explain to the public complex or esoteric issues that are within the scope of an academic public intellectual's scholarly expertise but that even specialized journalists may have particular difficulty understanding because the issues have arisen suddenly, and are unfolding rapidly, as part of a current controversy. We could observe a little of this useful activity in regard to the issues of election law, constitutional law, judicial procedure, and statistics that roiled the nation in the aftermath of the 2000 presidential election—along with, however, a good deal of tendentious, opinionated, even scurrilous public-intellectual commentary that I discuss in Chapter 3, plenty of erroneous predictions, and much obtuse commentary. A consensus quickly emerged among the constitutional-law professors who were commenting to the media on the unfolding crisis that the U.S. Supreme Court would not intervene. The consensus was based in part on a failure to foresee how badly the Florida supreme court would screw up the recount process, but less excusably on oblivion to the possibility that the clause in Article II of the Constitution that directs each state to pick its presidential electors "in such Manner as the Legislature thereof shall direct"[42] might provide a basis for Supreme Court intervention. Nor were the experts sensitive to the possibility that the Court might intervene not for base political reasons but rather out of concern with the harm to the nation were the deadlock to be left unresolved until Congress met to count the electoral votes in January 2001. Even after the Supreme Court, in its first opinion, rendered December 4, flagged the Article II issue,[43] most academic commentators did not expect the Court to play the decisive role in resolving the deadlock. Typical was public-intellectual law professor Akhil Reed Amar's response to the opinion. Asked on December 5 what the Supreme Court's role would be, Amar replied, "Basically, minimal. The Supreme Court made a brief cameo appearance on stage and has now I think rather gracefully bowed out."[44] A week later the Supreme Court ended the deadlock by its decision terminating the Florida recount.

Another especially questionable genre of public-intellectual expressive activity is *prophetic commentary*, such as that of the economic and ecological pessimists, though there are optimists in this group, like Marshall McLuhan, George Gilder, and Alvin Toffler. The prophetic commentary of cultural pessimists I discuss separately under the rubric of the *jeremiad*, a public-intellectual genre that has particularly rigid conventions. Closely related is *general social criticism*, for example that of Richard Rorty, who differs from the Jeremiahs only in employing the doomsday trope less insistently. Rorty, and to a greater extent Mar-

42. U.S. Const. art. II, § 1, cl. 2.

43. Bush v. Palm Beach County Canvassing Board, 531 U.S. 70 (2000) (per curiam).

44. National Public Radio, *Morning Edition*, Dec. 5, 2000.

tha Nussbaum, whom I discuss together with him in Chapter 9, also make concrete proposals for *social reform*. Such proposing differs from *own-field policy proposing* in ranging outside the boundaries of the public intellectual's primary discipline. Nussbaum relates her proposals dealing with education, homosexual rights, and oppression of women in the Third World to her academic fields of classics and philosophy, but the relation is sufficiently attenuated to place the proposals outside the disciplines themselves.

About the remaining genres mentioned in the Introduction—*specific social criticism, politically inflected literary criticism, political satire,* and *expert testimony*—only the last requires further elaboration here. It illustrates the overlap between genres and formats. Commenting on an ongoing controversy belongs to the genre of real-time commentary, but the format might be an op-ed piece, a book review, an appearance on a radio or television talk show, participation in a teach-in, or a full-page paid advertisement. In principle, the same commentary on a public issue could take the form of an article or of an affidavit in a legal case. Expert testimony might therefore be classified as a format rather than a genre of public-intellectual work. So distinctive are the rules and usages of the legal process, however, that, as we'll see in Chapter 10, testimony by public intellectuals constitutes its own, tiny but fascinating and dubious, genre of public-intellectual expression.

There are, finally, the different styles of public-intellectual argument. Examples are the polemical; the "splitting the difference" or "above the fray" style that I discuss in Chapter 3; the obscurantist style; the journalistic; the confessional; the scholarly—and the pseudo-scholarly.

～ 2

The Market for
Public Intellectuals

We [public intellectuals] profit while we prophet.[1]

$\mathcal{B}$EING AN academic public intellectual is a career,[2] albeit a part-time and loosely structured one, and like other careers it can be analyzed in terms of markets. There is a market for public intellectuals where demand and supply cross. One can investigate each side of the market, asking about the factors that create a demand on the part of the general public to read or hear what academics have to say about issues of general interest and about the factors that determine the supply response to this demand. And one can attempt to evaluate the performance of the market. I am not aware of a previous effort to study the public intellectual from an economic standpoint, but since to a significant extent, as we'll see, public intellectuality is a celebrity phenomenon, the nascent economic analysis of fame and reputation is pertinent.[3]

While reading this and the following three chapters, bear in mind that intellectual content ("information" for short) is not necessarily the only valued feature of public-intellectual work. Products often have multiple dimensions of value to the consuming public. Food is valued primarily for nutrition but also for taste and as a signal of wealth, refinement, and sometimes even of ideology, as in vegetarianism or in observance of religious restrictions on what may be eaten. Gambling is

1. Michael Eric Dyson, *Race Rules: Navigating the Color Line* 70 (1997).

2. Amusingly lampooned in David Brooks, *Bobos in Paradise: The New Upper Class and How They Got There* 153–177 (2000).

3. See, for the most recent study (which cites the earlier ones), Tyler Cowen, *What Price Fame?* (2000). The sociological approach to celebrity, on which I also draw, as does Cowen, is well illustrated by Joshua Gamson, *Claims to Fame: Celebrity in Contemporary America* (1994).

41

valued by risk preferrers for its expected utility but by other people for its excitement and its ambience. The writings and other expressive products of public intellectuals are valued as information but also as entertainment and as "solidarity goods," symbolic goods that provide a rallying point for like-minded people.[4] Truth and quality are not synonyms even when one is discussing symbolic goods and even if one is not a postmodernist truth skeptic. My emphasis will be on the informational aspect of public-intellectual work. Such issues as commitment, credibility, and quality that I shall be discussing at length are significant primarily with regard to that aspect. It is also the aspect emphasized by public intellectuals themselves and the one most likely to generate social rather than purely private benefits or costs. But the other aspects are important too and I will recur to them frequently.

Demand

The proximate demand for the expressive output of public intellectuals, as distinct from their consulting and other private services, comes from magazine editors (including editors of online magazines), the editors of newspaper op-ed pages, book publishers (including academic as well as commercial presses, the former being eager these days to expand their market beyond the purely academic), reporters seeking quotable commentary, colleges seeking commencement speakers, and producers of radio and television talk shows[5] and documentaries. The outlets through which public intellectuals are able to reach the general public have expanded greatly in recent decades. Consider, besides the increase in the number of television channels and the rise of the Internet, the number of new journals since 1960 that publish the writings of public intellectuals, such as the *New York Review of Books, Public Interest, First Things, Lingua Franca, New Criterion, American Prospect, Boston Re-*

4. See Cass R. Sunstein and Edna Ullmann-Margalit, "Solidarity Goods," *Journal of Political Philosophy* (forthcoming); cf. Gary S. Becker, "A Note on Restaurant Pricing and Other Examples of Social Influences on Price," in Becker, *Accounting for Tastes* 195 (1996); Eric A. Posner, *Law and Social Norms*, ch. 11 (2000); Eric A. Posner, "The Regulation of Groups: The Influence of Legal and Nonlegal Sanctions on Collective Action," 63 *University of Chicago Law Review* 144 (1996).

5. I have in mind the serious, news-oriented talk shows rather than the celebrity talk shows, on which see Gamson, note 3 above, at 101–104. On both types, see Howard Kurtz, *Hot Air: All Talk, All the Time* (1996), esp. ch. 7.

view, Weekly Standard, and *National Interest,* while the older such journals (for example, the *New Yorker, Nation, New Republic, National Review, Foreign Affairs, American Scholar, Commentary, Partisan Review,* and *Dissent*), with the principal exception of *Encounter,* continue to publish.

Whether the increased access of public intellectuals to the public is a response to a greater public demand for the work of public intellectuals or to greater competition in the media, or to both, is unclear. It is probably both but with the first predominant. The media are conduits for the demand of the general public rather than primary demanders themselves. They wouldn't fill up newspaper and magazine space and airtime with the words of intellectuals unless the public wanted to read and hear those words. Despite all the criticisms of American education, about as large a fraction of Americans seem interested in and reasonably well informed about current issues of a political, economic, and social character as used to be the case;[6] and this, along with sheer growth in population, the increased years of schooling of the average American,[7] the growing number of leisured, educated elderly persons, and the increase in the size of government (for remember that part of my definition of the public intellectual is that he writes about matters that have a political or ideological dimension), may explain the growing market for the public intellectual.

May, not must. For while it might seem obvious that the educated public would want to read or hear what academic experts have to say about the issues that interest that public, a moment's reflection will dispel this impression. The public wants to know what the experts think about the matters that interest it, but why should it want the experts' own exposition of their thoughts? If economists unanimously believe that rent control is inefficient, this is a datum that the general public has or should have an interest in. But it is a datum that can be adequately reported by a reputable journalist, who might be supposed to

6. See, for example, Robert D. Putnam, *Bowling Alone: The Collapse and Revival of American Community* 35–36 (2000).

7. Between 1960 and 1998, the percentage of the adult U.S. population that had completed at least four years of high school rose from 41.1 percent to 82.8 percent, and the percentage who had completed at least four years of college rose from 7.7 percent to 24.4 percent. U.S. Census Bureau, *Statistical Abstract of the United States 1999* 169 (tab. 263) (119th ed. 1999).

be the greater expert in communicating experts' findings to the public than an academic economist would be. Reporting in terms intelligible to lay people the academic findings that have some relevance to their lives, or that even just stimulate or satisfy their curiosity, is its own specialty distinct from academic research, and it is the specialty cultivated by journalists, editors, popular writers, politicians, and people who work in public relations and advertising. For the academic to be his own popularizer sounds like underspecialization, a refusal to recognize the benefits of the division of labor. It's like a manufacturer doing his own retailing. This degree of what industrial-organization economists call "vertical integration" is not unknown; but it calls for explanation.

Here is a stab at explanation. If the academic findings in which the general public has a potential interest are sufficiently recondite, a person untrained or only superficially trained in the discipline may be unable to get up to speed sufficiently to write intelligently about them. This is especially true if the findings in a particular field or subfield of the academy have only intermittent public interest. The impeachment of President Clinton illustrates this point. Presidential impeachments are so rare that it would not pay any journalist to become sufficiently expert in the law and political science of impeachment to be ready to opine on a presidential impeachment should one occur. And academic interest in the subject was so limited when the issue arose that there was very little in the way of a ready-made body of academic writing on which journalists could draw. The antitrust case brought by the Department of Justice and a number of states against Microsoft Corporation, which consumed so much public attention in 1999 and 2000, is a similar example. The public has little interest in antitrust law in general, and academics had not paid much attention to the novel issues presented by the application of antitrust law to Internet-related activities. A third example is the controversy over the deadlocked 2000 presidential election. The controversy raised esoteric issues of election law and constitutional law that academics had paid little attention to. Just as the last presidential impeachment occurred more than a century before Clinton's impeachment (1868), so the last deadlocked presidential election occurred more than a century before the 2000 election (1876).

There are two points here, not one, and both bear on the demand for the work of the academic public intellectual. The first is the sheer impracticability of creating a corps of journalists who know enough about the range of academic disciplines that produce knowledge or opinion in which the general public has a potential interest to be able to write competently about them. The second is the possibility that an issue of great interest to the public may erupt in which the academy has until that time taken little interest, though the issue lies within the domain of some academic field. The need is then not for translation of an existing body of academic thinking into words that the laity can understand, but for the application of a body of specialized academic knowledge to an issue to which it has not been applied before. That application requires academic expertise and so is beyond the capacity of the journalist or other specialist in communication to supply.

In a society undergoing rapid change, such cases are apt to be frequent. I mentioned the Internet. Its rise and that of everything connected with it, from e-mail to the World Wide Web and e-commerce, has taken place too rapidly to have become the subject of a mature scholarly literature in sociology, economics, political science, psychology, law, or cultural studies that has only to be translated into terms the general public can understand. The academics in these fields were taken by surprise by the Internet and the social and economic changes it has spawned, and they are scrambling to apply their knowledge capital to these phenomena. The same was true when the Cold War suddenly ended in 1989 and the Soviet Union and its satellite regimes collapsed shortly thereafter. While the experts are struggling to make up their minds about some issue, journalists are not going to be able to report an academic consensus. They can report the struggle but they cannot tell the public what to think about it. In these circumstances there is a demand to hear from the horse's mouth.

We can therefore expect a demand for the views of academic public intellectuals in areas in which novel issues around which an academic consensus has not yet formed are agitating the general public. And then there are the old issues on which no academic consensus has formed yet the interest of the public remains great—such hardy perennials as the proper balance between liberty and equality, the role of the state in regard to religion and the family, issues of sexual and reproductive freedom, the optimal severity of criminal punishment, our relation to the natural environment, and the proper treatment of minorities. When there is no academic consensus to report, the role of the journalist as translator is curtailed. He is reduced to reporting a fight, and the public wants to see the fighters.

In short, the media's demand for public intellectuals is derived from the demand of the educated general public for intellectual information *best supplied by public intellectuals* concerning issues of a broadly political character. To the extent that intellectual ideas can be competently translated for the general public by journalists, there is no reason to hire the originator of the ideas to be his own publicist. But this point is pertinent mainly to the information function of public-intellectual work. Its entertainment and solidarity functions may be best performed by the intellectual himself rather than by a journalist translator.

Let us consider the attributes that an academic is likely to need if he is to be marketable to the demanders of public-intellectual work. First he'll need communication skills, though this cannot be regarded as an absolute requirement when one considers what a poor writer yet important public intellectual John Dewey was. We must distinguish, however, between unclear writing and bad, or ineffective, writing. The oracular obscurity of a Heidegger and a Derrida, the elliptical style of Camille Paglia, and the dense academic style of Allan Bloom all proved effective vehicles for prominent public intellectuals. (Dewey, in contrast, had no style.) Increasingly the requisite communication skills include communicating via television. This has been a factor in Paglia's rise to prominence as a public intellectual, though her prominence may also be related to the entertainment dimension, in which she excels, of public-intellectual work.

The academic who aspires to play the role of public intellectual will also need (though again I would not describe this as an absolute prerequisite) *authority*. Almost by definition of academic expertise, and by the assumption that the public intellectual is addressing either a novel issue or an old one that continues to be contested, his audience will be unable to verify at first hand the truth of what he says. The logic and clarity of his exposition, or in a few cases the vatic or incantatory power of an obscurantist rather than limpid style, will provide some perceived warrant of the soundness of his views. This is a function of style that is distinct from communication. For we are in the domain of "rhetoric" in Aristotle's sense,[8] the suite of tactics for persuading people to take

8. See Aristotle, *Rhetoric* (W. Rhys Roberts trans.), in *The Complete Works of Aristotle: The Revised Oxford Translation*, vol. 2, p. 2152 (Jonathan Barnes ed., 1984); *Essays on Aristotle's*

one side or the other of issues that cannot be resolved by the application of logic, mathematics, controlled experiments, or other methods of exact reasoning. Almost all political and ideological issues fall into that domain, where one can do no better than to weigh probabilities and will often grasp at anything that provides a rational basis (sometimes we waive even this requirement) for shifting the balance.

Aristotle thought rhetoric on the whole a good thing, a way of getting closer to the truth in areas of ineradicable but not irreducible uncertainty. I prefer the neutral definition of rhetoric as "the art of persuasion using language," which implies that "rhetoric is not committed to using good arguments."[9] The test of good rhetoric is efficacy, not veracity.

Rhetoric has an economic interpretation. Economists distinguish between "inspection" and "credence" goods.[10] A good whose quality the consumer can determine by inspection (as by squeezing a melon to determine its ripeness) is unproblematic. But many goods have to be taken on faith, because their quality cannot be determined in advance of purchase or, what often amounts to the same thing, in normal use—cannot in fact be determined until it is too late for the consumer to avert a substantial loss. Examples are education in a particular private school, a chemical designed to make a house termite-proof, and a face lift designed to last a lifetime.

The market has a number of devices for increasing the buyer's trust in sellers of credence goods. One, the least reliable (except when it is linked to the fifth device, discussed below), is advertising. Another is the legally enforceable warranty. A third is reputation based on the experience of previous consumers. Even if most consumers never discover the product's defects and those that do discover them are too late to do anything about them, the cumulative effect of these consumers' bad experiences may register in the consciousness of other consumers, deterring them from buying the product. A fourth device is the consumer intermediary, such as a department store, a broker, an invest-

---

Rhetoric (Amélie Oksenberg Rorty ed., 1996); Brian Vickers, *In Defence of Rhetoric* (1988); Richard A. Posner, *Overcoming Law*, ch. 24 (1995).

9. John Shand, *Arguing Well* 23 (2000).

10. See, for example, Michael R. Darby and Edi Karni, "Free Competition and the Optimal Amount of Fraud," 16 *Journal of Law and Economics* 67 (1973); Asher Wolinsky, "Competition in Markets for Credence Goods," 151 *Journal of Institutional and Theoretical Economics* 117 (1995). See generally Dennis Carlton and Jeffrey M. Perloff, *Modern Industrial Organization*, pt. 4 (3d ed. 2000).

ment advisor, or a product-rating service such as *Consumer Reports* or the Michelin guides. Refereed journals and academic presses play this role in the market for scholarship. A fifth device is the seller's hope for repeat business, or more precisely the cost to him of losing future profits by pursuing a short-term strategy: the cost, in other words, of exit from the market. The more he has to lose if he is discovered to be cheating consumers (the more costs that he has "sunk" in this market in the sense that he cannot recover them if he is driven out) and thus acquires a bad reputation, the less likely he is to cheat.[11] Knowing or sensing this, consumers will have a justifiably greater confidence in the quality of this seller's product. The relation to advertising comes from the fact that one way of sinking costs is to spend a lot of money creating a popular trademark that may become valueless if the consumer discovers that the product is not as good as it was represented to be.

A distinction that parallels the one between inspection goods and credence goods is the distinction between monitoring output and monitoring inputs. If the quality of a seller's output can be determined readily, potential buyers have no reason to interest themselves in the quality of the inputs. But if the quality of the output cannot be determined readily, the next best way of ascertaining quality may be to monitor input quality. Careful screening of candidates for life-tenured federal judgeships is an example of input monitoring in a market in which the quality of the output is difficult to measure. To take another example, were we confident that courts could reliably determine the social costs of a traffic accident and of the measures that might have been taken to avert the accident, we could rely entirely on the tort system to optimize the number of accidents, viewed as an output of the use of the roads. Lacking such confidence we insist on regulating the inputs as well, such as the speed at which people drive. Similarly, in the case of credence goods we pay a lot of attention to the sellers' incentives and ability to produce a high-quality good rather than attempting to determine the quality of the good directly. Sometimes the law works on those incentives. I gave the example of enforceable warranties. Another example is punishment for fraud. In the market for judicial decisions, a classic credence good as I have noted, the law surrounds judges with

11. See Benjamin Klein and Keith B. Leffler, "The Role of Market Forces in Assuring Contractual Performance," 89 *Journal of Political Economy* 615 (1981). See generally *Reputation: Studies in the Voluntary Elicitation of Good Conduct* (Daniel B. Klein ed., 1997).

rules governing compensation, tenure, and conflicts of interest that are designed to reduce their incentive to market a defective product.

The opinions that public intellectuals "sell" are classic credence goods insofar as the informational as distinct from the entertainment and solidarity dimensions of public-intellectual work is concerned. Unable to monitor the quality of public-intellectual work reliably, the public—and its agents, the media—pay close attention to the quality of the inputs, that is, of the public intellectuals themselves. The consumers do not make a direct assessment of whether what the public intellectual says is true but instead decide whether the public intellectual is persuasive. Rhetoric is a set of devices for demonstrating the quality of the inputs into the production of credence symbolic goods. It thus bears the same relation to science as credence goods do to inspection goods. Or we might put it that rhetoric is to symbolic goods as advertising is to ordinary goods; the classic devices of rhetoric are well understood by Madison Avenue.[12]

Aristotle's theory of rhetoric emphasizes the "ethical appeal," which means trying to persuade your audience that, quite apart from the intrinsic merit of your argument, you are the type of person who is worthy of belief. The relation to input monitoring is direct. The ethical appeal is an appeal to the authority of the speaker or writer. Credentials, style, appearance, character—an audience's belief in the quality of these inputs into the speaker's output can enhance the credibility of the output with that audience.

The ethical appeal is in tension with the conventional view that *ad hominem* arguments—ones addressed to the character of the arguer rather than to the soundness of his arguments—are illegitimate. *Ad hominem* argumentation is the converse of the ethical appeal, so if the latter is legitimate, as Aristotle and later theorists of rhetoric have argued, why should the former be thought illegitimate? It should not be, at least not always. The conventional view rests on a confusion of domains. *Ad hominem* arguments are out of place in debates that can be settled definitively. But debates over politics and ideology, the domain of the public intellectual, are not of that character. When the debater's arguments must be taken, to a degree anyway, on faith, it is as

12. Larry Percy and John R. Rossiter, *Advertising Strategy: A Communication Theory Approach* 75–92 (1980). On the economics of rhetoric generally, see Posner, note 8 above, ch. 24.

rational to consider his general trustworthiness as it is to consider the general trustworthiness of any seller of credence goods. So if an adulterer writes an article denouncing adultery, we are entitled to consider whether his motivation may be guilt or an attempt to conceal his adultery or both. For if either or both motivations is operative, the denunciation is less likely to be the product of a sincere and well-reasoned belief in the wrongness of adultery and therefore somewhat less likely to be sound. Doubts about a public intellectual's character may thus give rise to rational doubts about the soundness of his views.

To take a positive example, when Orlando Patterson writes, "What is disturbing about Mr. Gore's [2000 presidential] campaign is that he has yielded to the established minority leadership (like the Congressional Black Caucus and some minority mayors), which is now committed to a conception of inclusiveness that eschews genuine social and cultural integration,"[13] the fact that Patterson is a politically liberal black confers additional credibility on his statement, beyond that conferred by his credential as a professor of sociology at a leading university.

All this is not to say that every mode of ethical appeal, or its mirror, *ad hominem* argumentation, is legitimate, even in areas to which the methods of exact inquiry cannot be applied. The academic public intellectual's most common mode of ethical appeal is simply to display his or her academic credentials, and this is neither as effective nor as innocent as it may seem. Academic credentials are both less important to the public than might be supposed and more important in the eyes of the public than they should be. They are less important in fields such as philosophy, history, sociology, political science, and law where there is no Nobel prize to provide dramatic validation and where as a result a large number of academics have credentials that are equally impressive in the eyes of a lay audience.

The more interesting point is that the public gives more weight to credentials than it should when an academic is opining outside of the area of his expertise. One reason is the tendency to exaggerate the degree to which a given human being is a unity—a single, consistent self whose behavior follows a predictable pattern. He is "good" or "bad," "kind" or "cruel," "wise" or "foolish," a "genius" or an "intellectual

---

13. Orlando Patterson, "The G.O.P. Isn't the Only Party to Dissemble on Race," *New York Times*, Aug. 6, 2000, § 4, p. 15.

lightweight," and so forth. The tendency is fostered by literature and the other arts, both popular and elite, which tend to depict "characters," the fictional counterparts of people, as unities, as types, consistent with Aristotle's thesis in the *Poetics* that fiction shows us what is probable and history what is actual. Most people, including most academics, are confusing mixtures. They are moral and immoral, kind and cruel, smart and stupid—yes, academics are often smart *and* stupid, and this may not be sufficiently recognized by the laity. They are particularly likely to be both smart and stupid in an era of specialization, when academic success is likely to crown not the person of broad general intelligence but rather the person with highly developed intellectual skills in a particular field, and both the field and the skills that conduce to preeminence in it may be bulkheaded from the other fields of thought. The brilliant mathematician, physicist, artist, or historian may be incompetent in dealing with political or economic issues. Einstein's political and economic writings are a case in point.[14] Picasso's artistic, or Sartre's literary and philosophical, or George Bernard Shaw's dramatic genius did not inoculate them against Stalinism, or Heidegger's philosophical genius against Nazism. But if the compartmentalization of competence, and the underlying disunity of the self, are not widely recognized—and they are not—a successful academic may be able to use his success to reach the general public on matters about which he is an idiot. It doesn't help that successful people tend to exaggerate their versatility; abnormal self-confidence is a frequent cause and almost invariable effect of great success.

The public is not irrational in giving credence to distinguished academics when the latter speak outside their field. It is rational not to be

---

14. Of Einstein's 1949 essay "Why Socialism?" (published in *Monthly Review*, May 1949, p. 9), a shallow Marxist tract (see also Einstein, *The World as I See It* 69–78 [1949]), it has been remarked: "Its low quality should help cure the occupational arrogance of natural scientists, physicists particularly, who pontificate amateurishly on social problems in a 'me for dictator' vein. Unfortunately, those natural scientists who read Einstein's essay are apt to be misled by the author's eminence and authority in his own field and will not investigate the essay's inadequacies." Martin Bronfenbrenner, "Radical Economics in America: A 1970 Survey," 8 *Journal of Economic Literature* 747, 762 (1970). Einstein advocated the creation of a world government to which the United States, the Soviet Union, and Great Britain would commit all their military strength, including the atomic bomb, at that time a U.S. monopoly. Albert Einstein as told to Raymond Swing, "Einstein on the Atomic Bomb," *Atlantic Monthly*, Nov. 1945, p. 43. See generally *Einstein on Peace* (Otto Nathan and Heinz Norden eds., 1960).

well informed about matters of no great moment to oneself, because it takes time and effort to become well informed, and these costs must be balanced against the benefits. We'll see in Chapter 4 that there is little evidence that public intellectuals are highly influential. If this is right, there is little payoff to the public as a whole in becoming well informed about the limitations of academic expertise and even less to an individual member of the public; a single individual's opinion on an issue of public moment is unlikely to be influential—which is why voters tend to be poorly informed about such issues.

The noninformational dimensions of the public intellectual's product are pertinent here. One buys a melon for its taste or nutritional value or both, and so the *quality* of the melon is directly instrumental to one's purposes. But often one will read an article by a public intellectual not to acquire information on which to rely but to be entertained or amused or to be reassured about or reinforced in one's opinions. To the ends of entertainment and solidarity the quality of the public intellectual's ideas may be secondary to his "star" quality or his rhetorical gifts ("rhetorical" now in the pejorative sense). The solidarity dimension of public-intellectual work may clash with the informational dimension in another way as well. It promotes the division of public intellectuals into warring camps, and thus undermines their credibility by underscoring their partisanship.

Several of the points I've been making are related to specialization, which is multiply threatening to the quality and impact of intellectuals' interventions in public debate as well as important in explaining the growing domination of the public-intellectual market by academics. Specialization of knowledge reduces the ability of academic intellectuals to speak clearly to general public issues, of nonacademic intellectuals to get a public hearing, and of the general educated public to understand arguments about public issues. Specialization also challenges the vertical integration of which I spoke earlier. Let me elaborate on all four of these points.

Specialization makes it difficult for an intellectual to write for a general audience. His orientation is toward writing for his fellow specialists on narrow topics in an esoteric jargon. For jargon is the natural tendency of language when people communicate primarily with members of an in-group—and so we witness the increasing mathematization of economics and the obscurity of word and syntax of much of the current writing in the humanities. The modern academic intellectual usually cannot, as earlier generations of intellectuals could and did, pitch his writing at a level that is accessible to a general audience yet does not strike the author's peers as lacking in rigor—he needs two styles of writing, one for the public and one for his peers. Tenure and the sheer size of the academic community[15] have liberated academics from having to learn to communicate with anyone outside their in-group. If they want to reach a broader audience, they must make an extra effort to do so.

The increasing specialization of knowledge has also made it more difficult for an intellectual who *can* write for a general audience to obtain the credentials that will impress that audience. He will first have to become an academic specialist. He will have to learn to walk the walk and talk the talk. This generally requires a tedious and time-consuming apprenticeship repulsive to many intellectuals; Richard Rorty has spoken aptly of the "introverted hyperprofessionalism" of the modern academic.[16] A related point is that specialization makes it difficult for an intellectual to pursue a nonacademic career; it pushes him into the academy. I mentioned in the preceding chapter that journalists are not in a good position to acquire specialized knowledge and here I add that neither are writers of fiction, traditionally an important source of public intellectuals—think only of Hugo and Zola, Harriet Beecher Stowe, George Bernard Shaw, Thomas and Heinrich Mann, Albert Camus, Norman Mailer, Saul Bellow, and James Baldwin. As knowledge becomes more complex, the areas in which writers can contribute to it shrink. *Moby-Dick* is among other things a competent (for its time) natural history of the whale, and writers as diverse as Edith Wharton, William Faulkner, and Ralph Ellison were skilled ethnologists; Swift, Dickens, and Orwell superb political satirists; and Tolstoy and Solzhenitsyn distinguished fictionalizing historians. As the natural and social sciences mature, the room for amateur contributions contracts.

15. Total faculty in American institutions of higher education rose from fewer than 6,000 in 1869 to more than 380,000 in 1959 and more than 900,000 in 1995. National Center for Education Statistics, "Fall Staff in Postsecondary Institutions, 1995" E-3 (March 1998) (tab. E–1).

16. Richard Rorty, "When Work Disappears," *Dissent*, Summer 1997, p. 111. He was speaking of the social sciences, but his term is equally applicable to the humanities. On the professionalization of philosophy, for example, see the tart observations in Liam Hudson, "Oxford Attitudes," *Times Literary Supplement*, June 9, 2000, p. 28.

Specialization narrows the mind at the same time that it sharpens it. Intellectual tasks are broken up into smaller and smaller packets, and intellectual workers just like factory workers achieve proficiency by concentrated, repetitive application to narrowly circumscribed tasks. One symptom is the growth of collaborative authorship in academia[17]—academic work increasingly is teamwork, just like industrial production, where each team member performs only a part of the overall productive function. The modern academic thus buys intellectual power at the expense of scope. A public intellectual is a generalist, but in an age of specialized knowledge the generalist is condemned to be an amateur; and the views of amateurs carry little weight with professionals.

Before literary criticism became an academic specialty—when the academic study of literature was historical or philological rather than critical—nonuniversity critics could compete on equal terms with university ones; both types were amateurs in a field that had no professionals. Philosophy, economics, sociology, psychology, anthropology, and history are all fields that, like literary criticism, or for that matter astronomy, were once far less technical and specialized, thus far more open to intelligent contributions from amateurs, than they have become. The professionalization of knowledge has made it much more difficult for intellectual freebooters to range across different fields, in the manner, say, of George Orwell. Orwell wrote literary criticism, satiric novels, sociological and ethnographic commentary, political science, and economics, all in lucid nonspecialist prose—and he had not even attended university. The scope for the public intellectual shrinks as more and more areas of knowledge are withdrawn from the amateur arena and become academized, and likewise the range of individuals from which the public intellectual is drawn shrinks. The public-intellectual market has become dominated by academic specialists who venture outside the walls of their specialty from time to time to cross

17. See, for example, David N. Leband and Robert D. Tollison, "Intellectual Collaboration," 108 *Journal of Political Economy* 632 (2000); Siva Nathan, Dana R. Hermanson, and Roger H. Hermanson, "Co-Authoring in Refereed Journals: Views of Accounting Faculty and Department Chairs," 13 *Issues in Accounting Education* 79–80 (1998); F. Ellen Netting and Ann Nichols-Casebolt, "Authorship and Collaboration: Preparing the Next Generation of Social Work Scholars," 33 *Journal of Social Work Education* 555, 556 (1997); Jean Louis Heck and Peter A. Zaleski, "Trends in Economic-Journal Literature: 1969–89," *Atlantic Economic Journal*, Dec. 1991, pp. 27–28.

swords on the field of political and ideological battle, a battlefield not yet academized.

My third point is that the specialization of knowledge that has given the modern university its distinctive character has also affected the knowledge base of the public intellectual's audience. We are all specialists now. No longer is there a common intellectual culture, the possession of a versatile and influential intellectual elite. The academic public intellectual is an expert speaking to an educated audience few members of which will know enough about his subject—whether it is ecology, penology, national defense, foreign policy, technology, sexual minorities, or presidential impeachment—to catch his errors. Consumer intermediaries have not emerged that would make up for the knowledge deficits of the consumers of public-intellectual work. The media do some screening, but not much.

Another way to put this is that credence goods are such only in virtue of the limitations of their buyers' knowledge. As knowledge become more specialized, more goods are credence goods. The character of public-intellectual work as a credence good is much more pronounced than it was half a century ago.

Fourth, increasing specialization poses a threat to the continued existence of the least problematic of public-intellectual genres, the one I have dubbed "self-popularizing." I mentioned earlier in this chapter that it is unusual for a manufacturer to do his own retailing. Yet that is what an academic does who "retails" his academic work to the general public by writing it up in a form accessible to nonspecialists. As a market expands in size, there is a tendency for the various functions that go into producing its end product to be contracted out to specialized producers rather than remaining within a single producer.[18] Specialization lowers costs, provided the market is large enough to enable the specialized producers of the various components of the market's end product to achieve an efficient scale of operations. The end product of the toothpaste market is the retail sale of a tube of toothpaste and is produced by the combined efforts of the manufacturer of the toothpaste (who no doubt buys many of the components, the container for example, from other manufacturers), the wholesaler, and the retailer. As the

18. George J. Stigler, "The Division of Labor Is Limited by the Extent of the Market," in Stigler, *The Organization of Industry* 129 (1968).

public-intellectual market expands—and it is expanding, as we'll see—
we can expect the retail function, which is to say the translation of academic ideas into a form accessible to the general public, to be taken
over increasingly by specialized journalists rather than remaining a
function performed by the academic creator of the ideas.

The trend toward ever-greater specialization of knowledge has not
gone unchallenged. The rise of interdisciplinary research, and the concomitant blurring of disciplinary boundaries (sociology, anthropology,
political science, and political philosophy are, for example, increasingly
difficult to distinguish from one another), can be seen as reactions
against excessive specialization. But interdisciplinarity and public intellectuality are not the same thing. A book by a literary critic on confessions in the criminal law can be as daunting an academic work as a book
by a literary critic on confessions in works of literature.[19] This book is
interdisciplinary but academic, though I hope not dauntingly so. And
interdisciplinarity often signifies merely the proliferation of specialized
fields: "law and economics" (that is, economic analysis of law) and
"public choice" (economic analysis of politics) are, for example, specialized fields with their own scholarly associations and journals.

In considering the market demand for public intellectuals, we must
not make the mistake of thinking that every academic, even every distinguished academic, could become a public intellectual just by deciding to put on a second hat. In a society in which intellectuality and
academic prowess are not very highly regarded, sterling academic credentials may not be enough to command public attention. (To the extent that they are neither sufficient nor necessary, however, this creates
some room for the nonspecialist to flourish as a public intellectual.)
Life experiences may be important. One reason so many well-known
public intellectuals are black, such as Anthony Appiah, Stephen Carter,
Michael Eric Dyson, Henry Louis Gates Jr., Lani Guinier, Thomas
Sowell, Shelby Steele, Cornel West, Patricia Williams, and William
Julius Wilson, is that blacks are believed to have life experiences that
give them insights denied the ordinary white male academic. Yet *all* the
black public intellectuals whom I have mentioned are academics. This
illustrates how the market for public intellectuals is becoming dominated by academics at the same time that the growth of academic spe-

---

19. Peter Brooks's book *Troubling Confessions: Speaking Guilt in Law and Literature* (2000),
is both.

cialization has made it increasingly difficult for academics to fill the public-intellectual role.

Two other warrants of authority, of credibility, besides academic credentials are particularly important for the modern public intellectual: *celebrity* and *commitment*. They can be regarded as additional aspects of a public intellectual's ethical appeal. We are more likely to give credence to the views of someone we know, or think we know, than to those of a complete stranger because we feel, perhaps mistakenly, that we can size up a person if we meet him. Television gives us the illusion of knowing celebrities.[20] We don't actually meet or talk to them, but we see them being interviewed by people much like ourselves and asked the questions that we might ask if we knew them. When Robert Bork was grilled by the Senate Judiciary Committee in 1987 after President Reagan had nominated him for the Supreme Court, those who watched the televised proceedings had a chance vicariously to "interview" Bork and form an impression of him that gave his later writings as a public intellectual (see Chapter 8) added weight. Moreover—turning now to commitment—just as Catharine MacKinnon's inability to obtain tenure until late in her academic career, long after she had become one of the most influential legal academics in the United States, was evidence of the seriousness of her commitment to her unpopular views, so the fact that Bork "paid" for the views he expounded in the confirmation hearing by being denied confirmation was evidence of his integrity.

A parallel example of commitment is Lani Guinier, a previously obscure University of Pennsylvania Law School professor whose nomination to be head of the civil rights division of the Justice Department at the outset of the Clinton administration was withdrawn by the president when her views were criticized as extreme. Her rejection drew national attention to her and the views for which she had been "martyred" and became the launching pad for a very successful career as a public intellectual writing about issues of race, feminism, and education. Eco-catastrophist Paul Ehrlich demonstrated his commitment to fighting overpopulation by having himself sterilized after fathering one child.[21] The *reductio ad absurdum* of the academic public intellectual's striving to demonstrate commitment is the photograph of Edward Said

---

20. Cf. Putnam, note 6 above, at 242.
21. Paul R. Ehrlich, "People Pollution," *Audubon*, May 1970, pp. 1, 8.

throwing a stone at Israeli soldiers from across the Lebanese border after Israel evacuated the zone in southern Lebanon that it had occupied for many years.[22] He was taking no risks; the Israelis weren't shooting back. Guinier, Ehrlich, and Said are our Havels and Solzhenitsyns, writ small.

Talk is cheap; when the talker is willing to pay a price, we listen with greater attentiveness because we know that the views expressed are not held merely casually or opportunistically ("commitment" meaning just that there is a price to be paid for relinquishing them). The literal martyr is merely the extreme example of the person who puts his money where his mouth is, which is what the seller of an ordinary credence does when he operates his business in such a way that should consumers become dissatisfied and turn away from him he will incur large costs. Sinking costs to make exit costly is a method of commitment.

The academic public intellectual lacks effective methods of voluntary commitment, although we'll encounter in Chapter 4 a rare instance in which a pair of public intellectuals bet money on their respective predictions, though not enough for a loss to hurt. Failure as a public intellectual will not jeopardize the public intellectual's academic employment; intellectual bankruptcy rarely has grave financial implications. The costs of exit from the public-intellectual market are thus, for an academic, very low. In addition, the public intellectual cannot issue a legally enforceable warranty of the validity of his statements. Deprived of two of the most effective tools by which sellers of credence goods build credibility, the public intellectual finds it more difficult than the seller of an ordinary credence good to persuade the public that his product is of high quality. This is a factor in the very limited influence that public intellectuals appear to have over public opinion, as we shall see in Chapter 4. Just as legalizing the burning of the American flag weakens the act's rhetorical impact by cheating the flag burner of "martyrdom," so academic tenure in a society that extravagantly protects freedom of expression (the Supreme Court has held that it is *unconstitutional* to punish flag burning) makes it difficult for the public intellectual to cut an impressive figure. "The angry and alienated social critic bangs his head against a rubber wall. He encounters infinite tolerance

22. See "Representation of an Intellectual," *New Republic*, July 24, 2000, p. 10; Karen W. Anderson, "Columbia Breaks Silence on Prominent Professor's 'Symbolic' Stone-Throwing," *New York Times* (national ed.), Oct. 19, 2000, p. A27.

when what he would like is the respect of resistance."[23] "Intellectuals often trumpet their marginality, but their marginality is more and more marginal . . . Marginality is a pose and . . . the self-defined outsiders are, and are glad to be, consummate insiders."[24]

There is a double sense of marginality worth noting here. It is brought out in Leon Fink's observation that "even the most well-intentioned and sensitive intellectuals have trouble dislodging themselves from their own sheltered perches to make honest, let alone efficacious, contact with the world of ordinary citizens,"[25] and in Cornel West's statement that "caught between an insolent American society and insouciant black community, the Afro-American who takes seriously the life of the mind inhabits an isolated and insulated world."[26] In one sense that is obviously not true of West himself, a full professor at Harvard after many years as a full professor at Princeton. But in another sense it is true of him and of most academic public intellectuals. There is a lack of efficacy in their public-intellectual work that makes that work marginal to the society. Part of the reason is the cocooned life of a tenured professor at a prestigious university. West wants to help his fellow black Americans, but it is apparent from his writings that he is much more comfortable talking about Hegel, Gramsci, Lyotard, Jameson, and other intellectual notables unknown to nonacademic people of any color than formulating or articulating social reforms that might help such people. He made little impression on black Americans by his active support of Bill Bradley for the Democratic presidential nomination in 2000; blacks supported Gore overwhelmingly—and not because West's Harvard colleague Henry Louis Gates Jr. was equally active in support of Gore![27]

23. Michael Walzer, *The Company of Critics: Social Criticism and Political Commitment in the Twentieth Century* 16 (1988) (a quip Walzer attributes to Irving Howe).

24. Russell Jacoby, *The End of Utopia: Politics and Culture in an Age of Apathy* 122–123 (1999).

25. Leon Fink, *Progressive Intellectuals and the Dilemmas of Democratic Commitment* 285 (1997).

26. Cornel West, "The Dilemma of the Black Intellectual," in West, *The Cornel West Reader* 302 (1999).

27. See Carey Goldberg, "Bradley and Gore Campaigns Split Harvard's Top Black Scholars," *New York Times* (late ed.), Jan. 15, 2000, p. A10. On the situation of the black public intellectual, see Dyson, note 1 above, ch. 2; Sidney I. Dobrin, "Race and the Public Intellectual: A Conversation with Michael Eric Dyson," in *Race, Rhetoric, and the Postcolonial* 81 (Gary A. Olson and Lynn Worsham eds., 1999).

So public intellectuals may be "marginal" after all, but not in the dangerous sense in which Socrates found himself marginalized. This is not to deny the existence of censorship and discrimination in American universities. But nowadays the victims tend not to be academic public intellectuals, simply because most academic public intellectuals are liberal. Today's censorship is mainly of the "political correctness" variety, which rules out frank discussion of race, ethnic, and gender differences and of sexual orientation.[28] There is a decided degree of intolerance of conservative, but not of liberal or even extreme left-wing, views and speakers,[29] while the covert but widespread discrimination in favor of blacks and women in faculty hiring constitutes a diffuse but cumulatively significant discrimination against white male academics. Since, as we'll see in Chapter 5, the public-intellectual market is dominated by left-leaners, most intellectuals take no risks in expressing their views publicly.

I qualified my statement that academics have difficulty demonstrating commitment by inserting "voluntary" before "commitment." Catharine MacKinnon did not want to be delayed in getting tenure any more than Bork wanted to be turned down for appointment to the Supreme Court or Guinier for appointment as head of the civil rights division. When the only forms of credible commitment are involuntary, luck is bound to play a large role in determining who achieves prominence as a public intellectual. Not that MacKinnon, Bork, or Guinier felt lucky to encounter professional setbacks; but the setbacks did (perhaps unforeseeably) provide platforms for the launching of a successful career as a public intellectual, in the case of Guinier, and for enhanced prominence in that career in the case of the other two. The greater the effect of luck on a career, the weaker the correlation between success and quality.

28. See, for example, John Leo, *Incorrect Thoughts: Notes on Our Wayward Culture*, pt. 2 (2001); Richard J. Ellis, *The Dark Side of the Left: Illiberal Egalitarianism in America* 214–222 (1998).

29. As documented in Paul Hollander, *Anti-Americanism: Critiques at Home and Abroad 1965–1990*, ch. 3 (1992). Hollander is a serious scholar; his work is not to be confused with the polemical accounts of leftist domination of American higher education that have drawn the scorn of left-leaning academics.

Supply

In turning now to the supply side of the market for public intellectuals, I emphasize the intellectuals themselves rather than the communications media, the conduits. But it is relevant to note that the cost of these conduits appears to be falling as a consequence of increased media competition (a result in part of deregulation and in part of technological advances), which has given intellectuals greater access to the public. With hundreds of television channels to fill, with the Internet a growing medium for the communication of news and opinion, and with newspapers becoming ever more like magazines in an effort to maintain readership in the face of the lure of continuously updated news on television and over the Internet, the opportunity cost to the media of providing a platform for public intellectuals has shrunk.

The media have a symbiotic relationship with public intellectuals. The media need to fill up a great deal of print and electronic space. Public intellectuals want publicity both for its own sake and as advertising for their books and public lectures,[30] and so they are willing to appear on television or radio talk shows and to write op-ed pieces for nothing, though newspapers sometimes pay the author of an op-ed piece and some public intellectuals now charge foreign journalists for television and radio interviews.[31] Of course, were there very little public demand for what public intellectuals have to say, the media would not use them to fill space on a page or take up airtime unless they *paid* to appear. That is not quite so far-fetched a suggestion as it may seem. It would perfect the advertising analogy. Consumers are not utterly uninterested in advertising—it does help them decide what to buy—but they won't incur even the modest time costs of watching television commercials without being paid to do so, as through the interleaving of commercials with free entertainment.[32]

Soon, with the rise of Internet-enabled distance learning[33] that will

30. For which they are often paid handsomely. See, for example, Kurtz, note 5 above, at 226.

31. Id. at 226–227.

32. See Gary S. Becker and Kevin M. Murphy, "A Simple Theory of Advertising as a Good or a Bad," in Becker, *Accounting for Tastes* 203, 223–224 (1996).

33. See, for example, Ann Grimes, "A Matter of Degree: After a Slow Start, Universities

allow professors to multiply the number of their students by orders of magnitude and the most successful professors to command salaries commensurate with those of true media celebrities, status as a public intellectual—a status that draws students, who don't know any better and often don't care—will enable a number of professors to reap huge monetary rewards. Being a public intellectual will *really* pay. Maybe a time will come when academics *will* pay to appear on television talk shows.

The pool of academic public-intellectual eligibles—academics for whom there is sufficient potential demand in the public-intellectual market to induce the media to give them a platform if they want it—is larger than the actual number of "performing" public intellectuals. This implies that there are costs involved in being a public intellectual. The principal costs are two. The first is the opportunity cost: the time that is expended on writing for or engaging in other expressive activities oriented toward the general public is unavailable for teaching, scholarly research, consulting, and leisure. All these activities—the last obviously, the third rarely—yield nonpecuniary benefits, and it is primarily these that are sacrificed to doing public-intellectual work, since the celebrity yielded by that work may generate an increase in one's academic salary and one's hourly consulting fee, though it can also reduce the former by lessening the academic repute in which the professor is held.

Other things being equal, therefore, we would expect the ablest scholars to be the least drawn to the career of a public intellectual, because the value of their forgone academic output, an important part of the full (that is, nonpecuniary as well as pecuniary) income of a productive scholar, would be greatest. But other things are not equal. The ablest scholars are likely to have more energy and better expository skills than the average academic, as well as more impressive credentials. We should expect the ranks of public intellectuals to be especially rich in able scholars who are in the twilight of their academic career; Albert Einstein and Bertrand Russell were examples. Because reputation tends to lag achievement, a scholar is apt to reach the zenith of his reputation

---

Are Going on the Offensive against Virtual U's. They Get High Marks for Effort," *Wall Street Journal*, July 17, 2000, p. R29; Michael Heise, "Closing One Gap but Opening Another?: A Response to Dean Perritt and Comments on the Internet, Law Schools, and Legal Education," 33 *Indiana Law Review* 275, 289–290 (1999).

when he is past the zenith of his scholarly productivity. His prospects for success as a public intellectual will thus be brightening at the same time that the opportunity cost of diverting his energies from scholarship is declining.

That cost has both pecuniary and nonpecuniary elements. The first are easier to study, and it has been found that the pecuniary returns to scholarly publication indeed diminish both with age and with output.[34] In contrast, a person's writing style will often continue improving, and certainly will not deteriorate, until long after his analytical or creative energies have begun to flag.[35] A young person, moreover, will rarely have accrued sufficient indicia of authority to break into the public-intellectual market, will often lack the rhetorical skills to perform effectively in that market if he does enter it, and will usually incur prohibitive opportunity costs of entering it, given the higher incomes and greater job security of academic public intellectuals compared to independent public intellectuals. We can expect the vast majority of living public intellectuals to be middle-aged or elderly.

The second cost of being a public intellectual is the risk of making a fool of oneself by making public comments in advance of complete knowledge of the events being commented on. A scholar works within a well-defined groove and so long as he adheres to the norms of his calling is unlikely to make many embarrassing errors. But the public intellectual operates without a safety net. He has to decide whether to be for or against communism, or avant-garde art, or capital punishment, or military intervention, or impeachment of the president, or public school vouchers, or the teaching of evolution when these are issues occurring in "real time" and therefore in circumstances often of radically incomplete knowledge. History may show him up as a fool, and quickly too, as we shall be seeing throughout this book. This risk may deter able academics from entering the public-intellectual arena. But we'll also see that public intellectuals who do not expect to undergo the close scrutiny of a biographer pay little cost in reputation even for being repeatedly proved wrong by events.

The academic-turned-public-intellectual pays another price: that of being derided by his academic colleagues. (The counterpart phenome-

34. Howard P. Tuckman and Jack Leahey, "What Is an Article Worth?" 83 *Journal of Political Economy* 951 (1975).

35. Richard A. Posner, *Aging and Old Age* 167–169 (1995).

non, in the case of the nonacademic public intellectual, is to be patronized by academics—the fate of T. S. Eliot, for example.)[36] In the words of the distinguished economist George Stigler, echoing Weber's dictum that "limitation to specialized work, with a renunciation of the Faustian universality of man which it involves, is a condition of any valuable work in the modern world,"[37]

> specialism is the royal road to efficiency in intellectual as in economic life. The widely trained individual simply cannot hold his own in any field with the individual of equal ability and energy who specializes in that field. Indeed, the individual who now attempts to survey a whole science or discipline is viewed as a popularizer ("journalist") or even as a charlatan, but definitely not as a creative scholar.[38]

Stigler's argument is not airtight. He ignores the possibility that a person of superior ability who does not specialize may outperform the specialist; he has no concept of optimal specialization; and he oddly assumes that the intellectual world is divided into journalists, charlatans, and creative scholars. The essay is also self-referential, since Stigler does not claim to be a specialist in the theory of scholarly specialization. Stigler himself—and not only in this essay and the book of which it is a part—was both less specialized, and more interesting, than the current crop of economists, few of whom (like few engineers or physicians) would be considered an intellectual, as Stigler undoubtedly was. Yet in the essay that I have just quoted from he describes himself as a specialist and his field of specialization as "homogeneous oligopoly,"[39] ignoring among other things his important contributions to the unrelated field of the history of economic thought. Years later Stigler *became* a public intellectual. But in deriding the generalist, Stigler was express-

36. For an excellent discussion, see William Arrowsmith, "Eliot's Learning," 2 *Literary Imagination* 153 (2000).

37. Max Weber, *The Protestant Ethic and The Spirit of Capitalism* 180 (Talcott Parsons trans., 1958). See also Weber, "Science as a Vocation," in *From Max Weber: Essays in Sociology* 129, 135 (H. H. Gerth and C. Wright Mills trans., 1946).

38. George J. Stigler, "Specialism: A Dissenting Opinion," in Stigler, *The Intellectual and the Market Place, and Other Essays* 9, 11 (1963).

39. Id. at 10.

ing a common academic view, and that is all I'm interested in showing here.

The supply of public intellectuals is of course a function of the benefits as well as the costs of a career as a public intellectual. The benefits are pecuniary as well as nonpecuniary. Distance learning to one side, public intellectuals often write books that sell well and give lectures for which they are paid, sometimes very handsomely; even some public intellectuals in the humanities have been known to receive lecture fees in five figures. And often the same ones who command large lecture fees also receive generous research grants from foundations or think tanks that value their public-intellectual work. A sampling of public intellectuals in 1969 revealed that their incomes were higher than that of the average professor.[40]

Granted, we must distinguish between expected and realized gains. Allan Bloom made millions of dollars in royalties from *The Closing of the American Mind*, but neither he nor his publisher expected the book to be a bestseller, and no doubt he would have sold his copyright in advance of publication for a small fraction of the ultimate royalties. Still, the pecuniary rewards of public intellectualhood are not trivial. Robert Putnam, the professor of political science who wrote *Bowling Alone*, which I discuss in Chapter 8, received an advance of several hundred thousand dollars from his publisher, Simon and Schuster. An advance is pretty good evidence of the ex ante monetary value of a book to the author. Academic presses rarely pay large advances, and trade presses rarely publish a book aimed at only an academic audience. Most of the books by public intellectuals that I discuss in this book were published by trade presses rather than by academic presses.

The academic who publishes with a trade press gives up a lot; this is part of the opportunity cost to a scholar of becoming a public intellectual. He loses the benefits of peer review, of review by a faculty board, and of careful editing by acquisition and manuscript editors who understand and value scholarship. In addition, trade presses usually remainder a book after a year—a symbol of the ephemeral quality of most nonscholarly work—whereas academic presses generally keep their books in print for many years despite small annual sales. And trade presses often push their academic authors to tart up their books

40. Charles Kadushin, *The American Intellectual Elite* 340 (1974).

with "human interest" touches that offend the fastidious, a class that may include the author. Lately, however, the two types of press show signs of convergence, with trade presses establishing academic divisions and academic presses establishing trade divisions and hiring "developmental editors" to rewrite academic books to give them wider appeal.

For most public intellectuals, the pecuniary benefits of public-intellectual work are modest and probably are dwarfed by the nonpecuniary benefits of public admiration or attention, which for many are substantial. Most people are known only to a small number of individuals besides the members of their family. Academics are known more widely, especially if they publish. Nevertheless their circle too is a constricted one, especially in an age of academic specialization. Philosophers, someone has said, are no longer famous—except among philosophers. Yet many people, including many academic and other intellectuals, derive great pleasure from being known to a broader public, even a nondiscerning and uncritical one—that is, from being celebrities, even minor ones. Henry James spoke of "*the* greed, the great one, the eagerness to figure, the snap at the bait of publicity."[41] Whether they are admired is secondary; for many people it is enough to be notorious. There is also the pleasure that comes from influencing the course of events—in other words, from exercising power. Few public intellectuals have any power to speak of, but writing and being written about create for many people the illusion of power.

Not to be overlooked is the private satisfaction derived from writing well and clearly, which may be a welcome relief from the conventions that govern academic writing, especially for professors who are becoming academically superannuated. And some professors write as public intellectuals out of passionate conviction, a felt duty to "bear witness" regardless of the likely impact of their public-intellectual work. How else to explain the enormous volume of Noam Chomsky's political writings (see next chapter), which has taken a great deal of time away from his immensely distinguished academic career and yet has received little public attention, much of it derisory? Of course, Chomsky may simply have an exaggerated sense of his influence, or believe that, as in

41. Henry James, "The Papers," in James, *Complete Stories 1898–1910* 542, 546 (1996) (emphasis in original).

the case of some other dishonored prophets, his influence will be great in the long run.

With the rise of distance learning and the general expansion of electronic media of communication, the size of the audience for, and hence both the pecuniary and the nonpecuniary rewards of, the most successful public intellectuals should be increasing. This trend might be expected to draw more and abler academics into the public-intellectual market. But the qualification "most successful" must be emphasized. A technological or economic change that reduces the cost at which producers of intellectual property can reach potential customers will lead to an increase in the incomes of the most successful producers, but not necessarily to an increase in average incomes, or even in the number of producers.[42] The advent of the compact disc may have led to a (further) decline in the number of orchestras, since the best orchestras could now compete for audiences all over the world; they became closer substitutes for average orchestras. Such an outcome is not certain; a reduction in the cost of reaching an audience may create niches for new orchestras that will cater to the tastes of a widely dispersed minority.[43] Similarly, many public intellectuals may lose market as their most successful rivals obtain greater access to a national or international audience through the electronic media and as these media become a more important outlet for public-intellectual work compared to books and magazines, while at the same time the expansion of the media creates new opportunities for less prominent public intellectuals to reach niche audiences. Since success in the electronic media is not well correlated with intellectual quality, there is no reason to expect the expansion of the media to lead to an increase in either the number or the quality of public intellectuals, though it should increase the aggregate output of the public-intellectual market.

The foregoing discussion should dispel any mystery about the fact that an ample supply of public intellectuals is forthcoming in response to the demand. And ample it is. Far from there being any shortage of public intellectuals, we are awash in them. The "superstar" phenomenon discussed in the preceding paragraph has boosted the pecuniary and nonpecuniary earnings of the most prominent public intellectuals

42. See Sherwin Rosen, "The Economics of Superstars," 71 *American Economic Review* 845 (1981).

43. See Cowen, note 3 above, at 101–108.

without thinning the public-intellectual ranks. The only shortage is of unaffiliated, and specifically of nonacademic, public intellectuals. Increased specialization of knowledge has made it harder for nonspecialists to write or speak with authority on intellectual matters; increasingly when they do so they are treading on the toes of a jealous specialist. But this is not a complete explanation if we assume that the academic public intellectual does not satisfy the demand for public-intellectual work as well as the independent intellectual does (or did). For in that event there would be a separable demand for the independent public intellectual. Something other than a paucity of demand must be drying up the supply of independent public intellectuals. That something is the vast increase in the size, wealth, and inclusiveness of the university sector, factors distinct from though closely related to the growing specialization of knowledge. The faculties of colleges and universities were once not only small but also hostile to Jews, blacks, women, and left-wingers—all groups well represented among modern public intellectuals—and paid lousy salaries. There was a time when an intellectual could do as well (or rather no worse) for himself financially by writing books and articles as by being a professor. That time is largely past. The opportunity cost of being an independent public intellectual has skyrocketed because of the greatly increased economic opportunities in the academic market.

Of course there is a "shortage" of independent public intellectuals in an economic sense only if there is unsatisfied demand, but there may be. Not private demand, but social demand if independent public intellectuals make a distinctive and on the whole useful contribution to social thought and progress, as they may.

The Market Equilibrium

We must now put together the demand for and supply of public intellectuals. This is done in Figure 2.1.

Line *D* represents demand. It slopes downward to indicate that the more public intellectuals there are, the less the public will "pay" for the last, the marginal, one (more precisely the last unit of output), where pay is understood to include both pecuniary and nonpecuniary income. The immediate demanders, remember, are not the public but the media, both print and electronic, but theirs is a derived demand—derived

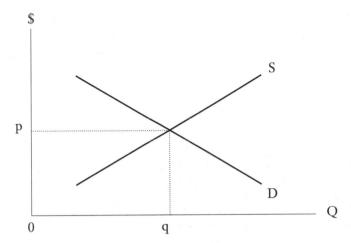

Figure 2.1 Demand for and supply of public intellectuals

from the demand of the public for public-intellectual work. Line *S* represents the supply of that work. It slopes upward to indicate that the cost of supplying public-intellectual services increases with the quantity supplied. The intersection of *D* and *S* determines the quantity of public-intellectual services produced (*q*) and the "price" (*p*) in money and other (call it psychic) income that the producers receive.

The principal cost of supplying public-intellectual services is the opportunity cost of the individual's time. Some public intellectuals have very low opportunity costs of time, and if only a small quantity of public-intellectual services is demanded they will supply it at low cost, on the left-hand side of the diagram. As a greater and greater quantity is demanded, public intellectuals having higher opportunity costs of time are drawn into the market, provided the public is willing to cover those costs. The suppliers include both academics and nonacademics. But the opportunity costs of academics tend to be lower, because academic employers do not buy an academic's full working time and because of complementarities between, for example, teaching and public-intellectual work.

With the expansion of universities, higher academic salaries, lighter teaching loads,[44] shorter academic years, and less discrimination (par-

44. More precisely, more faculty "discretionary time," time available for "pursuing professional and personal goals, largely by loosening their institutional ties and responsibilities." William F. Massy and Robert Zemsky, "Faculty Discretionary Time: Departments and the

ticularly against Jews, who as we'll see in Chapter 5 account for a high percentage of public intellectuals), an increasing percentage of public intellectuals are academics. Put differently, the opportunity costs of an academic career, in terms of alternative careers forgone, have been falling. And we have seen that academics have a natural cost advantage over nonacademics in the public-intellectual market. So not only do we expect a growing share of the supply in that market to come from academics (as indeed appears to be the case, as we'll also see in Chapter 5), but the cost of that supply should be proportionately lower at every level of output. Thus lighter teaching loads and shorter academic years have a dual significance: as making an academic career more attractive and as giving academics more time in which to do public-intellectual work.

The reduction in the cost of supplying public-intellectual services could be shown in Figure 2.1 by rotating S downward from its intersection with the vertical axis. When this is done, S intersects D at a lower point, implying a lower market price and a greater output. But at the same time that S has been falling (not supply, but the cost of supply at any given output), D has been rising for reasons explained earlier. This could be shown in Figure 2.1 by rotating D upward from its intersection with the vertical axis. When D rises and S declines at the same time, the unequivocal effect is greater output, but whether price rises, falls, or stays the same depends on the relative shifts of D and S.

Undoubtedly the aggregate amount of public-intellectual work has increased in the last half century. It is less clear whether the average price paid for that work has increased. Price and income must be distinguished. The larger audience that the most successful public intellectuals can reach today should lead to an increase in their full income, both pecuniary, since it costs only trivially more to disseminate intellectual property to a large audience than to a small one (and so the larger revenue generated by reaching a larger audience is not offset by a commensurate increase in cost), and psychic, since fame as well as revenue is a function of the size of one's audience.[45] But to the extent

---

'Academic Ratchet,'" 65 *Journal of Higher Education* 1, 2–3, 21 (1994). However, Jeffrey F. Milem, Joseph B. Berger, and Eric L. Dey, "Faculty Time Allocation: A Study of Change over Twenty Years," 71 *Journal of Higher Education* 454 (2000), find no overall decrease in teaching loads, except for a statistically nonsignificant decrease in research universities.

45. I emphasize that fame and revenue are practically as well as conceptually distinct. A

that the superstar public intellectual's income has risen because of a rise in his output, which is a function not only of how much he writes but of how many readers (or viewers or listeners, if he makes radio or television appearances) he has (a writer's output is not the number of books he writes, but the number of copies of them he sells), there is no implication that price per unit of output has risen. The average price of that output may not have risen at all (in real, that is, inflation-adjusted terms), may in fact have fallen, just as the incomes of successful entrepreneurs in the computer software business are negatively correlated with the price of software, which has been falling steadily.

As I noted earlier, the effect of the larger potential audience for public-intellectual work in increasing the incomes of the more successful public intellectuals may be offset by diminished prospects for the less successful ones, who lose their protected markets and must now face the competition of the star public intellectuals. But that does not imply that the price of public-intellectual work has risen—rather the contrary.

Market Failure?

Russell Jacoby has written that "younger intellectuals no longer need or want a larger public; they are almost exclusively professors."[46] The second clause is correct, but not the first. Plenty of professors want to reach a larger public than the merely academic. When people speak of the decline of the public intellectual, and are not merely being "declinists" (the kind of handwringer we'll meet in Chapter 8), they are referring to quality rather than quantity, to the possibility that the distinctive social value of the public intellectual may not be fully compatible with a full-time career as an academic. We must consider whether the market for public intellectuals is functioning well in the sense of producing a socially valuable product. ("Functioning well relative to what?" is a fair question, but one that I'll defer.) There are two related reasons to doubt this unless the noninformational value of public-intellectual work, as an entertainment or solidarity good, is emphasized.

---

public intellectual who receives no fee for writing an op-ed piece that is read by millions of people earns fame from the piece, but not revenue.

46. Russell Jacoby, *The Last Intellectuals: American Culture in the Age of Academe* 6 (1987).

The reasons are the character of the modern university and the absence of quality controls in the public-intellectual market.

Increased specialization of knowledge, and the safety and security of the modern academic career, are the principal but not the only characteristics of modern university life that imperil the quality of public-intellectual work. Another such characteristic is that the academic community rewards professors for being original, that is, for advancing novel ideas. To call an idea "fashionable" is an academic put-down. Nothing is derided so much as "the conventional wisdom" on a topic. Many an academic poses, however absurdly, as a genius, an outsider, an "original." This helps to explain why, as we'll see throughout this book, academic public intellectuals tend to be found at or near the extremes of the political-ideological spectrum—and for two further reasons. First, taking an extreme position stirs controversy and thus increases the drama of public debate. That is a desideratum of entertainment, and to a considerable extent the public-intellectual market is a branch of entertainment. Second, to obtain "brand identification" in the public-intellectual marketplace, it helps to have a distinctive position. This is more difficult to achieve in the crowded mainstream of opinion on a topic; all the niches may be filled there. (The impetus that this gives to wild predictions is a theme of Chapter 4.) Because there is no correlation between the originality and the political or social utility of an idea, the academic emphasis on originality, and the superior marketability of extreme positions in the market for public-intellectual work, are frequently at war with the accuracy, utility, and practicality of the academic public intellectual's predictions and recommendations.

The charm that novelty holds for intellectuals helps to explain why so many of them were mesmerized by communism for so long, and thus illustrates the danger that a hankering after originality poses for the socially responsible performance of the public-intellectual role. It is true that fascism, the equal and opposite extreme of communism, attracted many fewer intellectuals than communism did. But the main reason, apart from the strong antisemitic vein in most versions of fascism, which is pertinent because of the high proportion of Jewish public intellectuals, is that fascism is anti-intellectual while communism is based on "scientific" theories. Communism, and Marxism more generally, is a book-based creed, like Judaism, Christianity, and Islam. It provides rich opportunities, therefore, for exegesis and learned elaboration.[47]

Taking and defending intellectually bold positions is, as philosophers of science from Mill and Peirce to Popper and Kuhn have emphasized, vital to the advancement of science and of scholarship generally. But it has no particular merit in the realm of the political and the ideological. Scientific revolutions benefit humankind; most political and social revolutions do not. Much of the best public-intellectual work in the past has consisted of seeing through the big new political and economic nostrums. The exemplary figure is again Orwell. Patronized by some academic intellectuals as not having been a "genius,"[48] he indeed was not a genius in an academic sense; he didn't have a phenomenal memory, lightning-fast analytical capabilities, a taste for theory, or bold new ideas. What he had mattered more from the standpoint of writing for the general public about politics: the ability to see what was before his eyes and to describe what he saw in unforgettably vivid prose.

These are not typical academic gifts. The academic is not oriented toward writing for a general audience; unlike an Orwell, he doesn't depend for a living on being able to interest the general public in what he writes. But the more interesting point is that academics are not tuned to political reality either. They tend to be unworldly. They are, most of them anyway, the people who have never left school. Their milieu is postadolescent. Because they are tenured and work mostly by themselves rather than with others (though this is changing), they don't have to get along with colleagues; some of them don't get along well with anybody. People who live this way have difficulty grasping the distinctive and essential constituents of *political* morality,[49] comprising the qualities necessary in a statesman or other leader. Those qualities are strategic and interpersonal (manipulative, coercive, psychological) in character. They are quintessentially *social*. They constitute the moral-

47. The difference in this regard between communism and Nazism is, however, one of degree rather than of kind. Nazism had its own "science," that of race, and its own bible, *Mein Kampf*.

48. See, for example, Lionel Trilling, "Introduction," in George Orwell, *Homage to Catalonia* v, viii (1952).

49. See Richard A. Posner, *An Affair of State: The Investigation, Impeachment, and Trial of President Clinton* 133–135 (1999), and references cited there.

ity, misunderstood as cynicism, expounded by Machiavelli, the morality that Weber contrasted with an "ethic of ultimate ends,"[50] his term for the uncompromising, absolutist ethics that one finds, for example, in the Sermon on the Mount. The ethics of political responsibility implies a willingness to compromise, to dirty one's hands, to flatter and lie, to make package deals, to forgo the prideful self-satisfaction that comes from self-conscious purity and devotion to principle.[51] It requires a sense of reality, of proportion, rather than self-righteousness or academic smarts. The politician must have an "ability to let realities work upon him with inner concentration and calmness."[52]

Without these qualities, social reform is impossible. They are qualities that are remote from the ideals of scholarship and that many academics despise and few cultivate (and those few are ashamed—the term "academic politics" is a pejorative). Despising these qualities, academics, especially those who have achieved success in difficult and abstract fields, think politics is easy because they observe that the people who succeed in it are generally undistinguished intellectually as well as often being deficient in personal ethics. The absurd public-intellectual slogan "speaking truth to power" epitomizes this arrogance, as well as exaggerates the public intellectual's courage. Public intellectuals in the United States and other democratic nations incur no risk in abusing politicians, and do not realize that politicians have their own truths, truths without which nothing can be accomplished in the political world. Academics are not apolitical; would that they were. Rather, they are political naïfs, prigs about power. (Not all of course, to repeat an obvious but crucial qualification of everything I say about the academic public intellectual.)

They tend also to underestimate the world's recalcitrance to efforts at improving it. The world of theory operates without friction. The gap between origination and implementation, which makes the law of unintended consequences fundamental to a realistic understanding of historical causality and political efficacy, is hidden from the theoretician. The result is the impatience and unrealism with which public intellectuals advocate reform and their weakness for causal theories of

50. Max Weber, "Politics as a Vocation," in *From Max Weber: Essays in Sociology*, note 37 above, at 77, 120.
51. See id. at 118–128.
52. Id. at 115.

history and of the future (the Roman Empire fell because . . . ; the Soviet Union will triumph over the United States because . . .). It is notable that until recently economics was a much less theoretical discipline in Europe than in the United States, and that as a by-product of the more practical emphasis of European economists they were much more likely to enter politics than U.S. economists were or are.[53]

A proclivity for taking extreme positions, a taste for universals and abstraction, a desire for moral purity, a lack of worldliness, and intellectual arrogance work together to induce in many academic public intellectuals selective empathy, a selective sense of justice, an insensitivity to context, a lack of perspective, a denigration of predecessors as lacking moral insight, an impatience with prudence and sobriety, a lack of realism, and excessive self-confidence. The "on the one hand, on the other hand" approach to politically or ideologically charged issues—the kind of approach that can understand slavery in its historical context, that sees the bad along with the good in abolitionists, that seeks a functional explanation for (to us) bizarre practices such as clitoridectomy and infibulation, that acknowledges that Nazis were fervent environmentalists and public-health fanatics and that Bill Clinton was the consolidator of the Reagan Revolution—this approach is uncongenial to the academic temperament. The typical academic is a Platonist, not an Aristotelian.

The factors I have emphasized so far relate primarily to academic public intellectuals. The next set of factors I discuss, which relates back to my earlier discussion of credence goods, affects the public-intellectual market in general, and not just its academic participants.

The market is competitive in the superficial sense that there are many actual and potential demanders and suppliers and that entry is not restricted—there is no requirement of obtaining a license. Ordinarily we think that if a market is competitive, quality will take care of itself. And this is true of markets for products or services the quality of which either is observable by the consumer or can be guaranteed in other ways, such as by explicit warranties or producers' sunk costs. In some markets, however, such as medicine and law, where uncertainties about quality loom especially large, market incentives seem in-

53. Reiner Eichenberger and Bruno S. Frey, "Academia: American and European Economics and Economists," in Frey, *Economics as a Science of Human Behaviour: Towards a New Social Science Paradigm* 133 (2d ed. 1999).

adequate and the consequences of the market's failure to deliver a dependable product are grave. So government, often prodded by the providers of the service, who want protection from competition, steps in and requires that sellers be licensed. Licensure is not the only way in which markets riven by uncertainty are regulated. The market that most closely resembles the public-intellectual market—namely, the market for expert witnesses (examined in Chapter 10), where academics and other knowledge workers are engaged in expounding their views to a lay audience, a judge or jury—operates under rules designed however imperfectly to screen out the incompetent and the dishonest. The important point is that there are rules; the expert-witness market is not a free-for-all.

The market for public intellectuals operates without any rules or norms, legal or customary (the First Amendment would of course be a serious impediment to the former kind), and, unlike some other information markets, with little in the way of gatekeeping consumer intermediaries. The print and electronic outlets through which public intellectuals reach their audience do little screening for quality. Little is not none, but little may not be enough, especially given the multidimensionality of the public-intellectual product—the fact that it is bought for entertainment and to create solidarity, and not just for information, so that the truth value of the product must compete with other consumption values. Trade presses and nonacademic journals do not submit manuscripts for review by scholars, and while some nonacademic magazines have able and selective editors, few editors are competent across the entire range of subjects covered by their magazine. The highly competitive environment of modern book publishing prevents most commercial publishers from paying much attention to quality except as it translates into marketability (which is not to deny that they publish many good books, since authors of good books may have reasons, good or bad, to prefer being published by a commercial press), and this is where the multidimensionality that I have mentioned takes a big bite. Even academic publishers are under financial pressure to publish "trade" books (books that will sell beyond a narrow academic market), as well as just scholarly monographs. This pressure has led to some easing of standards for the publication of public-intellectual work by academic presses.

So *unfiltered* media are one reason to worry about the quality of public-intellectual work,[54] and another and more basic reason (since the media are unfiltered only because the public does not demand filtration) is that virtually no one is marching to a public intellectual's tune, as we'll see in Chapter 4. Not taking seriously a seller's claims about his product is one way of defending oneself against uncertainty about the product's quality. But it creates a chicken and egg problem. The less reliance the public places on the public intellectual's pronouncements, the less pressure the market exerts on the public intellectual to be careful and accurate in those pronouncements. Since no one is paying close attention, academics who do not worry much about being fools in history pay only a small price for mouthing off irresponsibly on matters of current interest to the lay public; their academic reputation is unlikely to be affected by their ventures into the public arena. The audience is not only inattentive but undiscerning; academics rarely make clear when they are speaking in the public-intellectual role *ex cathedra* as it were and when as rank amateurs; and the incentives for anyone to keep a record of what public intellectuals say, in order to provide a benchmark for evaluating the quality of their current and future interventions, are weak. Missing are the conditions that ensure reasonable quality in other markets for credence goods. In the public-intellectual market there are no enforceable warranties or other legal sanctions for failing to deliver promised quality, no effective consumer intermediaries, few reputational sanctions, and, for academics at any rate, no sunk costs—they can abandon the public-intellectual market and have a safe landing as full-time academics.

This would be less troublesome if the only or principal motive for becoming a public intellectual were to furnish the public with truthful information. But apart from the fact that certitude is not the test of certainty—that many people who believe they have a pipeline to the truth are deluded—we have seen that the motives for embarking upon a public-intellectual career are various. The typical public intellectual's utility function includes the desire to inform but also the desire for money, for acclaim, for power, and to help people, as well as the intrinsic utility of self-expression. So selfish and altruistic motives are mingled in proportions that vary across public intellectuals, and there can be no confidence that the utility the public intellectual derives from speaking

---

54. Cf. Cowen, note 3 above, at 72–92, on "gatekeeper critics" in the market for fame.

truth dominates. In addition, truth is an elusive goal in political and ideological controversy, and where objective verification is not possible claims of truth may be strongly, though often unconsciously, influenced by self-interest. It doesn't increase the truth quotient of public-intellectual work that academics tend to be disdainful of the general populace and of the media that cater to that populace. This is part of their broader disdain for people less intellectually acute than themselves. (It is natural for people to give pride of place to whatever it is they happen to excel in.) In dealing with such seas of ignorance they often find it neither feasible nor necessary to be scrupulous and nuanced. They are on holiday. They have slipped the reins that govern them in their scholarly work, and at the same time they have entered an arena in which an absence of deterrents to inaccurate and misleading arguments is more than usually damaging to the quality of intellectual activity because of the emotional character of so many of the controversies in which public intellectuals intervene.

Against all this it might be argued that the marketplace of ideas—Holmes's famous metaphor for freedom of speech[55]—can be relied upon to ensure that in the long run the soundest ideas will prevail. But such an argument would misunderstand both Holmes's meaning and the economics of competition. Holmes was a moderate skeptic, who believed that as a practical matter truth was a consensus that emerged from letting competing ideas duke it out in the court of public opinion rather than something that a judge or a board of censors could determine. (In this he was closely following Mill.)[56] This was not to suggest, however, that a *reliable* consensus would always emerge from a free market in ideas and opinions. Such a market is at most a necessary rather than a sufficient condition for the production of truth. Not all markets, however free of unwarranted government interference, deliver a quality product. Markets in ordinary credence goods would not were it not for incentives and constraints that happen to be missing

55. See Abrams v. United States, 250 U.S. 616, 630 (1919) (dissenting opinion).

56. "The beliefs which we have most warrant for have no safeguard to rest on but a standing invitation to the whole world to prove them unfounded. If the challenge is not accepted, or is accepted and the attempt fails, we are far enough from certainty still; but we have done the best that the existing state of human reason admits of; we have neglected nothing that could give the truth a chance of reaching us . . . This is the amount of certainty attainable by a fallible being, and this the sole way of attaining it." John Stuart Mill, *On Liberty* 30 (1955 [1859]).

from the public-intellectual market. Imagine how common product defects would be if sellers of defective products were not accountable for the defects, whether directly, through warranty enforcement or other legal actions, or indirectly, through costly reputation losses.

Maybe, though, the market in physical goods is not the proper benchmark. Maybe the question should be whether public intellectuals are any less accountable than other producers of symbolic goods, such as novelists and newspaper reporters, pundits and politicians. Probably they are. Although there are complaints about the quality of the news media and about the modern novel, both elite and popular, and about the arts in general, virtually no one wants to do anything about these forms of expression beyond the occasional libel suit or obscenity prosecution. Nor is it even clear that the incessant despairing complaints about the contemporary situation of "culture" are well founded.[57] So is it *only* the intellectuals' contribution to public discourse that is to be criticized? And isn't that paradoxical? Would not public discourse be immeasurably impoverished if left entirely to journalists and politicians? And if there is a problem either with public discourse in general or the contribution of public intellectuals in particular, ought not the blame be placed to a considerable extent on the public itself, for its short attention span, its philistinism, its embrace of a "sound bite" culture? Should the people who are trying to combat these tendencies in the culture be blamed?

There is reason to believe that competition may indeed be less effective in producing a quality product in the public-intellectual market than in other markets in symbolic goods, especially though not only the academic market, and this despite the fact that academics increasingly dominate the public-intellectual market as well. Consider the matter of the public's short attention span. People are very busy today, and information overload is a reality, not a cliché, as indicated by the dramatic increase in the number of television commercials per viewer, the equally dramatic reduction in the average length of these commercials, and the concomitant shift from informational to rhetorical advertising content.[58] The many competing uses for a modern American's time crowd the time available for the consideration of public issues at

57. See Tyler Cowen, *In Defense of Commercial Culture* (1998).
58. Sarah C. Hann, "The 'Persuasion Route' of the Law: Advertising and Legal Persuasion," 100 *Columbia Law Review* 1281, 1287–1289 (2000), and studies cited there.

the same time that the complexity of those issues has grown. The limited time of the "consumers" in this market implies limited capacity to evaluate the wares of the sellers (the public intellectuals) and so invites exploitation. And the sellers, at least the majority that are academics, are uniquely insulated from the retribution of disappointed consumers by virtue of being part-timers, able at any moment to leave the public-intellectual market at low cost.

The combination of an undiscriminating consumer facing a seller who can exit the market cheaply if the shoddiness of his product is discovered is uncommon even in the domain of symbolic goods. There is a norm of accountability in journalism that has no counterpart in academics' public-intellectual activities. Newspapers employ ombudsmen, publish corrections and retractions, and publish critical letters from readers. They worry about criticism for being biased or inaccurate, and about the occasional libel suit. They realize that they are in the public eye, that they are suspect in some quarters, and that they are inviting targets. Reporters report the news of the day, and if their reports are grossly inaccurate this is discovered eventually and they are fired. Reporters who make things up get the boot as soon as their embroidery is discovered. The media have a reputational stake in accuracy, and we know that that is one of the things that gives sellers an incentive to be honest. Politicians operate in a fiercely competitive market, and like journalists they are distrusted. Novelists and other creative artists produce goods that the consuming public, or fractions of it, like or don't like; but the public is not *fooled* into liking what it likes, although it may be slow to cotton to really novel work. Scholars and other technical writers produce for an expert audience. And again, journalism, politics, novel writing, and scholarship are full-time or at least principal careers. Failure imposes real costs. All these constraints are missing from the marketplace for academic public intellectuals.

Perhaps closest to the public intellectual in expressing political or ideological opinions without any market discipline are those movie stars, such as Jane Fonda, Barbra Streisand, Warren Beatty, Charlton Heston, and Robert Redford, who offer their political opinions to the general public. Their celebrity guaranties them an audience—there is no filtering by the media—and they pay no career price for their political "work," however strident and unpopular. (Jane Fonda is a good example.) But the public protects itself from them by refusing to take them seriously. Even after the Reagan presidency, the notion of an ac-tor's having anything worthwhile to say about public matters is consid-ered by most people faintly absurd. Charlton Heston is an impressive spokesman for the National Rifle Association, but it is doubtful that his statements about gun policy carry any independent weight. We shall see in Chapter 4 that the public inoculates itself against the statements of public intellectuals in much the same way. Newspaper readers too: they know that reporters write to tight deadlines and therefore cannot be trusted to be highly accurate, and so take journalistic accounts with a grain of salt.

Public intellectuals target a more highly educated audience than the politician, the popular writer, the politically active movie star, or the average journalist. But as knowledge expands and becomes increasingly compartmentalized, the *broadly* educated public, the public whose aver-age member used to be called the "general reader," shrinks. No longer is there a shared pool of knowledge from which the public intellectual draws along with his audience and which the latter can therefore use to test the soundness of the intellectual's arguments. No longer is there an intellectual elite each of whose members knows enough science, enough history, enough political theory, enough economics to be able to evaluate intelligently the science writer or the social critic. Almost no one has that breadth of knowledge any more. No longer is there a public that knows whether to trust or distrust the public intellectual—that knows how to evaluate his credentials, his ethical appeal. Writing for an incurably undiscriminating public, the modern public intellec-tual is likely to find his readers mostly among persons predisposed to agree with him. According to Bayes's Theorem and common sense alike, as between two equally persuasive debaters you'll side with the one with whom your priors agree. The modern public intellectual is more likely to solidify than to dissipate prejudices.

The contrast between scholarly and public-intellectual publication is particularly striking. Scholarly publication involves three levels of fil-tering. The norms of the academy, norms enforced by tenure and sal-ary review, impose a discipline on its members. The scholarly jour-nals and academic presses use peer review, and in the case of the presses also faculty review boards and specialized acquisition editors, to ensure high standards in published work. And the audience for academic writ-ing is an audience of experts. All three levels of control are missing from the public-intellectual market. Of course this is true whether or not the public intellectual is an academic. There are plenty of examples of bad work by nonacademic public intellectuals.[59] That is only to be expected. Yet unusual life experiences or unusual literary skills may redeem at least a fraction of public-intellectual work, and these attributes are more likely to be found outside than within the academy.

All this said, "market failure" may be too fell a term for this market, and even "inefficient" may be misplaced, or at least imprecise. I return to this question in Chapter 4.

59. A majority of the fellow-traveling public intellectuals pilloried in Paul Hollander, *Political Pilgrims: Travels of Western Intellectuals to the Soviet Union, China, and Cuba 1928–1978* (1981), were not academics. But Hollander's definition of "intellectual" is promiscuously broad, extending as it does to Jane Fonda and Shirley MacLaine.

~ 3

Care and Insight

Academic legitimacy in the public arena is a tenuous matter.[1]

*T*HIS CHAPTER begins empirical inquiry into the value, or quality, of public intellectuals. The next discusses the interrelated questions of influence and predictive accuracy. The chapter after that brings statistical analysis to bear on the issue of value, though it is not limited to that issue but is also concerned with simply providing a more exact description of the public-intellectual market. The value I have in mind in these chapters is what might loosely be called "truth value"; that is, I am concerned with the efforts of public intellectuals to shape public opinion rather than either to entertain the public or to build solidarity with like-thinking persons.

Two senses of value should be distinguished. One is avoidance of serious mistakes, and is achieved mainly by being careful in investigating the facts and cautious in stating conclusions. The other and more interesting sense of value is insight or distinction, the filling of some gap in intellectual space, and let me begin with an example of that.

A famous bit of politically charged literary criticism that an academic public intellectual could *not* have written, or that if written by one would have had little or no impact, is George Orwell's criticism of the phrase "necessary murder" in "Spain 1937," a poem about the Spanish Civil War written by W. H. Auden in his communist phase. The stanza preceding the one containing "necessary murder" begins "Tomorrow for the young, the poets exploding like bombs," and continues in this idyllic vein, ending, however, with "But today the struggle." And then we read

1. Alan Wolfe, "Academics, Ads, and Questions of Credibility," *Chronicle of Higher Education*, Dec. 1, 2000, p. B24.

Today the deliberate increase in the chances of death,
The conscious acceptance of guilt in the necessary murder;
　　Today the expending of powers
On the flat ephemeral pamphlet and the boring meeting.

About this Orwell comments acidly:

The second stanza is intended as a sort of thumbnail sketch of a
day in the life of a "good party man." In the morning a couple of
political murders, a ten-minutes' interlude to stifle "bourgeois"
remorse, and then a hurried luncheon and a busy afternoon and
evening chalking walls and distributing leaflets. All very edifying.
But notice the phrase "necessary murder." It could only be written
by a person to whom murder is at most a word. Personally I would
not speak so lightly of murder. It so happens that I have seen the
bodies of numbers of murdered men—I don't mean killed in battle, I mean murdered. Therefore I have some conception of what
murder means—the terror, the hatred, the howling relatives, the
post-mortems, the blood, the smells. To me, murder is something
to be avoided. So it is to any ordinary person. The Hitlers and
Stalins find murder necessary, but they don't advertise their callousness, and they don't speak of it as murder; it is "liquidation,"
"elimination" or some other soothing phrase. Mr. Auden's brand
of amoralism is only possible if you are the kind of person who is
always somewhere else when the trigger is pulled. So much of left-
wing thought is a kind of playing with fire by people who don't
even know that fire is hot.[2]

In response to this criticism Auden changed "necessary murder" to
"fact of murder."
　　It is an exceptionally powerful bit of criticism and both the criticism
and the power are inseparable from Orwell's having not led a sheltered,
academic life. He had been a policeman in Burma and so knew murder
at first hand. He had fought in Spain with the anarchists, had been seriously wounded, and had narrowly escaped being killed by the Stalinists.

2. George Orwell, "Inside the Whale," in *Collected Essays, Journalism and Letters of George
Orwell*, vol. 1, pp. 493, 516 (Sonia Orwell and Ian Angus eds., 1968).

The essay in which the criticism of Auden's poem appears was first published in 1940, after the outbreak of World War II—Auden having removed himself to the safety of the United States while Orwell, his desperate attempt to join the British army spurned because of his terrible health, was serving as an air raid warden during the London Blitz. It is not just that Orwell's life experiences enabled him to speak with great moral authority about political murder, but that they enabled him to notice an odious phrase in Auden's poem that would have escaped the notice of anyone for whom a political murder was the abstraction that it was for Auden. And we must remember that Orwell was a journalist and a novelist, as well as an essayist; the passage I quoted from his essay is a brilliant polemic. So this is powerful but also, and more important, *distinctive* criticism, whereas about all that we can expect from an academic who writes literary criticism with a political inflection for a general audience is a diluted version of academic literary criticism.[3]

The example of Orwell suggests that to be a really effective public intellectual is a *charismatic* calling. It isn't primarily a matter of being intelligent and well informed and writing clearly, but of being able through force of rhetoric or the example of one's life (related points—an exemplary life being a particularly effective form of the ethical appeal) to make fresh, arresting, or heterodox ideas credible to the general, or at least the educated, public. The charismatic public intellectual is disappearing as a consequence of the absorption of intellectuals into university faculties in an era of specialization and professionalization.

One might think that academic public intellectuals would at least be accurate, meticulous, and responsible, with a clear sense (not always honored in Orwell's journalism, by the way) of the difference between fact and fiction, proof and speculation. Not so, for the reasons suggested in the preceding chapter. Consider Noam Chomsky, the most influential figure in modern linguistics, and probably in cognitive science as well. In book, pamphlet, lecture, and interview, he repeatedly

3. A similar point is made by (is in fact the theme of) Morris Dickstein's book *Double Agent: The Critic and Society* (1992). His term "public critic," while it includes many academic as well as nonacademic literary critics (notably, among the academics, Lionel Trilling), is weighted toward the latter, and toward academic literary critics such as Philip Rahv, Alfred Kazin, and Irving Howe who either lacked the standard academic credentials or flouted the conventions of academic scholarship.

denounces the United States for violent, lawless, repressive, and imperialistic behavior as black as that of Hitler's Germany and worse than
that of Imperial Japan or that of any communist regime past or present, including Stalin's Soviet Union. Chomsky is not a communist and
doesn't admire any of the communist regimes. He just thinks that the
United States is more violent, more aggressive, more imperialistic, and
more dangerous than any of them ever was. He thinks that "Stalin and
his successors would have been willing to accept the role of junior managers in the US-dominated world system,"[4] though he doesn't explain
why we were unwilling to give them that role. Chomsky describes
North Korea as a helpless victim of American imperialism during the
Korean War and blames the United States not only for the Cold War
but also for Japanese aggression *before* our embargo on the export of oil
to Japan precipitated Japan's decision to attack us. And the embargo, as
he neglects to point out, was not an act of unprovoked aggression but
a response to Japanese aggression in China and French Indochina.
Chomsky intimates that the sole effect of World War II was to create
an American empire every bit as evil as the fascist powers that the
United States and its allies had conquered.[5] He questions whether, had
Japan not surrendered, we would have been justified in invading it:
"The fact that Japan had attacked two military bases in two U.S. colonies hardly gives us a justification for occupying it."[6]

Chomsky made elaborate excuses for the Soviet invasion of Afghanistan.[7] These were part of his determined effort, which continues, to
blame the United States not only for the Cold War but for everything
else that is wrong with the world, even Pol Pot's massacres (which he
now acknowledges, though belatedly as we're about to see),[8] and to depict the Soviet Union as a harmless and unaggressive, though internally

4. Noam Chomsky, *Year 501: The Conquest Continues* 72 (1993). Year 1 was 1492.

5. See, for example, Noam Chomsky, *American Power and the New Mandarins* (1969).

6. Noam Chomsky, *Class Warfare: Interviews with David Barsamian* 67 (1996). See also
Chomsky, note 4 above, at 239–242. One of the bases in one of the "colonies" presumably was
Pearl Harbor, since Hawaii was not yet a state. The Japanese attack on the other "colony,"
however, by which Chomsky presumably means the Philippines, was not limited to a single
military base. The Japanese attacked other U.S. Pacific territories as well—including Guam,
Wake Island, and Midway Island—and also bombarded the Pacific coast of the United States.

7. Noam Chomsky, *Towards a New Cold War: Essays on the Current Crisis and How We Got
There* 374 n. 23 (1982).

8. Id. at 382 n. 73.

repressive, pretext for American imperialism. Chomsky's writings are peppered with such dicta as that the United States is "the center of international terrorism"[9] and that "corporations are just as totalitarian as Bolshevism and fascism."[10] He believes that Saddam Hussein's reasons for bombarding Israel with missiles during the Persian Gulf War in 1991 were as good as George Bush's reasons for seeking to expel Hussein from Kuwait by force[11] and that the nations of Central America are more repressive than the communist nations of Eastern Europe ever were.[12] He says that "there are many terrorist states in the world, but the United States is unusual in that it is *officially* committed to international terrorism, and on a scale that puts its rivals [such as Iran, Iraq, Libya, Syria, the Sudan, and North Korea] to shame."[13] He regards Arab hostility to Israel as entirely a product of Israeli aggression—he does not acknowledge that Israel has *any* legitimate security concerns or that any of its wars with the Arab states can be described as defensive on Israel's part.[14] He dismissed reports that the Khmer Rouge in Cambodia had killed more than a million people, saying that "highly qualified specialists . . . concluded that executions have numbered at most in the thousands; that these were localized in areas of limited Khmer Rouge influence and unusual peasant discontent, where brutal revenge killings were aggravated by the threat of starvation resulting from the American destruction and killing."[15] He never acknowledges error.

Not that Chomsky's dozens of books and pamphlets contain no use-

9. Id. at 52.

10. Noam Chomsky, "You Say You Want a Devolution," *Progressive*, March 1996, pp. 18, 19. He adds, "They [the corporations] come out of the same intellectual roots, in the early Twentieth Century." Id. Actually, corporations are not a twentieth-century invention.

11. Noam Chomsky, *Media Control: The Spectacular Achievements of Propaganda* 53–54 (1997).

12. Noam Chomsky, *World Orders Old and New* 39–40 (1994).

13. Noam Chomsky, *Pirates and Emperors: International Terrorism in the Real World* 178 (rev. ed. 1991) (emphasis in original).

14. See, for example, Noam Chomsky, *Fateful Triangle: The United States, Israel and the Palestinians*, ch. 4 (updated ed. 1999).

15. Noam Chomsky and Edward S. Herman, "Distortions at Fourth Hand," *Nation*, June 25, 1977, pp. 789, 791. See further, on Chomsky's view of the Cambodian massacres, Paul Hollander, *Political Pilgrims: Travels of Western Intellectuals to the Soviet Union, China, and Cuba 1928–1978* 68–69, 446–447 n. 62 (1981). The "*at most* in the thousands" is significant, since the article by Chomsky and Herman suggests that the executions may have numbered only in the hundreds.

ful information and interesting half-truths, as when he calls Theodore Roosevelt a "racist fanatic and raving jingoist."[16] But the tone and the one-sidedness of this characterization are all too typical. Chomsky's use of sources is uncritical, and his methodology unsatisfactory—it consists simply of changing the subject. If someone argues that military intervention in Kosovo was a morally worthy if ineptly implemented effort to avert a genocide of the Albanian population, Chomsky replies by asking what about our failure to protect the Kurds from the Turks, the East Timorese from the Indonesians, or the Palestinian Arabs from the Israeli Jews?

Resort to force is never justified, in his view, because no nation has completely clean hands. But it may be excused when it is by a nation or group that is neither the United States nor allied with it. Chomsky is an anarcho-pacifist. His embrace of that creed—which he treats as self-evidently correct and so doesn't attempt to defend—illustrates the academic public intellectual's common mistake of confusing political with personal ethics.[17] A private citizen of the United States can go through life without killing anybody or governing anybody; it does not follow that a large nation can get through its life without governing and without causing people to be killed.

Although most of Chomsky's political writings concern U.S. foreign policy, they are anchored in an economic theory, Marxian in character, that denies that capitalism is a viable economic system. It can be kept afloat, he believes, only by exploiting, deceiving, and intimidating workers; dominating and exploiting backward countries; suppressing all experiments with alternative economic systems, such as socialism; and harming families and children.[18] Chomsky predicted that the rise of free-market economics in the wake of the collapse of the Soviet system would impoverish Eastern Europe, Australia, Canada, and numerous other countries; would cause the wealthy countries of the West, including the United States, to become more like the Third World; and,

16. Noam Chomsky, *The New Military Humanism: Lessons from Kosovo* 91 (1999).

17. "If it is said, in line with the acosmic ethic of love [the ethic of Jesus, the apostles, St. Francis, and their like], 'Resist not him that is evil with force,' for the politician the reverse proposition holds, 'thou *shalt* resist evil by force,' or else you are responsible for the evil winning out." Max Weber, "Politics as a Vocation," in *From Max Weber: Essays in Sociology* 77, 119–120 (H. H. Gerth and C. Wright Mills trans., 1946).

18. See, for example, Chomsky, note 4 above, ch. 2.

in short, would lead to a worsening of economic conditions around the globe.[19] He claimed that central planning, protectionist trade policies, and other state interventions in the economy were critical to the survival of capitalism, pointing to statist policies in Japan and Germany that he regarded as crucial to those countries' economic success.[20] He attributes our hostility to Castro's regime to the regime's economic and humanitarian successes. Our "terrorist war" against Cuba was "launched by John F. Kennedy. It had nothing to do with communism. There weren't any Russians around. It had to do with things like the fact that these people were devoting resources to the wrong sectors of the population. They were improving health standards. They were concerned with children, with malnutrition. Therefore we launched a huge terrorist war."[21]

Chomsky is an irresistible example of the quality problem that besets the market for academic public intellectuals.[22] But he may not be the best example. The establishment press generally does not publish his public-intellectual work,[23] though whether by his choice or theirs I don't know. He has, however, a following on college campuses, where he speaks frequently, and abroad, where his anti-Americanism is welcome. And he is mentioned frequently enough in the media, and mostly for his political views, to be among the one hundred most frequently mentioned public intellectuals.[24]

At a more responsible level than Chomsky, but illustrative of the same propensity of academic public intellectuals to venture imprudently beyond their areas of specialized academic knowledge, we have the distinguished physicist Steven Weinberg setting himself up in the pages of the *New York Review of Books* as a philosopher of science, a sub-

---

19. Id. at 55–61, 76–86.

20. Id. at 100–106, 111–112.

21. Noam Chomsky, *Chomsky on MisEducation* 52 (Donaldo Macedo ed., 2000); see also Chomsky, note 4 above, at 151–152.

22. He and other far-left public intellectuals, such as Sartre and Bertrand Russell (though Russell veered to the right at times, as when he advocated preventive nuclear war against the Soviet Union), are effectively pilloried in Paul Johnson, *Intellectuals* (1988). See also, in similar vein, Hilton Kramer, *The Twilight of the Intellectuals: Culture and Politics in the Era of the Cold War* (1999). But Johnson incorrectly implies that extreme and irrational political views are more likely to be found among far-left intellectuals than among far-right ones.

23. The principal exception is the publication by Columbia University Press of his book *World Orders*, note 12 above.

24. See Table 5.3 in Chapter 5.

ject about which he admits knowing very little, and uttering such philosophically dubious apothegms as that the laws of physics are real in the same sense that rocks are real.[25] Defending himself against the charge that this particular apothegm is philosophically naïve, he has pointed out that when he said that rocks and the laws of nature are real "in the same sense" he had added "whatever that is."[26] That is a damaging admission. If he doesn't know in what sense rocks and the laws of nature are real, how does he know they're real in the same sense? They don't *seem* real in the same sense. Rocks are physical objects, while laws of nature are relations or regularities that we believe to hold throughout some given domain. Rocks are observed; laws of nature are inferred. Rocks are to laws of nature as a car's engine is to its horsepower.

What physicist Weinberg tried to do to the adjacent "soft" (or softer) subject of philosophy of science, biologist Stephen Jay Gould has tried to do to the "soft" field of theology, arguing that science and religion occupy nonoverlapping domains—fact in the case of science, value in the case of religion.[27] It follows that every factual assertion made by a religion that is inconsistent with scientific theory or observation is out of order, a trespass on science's domain. This begs the question of scientific versus religious truth. In fact it is just a variant of Weinberg's fallacious philosophical reasoning. Both reflect a naïve scientific realism. What is correct is that such claims put forth by some religious sects as that the earth is only six thousand years old or that the fetus is ensouled at conception are either scientific errors (such as the claim about the age of the earth) or have no scientific standing because, as in the case of fetal ensoulment, they are not testable by any procedure known to sci-

25. Steven Weinberg, "Sokal's Hoax," *New York Review of Books*, Aug. 8, 1996, pp. 11, 14–15, skewered in Richard Rorty, *Philosophy and Social Hope* 182–188 (1999). Weinberg's article is an attack on postmodernism, the ideologically tinged controversies over which warrant classifying the article as public-intellectual work rather than merely as an attempt to explain science to a lay readership. Right-wing declinists (see Chapter 8), which Weinberg however is not, regard postmodernism as cause or symptom of the nation's "decadence."

26. Steven Weinberg, "The Revolution That Didn't Happen," *New York Review of Books*, Oct. 8, 1998, pp. 48, 52.

27. Stephen Jay Gould, *Rocks of Ages: Science and Religion in the Fullness of Life* (1999). Gould is a leftist, but efforts to reconcile science with religion are not a monopoly of the Left. "Combining a particle and a wave, it [quantum theory] joins the definite to the infinite, a point of mass to an eternal radiance. In this light, we can comprehend the paradox of the brain and the mind, the temporal and the divine, flesh and the world, freedom and fatality." George Gilder, *The Meaning of the Microcosm* 104 (1997).

ence. But to pronounce these claims false or meaningless is possible only if scientific criteria of validity are accepted as trumps, and the decision to do this can't be derived from science. Science cannot establish that science is a higher authority than the Bible. Gould isn't even aware of this as an *issue*.

He also seems unaware of a point that Freud made long ago: a division of responsibilities between science and religion that assigns fact to science, leaving consolation, ethics, and "higher truths" to religion, deprives religion of its authority.[28] Gould's appearance of evenhandedness is thus a pretense. Deprived of the authority to assert as fact that God created the universe and man, that Jesus Christ did not have a mortal father, and that human beings have souls that outlive the death of the body, Christianity becomes a myth, a fairy tale; its moral precepts, rituals, and clergy become the doctrines, the customs, and the managers of a fraternity or other social club. The other religions undergo a similar deflation. It is impossible to believe that Gould takes religion seriously.

Gould's book illustrates the style of public-intellectual work that might be called "splitting the difference" or "above the fray," in which a partisan of one side of a hotly debated topic professes to be navigating a middle course between extremes that he disparages for their extremism, but in fact he gives all the good arguments to his own (undisclosed) side. The prominent law professor and public intellectual Laurence Tribe wrote a book on abortion purporting (as its subtitle suggests) to find a middle way between the pros and the antis, but in fact coming down hard in favor of the pros.[29] A review by Michael McConnell pointed out that "Professor Tribe is too little informed about the ethical, scientific, and legal arguments of opponents of abortion to be able to explain them, too unacquainted with pro-life people to understand their motivations or address their concerns, too committed to his own perspective to see things through the eyes of the other side, and too much a lawyer to put aside, even for a moment, the opportunity to argue his case."[30] Tribe published a second edition of his book in 1992. Although the second edition discusses a case decided in

28. Sigmund Freud, "The Question of a Weltanschauung," in Freud, *New Introductory Lectures on Psycho-analysis* 158, 172 (James Strachey trans., 1965).

29. Laurence H. Tribe, *Abortion: The Clash of Absolutes* (1990).

30. Michael W. McConnell, "How Not to Promote Serious Deliberation about Abortion," 58 *University of Chicago Law Review* 1181, 1182–1183 (1991).

June of that year, almost a year after McConnell's review was published, Tribe does not mention the review or attempt to meet any of McConnell's criticisms.

Gould's best-known book, *The Mismeasure of Man*,[31] the first edition of which sold more than one hundred thousand copies, attempts to debunk claims made mainly by long-dead psychologists and evolutionary biologists that variations in human intelligence are determined by heredity and vary with race. Since Gould is a biologist, he may seem to have been writing within his field. The appearance is deceptive. He is a paleontologist and not an expert on the problem of intelligence. He is not writing as far out of his field as Elaine Scarry, a professor of English who writes about the technical causes of celebrated airplane crashes,[32] but outside of his specialty nevertheless. The book was criticized by scholars for tendentiousness, political bias, sundry distortions, and, in particular, for denying that there is any such thing as IQ (that is, general intelligence having a substantial hereditary component).[33] Gould calls the belief that IQ exists "reification," on the ground that you cannot point to anything in the brain as IQ. That is the equivalent of denying the existence of horsepower, or of any other abstraction. "Reification" is a philosophical rather than a scientific concept, however, so we should not expect Gould to be able to handle it deftly.

The book has a self-reference problem: the mistakes of earlier writers on intelligence are blamed on their having been racists, but Gould, while acknowledging that he is a Marxist, denies that his political predilections have influenced his analysis, while at the same time noting the Marxian character of his concept of evolution—punctuated equilibrium, which he analogizes to political revolution.[34] He is troubled by

31. Stephen Jay Gould, *The Mismeasure of Man* (1981).

32. See, for example, Elaine Scarry, "Swissair 111, TWA 800, and Electromagnetic Interference," *New York Review of Books*, Sept. 21, 2000, p. 92; Scarry, "The Fall of EgyptAir 990," *New York Review of Books*, Oct. 5, 2000, p. 49. Professor Scarry believes that she has discovered an electromagnetic "Bermuda Triangle" in the North Atlantic that caused these crashes. The experts do not agree with her. See Emily Eakin, "Professor Scarry Has a Theory," *New York Times Magazine*, Nov. 19, 2000, p. 78.

33. See Lloyd Humphreys, Review, 96 *American Journal of Psychology* 407 (1983); John B. Carroll, "Reflections on Stephen Jay Gould's *The Mismeasure of Man* (1981): A Retrospective Review," 21 *Intelligence* 121 (1995); Kevin B. Korb, "Stephen Jay Gould on Intelligence," 52 *Cognition* 111 (1994); Frank Schmidt, Review, 50 *Personnel Psychology* 485 (1997). For evidence that IQ is determined by brain structure, see John Duncan et al., "A Neural Basis for General Intelligence," 289 *Science* 457 (2000).

34. Stephen Jay Gould, "Life in a Punctuation," 101 *Natural History* 10 (1992). See Daniel

the antithesis of evolution as ordinarily understood (a very gradual process) to revolution, since Marxism celebrates revolution. Wearing his politics on his sleeve as he does—having, indeed, married his politics to his science in the concept of punctuated equilibrium—Gould might have been expected to be more sympathetic to politically motivated intelligence testers.

Gould also intimates that because scientists have been wrong in the past about IQ, they can't be trusted to be correct now. Again he excuses himself from this possibility.

Gould published a second edition of *The Mismeasure of Man* in 1996. The second edition does not respond to the criticisms that scholars had made of the first. Gould explains that the occasion for the second edition was the publication of Richard Herrnstein and Charles Murray's *The Bell Curve*, and indeed the only substantial change in the second edition is the addition of criticisms of that work. *The Bell Curve* is an effort by a psychologist and a political scientist to establish *contra* Gould the reality and heritability of general intelligence. Its most controversial feature, which incenses Gould, is the claim that the substantial difference in average IQ between blacks and whites (the average black IQ is about one standard deviation less than the average white IQ, that is, 85 versus 100) may have a genetic component.[35] Gould makes a number of technical criticisms of Herrnstein and Murray's argument, but what is most notable is his insistence that their book is a "manifesto of conservative ideology."[36] This is the pot calling the kettle black. The introduction to the second edition of *The Mismeasure of Man* is emphatic in drawing attention to Gould's own politics and acknowledging the political motivation for the preparation of a second edition (pp. 38–39). He writes admiringly of Chomsky as a "great humanist" (p. 45).

The *scientific* disagreements between Gould on the one hand and Herrnstein and Murray on the other are smaller than meet the eye, which is typical of public-intellectual work. Both *The Mismeasure of Man* and *The Bell Curve*, though scholarly, were published by commer-

---

C. Dennett, *Darwin's Dangerous Idea: Evolution and the Meanings of Life* 309 (1995); Humphreys, note 33 above, at 408–409.

35. Richard J. Herrnstein and Charles Murray, *The Bell Curve: Intelligence and Class Structure in American Life*, ch. 13 (1994).

36. Stephen Jay Gould, *The Mismeasure of Man* 37–38, 376 (revised and expanded ed. 1996). Subsequent page references are to this edition.

cial presses and are aimed at the general educated public, and they make strong, attention-arresting, politically charged claims for their opposing positions. But what is really at stake?

The concept of "general intelligence" derives from the observation that an individual's performances on various mental tests (verbal, spatial, mathematical, memory) that try to abstract from differences in test subjects' education or information tend to be positively correlated. This correlation implies the possession of a set of mental abilities that is highly versatile and so can predict the person's likelihood of doing better or worse than average across a wide range of occupations and activities—almost anything in fact in which the mental predominates over the physical. The correlation among the outcomes of the various mental tests, and so presumably among the mental skills they are testing, is imperfect. That is one reason why it is perilous for a mathematically gifted person to think that he can make insightful analyses of U.S. foreign policy, though the more important reason is that training and experience in a particular field may be a necessary though not a sufficient condition of making a significant contribution to it. IQ and general knowledge may not be enough, especially in an age of specialized knowledge.

Although denying that general intelligence (IQ) is a "thing," Gould does not deny the correlation among the different mental tests or suggest that it is meaningless or even misleading to call one person "more intelligent" than another. He does not regard IQ as a meaningless *concept*. Nor does he doubt that differences among persons in intelligence have a heritable component (pp. 33–35, 37), or deny the one-standard-deviation difference between the average black IQ and the average white IQ. Gould thinks the heritable component of IQ is smaller than do Herrnstein and Murray, and given how mixed the races are he believes that the racial difference in IQ is not genetic at all. He also doubts that IQ is as good a predictor of worldly success as Herrnstein and Murray believe. He may well be right.[37] He is right to criticize Herrnstein and Murray (as others have done) for having created an exaggerated impression of the statistical robustness of their correlations between IQ and worldly success or failure (pp. 374–376).

37. See, for example, James J. Heckman, "Lessons from the Bell Curve," 103 *Journal of Political Economy* 1091, 1103–1110 (1995); Derek A. Neal and William R. Johnson, "The Role of Premarket Factors in Black-White Wage Differences," 104 *Journal of Political Economy* 869, 890–891 (1996).

But Gould mischaracterizes their book when he describes it as "little more than a long brief" for "the theory of intelligence as a unitary, rankable, genetically based, and minimally alterable thing in the head" (pp. 35–36). Herrnstein and Murray believe that the heritable component is 60 percent of IQ,[38] which leaves a good deal of room for cultural and other environmental effects to alter intelligence. Sixty percent may be too high an estimate. Gould obviously thinks so, but offers no estimate of his own, so one is left in considerable doubt concerning the actual disagreement between the warring parties. If their debate were confined to scholarly journals rather than spilling over into the public arena, it would be recognized for what it is when the political overtones are removed: a technical disagreement that cannot be, or at least has yet to be, definitively resolved.

James Heckman, winner of the Nobel prize in economics for 2000, liberal in racial matters, and severe critic of *The Bell Curve*, has said of *The Mismeasure of Man* and a similar book by Leon Kamin that they "rely heavily on innuendo and arguments based on guilt by association and neither acknowledges the well-established facts that IQ has both predictive power in the labor market and a substantial heritable component."[39]

Since Herrnstein and Murray were writing for a general audience, it is appropriate to point out that their decision to include a chapter on IQ and race was a rhetorical error, unless (as I doubt) their primary motive in writing the book was financial. A book that argues that IQ has a large heritable component and that the average black IQ is substantially lower than the average white or Asian IQ is likely to be read as arguing that blacks are an inferior race. Actually the premises do not support the conclusion. The heritable component of IQ might be the same across races, yet if the environmental conditions of blacks were far less propitious than those of the other races there would be a systematic racial difference in IQ. Only it would be remediable. *The Bell Curve*'s discussion of race, quite apart from its inflammatory potential, is thus largely moot, since, as the Thernstroms point out, "almost all young people are capable of learning more than schools demand of them today."[40] They argue that the educational potential of blacks is

38. Herrnstein and Murray, note 35 above, at 105.

39. Heckman, note 37 above, at 1096.

40. Stephan Thernstrom and Abigail Thernstrom, *America in Black and White: One Nation, Indivisible* 353 (1997).

being depressed by unwise social policies.[41] When those policies are corrected, it will be time enough to decide whether some residual racial difference in the heritable component of IQ would place a limit on the fraction of particular jobs occupied by members of particular races in an economy of wholly meritocratic hiring and promotion.

Chomsky, Weinberg, and Gould (not to mention Einstein!—see Chapter 2) are able academics writing outside their fields for a general audience. But it would be a mistake to infer from this that to be an able academic writing *within* one's field for a general audience is a guarantee of consistently high quality. Paul Krugman, a highly respected economist specializing in international trade, has long written on economics for the general public and recently became the principal economic columnist of the *New York Times*. In a book published in 1994 he argued that the fact that a particular country has a commanding share of some world market is often a matter of historical accident rather than of superior efficiency.[42] The economic theory that shows this, and that he thinks may have implications for whether nations should embrace policies of free trade—and specifically may suggest that "there are times when aggressive support of a domestic industry against its foreign competitors can be in the national interest" (p. 238)—he calls "the QWERTY revolution" (p. 244) in tribute to a paper by the economic historian Paul David.

According to David, the QWERTY keyboard that we all use for typing and for interfacing with computers was designed to limit typing speed in order to prevent constant jamming of the keys. The problem disappeared with the advent of electric typewriters and word processing, yet we are stuck with the old keyboard because the costs of getting agreement among manufacturers on a new, more efficient keyboard and of retraining the many millions of people who have become habit-

41. And, Orlando Patterson adds, by a dysfunctional black culture that has contributed to "chronic anti-intellectualism among Afro-American youth." Patterson, *Rituals of Blood: Consequences of Slavery in Two American Centuries* 278 (1998). Also, Dan Subotnik adds, by the campaign against standardized testing and merit-based hiring and promotion policies in education. Subotnik, "Goodbye to the SAT, LSAT? Hello to Equity by Lottery? Evaluating Lani Guinier's Plan for Ending Race Consciousness," 43 *Howard Law Journal* 141 (2000). See also Shelby Steele, *A Dream Deferred: The Second Betrayal of Black Freedom in America* (1998).

42. Paul Krugman, *Peddling Prosperity: Economic Sense and Nonsense in the Age of Diminished Expectations*, ch. 9 (1994).

uated to the old one are prohibitive.[43] This shows that even large positive benefits of changing may be swamped by the costs if a great many
people will have to change their behavior (especially habitual and other
deeply entrenched behavior) more or less at once.

Krugman places enormous weight on David's paper, totally ignoring the severe criticisms of the paper by two other economists—Stan
Liebowitz and Stephen Margolis—who argue that David got his history all wrong and that the alternative keyboard that he touted as more
efficient than QWERTY is not, though its inventor claimed it was.[44]
Leibowitz and Margolis may be right or wrong, but by not mentioning
their critique (which, as far as I have been able to determine, has never
been answered)[45] Krugman leaves his readers in doubt as to whether he
was even aware of it when he wrote his book. For all they can know, his
argument rests on a paper that unbeknownst to him has been refuted.

He doesn't help himself with the following bit of anecdotal evidence
for the QWERTY revolution and for strategic trade policy (p. 229) in
lieu of free-trade policy:

> Britain was once a leading aircraft producer. During World War
> II, the Spitfire fighter was technologically superior to anything
> Germany or for that matter the United States could put in the air,
> and the first commercial jet aircraft was actually British rather
> than American . . . Why did Britain lose its aircraft capacity? . . .
> Huge orders by the U.S. military during the 1950s helped give

43. Paul A. David, "Clio and the Economics of QWERTY," 75 *American Economic Review Papers and Proceedings* 332 (May 1985).

44. See S. J. Liebowitz and Steven E. Margolis, "The Fable of the Keys," 33 *Journal of Law and Economics* 1 (1990); Liebowitz and Margolis, "Path Dependence, Lock-In, and History," 11 *Journal of Law, Economics, and Organization* 205 (1995). The second of these papers was published after Krugman's book; the first, however, was published years before.

45. See Peter Lewin, "Introduction: Two Approaches to the Market Process and the Economics of QWERTY," in *Microsoft and the Economics of QWERTY: History, Theory and Policy: Essays by Stan J. Liebowitz and Steven E. Margolis* (Macmillan and New York University Press, forthcoming). In an expanded version of his QWERTY paper published in 1997, David did not refer to the criticisms by Leibowitz and Margolis. See Paul A. David, "Understanding the Economics of QWERTY: The Necessity of History," in *Economic Growth in the Long Run: A History of Empirical Evidence*, vol. 3, p. 30 (Bart van Ark ed., 1997). And while in an unpublished paper David accuses Liebowitz and Margolis of mischaracterizing the facts concerning the history of typewriter keyboards, he offers no particulars or references in support of the accusation. Paul A. David, "At Last, a Remedy for Chronic QWERTY-Skepticism!" (Stanford University and All Souls College, Oxford, Sept. 1999).

American firms a decisive edge in jet technology. Once Britain had
been driven out of the world aircraft market, it lacked the base of
knowledge, suppliers, and skilled workers that would have allowed
it to reenter. (p. 238 n. 4)

What is true is that in 1940, during the Battle of Britain, the Super-
marine Spitfire was as good a fighter plane as the Messerschmidt 109[46]
and better than any fighter produced by the United States, which was
just gearing up its military aircraft production. By the end of the war,
American fighters were superior to the British ones, and Germany had
begun producing the first jet fighter. The Spitfire was a small, single-
engine plane, not a possible prototype for commercial airliners. Britain
did make four-engine bombers during the war, but none matched the
B-29, which went into service with the U.S. Air Force in 1944. And the
scale of U.S. aircraft production in World War II vastly exceeded that
of Britain. In 1944, the peak year of wartime aircraft production for
both countries, the United States produced 96,000 aircraft and 257,000
aircraft engines, Britain only 26,000 aircraft and 57,000 aircraft engines.[47] Even before the war, moreover, when military orders were few,
the United States was far ahead of the other industrial nations in the
manufacture of civilian transport aircraft.[48]

Military orders may have played a role in America's postwar aircraft
manufacturing prowess, but the suggestion that this statist factor destroyed the British industry is not supported by the literature.[49] More
important was the failure of Britain's Labour government, having na-
tionalized the British airline industry, to "us[e] its substantial power, as

46. See Richard Hough and Denis Richards, *The Battle of Britain: The Greatest Air Battle of
World War II* 44–45 (1989). The authors give a slight overall edge to the Spitfire, while recognizing the superiority of the Me 109 in several important respects. The Me 109's principal de-
fect was its short range. See also Horst Boog, "The Luftwaffe's Assault," in *The Burning Blue:
A New History of the Battle of Britain* 39, 46–48 (Paul Addison and Jeremy A. Crang eds.,
2000). The Spitfire was soon surpassed by U.S. and German aircraft. *Aircraft of the Second
World War: The Development of the Warplane 1939–45* 69, 71 (Philip Jarrett ed., 1997).

47. R. J. Overy, *The Air War 1939–1945* 150 (1980) (tab. 12).

48. Peter W. Brooks, *The Modern Airliner: Its Origins and Development*, ch. 3 (2d ed. 1981)
(by an English pilot and aviation executive!). See also Ronald Miller and David Sawers, *The
Technical Development of Modern Aviation* 66–71 (1970).

49. See Miller and Sawyers, note 48 above, at 277–281; M. Y. Yoshino, "Global Competition in a Salient Industry: The Case of Civil Aircraft," in *Competition in Global Industries* 517,
518–521 (Michael E. Porter ed., 1986). Neither work assigns primacy to that factor.

owner and overseer of BEA and BOAC [the government-owned air-
lines], to encourage the emergence of manufacturers big enough to
take on the American aircraft builders."[50] And while it is true that Britain manufactured the first jet airliner, the Comet, that aircraft, in addition to being uneconomical like its eventual successor, the Concorde,
had a terrible safety record that caused it to be withdrawn from service.[51]

My point is not that Krugman is wrong in his analysis of international trade; I am not competent to say. Nor is it that path dependence
is a nonexistent or unimportant phenomenon. My purpose is to draw
the reader's attention to the casualness with which evidence is handled
in much public-intellectual work because of the absence of the usual
gatekeepers who filter and police academic publication. I should add,
lest I give a misleading impression either of Krugman's views or of my
opinion of him as an economist, that he is not a protectionist, that he
does not consider strategic trade policy something the United States
ought to pursue even though it might have some theoretical economic
appeal, and that he is highly critical of what he calls "competitive internationalism," the idea promoted by Lester Thurow and other public-
intellectual economists that America's economic health is critically
dependent on international competition and hence on international-
trade policy.[52]

For some years now, Gary Becker, an immensely distinguished economist who received the Nobel prize in economics in 1992, has been
writing a column for *Business Week*. Most of the columns fall in the cat-
egories of public-intellectual work that I have dubbed "self-popularizing" and "own-field policy proposing" and have described as relatively
unproblematic. The unusual breadth of Becker's academic work enables him to range across an enormous variety of policy issues without straying outside his areas of expertise. But even Becker's academic
competence has limits, which he exceeded in a column urging a consti-

50. Peter J. Lyth, "'A Multiplicity of Instruments': The 1946 Decision to Create a Separate British European Airline and Its Effect on Civil Aircraft Production," *Journal of Transport
History*, no. 2, pp. 1, 15 (1990).
   51. Brooks, note 48 above, at 180.
   52. All these are themes of Krugman's excellent book *Pop Internationalism* (1996). The
book is peppered with cogent criticisms of the factual accuracy and economic logic of
Thurow's public-intellectual writings (see index references to Thurow in id. at 219), which I
discuss in the next chapter.

tutional amendment that would limit the terms of federal judges to twelve years, or sixteen in the case of Supreme Court justices.[53]

The column claims that while in the nineteenth century "judges generally took a rather limited view of their purpose," this is no longer the case. Judges now cannot resist "mak[ing] laws through creative readings of precedents, statutes, and constitutional provisions" (p. 236), and as a result "the judiciary has, in effect, become a second legislative body" (p. 237). So far there is no economics; and lawyers will have no difficulty naming nineteenth-century cases in which federal judges took a broad, in fact extravagant, view of their proper role, of which the Dred Scott case is only the most notorious. But the column goes on to say that "like other professionals, judges are influenced by a desire to be popular with friends and the media, by prevailing views of what is fair and the proper role of governments, and by other ideas they have been exposed to as students and practicing attorneys" (pp. 236–237), and this could be thought an allusion to an economic conception of the judge as a self-interested rather than public-interested actor. But it is left unexplained why the judicial utility function thus sketched should lead judges to be willful (or why the judicial utility function was different in the nineteenth century). No doubt judges want to be liked by their friends and their professional peers; but judges' peers, and even their friends, are mostly other judges. Some want to be admired by the media, but the media are not monolithic; there are a number of conservative magazines, talk-show hosts on television and particularly radio, and the Federalist Society and the Liberty Fund to provide warm support to conservative judges. There is no single prevailing view of "what is fair and the proper role of government" either; one influential view is precisely that the judges should be self-restrained in the exercise of their powers—and that is also one of the ideas to which judges will have been exposed as students and as practitioners.[54]

Nor is it explained how term limits would make federal judges more restrained. It is true that term limits would give presidents "the opportunity not to reappoint judges who are ill or incompetent, who issue

53. Gary S. Becker, "Life Tenure for Judges Is an Idea Whose Time Has Gone," in Gary S. Becker and Guity Nashat Becker, *The Economics of Life: From Baseball to Affirmative Action to Immigration, How Real-World Issues Affect Our Everyday Life* 236 (1997).

54. See further, on the judicial utility function, Richard A. Posner, *Overcoming Law*, ch. 3 (1995) ("What Do Judges Maximize?"), and references cited there.

outrageous opinions, or who use unreasonable interpretations of statutes and the Constitution to oppose consistently popular views of the
vast majority of the people" (p. 237). Equally, however, term limits
would empower presidents not to reappoint judges who hewed to the
unpopular course of judicial self-restraint; Becker himself seems to regret that the Supreme Court "has not yet discovered constitutional
constraints on the size of damages."[55] In another *Business Week* column,
written the same year as the one advocating term limits for federal
judges, Becker had opposed term limits for members of Congress, noting that "members who cannot look forward to a long tenure will take
less interest in their work and spend their time arranging future careers."[56] Why wouldn't the same be true of federal judges?

Becker has emphasized the importance of legal stability in business
cases.[57] But shortening federal judges' terms would, by increasing judicial turnover, reduce legal stability. It would also make it more difficult
to attract able people to a career in the judiciary. Secure tenure is an
important part of a federal judge's compensation.

Had Becker confined his proposal to the Supreme Court, the current
diet of which is indeed dominated by politically charged constitutional
cases, he would have been on firmer ground. Germany, for example,
has a special supreme court for constitutional cases, and the judges of
that court have nonrenewable ten-year terms. But Becker wants Supreme Court justices to have *longer* terms than other federal judges.

Paul Krugman, too, has ventured into commentary on a legal subject. Discussing price discrimination by the Internet retailer Ama-
zon.com,[58] Krugman points out that this discrimination may be good
for the book industry. The making of books involves heavy fixed costs
relative to marginal costs. A book is costly to produce, but, once it is
produced, running off another copy is cheap. If the consumers who
value the book highly can be charged a high price that will enable the
producer to recover his fixed costs from them, he can sell the book to

55. Gary S. Becker, "The High Court Debate Isn't High—or Broad—Enough," in Becker
and Becker, note 53 above, at 234, 235.

56. Gary S. Becker, "Reforming Congress: Why Limiting Terms Won't Work," in id. at
213, 214.

57. Becker, note 55 above, at 235.

58. Paul Krugman, "What Price Fairness?" *New York Times* (national ed.), Oct. 4, 2000,
p. A31.

other consumers at a price closer to his low marginal cost, and this will enable him to increase his profits. Analysis is complicated by the fact that it is the retailer, Amazon.com, not the publisher, that is doing the discrimination. Krugman does not discuss the mechanism by which the benefits (or a substantial fraction of them) will inure to publishers. But assume they will; I am concerned with something else. Toward the end of his column Krugman states that Amazon.com's discriminatory pricing of books is "undeniably unfair: some people pay more just because of who they are," and "it looks to me as if the Robinson-Patman Act, which outlaws price discrimination across state lines (though strictly speaking only if it hurts competition), could be invoked to prevent" such discrimination.

He is wrong about the Robinson-Patman Act. It does not outlaw price discrimination; if it did, examples that Krugman gives of commonplace, unexceptionable price discrimination in the publishing industry, such as the price difference between the hardback and paperback versions of a book, a difference that invariably exceeds any difference in the cost of publishing the two versions, would be examples of unlawful activity. What the Robinson-Patman Act primarily forbids (with exceptions unnecessary to get into) is price discrimination in sales to dealers or other middlemen. The concern is that such discrimination may impair competition in the distribution of goods. That is the significance of the statutory requirement that the discrimination be shown to have a competitive effect.[59] The Act is not concerned with discrimination in sales to consumers except in the rare case in which that discrimination might be a form of predation against the competitors of the price-discriminating seller, which is not the character of Amazon.com's discriminatory pricing either.

In addition, Krugman's statement that discriminatory pricing is "unfair" is highly questionable, given that price discrimination is extremely common yet for the most part tolerated without protest. I mentioned the difference in the prices of hardback and paperback books. Other examples are the difference in ticket prices between first-run and subsequent-run theaters and the differences between advanced-purchase and regular, weekend and weekday, and discount coach and first-class airplane fares. The examples can be multiplied at will.

59. See Clayton Act (as amended by the Robinson-Patman Act), § 2(a), 15 U.S.C. § 13(a); FTC v. Morton Salt Co., 334 U.S. 37 (1948).

Krugman evinces no disapproval of these other forms of price discrimination. But he worries that Amazon.com's form of discriminatory pricing (which the industry calls "dynamic pricing") causes "some people [to] pay more *just because of who they are*": the company "uses a potential buyer's electronic fingerprint—his record of previous purchases, his address, maybe the other sites he has visited—to size up how likely he is to balk if the price is high. If the customer looks price-sensitive, he gets a bargain; if he doesn't he pays a premium" (emphasis added). In the more common types of price discrimination, the seller sets different prices to different classes of consumer and each consumer decides which class to join (for example, whether to buy the hardback version of a book or wait for the paperback version to be published). The difference, however, is gossamer thin. The consumer who has to pay full fare to travel to a funeral is discriminated against because of his special need, and likewise the consumer who must buy the hardback version of a book because he needs it for a course and the paperback version has not been published yet. Maybe those instances of price discrimination are "fairer" than what Amazon.com is doing. Krugman evidently thinks so. It is his claim that ordinary price discrimination (though he thinks it unlawful!) is undeniably fair and what Amazon.com is doing is undeniably unfair that is extravagant.

Camille Paglia is a substantially less distinguished academic than any I have mentioned thus far, and she writes really wild public-intellectual stuff—though no wilder than Chomsky's. Yet she has become a greater media celebrity than any of the academics whom I have mentioned thus far in this chapter except Stephen Jay Gould (see Table 5.3 in Chapter 5). The book that launched her meteoric career as a public intellectual is a 718-page scholarly work entitled *Sexual Personae*, published by a leading academic press (Yale).[60] Its subject is sexual decadence in pictorial art and, particularly, literature. It is an insightful book, written in a lively manner, though opinionated, uneven, and often difficult to follow. Like *The Closing of the American Mind* it is one of those difficult academic works that mysteriously strike a chord with a broad public. Within a short time after its publication the author was a media star, opining in print but particularly on television on almost every subject under the sun[61] and in increasingly wild and whirling words. In 1994

60. Camille Paglia, *Sexual Personae: Art and Decadence from Nefertiti to Emily Dickinson* (1990).

61. Including Clinton's impeachment, in regard to which she said that "most Americans

she published *Vamps and Tramps: New Essays*, and the first essay in the collection, "The Penis Unsheathed" (actually the transcript of a television show broadcast in England), begins with her saying "The penis. Should we keep it? Or should we cut it off and *throw it away?*" (p. 3, emphasis in original). The book continues in this vein, with essays having such titles as "Kind of a Bitch: Why I Like Hillary Clinton" (p. 176) and ending with a collection of cartoons of Paglia that have been published in various newspapers and magazines and sixty pages of brief synopses of articles about her.

Paglia presents herself as a bisexual hostile to feminism and all other forms of political correctness ("Because I am a pornographer, I am at war with Catharine MacKinnon and Andrea Dworkin," p. 107—from an article first published in *Playboy*). Thus occupying her very own niche in the public-intellectual ecosystem (and therefore free from the competition that a close substitute would provide), relentless in self-promotion,[62] and lacking any verbal restraint, Paglia has become one of the intellectuals best known to the general public in the United States. Not that there isn't method in her madness. Wild it may be, but no one will deny a certain justness to her description of the French post-modernist Jacques Lacan: "Lacan: the French fog machine; a gray-flannel worry-bone for toothless academic pups; a twerpy, cape-twirling Dracula dragging his flocking stooges to the crypt. Lacan is a Freud T-shirt shrunk down to the teeny-weeny Saussure torso."[63] And she is right on point when, reviewing two books of gay studies, she complains of the "political packaging" of the books—of the fact that both state that a portion of the profits from them will be given to an AIDS foundation—and remarks "the hypocrisy and Phariseeism of public announcements of one's own charity" and the subtle coerciveness of

---

would probably prefer being governed by a charming, oafish philanderer [President Clinton] than by a simpering, shilly-shallying, fascist milquetoast like Special Prosecutor Kenneth W. Starr, who has a face like creamed corn and the brains to go with it." Camille Paglia, "Ask Camille: Linda Tripp, the White House's Ghoulish Bad Conscience," *Salon Magazine*, July 7, 1998, http://www.salonmagazine.com/col/pagl/1998/07/07pagl.html.

62. "Playing off the stereotype of the pompous man or woman of letters, Paglia, decked out in leather and flanked by muscular young bodyguards, may have been the first intellectual to assume the pose of rock star." Neal Gabler, *Life the Movie: How Entertainment Conquered Reality* 140 (1998). Gabler regards Paglia as the prototype of the contemporary intellectual, id. at 140–142, but that is inaccurate.

63. Camille Paglia, "Junk Bonds and Corporate Raiders: Academe in the Hour of the Wolf," in Paglia, *Sex, Art, and American Culture: Essays* 170, 241 (1992).

"implying: don't give these books a bad review, or you will hurt sales and cause more people to die."[64] And maybe I am judging her by the wrong criteria—maybe her public-intellectual work should be categorized and assessed as entertainment rather than as an effort to contribute to knowledge. But even if it is placed in the second category, its quality is no lower than that of Chomsky, or of Gould in his book on science and religion. Yet Chomsky and Gould are scientists (Chomsky's brand of linguistics is a form of cognitive science). High up in the norm hierarchy of the scientific community are accuracy, open-mindedness, disinterest, and logicality, norms that Chomsky and Gould regularly (and Paul Krugman, a distinguished scientific economist, occasionally) flout in their public-intellectual work. This supports my claim that academics tend to think of themselves as being on holiday when they are writing for the general public.

But let us not lose perspective. Academic public intellectuals have written many fine books and articles that helped enlighten the public on important issues, though most of this work has been devoted to undoing the damage caused by other public intellectuals and some of the best of it had trouble getting a hearing. No public-intellectual work has dated less than Milton Friedman's book *Capitalism and Freedom* (1962). Yet when it was first published no major publication would review it.[65] Some public-intellectual writings, as we'll see in Chapter 7, have great literary distinction. Others are superb reads even if completely wrongheaded, such as Edmund Wilson's history of communism *(To the Finland Station)* and Walter Benjamin's memoir of his visit to Moscow in 1927.[66] But literary distinction is rare among *academic* public intellectuals.

What complicates evaluation is that while the average quality of public-intellectual work is not high, the variance around the mean is great, sometimes even within the same book. In a brilliant article first published in 1952, David Riesman, one of the nation's best-known academic public intellectuals,[67] argued both that Orwell's novel *Nineteen Eighty-Four* had exaggerated the efficacy of totalitarian brainwash-

64. Id. at 171–172.

65. See preface to 1982 reprinting, at vi.

66. "Moscow," in Walter Benjamin, *Selected Writings*, vol. 2: *1927–1934* 22 (Michael W. Jennings, Howard Eiland, and Gary Smith eds., 1999).

67. One of the best known to other intellectuals, at any rate, for the popular media seem to have lost interest in him. See Table 5.1 in Chapter 5.

ing and that corruption would eventually undermine the Soviet Union's ideological claims and political integrity.[68] He was right on both counts, as we shall see with reference to the first in Chapter 7, though he was wrong to attribute the novel's exaggeration of totalitarianism's staying power to Orwell, as we'll also see. But in the same volume is another essay—the title piece, no less—predicting (in 1957) that Americans' desire for material goods was rapidly approaching satiation.[69] All one can say in Riesman's defense of such nonsense is that he was in distinguished company. A year later, we find Hannah Arendt attributing Germany's postwar economic "miracle" to the fact that destruction and production are the same thing: "In Germany, outright destruction took the place of the relentless process of depreciation of all worldly things, which is the hallmark of the waste economy in which we now live. The result is almost the same: a booming prosperity which, as postwar Germany illustrates, feeds not on the abundance of material goods or on anything stable and given but on the process of production and consumption itself."[70] In other words, war and consumption are the same thing—a curious view, connected to the widespread belief in the 1950s that prosperity depended on a high level of military spending, that is, spending on "goods produced to be wasted either by using them up in destruction or . . . by destroying them because they soon become obsolete."[71]

Another well-known public intellectual, Richard Sennett, a sociologist like Riesman, made a similar point some years later (and so with even less excuse) in a book advocating the abolition of *all* material and moral incentives to productivity and achievement: "The problem confronting an affluent capitalist society is not how to make more things, but how to get rid of what it has."[72] This is the "overproduction" critique of capitalism. As we shall see in Chapter 7, it is one of the persistent public-intellectual fallacies.

68. David Riesman, "Some Observations on the Limits of Totalitarian Power," in Riesman, *Abundance for What? And Other Essays* 80 (1964).

69. David Riesman, "Abundance for What?" in id. at 300. I discuss Riesman further at the end of Chapter 8.

70. Hannah Arendt, *The Human Condition* 229 (1958). See also id. at 116–117.

71. Id. at 364 n. 3.

72. Richard Sennett and Jonathan Cobb, *The Hidden Injuries of Class* 261 (1972).

⌒ THE QUALITY of public-intellectual work is particularly at risk in situations in which an academic (and remember that the focus of this book is on the *academic* public intellectual) is being asked to comment on controversies *in medias res*. Academic time is not real time. The academic is accustomed to conducting research in depth, at his leisure, before formulating a conclusion. He is a fish out of water when asked to opine on events that are unfolding before his eyes as he speaks. There are exceptions, of course;[73] but I think I've identified the tendency correctly. It has been observed (without limitation to academics) in connection with the Kosovo campaign that "running parallel to the reporting is the opinion barrage of politicians, commentators, experts, writers, and other public intellectuals . . . These opinion pieces are generally of minimal use for working out what happened and why. The world-historical reflections of a Nobel Prize winner prove more ephemeral than the hurried news story of a nineteen-year-old reporter."[74]

Let us recall some of the contemporaneous comments of public intellectuals on the Clinton impeachment. For David Frum, a conservative public intellectual, what was "at stake in the Lewinsky scandal . . . [was] the central dogma of the baby boomers: the belief that sex, so long as it's consensual, ought never to be subject to moral scrutiny at all,"[75] while for liberal public intellectual Arthur Schlesinger Jr., "All the Independent Counsel's charges thus far derive entirely from a President's lies about his own sex life . . . Lying about one's sex life is not a monstrous crime . . . Gentlemen always lie about their sex lives. Only a cad tells the truth about his love affairs."[76] For Frum, then, Clinton was a sexual immoralist; for Schlesinger, he was a gentleman. Both allowed their disagreement over sexual morality to obscure the conduct actually at issue—conduct to which sex was merely the catalyst—involving vari-

73. For example, Kenneth Anderson's brilliant contemporary denunciation of the inconsistency of "family rights" conservative public intellectuals, such as George Will, in seeking to prevent the father of the Cuban child Elián González from taking his child back to Cuba. Kenneth Anderson, "A Great Betrayal: How American Conservatives Have Abandoned Parental Rights in the Case of Elián González," *Times Literary Supplement*, May 12, 2000, p. 14.

74. Timothy Garton Ash, "Kosovo: Was It Worth It?" *New York Review of Books*, Sept. 21, 2000, p. 50.

75. David Frum, "A Generation on Trial," *Weekly Standard*, Feb. 16, 1998, pp. 19, 23.

76. Arthur Schlesinger Jr., "The Background and History of Impeachment," statement before the House Judiciary Committee, Nov. 9, 1998.

ous obstructions of justice; reckless disregard for the dignity of the presidency; repeated lying to aides, Cabinet members, and the public; and slander, religious posturing, and phony contrition. If, as the passage that I quoted from Frum suggests, the core of the opposition to Clinton was not that he was a liar or even a criminal (for the Right displayed no indignation over the crimes committed by participants in the Iran-Contra affair), but that his personal conduct and attitudes were revolting, then the claim of his defenders to be warding off a Puritan assault on sexual liberty can't be dismissed as mere demagoguery.

Cornered by the press, speaking off the cuff, excited to have a chance to participate in electrifying events, academics commenting on the Clinton affair spoke without precision, nuance, or care. Here is the distinguished sociologist and prolific writer for the *New Republic* and other intellectual magazines Alan Wolfe on the scandal:

> The American people are forgiving. We like to give people a second chance, and Clinton will get one because he's been a naughty boy, and you have to forgive naughty boys . . . No one really knows the limits of our tolerance. When this all started, I thought we were living in Nathaniel Hawthorne's Massachusetts.[77]

Could Wolfe have been serious in dismissing Clinton's misconduct as the eminently forgivable actions of a "naughty boy" and supposing that the criticisms of it were the product merely of sexual Puritanism?

Writing for a general audience in the midst of Clinton's crisis, the liberal philosopher and public intellectual Thomas Nagel denounced "the shameful farce now being played out in Washington." He singled out for criticism "the sinister and obsessionally puritanical Starr," "the lurid and poisonous Linda Tripp," and "the fetishistic and infantile Monica Lewinsky."[78] These defamatory characterizations, published recklessly in advance of the evidence (just as when John Judis denounced the media for reporting "the entirely unsubstantiated rumor about Lewinsky's semen-stained dress"),[79] introduced an article

---

77. Quoted in Mary Leonard, "In Land of Second Chances, an Apology Can Suffice," *Boston Globe*, Aug. 18, 1998, p. A11.

78. Thomas Nagel, "The Shredding of Public Privacy: Reflections on Recent Events in Washington," *Times Literary Supplement*, Aug. 14, 1998, p. 15.

79. John B. Judis, "Irresponsible Elites," *American Prospect*, May-June 1998, pp. 14, 15.

excerpted from a much longer one that Nagel had published in an academic journal before the Clinton–Lewinsky affair came to light.[80] In that article, as in its popular condensation, Nagel argued unexceptionably that people are entitled to keep their sex lives private. But by juxtaposing in the shorter article that argument with references to the investigation of the Clinton–Lewinsky affair, Nagel, like Frum and Schlesinger, drew attention away from the issue that had precipitated the investigation and the impeachment inquiry: the issue of obstruction of justice.

Nagel forgot, moreover—as is common when an academic switches gears from academic to popular exposition—an important point that he had made in the longer article, which is that privacy is a duty as well as a right. The precondition of freedom to behave unconventionally in private is to avoid flaunting one's unconventionality; flaunting makes it a public issue.[81] Clinton did not want his affair with Lewinsky to become public. But he took a grave risk that it would. The result, as Nagel would have predicted, was to create a public issue of what Nagel argued in his academic article should be private conduct. American sexual morality is pluralistic. An enormous variety of attitudes—toward adultery, oral sex, phone sex, sex between a young woman and a middle-aged man, between employee and employer—coexist; and they coexist in part because of tacit agreement that these are (the last least securely) private matters. By forcing these attitudes into articulate competition, Clinton precipitated a rancorous *Kulturkampf.* Nagel neither remarked upon this nor tried to reconcile his condemnation of the Clinton–Lewinsky investigation with the statement in his academic article that "it is a good thing that sexual coercion of an employee or a student should be legally actionable."[82] Paula Jones was charging sexual coercion by an employer, and Clinton resorted to illegal tactics to thwart her effort to prove it.

Kant famously took a very hard line both against lying[83] and in favor

---

Judis's article failed to identify any errors in the media coverage of the Clinton–Lewinsky affair.

80. Thomas Nagel, "Concealment and Exposure," 27 *Philosophy and Public Affairs* 3 (1998).

81. Id. at 12–17, 26–30.

82. Id. at 27.

83. For example, "To be truthful (honest) in all declarations is, therefore, a sacred and unconditionally commanding law of reason that admits of no expediency whatsoever." Im-

of compliance with legal norms,[84] and these positions retain a following in modern philosophy.[85] A moral philosopher such as Nagel, a follower of Kant, might have been expected either to criticize the president forthrightly or to explain why lying and illegality aren't serious moral lapses either generally or in the case of President Clinton, since, as Sissela Bok has pointed out, "few lies are solitary ones . . . More and more lies may come to be needed; the liar always has more mending to do . . . The sheer energy the liar has to devote to shoring them up is energy the honest man can dispose of freely."[86] But Nagel did not criticize Clinton's lies; and another public-intellectual philosopher, Michael Sandel, opined in the *New Republic* that President Clinton might have been "justified" in falsely denying his sexual escapade with Lewinsky. Sandel cited Kant for the proposition that there is "a sharp distinction between lies and statements that are misleading but not, in the formal sense, untrue."[87] Kant declined to equate the duty not to lie to a duty to tell the truth on all occasions—a duty of complete candor. He recognized that some reticences are not deceptive and that some deceptions created by reticence are prudentially justified.[88] But what Sandel failed to mention is that Kant believed "we may *never* state outright that we *will* tell the truth when we have no intention of doing so. Oaths, for example, must be taken and kept with the utmost seriousness."[89] Clinton had denied his relationship with Lewinsky under oath.

The invocation of Kant is a good example of the futility of much public-intellectual writing. Kant has no resonance for Americans. Most of his writing is opaque. Only a tiny handful of Americans read him.

---

manuel Kant, "On a Supposed Right to Lie Because of Philanthropic Concerns," in Kant, *Grounding for the Metaphysics of Morals with On a Supposed Right to Lie Because of Philanthropic Concerns* 63, 65 (James W. Ellington trans., 3d ed. 1993).

84. "The moral requirement of obedience to actually existing law, Kant concluded, is 'absolute.'" Jeremy Waldron, "Kant's Legal Positivism," 109 *Harvard Law Review* 1535, 1545 (1996).

85. On lying, see, for example, Sissela Bok, *Lying: Moral Choice in Public and Private Life* (1978) (though she does not go so far as Kant). On compliance with legal norms, see, for example, Jürgen Habermas, *Between Facts and Norms: Contributions to a Discourse Theory of Law and Democracy* (1996); Ernest J. Weinrib, "Law as a Kantian Idea of Reason," 87 *Columbia Law Review* 472 (1987).

86. Bok, note 85 above, at 25.

87. Michael J. Sandel, "White Lies," *New Republic*, March 2, 1998, p. 10. A remarkable title in the circumstances.

88. Roger J. Sullivan, *Immanuel Kant's Moral Theory* 170–173 (1989).

89. Id. at 173 (emphasis in original).

His strong condemnation of lying under oath was no more an embarrassment for Clinton than his rejection of a duty of candor is a comfort for him.

Judis and Sandel were writing early in the crisis, before the DNA test on Lewinsky's dress and before the president's grand jury testimony and television address of August 17, 1998, in which he admitted the relationship with Lewinsky. Sandel's description of the president's conduct as "white lies," and Judis's criticisms of the press for inaccurate reporting, became completely untenable as Starr's investigation progressed. At some point it must have become evident to these commentators that they had misled the public. They had access to the same media in which their original comments had been published and could have issued appropriate retractions or modifications of their earlier statements, but they didn't.

A full-page advertisement in the *New York Times* signed by a large number of historians stated that "the current charges against [President Clinton] depart from what the Framers saw as grounds for impeachment."[90] No effort to support this conclusion was made; nor was there any argument that "what the Framers saw as grounds for impeachment" should resolve a current controversy. The "theory of impeachment" underlying the efforts to impeach Clinton was said to be "unprecedented in our history," but it was not said what that theory is. There were two possibilities. One was that it was the theory, for which the Nixon impeachment inquiry could be cited as a precedent, that obstruction of justice by the president is an impeachable offense. No lack of precedent there. The other possibility was that it was the theory of "political impeachment" that underlay the efforts of the Jeffersonian Republicans to impeach Federalist judges such as Samuel Chase and of the radical Republicans to impeach Andrew Johnson. That is a bad theory, but it is part of our history too, as any historian would have known who took the time to examine the history of impeachment.

One of the signers, Jack Rakove, had three weeks earlier published an article that, as the title suggests, contradicts the advertisement's central historical claim.[91] The article concludes that history couldn't answer the question whether Clinton's detractors were right or wrong in

90. "Historians in Defense of the Constitution," *New York Times*, Oct. 30, 1998, p. A15. Arthur Schlesinger Jr. was again among the signatories.

91. Jack Rakove, "Framers of Two Minds on Impeachment," *Newsday*, Oct. 11, 1998, p. B5.

arguing that his conduct constituted a high enough misdemeanor to justify impeachment. Professor Rakove has in conversation acknowledged the contradiction but explained that he considered the advertisement a political act rather than a statement of his actual views.

Just the fact that a large number of public intellectuals would permit their names to be affixed to a newspaper advertisement, open letter, petition, or brief (see Chapter 10) is a clue to the lack of quality standards in the public-intellectual market. Rarely do more than a small minority of the signers have firsthand familiarity with the position they are signing on to. And few of them would agree with the actual wording of a statement designed to paper over any disagreements among the persons whom the sponsors of the statement wish to enlist in its support.

In November of 1998, several hundred law professors, of whom few were experts on impeachment and most surely had only a superficial acquaintance with the facts bearing on the Clinton impeachment, asked Congress not to impeach the president. The letter stated that "*If the President committed perjury regarding his sexual conduct, this perjury involved no exercise of Presidential power as such*" (emphasis in original). But there was no "if" about it to anyone who had followed the investigation carefully; and those who had not—the vast majority—had no business signing a letter in their capacity as law professors, thus representing themselves to have a professionally responsible opinion.[92]

Cass Sunstein argues that those signatories who were not constitutional-law experts "probably believed that they knew enough—from training and from substantive conversations with colleagues—to have a reasonably informed opinion."[93] But with whom would they have had the substantive conversations? Very few law schools had a faculty member who knew anything about the esoteric field of impeachment law. As Neal Devins notes, the eighteen-hundred-page constitutional-law casebook of which Sunstein is one of the editors devotes only one page to impeachment.[94]

92. This point is also made in Neal Devins, "Bearing False Witness: The Clinton Impeachment and the Future of Academic Freedom," 148 *University of Pennsylvania Law Review* 165, 166–167, 170 (1999), and in Ward Farnsworth, "Talking out of School: Notes on the Transmission of Intellectual Capital from the Legal Academy to Public Tribunals," 81 *Boston University Law Review* 13, 30–41, 2001).

93. Cass R. Sunstein, "Professors and Politics," 148 *University of Pennsylvania Law Review* 191, 195 (1999).

94. Devins, note 92 above, at 170.

Devins mentions other letter-writing campaigns by law professors, including a 1987 campaign in which two thousand of them, roughly a quarter of the total legal professoriat in the United States, participated in opposing the confirmation of Robert Bork as a Supreme Court justice.[95] Law professors and historians are not the only offenders. In response to President Clinton's (postimpeachment) proposal for a national antimissile defense, fifty Nobel science laureates signed an open letter to the president stating that the proposed system "would offer little protection." Half the signatories were either biologists or chemists, and many of the others were in branches of physics unrelated to the science involved in trying to shoot down missiles without being fooled by decoys.[96] The opinion of these distinguished nonexperts was as pertinent to the debate over the antimissile defense as a celebrity endorsement. They were making a political statement rather than presenting an expert opinion, but they were pretending that it was the latter.

But the *reductio ad absurdum* of public-intellectual open-letter-writing is the full-page advertisement entitled "The Election Crisis" published in the *New York Times* just forty-eight hours after it was discovered that the November 7, 2000, presidential election had failed to produce a clear winner.[97] This ominous black-bordered document claimed that "there is good reason to believe that Vice President Gore has been elected President by a clear constitutional majority of the popular vote and the Electoral College." Overlooked is the fact that a popular-vote majority has no constitutional standing; only the vote of the Electoral College (or of the House of Representatives if the Electoral College fails to produce a majority vote for one of the candidates) counts. The term "clear constitutional majority of the popular vote" is thus gibberish.[98] The advertisement went on to state that "to preserve the dignity and legitimacy of American democracy, it is essential to remove any *hint* of inaccuracy in the final result" (emphasis added). But no tally in a political election is a completely accurate record of the intentions of the voters. It is not intended to be, since what is tallied is legal votes, not intentions. Even when the voting and counting machin-

95. Id. at 166–167. See also Farnsworth, note 92 above, at 14 n. 2.

96. See "I'm Not Gonna Pay a Lot for This Missile Defense," *New Republic,* July 31, 2000, p. 10.

97. "The Election Crisis," *New York Times* (national ed.), Nov. 10, 2000, p. A29.

98. As also noted by Wolfe, note 1 above.

ery is flawless, which of course can never be guaranteed, some ballots are spoiled by the voter (for example by accidentally voting for more than one candidate for the same office, or by misreading the instructions) and some voters make a mistake and vote for someone other than they meant to vote for. It would be impossible to remove any "hint" of inaccuracy from the process.

The advertisement stated that "as many as 19,000 Gore votes may have been nullified." The reference was to the number of votes thought to have been cast mistakenly for Patrick Buchanan in Palm Beach County owing to the design of the ballot used in that county (the "butterfly ballot"), rather than to the number of votes, unknown on November 10, that the machine count had missed. The butterfly ballot was the brainchild of the county's supervisor of elections, a Democrat. The purpose was to enable the names of the ten presidential candidates to be printed in large type, yet on facing pages, for the convenience of the elderly voters in the county.

The advertisement concluded by calling on the Florida Election Commission to "explore every option, including scheduling and supervising new elections in Palm Beach County. Nothing less, we believe, can preserve the faith of the people upon which our entire political system rests." The referent of "nothing less" is obscure, but the implication seems to be that nothing less than a revote would clear the air. Nothing was said, however, about the practicality of holding a new election before December 12, the deadline for the secure designation of Florida's electors in the Electoral College;[99] a new ballot would have to be prepared, a new election day designated, polling places reopened, arrangements made for staffing them and for counting the votes cast in the new election, the votes counted, and challenges to the outcome resolved. Nothing was said about whether such a remedy would be appropriate given that the voters in the reelection would be voting in light of knowledge not available to the original electorate, such as the

---

99. As long as a state submitted its electoral vote for president to the Electoral College no later than (for the 2000 election) December 12, the validity of its vote could not be questioned by Congress. 3 U.S.C. § 5. If the state missed this deadline, its vote could be challenged when Congress met in January to count the electoral votes. See 3 U.S.C. § 15. For a detailed analysis of the election deadlock and its resolution, see my book *Breaking the Deadlock: The 2000 Election, the Constitution, and the Courts* (2001). Chapter 4 of that book contains additional discussion of public-intellectual commentary on the deadlock.

outcome in other states. Nothing was said about whether the Democratic Party should be allowed to obtain an advantage from repudiating a ballot design that the responsible Democratic official had created. Nothing was said about whether recounts would be appropriate on similar grounds in other states.

A word on the significance of simultaneity: the presidential election is supposed to be simultaneous throughout the nation apart from time-zone differences, and when election results from the East Coast are broadcast before the polls have closed in other time zones there is widespread public indignation. A revote limited to Florida or to particular Florida counties would be contaminated by the voters' knowledge of the election outcome in the other states; there would be powerful moral pressure to ratify Gore's popular-vote majority.[100] A consensus soon emerged that there would be no reelection, and a suit seeking one failed in the Florida courts.

The advertisement was signed "Emergency Committee of Concerned Citizens 2000," and among the listed members were several prominent academic public intellectuals, such as Bruce Ackerman, Ronald Dworkin, Cass Sunstein, Michael Walzer, and Sean Wilentz, along with other professors, writers and journalists, and, remarkably, Broadway and Hollywood in the persons of Robert DeNiro, Bianca Jagger, Paul Newman, and Joanne Woodward. Here truly is the merger of the entertainment and academic worlds.

"The Election Crisis" lacks balance and depth. As a statement of the feelings and desires of Democratic Party supporters, such as the signatories from the entertainment world, it is unexceptionable. Obviously these people have a right to express their views. But what are the academics doing as signatories? The advertisement does not on its face reflect the conclusion of a process of academic inquiry; nor could the academic signatories, none of whom is an expert in election law, have formulated a responsible academic opinion in the few hours that elapsed between the emergence of the "crisis" and the composition of

100. Public-intellectual law professor Laurence Tribe's solution to this problem bordered on the comical: "A corrective election could be limited to people who voted the first time around, and those voting could be required to submit sworn affidavits that they will vote for whichever candidate they had intended to vote for on Election Day." Laurence H. Tribe, "Let the Courts Decide," *New York Times*, Nov. 12, 2000, § 4, p. 15. There would be no way to verify the truthfulness of such affidavits.

the advertisement. The opinion expressed in the advertisement, with its barely muffled call for a reelection in Palm Beach County, was not responsible. Ackerman, Dworkin, Sunstein, and Wilentz were all prominent in opposing Clinton's impeachment, but had denied they were acting out of political partisanship. Now they were appearing as signatories of an advertisement that whether justly or not was certain to be read as campaign literature for Gore's postelection presidential quest.

The next day, the same group, with some additional names but with DeNiro and Jagger mysteriously deleted, published a smaller advertisement in the *Times* pompously captioned "We the People." This advertisement removed the ambiguity of its predecessor concerning remedy and urged unequivocally that "those who voted [in Palm Beach County] on November 7 should be asked to vote again as soon as possible . . . and there should be an accurate hand count in certain counties under question."[101] Much ambiguity is concealed in the phrase "accurate hand count."[102] The count later sought by the Democrats involved highly subjective criteria incapable of removing ambiguity. And it was unsound to suggest that the hand recount be limited to the counties picked out by the Democrats, since a recount of ballots rejected by the machine count would be likely to favor the candidate with the most support in the electoral district in question.[103] "We the People" made a pretense of evenhandedness by remarking that "Republicans are aggrieved that premature assignment of Florida to the Democratic candidate, while the polls were still open, may have deterred Republican voters." But no remedy was proposed for that grievance. And, as I mentioned, the proposal for a reelection went nowhere.

The next day one of the academic signatories[104] sent an e-mail to a

101. "We the People," *New York Times* (national ed.), Nov. 11, 2000, p. A27.

102. See Glenn R. Simpson, Helene Cooper, and Evan Perez, "Florida Neighborhoods Deciding Fate of the Presidency: Tiny, Significant Gain Goes to Gore as Hand Count Often Becomes Surreal," *Wall Street Journal*, Nov. 13, 2000, p. A38.

103. Suppose that Candidate A has 700 votes, Candidate B 350, and 100 are erroneously not counted, so that A leads B by 350 votes. If the 100 are now counted, they can be expected to split in roughly the same proportion as the votes that were counted. The result will be to give A 67 more votes and B 33 more votes. Hence A's lead over B will rise from 350 to 404. If there is another district with identical statistics except with A's and B's numbers reversed, a hand count in that district can be expected to favor B to the same extent as the hand count in the first district favored A.

104. Cass Sunstein (see Sunstein, "Ad Hominem" [letter to the editors of the *New Republic*], *New Republic*, Dec. 11, 2000, p. 6), who along with Sean Wilentz and Todd Gitlin was the

number of his friends and acquaintances stating that he (and he believed also one or maybe even all of the other academic signatories, but definitely including Ronald Dworkin) had not seen or approved the November 11 advertisement before it was published, did not agree with it, and thought its call for a new election premature and irresponsible. Yet in a short article written a few days after that advertisement was published, Dworkin endorsed reelection, in the approximate format suggested by another public intellectual supporter of the Democrats, Laurence Tribe,[105] as the best remedy for the kind of deadlock that had arisen, though he implied without quite saying that it was too late to use it to resolve the current deadlock.[106] The article does not discuss any objections to the proposal.

Discussing the two advertisements and their aftermath, Timothy Noah drew the lesson "that the value of intellectual opinion—that it reflects greater knowledge and depth than you typically hear from a talk-radio caller—is lost when intellectuals shoot from the hip" and that "intellectuals look like asses when they attempt to make group pronouncements."[107] Alan Wolfe called the first ad "an exercise in spin," and thought the e-mail by Sean Wilentz soliciting signatures for it "a form of vote-grabbing"; the e-mail had said "get me as many famous names as you can to sign it by 1 P.M. today . . . Mainstream. Fa-

organizer of the committee and the draftsman of the original advertisement. See Tamar Lewin, "The Advocates: Confusion over Voting Has Stirred Wide Range of People and Mobilized Many to Act," *New York Times* (national ed.), Nov. 12, 2000, § 1, p. 18; Timothy Noah, "How Intellectuals Blew the Election 'Crisis,'" *Slate*, Nov. 14, 2000, http://slate.msn.com/Code/chatterbox/chatterbox.asp?Show=11/14/2000&idMessage=6497. In like vein, see Peter Berkowitz, "Nutty Professors: Intellectuals Whiff on the Recount," *New Republic*, Nov. 27, 2000, p. 11. In a letter sharply criticizing Berkowitz's article, Professor Sunstein, while disclaiming the second advertisement, defended the first and did not acknowledge any errors in it. Sunstein, "Ad Hominem," above.

105. See note 100 above.

106. Ronald Dworkin, "The Phantom Poll Booth," *New York Review of Books*, Dec. 21, 2000, p. 96. (For the reference to Tribe, see id. at 98 n. 6.) The article is dated November 15, but Dworkin knew that by the time the article was published it would be much too late to conduct a reelection. In contrast, another academic public intellectual, Stephen Gillers, argued that there was no deadline for resolving the deadlock, because, under the Twentieth Amendment to the Constitution, if Congress, when it meets on January 6 following the election to count the electoral votes, decides that no candidate has yet qualified for the presidency, it can appoint an acting president—Gillers's candidate was Clinton. Stephen Gillers, "Who Says the Election Has a Dec. 12 Deadline?" *New York Times* (national ed.), Dec. 1, 2000, p. A31. What an uproar that (probably unconstitutional) solution would have caused!

107. Noah, note 104 above, points out that the two ads cost $125,000, paid for by anonymous donors.

mous/recognizable."[108] Wolfe added that "whatever prestige academics have because of the depth of their scholarship is surely lost when it is linked to the glitter of celebrities," and that "in their rush to speak, the signers of the November ads resembled the squabbling politicians more than the dignified electorate."

But Wolfe failed to heed his own advice. For two weeks later we find him claiming that "Bush will be our first truly postmodern president, the first of whom it can be said that when asked how he came to be the winner, he can respond that it all depends on the perspective one brings to the question," because "he implicitly endorsed the notion that there was no truth [about who had actually won the presidential vote in Florida] even worth manipulating." "As a postmodern president, Bush will face a challenge to his authority far greater than Clinton's [challenged for lying too flagrantly even for a politician], for the foundation of his legitimacy will hinge on the proposition that ultimately it did not matter whether his victory was real or not . . . A president elected in a world beyond truth and falsity will not find it easy to govern."[109] Wolfe committed in this article both the ontological error of thinking that the question who won the presidential election in Florida is of the same order as the question how many telephone jacks I have in my office and the epistemological error of thinking that to deny that something is knowable is to deny that it exists. The question who really won in Florida depends in the first instance on what shall count as a vote, and that is a legal question; until it is answered, there is no fact of the matter as to who really won. And depending on whether, as the Democrats urged, a legal vote includes a barely dimpled ballot, it may be impossible to determine objectively who won even after we know what the definition of a legal vote is.

On December 5, 2000, Bruce Ackerman along with several other professors of constitutional law sent an open letter to the Florida legislature stating that the proposed special session of the legislature to appoint presidential electors was unlawful.[110] Federal law allows a state

108. Wolfe, note 1 above.

109. Alan Wolfe, "Hobbled from the Start: How Can George W. Bush Convince Americans to Trust Him When He Has Dismissed Such Notions as Truth and Justice?" *Salon Magazine*, Dec. 15, 2000, http://www.salon.com/politics/feature/2000/12/15/trust/index.html.

110. Ackerman presumably was the author, or at least the principal author; he had already testified in person before a committee of the Florida legislature, and he later published an op-

legislature to appoint presidential electors if the election "failed to make a choice."[111] The letter argued, however, that "if the Florida courts ultimately find that Vice President Al Gore won the state's electoral votes," after Florida's elections canvassing commission had on November 26 certified Bush the winner, "Florida will again not 'fail' to choose . . . Instead it will simply replace one choice with another. The federal law still does not authorize legislative intervention. Indeed, because a vote was held for presidential electors on November 7 that was lawful under the U.S. Constitution, federal law, and Florida law, there is no realistic circumstance under which Florida has or will 'fail' to make a choice under the provision of 3 U.S.C. § 2." Ignored is the possibility, a very live one on December 5, that by December 12, the "safe harbor" day for selection of a state's electors,[112] Florida's electoral choice would be completely up in the air, the controversy over who actually won not having been resolved. The "fail to choose" provision assumes that the state "has held an election for the purpose of choosing electors" (states are not required to) yet has somehow failed to choose electors. That is at least a plausible characterization of a situation in which a controversy over who won is still dragging on when the safe-harbor deadline arrives. The letter's failure to discuss this interpretation is remarkable, given the desirability of having some mechanism by which a deadlock over the selection of the president can be resolved in time to permit the selection to be made by the Electoral College without intervention by Congress.

The decision by the U.S. Supreme Court on December 12, 2000,[113] which brought on Gore's concession the next day and so ended the deadlock, caused paroxysms of intemperate public-intellectual commentary. Writing within days, perhaps hours, of the decision, public-intellectual law professor (and director of legal affairs for the *New Republic*) Jeffrey Rosen denounced the "four vain men and one vain woman" who had constituted the Court's majority for stopping the recount.[114] The allegation of vanity makes no sense. The article refers in-

ed piece that is an abridged version of the open letter. See Bruce Ackerman, "As Florida Goes . . . ," *New York Times* (national ed.), Dec. 12, 2000, p. A31.

111. 3 U.S.C. § 2.
112. See note 99 above.
113. Bush v. Gore, 531 U.S. 98 (2000) (per curiam).
114. Jeffrey Rosen, "Disgrace: The Supreme Court Commits Suicide," *New Republic*, Dec.

accurately to the "joint dissent" of the four liberal justices (p. 18); there were several dissenting opinions, but none to which all four subscribed. What is more, two of the "dissenters" joined the substantive ruling of the majority, disagreeing only on the remedy. (The five conservative justices believed that, under Florida law, December 12 was the deadline for a hand recount.) The majority opinion was per curiam, that is, unsigned; such opinions are common, and Rosen had no ground for saying that "the justices who handed the election to Bush—O'Connor and Kennedy—were afraid to sign their names" (id.). Rosen calls Justice O'Connor "addled" and "preening" (p. 20), and claims that the decision has "made it impossible for citizens of the United States to sustain any kind of faith in the rule of law as something larger than the self-interested political preferences of William Rehnquist, Antonin Scalia, Clarence Thomas, Anthony Kennedy, and Sandra Day O'Connor" (p. 18).

Rosen's tone is echoed in an editorial in the same issue of the *New Republic* that refers to "the Republican larcenists, in and out of robes, who arranged to suppress the truth about the vote in Florida and thereby to make off with the election of 2000."[115] A week later the publisher of the *New Republic* (who happens to be a close personal friend, diehard supporter, and former teacher of Gore) chimed in, calling Bush "the great usurper" and "the village idiot" and accusing Chief Justice Rehnquist of making a "career of limiting citizens' access to the voting booth."[116] In seeming contrast, Professor Dworkin, in an article strongly critical of the Supreme Court's decision that ended the Florida recount, urged his readers "not to compound the injury to the Court with reckless accusations against any of its members."[117] But he also said that it is "difficult to find a respectable explanation of why all and only the conservatives voted to end the election in this way."[118] He

---

25, 2000, p. 18. Although dated December 25, the issue was on the newsstands by December 18, so the article must have been written several days earlier.

115. "Unsafe Harbor," *New Republic*, Dec. 25, 2000, p. 9.

116. Martin Peretz, "All Too Human," *New Republic*, Jan. 1 and 2, 2001, p. 38.

117. Ronald Dworkin, "A Badly Flawed Election," *New York Review of Books*, Jan. 11, 2001, pp. 52, 54. A defender of what critics call "the imperial judiciary," Dworkin would not like to see the Supreme Court weakened by accusations that its members are partisan politicians in robes, as the *New Republic* suggested they are.

118. Id. at 53.

searches, finds none, and so implies that the accusation of rank partisanship is correct after all.

Judges care who their colleagues are, and even who their successors are, and so there is suspicion that the justices' votes, in a case that would determine who was to be the next president, may have been influenced consciously or not by a desire that future colleagues or successors, should there be vacancies in the next four years, be appointed by Bush or by Gore, depending on the justice's own ideological leanings. There is no more reason, however, to suppose this an inclination of conservative but not of liberal justices than to think that the senators who voted to acquit Clinton were less politically motivated than the senators who voted to convict him. The conflict of interest affected the two wings of the Court equally, and so is a wash and can be ignored in evaluating the decision.

Seven justices, including two of the liberals, thought that the hand recount ordered by the Florida supreme court four days earlier was, because of its lack of standards, a denial of the equal protection of the laws. This conclusion may be correct or incorrect, but it is not crazy or usurpative, as Rosen and the editorialist claim. Three justices (probably five, if the alternative ground, the one that attracted the two liberals, had been unavailable) thought that, in addition, the Florida supreme court had violated Article II of the U.S. Constitution, which in the second clause of its first section requires that each state appoint its presidential electors in the manner directed by the state legislature. The Court had been unanimous on December 4[119] in suggesting that this clause limits the power of a state court to alter by reference to the state constitution or otherwise the rules laid down by the state legislature for the appointment of electors; and it was arguable that this had been precisely what the Florida supreme court had done.[120] The argument was not demonstrably correct, but it was not so far out that it merited the intemperate abuse heaped upon it by one of our leading public-intellectual magazines before the abusers could have analyzed the issues in sufficient depth and with sufficient calm to write responsibly.

I have been focusing on the liberal commentators on the election deadlock and its resolution by the Supreme Court, because they were

---

119. Bush v. Palm Beach County Canvassing Board, 531 U.S. 70 (2000) (per curiam).
120. See Posner, note 99 above, ch. 3.

more numerous and more vociferous than the conservatives, who after all were content with the result though anxious at various points in the proceedings leading to it. But some conservative public intellectuals displayed a partisanship, and at times an irresponsibility, to match that of the liberal public intellectuals who commented on the matter. Consider the crudely titled article by two academic economists, "It's the Fraud, Stupid," which appeared in the *New York Post*, an angry conservative tabloid, in December.[121] The article contains no economics; it consists rather of a string of accusations of vote fraud and other electoral misconduct committed by Democrats. Among the accusations is that "some Chicagoans successfully register[ed] their cats to vote." As a Chicago cat owner, I am charmed by the suggestion. But it is irresponsible to throw charges of this nature about. No substantiation is offered for the accusations; unspecified "news stories from around the nation" are the primary source given. Such tabloid journalism is unworthy of academics.

Let me come back now to the Clinton impeachment, where again we meet Sean Wilentz, one of the draftsmen of the historians' pro-Clinton advertisement as well as a principal in the election advertisements. He testified on December 8, 1998, before the House Judiciary Committee and in his prepared testimony stated (emphasis in original):[122]

> It is no exaggeration to say that upon this impeachment inquiry, as upon all presidential impeachment inquiries, hinges the fate of our American political institutions. *It is that important.* As a historian, it is clear to me that the impeachment of President Clinton would do great damage to those institutions and to the rule of law— much greater damage than the crimes of which President Clinton is accused.

No exaggeration? But it could not have been *clear* to Wilentz, or to any historian, or indeed to anyone, that "the fate of our American political institutions" hinged on whether President Clinton was impeached. A

---

121. Stephen Bronars and John R. Lott Jr., "It's the Fraud, Stupid," *New York Post*, Dec. 20, 2000.

122. The only published version of his testimony that I've found is in a Westlaw database called "Congressional Testimony by Federal Document Clearing House," 1998 WL 18089985 (Dec. 8, 1998).

historian might speculate about these matters, but he would have to be clairvoyant to be entitled to speak with Wilentz's confidence. Several days after he wrote, Clinton *was* impeached, and the sky did not fall. (At this writing, two years after Clinton was impeached, there are still no signs that his impeachment weakened the presidency as an institution or even that it substantially impaired his ability to govern in the remainder of his term.) But neither did it fall when he was acquitted, though Robert Bork had warned that if Clinton was not removed from office "it will be a clear sign that we have turned a corner, that American morality, including but not limited to our political morality, is in free fall."[123]

Wilentz testified that the historical record was clear that only actions taken in the performance of official duties can be the basis of an impeachment. The record is not clear, and Wilentz himself was unwilling to stand by his assertion, because he admitted that a president who committed murder, "even in the most private of circumstances," should be impeached and removed from office. Wilentz testified that Andrew Johnson's "impeachment [in 1868] helped pave the way for the Gilded Age, an age of political sordidness and unremarkable chief executives." He offered no support for this vague assertion—vague because of the uncertain force of "helped pave the way" in this context. Although Johnson's successors as president during the remaining years of the nineteenth century were weak, the reasons are complex and many earlier presidents had been weak too. Indeed, though Johnson was an accidental president, not even of Lincoln's party, impeached by an overwhelming vote in the heated atmosphere of the aftermath of civil war, even he was acquitted, and his acquittal was thought to have made it "almost inconceivable that a future president will be impeached and removed."[124] So the Johnson impeachment may actually have strengthened the presidency, at least in the long run. And if in the short run the impeachment did weaken the presidency, by causing Johnson to back down from the assertion of presidential power that had precipitated the impeachment, this is because the issue in that impeachment was precisely the relative powers of the president and Congress. The issue in Clinton's impeachment was not whether he was usurping power that

123. Robert H. Bork, "Counting the Costs of Clintonism," *American Spectator*, Nov. 1998, p. 55.

124. Michael Les Benedict, *The Impeachment and Trial of Andrew Johnson* 180 (1973).

the Constitution reserves to Congress but whether he had so degraded the office of the presidency that he should be removed.[125]

Wilentz ended his testimony by warning that if the members of the House of Representatives, "defying the deliberate judgment of the people whom you are supposed to represent," went through with impeachment, "your reputations will be darkened for as long as there are Americans who can tell the difference between the rule of law and the rule of politics." There was no evidence that the people had made a "*deliberate* judgment," and in any event the Constitution assigns the responsibility for judgment to the Congress, not to the people; the Constitution does not authorize referenda. Defying public opinion polls, moreover, is not an obvious sign of political expedience. Nor was there any basis for thinking that political calculation played a smaller role in the Democratic response to the Clinton scandal and its aftermath than in the Republican response.

Wilentz's concern about the weakening of the presidency by impeachment might have been expected to lead him to be cautious about suggesting a rerun of the 2000 presidential election in Florida. Anything that cast doubt on the validity of the November 7 election, anything that extended the period of postelection uncertainty, would tend to weaken the president chosen in that election, and perhaps subsequent presidents as well if the bitterness and rancorous partisanship touched off by the electoral deadlock was extended for weeks, an inevitable consequence of a revote. Wilentz deployed concern for weakening the presidency in defense of Clinton, but was not willing to do so in defense of Bush.

But fairness to Wilentz requires mention that at a "Rally against Impeachment" held at New York University School of Law on December 14, 1998, at which a number of politicians and public intellectuals (among the latter Gloria Steinem, E. L. Doctorow, Thomas Nagel, Ronald Dworkin, Toni Morrison, and Arthur Schlesinger Jr.) gave short speeches denouncing the impending impeachment, Wilentz was the only speaker to criticize the president forthrightly, stating that his conduct had brought lasting shame on Clinton and damaged the presidency.[126] When he said this, there were titters from the audience—they

125. See Keith E. Whittington, "Bill Clinton Was No Andrew Johnson: Comparing Two Impeachments," 2 *University of Pennsylvania Journal of Constitutional Law* 422 (2000).

126. There is, to my knowledge, no transcript of the rally, but a videotape of it can be pur-

thought he was kidding. He assured them he was not, and they quieted. The incident conveys a sense of the atmosphere of the event, for which "rally" was the right name; rallying the troops—building solidarity—is a lot of what public-intellectual work is about. The lack of nuance, of balance, was notable, which is why Wilentz's concession startled the audience. Gloria Steinem distinguished "welcome sex" from sexual harassment, but the only ground she gave for disbelieving Paula Jones's charge of an unwelcome sexual advance by President Clinton was that Jones had refused to meet with the president of the National Organization for Women. Steinem also suggested, with what logic is unclear, that since women had elected Clinton, in the sense that he would have lost his two presidential elections had only men voted, they should oppose his impeachment. E. L. Doctorow argued that if Clinton was impeached and tried, it would mean a rebirth of Puritanism. He was wrong, just as the public intellectuals at the other end of the political spectrum were wrong to predict that the president's acquittal would usher in a new era of depravity.

Professor Alan Dershowitz of the Harvard Law School took a prominent role in the public commentary on the Clinton impeachment. He commended Clinton for adopting a "simple and elegant" defense: "He will admit to sex and claim it is private and non-impeachable. And left [leave?] it to the independent counsel to prove any impeachable offenses such as obstruction of justice or subornation of perjury. And since there will never be stains or tapes proving obstruction or subornation, the president will prevail."[127] The implication is that these crimes cannot be proved without either irrefutable physical evidence or taped admissions. That is false; but were it true, there would still be a difference that one might have expected a professor of criminal law to point out between not *being* guilty and not being *proved* guilty. It is an unsettling notion of "elegance" that associates it with the tactics by which guilty defendants can escape punishment.

In testimony before the House Judiciary Committee, Dershowitz

---

chased from C-Span Archives, P.O. Box 2909, West Lafayette, Indiana 47996–2909. For a critical commentary on the rally, with well-chosen quotations, see Walter Shapiro, "Intellectuals at the Barricades," *Slate*, Dec. 15, 1998, http://slate.msn.com/code/Chatterbox/Chatterbox.asp?Show=12/15/98&idMessage=273.

127. Alan M. Dershowitz, "Testimony Key, Not the Speech," *Boston Herald*, Aug. 20, 1998, p. 37.

took the Republican members of the Committee to task for ignoring what he told them was a more serious kind of perjury than the president's, namely, perjury by police officers in criminal prosecutions. It may be a serious problem, but its gravity does not lessen the president's guilt. Dershowitz might as well have said that since we mostly ignore genocides (for example in Rwanda, Cambodia, and, until it was almost too late, Bosnia), we shouldn't prosecute ordinary murderers. That is Chomsky-speak.

In his book *Sexual McCarthyism* Dershowitz did finally criticize Clinton, but mainly for the blunders Clinton had committed in trying to conceal his affair with Lewinsky and implicitly for his not having retained Dershowitz as a legal adviser. Dershowitz was scathing in his criticisms of the tactics employed by the president's lawyers, and in particular of Robert Bennett's failure (which Dershowitz claimed Bennett had admitted to him in a phone conversation)[128] to advise the president to default in the Paula Jones suit. Dershowitz made no criticism of Clinton for committing criminal acts or for undermining the rule of law, though he did criticize him for taking a hard line on crime in general—for lacking, as it were, empathy for his fellow criminals!

Dershowitz went on television and stated that "a vote against impeachment is not a vote for Bill Clinton. It is a vote against bigotry. It's a vote against fundamentalism. It's a vote against anti-environmentalism. It's a vote against the right-to-life movement."[129] I am sure he made other such statements, but, to sound a frequent note in this book, it is difficult to retrieve a public intellectual's broadcast statements.[130]

---

128. Alan M. Dershowitz, *Sexual McCarthyism: Clinton, Starr, and the Emerging Constitutional Crisis* 19 (1998).

129. Alan Dershowitz on *Rivera Live*, CNBC News Transcripts, Dec. 14, 1998.

130. During the period of uncertainty following the deadlocked 2000 presidential election, Dershowitz called the Florida secretary of state not merely a partisan Republican, but "corrupt," "bought and paid for," and a "crook." *CNN Breaking News*, Nov. 14, 2000, 8 P.M., Transcript # 00111438V00, p. 9; *Rivera Live*, CNBC News Transcripts, Nov. 14, 2000; Somini Sengupta, "The Florida Secretary of State: A Human Lightning Rod in a Vote-Counting Storm," *New York Times* (national ed.), Nov. 20, 2000, p. A17; Alan M. Dershowitz, "Justice May Be Blind, but It's Not Deaf," *Los Angeles Times*, Dec. 28, 2000, p. B11. He called the Supreme Court's decision in Bush v. Gore the "Dred Scott [decision] of the 21st century" (a wonderful absurdity, considering that when he said this the twenty-first century was only eleven months old), and suggested that all nine of the Supreme Court justices are political partisans but that four of the five justices in the majority also had financial motives for supporting Bush. *ABC: Good Morning America*, Burrelle's Information Services, Dec. 13, 2000.

These examples of public intellectuals' questionable interventions in the Clinton impeachment matter can be multiplied,[131] and there is very little to place in the balance on the other side.[132] They—along with the earlier examples in this chapter and the examples in the next one— show that many prominent public intellectuals, whether or not they are academics, are not prudent, careful, or sensible in their commentaries and predictions. The *emotionality* of the public intellectual, so well illustrated by the perverfid reactions of public intellectuals to the Clinton impeachment and the 2000 presidential election deadlock, stands in particularly striking contrast to the official image of the academic.

131. See Chapter 10.

132. Little, not nothing. See, for example, Kenneth Anderson, "The American Inquisition: How the Religious Right and the Secular Left Collude in the Growth of the Prosecutorial State," *Times Literary Supplement*, Jan. 29, 1999, p. 12; Jean Bethke Elshtain, "Politics and Forgiveness: The Clinton Case," in *Judgment Day at the White House: A Critical Declaration Exploring Moral Issues and the Political Use and Abuse of Religion* 11 (Gabriel Fackre ed., 1999); Elshtain, "Going Public," *New Republic*, March 23, 1998, p. 12; Stephen Gillers, "The Perjury Precedent," *New York Times* (national ed.), Dec. 28, 1998, p. A27; Gillers, "Clinton's Choice: Tell Truth or Dare to Gamble," *Los Angeles Times* (home ed.), Aug. 2, 1998, p. M1.

～ 4

Prediction and Influence

Among all forms of mistake, prophecy is the most gratuitous.[1]

On Not Keeping Score

Prediction is the stock in trade of the public intellectual. Yet, as we began to glimpse in the last chapter, the record of public intellectuals' predictions is poor. This is not well known; and (a closely related point) public intellectuals do not lose their standing in the public-intellectual market when their predictions are falsified by events. No one is keeping score. This is a puzzle, but also a clue to the question whether public intellectuals are influential, a question that feeds back, as we'll see, into the question of the quality of the public intellectuals' contribution to public discourse.

The first topic taken up in this chapter, stated more precisely, is the failure of the public and the media to keep *better* score of public intellectuals' *unconditional* predictions. By the qualifier *better* I acknowledge that public intellectuals' mistaken predictions and discredited assessments are sometimes publicized.[2] Public intellectuals who have a good record of predictions might be expected to publicize that record, but I

---

1. George Eliot, *Middlemarch* 110 (W. J. Harvey ed., 1965 [1871–1872]).

2. See, for example, Paul Hollander, *Anti-Americanism: Critiques at Home and Abroad 1965–1990* (1992); Lawrence F. Kaplan, "Fall Guys: Guess Who Hates America? Conservatives," *New Republic*, June 26, 2000, p. 22. Cf. Andrew Sullivan, "London Fog: Why Americans Go Soft in the Head for *The Economist*," *New Republic*, June 14, 1999, p. 25, reciting inaccurate predictions by the *Economist* magazine. See also note 5 below and accompanying text. Remarkably, George Soros, a public intellectual as well as a businessman, publicly announced his error in having predicted in 1998 that the global capitalist system was about to collapse. "His reversal is a highly unusual public about-face. Most incorrect prognosticators simply let their mistakes drift quietly through remainder piles and into the dustbin of history." David D. Kirkpatrick, "Soros Concedes Goof in Book. Global Economy Didn't Collapse," *New York Times* (national ed.), Aug. 12, 2000, p. B1.

know of only one instance in which that has been done.[3] A possible inference to be drawn from that singularity is that very few public intellectuals *have* a good record of predictions to publicize.

By *unconditional* predictions I mean to distinguish prophecies from conditional prophecies, especially warnings—unless society does thus and so, disaster will ensue. As warnings about the dangers of state power, George Orwell's *Nineteen Eighty-Four* and Friedrich Hayek's *The Road to Serfdom* were illuminating, though alarmist; but as prophecies they have been falsified by events. They had aspects of both. They implied, if only by being set in the future, that there was still time to avoid the forecasted catastrophes, something that eco-catastrophist Paul Ehrlich, of whom more shortly, has often failed to do. Nevertheless both books were importantly and not merely incidentally wrong: *Nineteen Eighty-Four* because, as we'll see in Chapter 7, it exaggerated the efficacy of thought control, and *The Road to Serfdom* because it claimed that Nazism was genuinely socialist and that the British Labour Party's brand of socialism would lead inevitably to totalitarianism.[4]

Now it is true that in evaluating the cogency of a prediction we should distinguish between the ex ante and the ex post perspective. The "best" prediction in the sense of the one based on the most evidence and the best reasoning may be disconfirmed by events and the worst prediction confirmed. Anyone who in 1985 had made an even-money bet that the Berlin Wall would no longer be standing in five years would have been foolish ex ante, though he would have seemed prescient ex post. It might be sensible to repose greater confidence in a

---

3. See Gary S. Becker and Guity Nashat Becker, *The Economics of Life: From Baseball to Affirmative Action to Immigration, How Real-World Issues Affect Our Everyday Life* 9–10 (1997).

4. In a favorable review of *The Road to Serfdom*, Orwell accurately summarizes Hayek's thesis: "Socialism inevitably leads to despotism, and . . . in Germany the Nazis were able to succeed because the Socialists had already done most of their work for them, especially the intellectual work of weakening the desire for liberty . . . Britain, he says, is now going the same road as Germany." George Orwell, "Review," in *The Collected Essays, Journalism and Letters of George Orwell*, vol. 3: *As I Please 1943–1945*, pp. 117, 118 (Sonia Orwell and Ian Angus eds., 1968). Hayek returned the compliment, as it were, in the preface to a 1956 reprinting of his book, noting that *Nineteen Eighty-Four* had been the "most effective" of the popular discussions of the problem with which *The Road to Serfdom* had been concerned. "Preface to the 1956 Paperback Edition," in F. A. Hayek, *The Road to Serfdom: Fiftieth Anniversary Edition* xxvii, xxxiii and n. 5 (1994). I'll note in Chapter 7, however, that *Nineteen Eighty-Four*, a work of fiction, is more pessimistic than its author was.

new prediction by the person who had bet that the wall would still be standing in 1990 than in a new prediction by the winner of the bet. Still, the ex post perspective is important. The wisdom of hindsight is not completely spurious. Unless one's predictions are confirmed more often than a random guesser's, we should be suspicious of their quality, however cogent they may have seemed when made.

Although keeping score on a forecaster thus is important after all to evaluating the quality of his insight, it is rarely done on public intellectuals. This may seem puzzling, considering the large target they present to anyone minded to keep track of their forecasts. Think of how many of them predicted that socialism would triumph and capitalism ("late capitalism") collapse; that Japan would bury us economically; that we would experience this or that demographic, environmental, political, or economic catastrophe; that we were too prosperous or too conformist (major 1950s themes).[5] One might have expected a lively industry in ridiculing and rejecting false prophets. It has not emerged. A public intellectual can be cast into the outer darkness for taking a politically incorrect position, in other words for offending people, but not for being wrong.

Yale professor Paul Kennedy had a distinguished but unglamorous career under his belt when he wrote *The Rise and Fall of the Great Powers*, predicting American decline. He was wrong, and hundreds of other commentators rose to say so, thus making him famous and turning his book into a bestseller. Francis Fukuyama wrote an essay called "The End of History," which seemed wrong to people who read only the title. Thousands of essayists wrote pieces pointing out that history had not ended, and Fukuyama became a global sensation.[6]

Economic pessimists such as John Kenneth Galbraith and Lester Thurow, and environmental pessimists such as Barry Commoner and Paul Ehrlich, have been consistently wrong for decades,[7] yet they re-

5. See Chapter 8; also Richard H. Pells, *The Liberal Mind in a Conservative Age: American Intellectuals in the 1940s and 1950s*, chs. 3–5 (1985).

6. David Brooks, *Bobos in Paradise: The New Upper Class and How They Got There* 163 (2000).

7. Consider, for example, Galbraith's prediction that the economy of the United States would come to resemble the socialist economy of the Soviet Union. John Kenneth Galbraith,

tain the public's respectful attention. In 1970, Ehrlich, who was and is a professor of biology at Stanford University, warned "that even Americans will probably be subjected to water rationing by 1974 and food rationing by the end of the decade, [and] that hepatitis and epidemic dysentery rates could easily climb by 500 percent in this country between 1970 and 1974 on account of crowding and increasingly polluted water."[8] In that year he also wrote that "most American women do not realize that by having more than two children, they are unknowingly contributing to the early death of those children."[9] He opined that DDT and other pesticides "may have already shortened by as much as a decade the life expectancy of every American born since 1946."[10] And that "the death rate will increase until at least 100–200 million people per year will be starving to death during the next ten years . . . If we're

---

The New Industrial State 332, 389–391 (1967). Consider Barry Commoner's claim in 1976 that the U.S. "energy crisis" could be overcome only if the United States replaced capitalism with socialism. Barry Commoner, *The Poverty of Power: Energy and the Economic Crisis* 243–249 (1976).

The way was paved for Ehrlich and other eco-catastrophists by Rachel Carson's book *The Silent Spring* (1962), an attack on the use of pesticides. "In part due to the precedent set by *Silent Spring*, the rhetoric of war, creating a climate of crisis, has been deployed by the environmental movement for more than three decades." Cheryll Glotfelty, "Cold War, *Silent Spring*: The Trope of War in Modern Environmentalism," in *And No Birds Sing: Rhetorical Analyses of Rachel Carson's* Silent Spring 157, 167 (Craig Waddell ed., 2000). *The Silent Spring* is a beautifully written book and identified real environmental problems that had been neglected, see, for example, *The Pesticide Question: Environment, Economics, and Ethics* (David Pimentel and Hugh Lehman eds., 1993), although it exaggerated the role of pesticides in causing human cancers. See Carson, above, ch. 14. Pesticides are harmful primarily to wildlife rather than to human beings; and controversy continues, therefore, over whether DDT should be banned in countries in which malaria is endemic. See, for example, A. G. Smith, "How Toxic Is DDT?" 356 *Lancet* 267 (2000).

8. David M. Rorvik, "Ecology's Angry Lobbyist: Dr. Paul Ehrlich Argues That the Chief Cause of Pollution Is Overpopulation," *Look*, April 21, 1970, p. 42.

9. Paul R. Ehrlich, "Are There Too Many of Us?" *McCall's*, July 1970, p. 46.

10. Id. at 46, 104. Other wild statements made by Ehrlich in 1970, the year of the first "Earth Day," are recited in Ronald Bailey, "Earth Day Then and Now," *Reason*, May 2000, p. 18, including that 65 million Americans might starve to death in the 1980s, that hundreds of thousands of Americans might die in "smog disasters" in the 1970s, and that Americans' life expectancy might well fall to 42 by 1980 because of DDT and other pesticides. I have not been able to verify the accuracy of these specific predictions—an example of the general difficulty of retrieving, in order to evaluate, public intellectuals' predictions. But they are in the spirit of the 1970s popular articles by and about Ehrlich from which I have quoted in the text and also of his books of that period, though the books are a tad less wild. See Paul R. Ehrlich, *The Population Bomb* (1968); Paul R. Ehrlich and Richard L. Harriman, *How to Be a Survivor: A Plan to Save Spaceship Earth* (1971).

really lucky, the steep increase in death rates might hold off until the 1980s."[11] He said, "It is conceivable that in a decade or two all marine fishing, both commercial and sport, will have ceased because of irreversible changes in the oceans."[12]

Yet his declaration that "the decade of the 1970's represents the last chance for both conservation and for man"[13] must have been made when he was feeling optimistic, because in an interview published the same month he said, "We're dead and we don't know it yet."[14] Two years earlier he had predicted "a drastic rise in the death rate in the next few decades" and "massive famines" by the early 1980s and had described as "optimistic" a scenario in which "only" half a billion people starved to death.[15]

Naturally, given his predictions, Ehrlich has repeatedly recommended the most radical environmental and population-control measures. He wants in fact to "de-develop the United States."[16] Deeming the United States the most overpopulated country in the world, he would like to see the U.S. population shrink to 135 million. That was its population during World War II, and therefore, Ehrlich argues, it is sufficient to meet any needs of national defense. Since he thinks we spend too much on defense, he would be untroubled by the fact (which he seems not to have noticed, however) that if our population were half what it is, the tax rate would have to be twice as high to support our present level of defense spending. Ehrlich would like to see the world's population fall to 500 million and (like Einstein) world government instituted. He "hints at a time when we might put temporary sterilants in food and water."[17]

11. Peter Collier, ". . . Ecological Destruction Is a Condition of American Life . . . : An Interview with Ecologist Paul Ehrlich," *Mademoiselle*, April 1970, pp. 189, 293.

12. Paul R. Ehrlich, "Population Overgrowth . . . The Fertile Curse," *Field and Stream*, June 1970, pp. 38, 58.

13. Paul R. Ehrlich, "People Pollution," *Audubon*, May 1970, pp. 5, 9. He also announced in that article the "demise" of the peregrine falcon, which today is alive and well—living, among other places, on the roofs and ledges of Chicago and New York skyscrapers, from which the falcons swoop down on pigeons flying below.

14. "Man Is the Endangered Species," *National Wildlife*, April/May 1970, p. 38 (interview with Paul Ehrlich).

15. Ehrlich, *The Population Bomb*, note 10 above, at 44–45, 69, 78–80.

16. Paul R. Ehrlich, Anne H. Ehrlich, and John P. Holdren, *Human Ecology: Problems and Solutions* 279 (1973).

17. Steve Weissman, "Why the Population Bomb Is a Rockefeller Baby," *Ramparts*, May 1970, pp. 42, 43.

Ehrlich bet economist Julian Simon in 1980 that the composite price of a menu of commercially valuable metals picked by Ehrlich would rise over the next decade because of a growing scarcity of raw materials. The price fell, so he lost the bet and had to pay Simon more than $500.[18] He had failed to consider that price is a function of cost as well as of scarcity in relation to demand; that technological progress brings many costs down; and that when a valuable resource begins to dwindle, any resulting increase in its price will both moderate demand and incite a search for ways of making the resource more plentiful and using it more economically by substituting other inputs for it. It is true as Ehrlich keeps saying that natural resources are not in infinite supply, but this is irrelevant, since demand is not infinite and substitutes exist or can be devised for virtually any resource. While it is also true, and more to the point, that pollution and other environmental costs (as distinct from costs arising from the scarcity of commercially valuable natural resources) are not internalized by the market, rising incomes and technological progress create the will and the way to control these costs. Health, and delight in nature, are what economists call "superior goods": demand for them rises with income. Technology enables the demand to be supplied at tolerable cost.

Although Ehrlich has moderated his predictions in recent years, having learned from his religious counterparts in the doomster business that it is risky to put a date on doomsday, he remains basically unrepentant.[19] Rather than acknowledge his errors, he attacks his critics.[20] He has never referred to publicly, let alone retracted, the predictions that he made in popular magazines in 1970.

It may seem that unlike Noam Chomsky, Paul Ehrlich at least is not writing for the general public outside his field of academic expertise.

18. Simon was the anti-Ehrlich. He saw our salvation in a rapidly growing population. He thought the world had a *shortage* of people. Julian L. Simon, *The Ultimate Resource* 40 (2d ed. 1996). A competent economist, he could not keep his own values out of his demography. See, for example, id. at xxxii–xxxiii.

19. See, for example, Paul R. Ehrlich and Anne H. Ehrlich, *The Population Explosion* 178–180 (1990); Paul R. Ehrlich and Anne H. Ehrlich, *Healing the Planet: Strategies for Resolving the Environmental Crisis* (1991). Ehrlich has, however, acknowledged that he underestimated the effectiveness of the Green Revolution, which he used to mock, in averting worldwide famine. Paul R. Ehrlich and Anne H. Ehrlich, *Betrayal of Science and Reason: How Anti-Environmental Rhetoric Threatens Our Future* 33–34 (1996).

20. In the book just cited, *Betrayal of Science and Reason*. It discusses the bet with Simon at pp. 100–104.

But that is incorrect. The essence of his public-intellectual work is economic analysis. He is an extreme Malthusian who like his great predecessor can't imagine that the economic system can cope with the increased demand for food and other resources exerted by a growing population. He has not learned from Malthus's errors or paid any attention to advances in economic analysis of the last two centuries. By repeatedly crying wolf, he has played into the hands of those who consider environmentalism a lunatic movement. I suspect that as a natural scientist Ehrlich considers economics a soft field that he can handle in his spare time, as it were.

The bet Ehrlich lost to Julian Simon illuminates the fundamental weakness in public-intellectual predictions: they are *trendy* in a literal sense. They are naïve extrapolations from existing trends. Part of the problem may be semantic. The word "trend," like the present progressive tense, equivocates between past, present, and future. To observe that per capita income "is growing" by 1 percent a year is, strictly speaking, merely to make an observation about what *has* been happening; but it implies that the growth will continue, that the observer has spotted a "trend." This equivocation may be related to what philosophers call the "fallacy of induction," which is the tendency to generalize from past to future without an adequate theoretical basis. If pollution is growing, it is predicted to continue to grow until we're all dead; if government is growing, it is predicted to grow until capitalism gives way to socialism; if the marriage rate is falling, the demise of marriage is predicted. (We'll encounter more of these predictions in Chapter 8.) There is little awareness that a bad trend often contains within itself the seeds of reversal, either because it will encounter diminishing returns or because the growing social costs that it imposes will incite a more effective search for and a greater receptivity to curative or ameliorative measures. Economists tend to be more sensitive to these possibilities than noneconomists. Simon realized that the increasing scarcity of raw materials would incite a search for substitutes and for better, cheaper methods of extraction and use. Tomas Philipson and I argued correctly that demographers were overpredicting the growth in the prevalence of HIV-AIDS in the United States by failing to perceive that the growing risk of infection would (as it did) induce behavioral modifications that would cause the epidemic to peak.[21]

---

21. Tomas J. Philipson and Richard A. Posner, *Private Choices and Public Health: The AIDS*

What made the collapse of the Soviet Union such an embarrassing falsification of predictions was not the collapse as such. Had the Soviet Union been destroyed by a meteor, no one could have faulted the students of Soviet communism for having failed to predict the system's collapse. What was crushing was the absence of external causes. The system collapsed for purely internal reasons—the very reasons one might have expected the experts to understand and track. Their failure to do suggests that the only reason the experts would not have predicted in 1985 that the Berlin Wall would no longer be standing five years later was that, lacking any understanding of the dynamics of communist society, the experts had no better method of prediction than to assume that the future would resemble the present. They were engaged in naïve extrapolation, a common sign of a lack of a causal theory.

There is nothing wrong with a *conditional* prediction based on naïve extrapolation—describing a current trend and explaining where we will be in ten, or twenty, or for that matter one hundred years if the trend continues. It is predicting that the trend *will* continue that is so often irresponsible. But maybe prediction by public intellectuals is better viewed as a rhetorical device than as a serious effort to chart the future. On this construal, to say that the United States will become a Third World country or that it will be destroyed by pollution is merely a dramatic way of saying that we're in a parlous state now. The public intellectual who makes predictions is thus a kind of science-fiction writer, taking liberties with present reality in order to paint a more arresting picture of his society. Perhaps, to the extent it makes predictions, most public-intellectual work, and not just the fiction of satirists like an Orwell or a Huxley, belongs to literature rather than to science, whether natural or social. If this is right, it will help us to understand why, as we'll see, public intellectuals' predictions are generally not heeded.

In a book published in 1991 and still in print in 2000, the well-known sociologist Robert Bellah offered gloomy forebodings about the American economy. Although not an economist, businessman, business consultant, or engineer, he asserted with a show of confidence that our commitment to free-market economics would discourage investment

---

Epidemic in an Economic Perspective (1993), esp. pp. 45, 57–68. We also pointed out that if a cure were discovered, the incidence of the disease might rise again, in much the same way that the discovery of a cure for syphilis (penicillin) appears to have led to an increase in the incidence of that disease. See id. at 82, 187.

in productivity-enhancing technologies because corporate raiders were stripping corporations of their assets, pursuing short-term gains at the expense of the long term, and destroying precisely the sense of community within corporations that a high-tech company must have to be successful.[22] Bellah predicted that if we remained "obsessed by an obsolescent economic ideology . . . it will be catastrophic for the United States, and finally for business as well, and in the not so very long run" (p. 278). In the decade since he wrote ("the not so very long run"), the ideology that he deplored has not diminished, has in fact intensified, yet contrary to his expectations there have been substantial gains in productivity, stemming largely from a breakneck pace of technological advance that he predicted would be impeded by the lack of a sense of community in high-tech companies.

In 1996 Bellah reprinted his best-known book, *Habits of the Heart*, with a new introduction actually gloomier than the original text of 1985.[23] Imprudently citing Lester Thurow (of whom more shortly) with approval, the new introduction portrays a nation on the verge of disaster: "for most Americans, growth of the global economy no longer means opportunity but, rather, 'downsizing,' 're-engineered' jobs, and the pink slip of dismissal . . . The result [of globalization] is not only income polarization, with the rich growing richer and the poor poorer, but also a shrinking middle class increasingly anxious about its future . . . [We are] a society in which most of the population is treading water, the bottom is sinking, and the top is rising."[24]

A high rate of mistaken prediction is not a danger limited to public intellectuals who write outside their academic field. Lester Thurow is a professor of economics at MIT's Sloan School of Management and was the dean of the school for some years. He has written a series of books aimed at a general audience, and they are full of mistaken economic descriptions and predictions. As recently as 1996, with the U.S. economy booming, he wrote: "The facts are clear. Income and wealth inequalities are rising everywhere. Real wages are falling for a large majority. A lumpen proletariat unwanted by the productive economy is growing. The social contract between the middle class and corporate America

---

22. Robert N. Bellah et al., *The Good Society* 94–100 (1991).

23. Robert N. Bellah et al., *Habits of the Heart: Individualism and Commitment in American Life* (updated ed. 1996). The only updating was the addition of the new introduction.

24. Id. at vii, xii, xvi.

has been ripped up."[25] In a book published just a couple of years earlier, coauthored with another well-known public-intellectual economist, Thurow had stated that America had fallen "seriously behind its competitors," mainly Japan and Germany, and had become the "least up-to-date member" of the group of economic leaders.[26] "New York, the city of the richest people in the world, lacks the money to keep its streets clear or safe . . . By the 1990s the only major area in which American economic preeminence was still widely acknowledged was in the production of airplanes . . . Its political cloud [*sic*—the authors mean 'clout'] in Europe all but disappeared . . . Both Europe and Japan laid in the basis for a new kind of more economically flexible, and more socially resilient capitalism, whereas we stood idly by . . . Our defensive, anti-public sector way shows no signs of being a winner."[27] And just two years before that, Thurow was writing that "Japan would have to be considered the betting favorite to win the economic honors of owning the twenty-first century . . . In head-to-head competition, its communitarian companies have been impossible to beat . . . One hundred years from now, historians looking back are most apt to say that the twenty-first century belonged to Japan."[28]

What is more censurable than Thurow's lack of percipience about Japan's serious economic problems is his assuming that it is possible to predict what nation will perform best over the course of the next century.

Unabashed by past mistakes, in 1999 Thurow published *Building Wealth*, in which we read that "Japan's economic system is stuck" and

25. Lester C. Thurow, *The Future of Capitalism: How Today's Economic Forces Shape Tomorrow's World* 313 (1996). Apparently the book was written as well as published in 1996. See id. at viii.

26. Robert Heilbroner and Lester Thurow, *Economics Explained: Everything You Need to Know about How the Economy Works and Where It's Going* 258 (rev. ed. 1994).

27. Id. at 256–257, 259.

28. Lester Thurow, *Head to Head: The Coming Economic Battle among Japan, Europe, and America* 247, 251 (1992). The idea that a special cooperative ethos was responsible for Japan's economic success was naturally very attractive to left-leaning economists. See also Amartya Sen, *Resources, Values and Development* 104–105 (1984). For an antidote to Thurovian gloom, see George Gilder, *Recapturing the Spirit of Enterprise* (rev. ed. 1992)—or, for that matter, see the 1999 model Thurow in the text below. And, for a far more astute appraisal of Japan's economy, made two years before Thurow predicted that the twenty-first century would belong to Japan, see Alvin Toffler, *Powershift: Knowledge, Wealth, and Violence at the Edge of the 21st Century* 431–437 (1990).

that until Japan demonstrates an ability to make big breakthroughs in technology it "will forever be playing catch-up, never the world economic leader."[29] Europe is an "also-ran"; "the technological gap between it and the United States grows larger every day" (p. xii). "America is back! In the 1990s it will be the best performer in the industrial world" (p. xiii). (Thurow has learned the advantages of postdiction.) Is he contrite? His only acknowledgment of past error concerns his failure to appreciate the significance of the Japanese stock market crash in 1990 (p. 57). He feels free to speculate about what historians in the year 3000 will say about our era (pp. 282–283).

Paul Krugman, whom we met in the last chapter, has criticized Thurow, even saying that Thurow arguably is "more deeply rooted in journalism than in academia,"[30] a remark to which Krugman's being hired subsequently as the economic columnist of the *New York Times* lends a note of irony. He was not hired by the *Times* for his record as a prophet. In a book published in 1990 he had offered as "the most likely forecast for the U.S. domestic economy in the 1990s . . . fairly slow growth, modestly rising incomes for most Americans, generally good employment performance, [and] a gradual acceleration of inflation" to 7 percent.[31] He predicted that by 2000 the United States would "have sunk to the number three economic power in the world," after Europe and Japan, and that the world economy would be less unified than it had been in the 1980s.[32] He published a "revised and updated" edition four years later, but retained these predictions.[33]

Thurow and Krugman are liberals, but bad economic prophecy is not a liberal monopoly. Consider Martin Feldstein's criticism of Clinton's economic plan. Writing shortly after its enactment in 1993, Feldstein stated that the plan would "hurt incentives, weaken the economy and waste investment dollars." He predicted that the increase in

29. Lester C. Thurow, *Building Wealth: The New Rules for Individuals, Companies, and Nations in a Knowledge-Based Economy* 87 (1999).

30. Paul Krugman, *Peddling Prosperity: Economic Sense and Nonsense in the Age of Diminished Expectations* 249 (1994). For other, and, in retrospect, equally ironic criticism of economist public intellectuals, see id. at 11–15.

31. Paul Krugman, *The Age of Diminished Expectations: U.S. Economic Policy in the 1990s* 191, 193 (1990).

32. Id. at 193–194.

33. Paul Krugman, *The Age of Diminished Expectations: U.S. Economic Policy in the 1990s* 225–228 (revised and updated ed. 1994).

income tax rates, by causing wealthy taxpayers to reduce their taxable incomes, "would end up producing only about $7 billion in extra tax revenue while permanently hurting the economy."[34] In fact, the plan appears to have contributed to the elimination of the federal budget deficit, in part by increasing federal tax revenues, and to keeping interest rates low, which helped fuel the expansion of the economy in the remainder of the decade.

Jeane Kirkpatrick, another distinguished conservative, argued in 1979 that communist regimes, unlike right-wing autocracies, would never evolve into democratic societies,[35] while liberal Daniel Bell wrote in his most famous book, published in 1960, that, as the subtitle suggests, the traditional ideologies of the West were exhausted.[36] He was wrong. Socialism retained considerable vitality for a time, a kind of anarcho-Marxism flourished in the late 1960s and the 1970s under the banner of the New Left, and the ideology of the free market began a comeback in the 1970s with the deregulation movement in the United States and became the world's dominant ideology in the 1990s. In 1976 Bell wrote that "the period of American economic dominance in the world has crested and that, by the end of the century, the United States, like any aging *rentier*, will be living off the foreign earnings on the investments its corporations made in the halcyon quarter century after World War II."[37] By the end of the century we would no longer be the "hegemonic" world power; indeed, we would have difficulty maintaining our "political stability."[38]

Bell's most substantial work, *The Coming of Post-Industrial Society: A*

34. Martin Feldstein, "Clinton's Revenue Mirage," *Wall Street Journal*, Apr. 6, 1993, p. A14.

35. Jeane Kirkpatrick, "Dictatorships and Double Standards," *Commentary*, November 1979, pp. 34, 37, 44–45. This was a common view on the Right. See, for example, Leon R. Kass, *Toward a More Natural Science: Biology and Human Affairs* 29 (1985): "it is the Soviets and their compatriots who have achieved a stable and efficient tyranny, seemingly impregnable and thus unrivaled in human history, not least because they are armed with sophisticated psychological and organizational techniques and elaborate devices for controlling the flow of information."

36. Daniel Bell, *The End of Ideology: On the Exhaustion of Political Ideas in the Fifties* 369–375 (1960). Therefore, he predicted erroneously, "Hayek could never become a convincing adversary of Keynesian thought." Id. at 80.

37. Daniel Bell, *The Cultural Contradictions of Capitalism: Twentieth Anniversary Edition* 215 (1996 [1976]).

38. Id. at 215–219.

Venture in Social Forecasting (1973), is sober and sensible,[39] and both generally cautious about prediction (despite its subtitle) and accurate in spotting a trend toward knowledge-based rather than resource-based industries, although his identification of services with information is unpersuasive. Technological advance, by enabling goods to be produced with fewer workers, frees up labor for the production of services; the services need not be information-intensive. But that is a detail.

Yet when Bell does venture in this rather good book into predicting, the predictions tend to be wrong to the extent that they can be verified, and otherwise reckless. For example, he predicts that the university will displace the business firm as the central institution of the next hundred years (p. 344). Fewer than a hundred years have elapsed since this prediction was made, so it cannot be falsified yet; but there is no indication that it is likely to be confirmed. Nor is there any sign that "the crucial decisions regarding the growth of the economy and its balance will come from government" or that "the entire complex of prestige and status will be rooted in the intellectual and scientific communities" (pp. 344–345). These predictions are inconsistent. If prestige follows power and government becomes more powerful, politicians, bureaucrats, judges, and lobbyists will accrue prestige, rather than scientists and engineers.

Anyway there is scant correlation between the "importance" of a job to society and the prestige of the jobholder. Industrial workers had little prestige in industrial society; why should knowledge workers have great prestige in the information society? In assuming they will, Bell is neglecting scarcity as a factor in labor value and associated social status. And in fact in our "postindustrial" society, contrary to his expectation, the ability to create a new firm, to manage a large enterprise, to scale the heights of the entertainment or sports worlds, to write a bestseller, or to conduct litigation involving large monetary stakes are all rewarded in both money and celebrity more highly than scientific or other purely intellectual skills. *The Coming of Post-Industrial Society* embraces John Kenneth Galbraith's hackneyed claim that capitalism and socialism (including communism) "may be converging in the pattern of their economies into some new kind of centralized-decentralized mar-

---

39. For example, in discussing the predictions of the eco-catastrophists. Daniel Bell, *The Coming of Post-Industrial Society: A Venture in Social Forecasting* 463–466 (1973).

ket-planning system" (p. 348). Bell's book *The Cultural Contradictions of Capitalism* was republished in 1996, long after its predictions had been falsified, with a gloomy afterword, *already* almost as dated as the original version, full of worries about "the unraveling of the middle class," corporate downsizing, greedy takeover artists, and "a sinking sense that the wave of History is moving to the Pacific Rim."[40]

Bell and Kirkpatrick remain respected public intellectuals. They must have *something* that commands respect, though it is not the gift of prophecy. They are well informed and forthright; they write confidently and well; they are interesting to read. (Paul Krugman has the same gifts, and I enjoy reading his column in the *New York Times*.) They are also "names," even celebrities; the brilliance of their fame blinds the public to their predictive inaccuracy. *The Coming of Post-Industrial Society* is not without prescience, and Kirkpatrick played a salutary role in the 1970s in opposing the inanities of the Left, though her anxiety about President Carter's having laid "the groundwork for a transfer of the Panama Canal from the United States to a swaggering Latin dictator of Castroite bent"[41] is as dated as her belief that while a democratic nation might become communist (as in the case of Czechoslovakia in 1948 and Chile in the early 1970s), a communist nation could never become democratic. Her mistake, we can now see, was to suppose the Soviet Union somehow immune from the brittleness that is the Achilles' heel of authoritarian regimes. They are often strong, but rarely resilient.

Edward Luttwak is the author of numerous books, articles, and op-ed pieces on military and economic affairs. He writes well and with authority (that is, with an air of great confidence) and knows a lot—he is a serious historian and defense analyst.[42] But writing as a public intellectual, he repeatedly ventures predictions that events falsify. In 1983, he pronounced the Soviet invasion of Afghanistan a success.[43] He also

---

40. "Afterword: 1996," in Bell, note 37 above, at 283, 314–318, 325–326.

41. Kirkpatrick, note 35 above, at 34.

42. See, for example, Edward N. Luttwak, *The Grand Strategy of the Roman Empire: From the First Century* A.D. *to the Third* (1976); Luttwak, *Strategy and Politics, Collected Essays* (1980).

43. "The resistance continues, but the Soviet Union shows no sign of being inclined to give up the fight." Edward N. Luttwak, *The Grand Strategy of the Soviet Union* 110 (1983). "The resistance is a small affair for the Soviet armed forces." Id. at 83. To the same effect, see Edward N. Luttwak, *The Pentagon and the Art of War: The Question of Military Reform* 111 (1984).

thought it likely that the Soviet Union would launch a limited war against China, especially if the West increased its military power (as it did in the 1980s, under Reagan).[44] Years later, and indeed just a few months before the Berlin Wall came down, Luttwak was worrying that Gorbachev's policies of *glasnost* and *perestroika* would augment the military power of the Soviet Union.[45] Instead those policies precipitated the end of the Cold War and the dissolution of the Soviet Union.

Writing in 1992, Luttwak described the United States as a country on the way down. He asked "When will the United States become a third-world country?" and answered: "One estimate would place the date as close as the year 2020. A more optimistic projection might add another ten or fifteen years. Either way, if present trends simply continue [but Luttwak expected them to worsen], all but a small minority of Americans will be impoverished soon enough."[46] He thought Japan had already surpassed us. He wrote that "we are indeed adapting to our fate, by acquiring the necessary third-world traits of fatalistic detachment. But they, of course, ensure that the slide will continue."[47] He has had to change his tune. His pessimism remains, but it is now based on predicting *dynamic* economic growth—which he believes brings in its train all sorts of ugly social consequences such as high crime rates and job insecurity—rather than a continued "slide."[48] His only constant is pessimism.

Shortly after the United States and its allies began bombing Iraq at the outset of the Persian Gulf War, Luttwak predicted that Sadam

44. See Luttwak, *The Grand Strategy of the Soviet Union*, note 43 above, at 101–107, 116.

45. Edward N. Luttwak, "Gorbachev's Strategy, and Ours," *Commentary*, July 1989, p. 29. (He consistently exaggerated that power. See, for example, Luttwak, *The Pentagon and the Art of War*, note 43 above, ch. 4.) For a much more insightful view, approximately contemporary with Luttwak's, see Paul Craig Roberts and Karen LaFollette, *Meltdown: Inside the Soviet Economy* (1990).

Goofiest of all Luttwak's predictions is one he made in 1970—that by 1977 the U.S. military might seize power. Edward Luttwak, "A Scenario for a Coup d'Etat in the United States," *Esquire*, July 1970, p. 60.

46. Edward N. Luttwak, "Is America on the Way Down?" *Commentary*, March 1992, p. 15. Notice the convergence in predictions between archconservative Luttwak and archradical Chomsky, writing at about the same time. See Chapter 3.

47. Id. at 21. See also, in similar but less apocalyptic vein, Edward N. Luttwak, "The Downside of Turbo-Capitalism: What the 'Experts' Don't Know about Economic Reality," *Washington Post*, March 10, 1996 (final ed.), p. C3.

48. See Edward Luttwak, *Turbo-Capitalism: Winners and Losers in the Global Economy* (1999).

Hussein would evacuate Kuwait after a week or two of bombing (the bombing continued for six weeks without inducing him to do so) and warned that the use of ground forces "could make Desert Storm a bloody, grinding combat with thousands of [U.S.] casualties."[49] The ground fighting lasted only four days, rather than the minimum of two weeks that Luttwak predicted, and U.S. casualties were minimal.[50] Writing a month into the bombing, Luttwak was no longer predicting heavy casualties but he still opposed a ground campaign. He thought it would lead inevitably to a military occupation of Iraq from which we would be unable to disengage without disastrous foreign policy consequences.[51]

One might have thought that someone whose predictions have so often proved to be so far off base would have lost a public platform for continuing to make predictions. That has not happened to Luttwak or to any other prominent public intellectual. I cannot prove this, but it is more than merely an impression. Amazon.com ranks the more than 2 million books in its inventory on the basis of sales (most very recent, because Amazon.com is a company of recent origin and rapidly growing sales) of the book to date.[52] It considers the ten thousand highest-ranking books its "best sellers," which is absurd puffing, but to have a book in that tier is highly respectable, especially if it is a serious work of nonfiction. Hardback and paperback versions of the same book are ranked separately, so if both are ranked the composite rank would be higher, but how much higher is not reported. Because most recent sales are of recently published books, a book that is several years old yet has a respectable ranking should be considered quite successful.

It is striking, in light of Lester Thurow's record of erroneous predic-

---

49. Edward N. Luttwak, "No Ground Assault," *Washington Post*, Jan. 19, 1991 (final ed.), p. A15. For equally dire predictions from the other end of the public-intellectual political spectrum, see Noam Chomsky, *Chronicles of Dissent: Interviews with David Barsamian* 262–264 (1992).

50. The total number of U.S. military deaths in the entire war, including the air war that preceded the ground fighting, was only 158.

51. Edward N. Luttwak, "Stop the Clock on the Ground War," *New York Times*, Feb. 20, 1991 (current events ed.), p. A27.

52. Barnes and Noble.com, the other principal online book retailer, also does rankings. They are generally, and on occasion strikingly, similar to Amazon.com's. For example, the paperback edition of Robert Bork's *Slouching towards Gomorrah* ranks 11,446th on Amazon.com's list and 11,157th on Barnes and Noble.com's.

tions, that the paperback edition of his latest book, *Building Wealth*,[53] which as we know is full of predictions, should rank 4,240th on Amazon.com's "best seller" list,[54] or that *Economics Explained*, rich in falsified predictions as we have seen, ranks 17,065th on Barnes and Noble.com's list (Amazon.com has no ranking for it). Or that Paul Kennedy's *The Rise and Fall of the Great Powers*, published in paperback in 1989 (ancient history for Amazon.com), should rank a respectable 13,398th, despite the falsification of its major thesis, the decline of the United States.[55] The 1996 edition of Bellah's *Habits of the Heart*, with its already falsified doom-prophesying introduction, ranks 6,188th on Amazon.com's list. Robert Bork's quickly dated *Slouching towards Gomorrah* (see Chapter 8), published in hardback in 1996 and paperback the following year, has very respectable Amazon.com rankings of 17,860th and 11,446th respectively; the composite ranking would undoubtedly be higher. Even though it should have been clear by 1980, long before Amazon.com existed, that Paul Ehrlich's predictions of ecological catastrophe had been dramatically falsified, Amazon.com lists fifteen editions of his books, and the latest *(Human Nature: Genes, Culture, and the Human Prospect)*, published in 2000, ranks a highly respectable 5,899th (5,821th on Barnes and Noble.com's list). These are clues to the ability of public intellectuals to survive the falsification of their predictions.[56]

There is evidence, however, that public intellectuals do pay at least a small price for making erroneous predictions. Table 4.1 compares the percentage increase in media mentions of eight prominent public intellectuals who have made serious errors in prediction or assessment (in the latter category is Sartre, with his notorious embrace of Stalinism, and Gould, with his tendentious rejection of IQ) to the increase in media mentions over the same period of a random sample of public intellectuals.[57] Both groups experienced an increase in media mentions,

53. Note 29 above.

54. The hardback edition ranks a much more modest 45,188th. The sales figures in this paragraph are current as of October 4 and 5, 2000. This is important to bear in mind because the figures are constantly updated—hourly, in fact, in the case of the ten thousand "best sellers."

55. See text at note 6 above.

56. It is true that *Human Nature* has only incidental references to ecological catastrophe; the book's subject is evolution. But its popularity is doubtless related to Ehrlich's fame, which he acquired as a prophet of ecological disaster.

57. For the population from which the sample was taken, and the concept and estimation of "media mentions," see next chapter.

Table 4.1 Media mentions of public intellectuals, 1989 and 1999

Test group	1989	1999
Daniel Bell	38	105
Robert Bellah	20	35
Robert Bork	848	483
Paul Ehrlich	116	141
John Kenneth Galbraith	249	310
Stephen Jay Gould	165	384
Edward Luttwak	44	398
Jean-Paul Sartre	261	410
Lester Thurow	126	353

Simple average increase: 159%
Weighted average increase: 40%

Control Group	1989	1999
Thurman Arnold	8	12
Harold Bloom	36	319
Stephen Breyer	20	878
Albert Camus	165	309
Robert Conquest	53	117
Jared Diamond	1	238
Richard Falk	6	9
Elizabeth Fox-Genovese	5	11
Nathan Glazer	38	50
Amy Gutmann	1	25
Richard Herrnstein	7	48
Robert Maynard Hutchins	28	33
Carl Kaysen	4	2
Hilton Kramer	48	57
Mary Lefkowitz	5	7
Arthur Liman	145	11
Janet Malcolm	60	50
Louis Menand	5	16
Daniel Patrick Moynihan	1,554	2,352
Conor Cruise O'Brian	113	81
William Philips	1	19
Jonathan Rauch	6	103
Ron Rosenbaum	5	67
William Shawn	35	124
Theodore Solotaroff	2	8
George Steiner	97	96
Michael Walzer	12	37
Walter Williams	21	83

Simple average increase: 1,461%
Weighted average increase: 108%

but the increase for the false prophets was only 40 percent, compared to 108 percent for the control group.[58]

The market response to public intellectuals' errors of prediction or assessment is mild, however; only Bork's media mentions actually declined, and they remain at a high level. The response would be greater if public intellectuals made predictions in order to establish their credibility by a method analogous to the scientific method. A scientist makes hypotheses (predictions) and tests them by experimental or other exact observation, and if falsified they are discarded. If the consequence is to discredit a theory on which the scientist has staked his career, his career is down the drain. Scientific theories are credence goods and hypothesis-testing is the canonical means of determining their quality. One can imagine public intellectuals' predictions being treated similarly, as scientific hypotheses to be tested empirically and rejected if they flunk. They are not so treated. They are not tested.

Why not? First, they are not *intended* to be tested. Most public intellectuals are identified with one or another ideological school, such as welfare liberalism, multiculturalism, social conservatism, or libertarianism. Most of their readers are members of the same school and are seeking to shore up their own preconceptions rather than to see them challenged. When a public intellectual's prediction goes awry, normally as a result of his having extrapolated from some current trend that his ideological confrères consider dire, they are reluctant to drop him. To do so would discredit their side of the ideological divide. Instead they close ranks around one who has fought the good fight, albeit unsuccessfully. So you don't find environmental radicals criticizing Paul Ehrlich for having predicted that the sky would have fallen by now, even though his Chicken Little alarmism may actually have harmed the environmental movement.

Second, the predictions made by public intellectuals are not conveniently collected in one place where their accuracy can be easily

58. These are weighted averages. That is, before the percentages are averaged, the percentage increase for each public intellectual is weighted by the number of media mentions that he received. The weighted averages for the two groups are therefore computed simply by adding up the 1989 and 1999 columns and determining the percentage increase. The difference in unweighted averages, as indicated in the table, is even greater. The unweighted averages are computed by adding up the percentage increase experienced by each public intellectual in each of the two groups and then dividing by the number of public intellectuals in each group.

checked. Some of Ehrlich's most decisively falsified predictions were made at Earth Day rallies and in popular magazines rather than in his books. The public intellectual's current writings will not dwell upon, and indeed will rarely mention at all, his failed predictions. Few readers will remember them and fewer still will be minded to do the research necessary to establish and evaluate his record of predictions.

The third reason there is little scorekeeping underlies the second: the views of public intellectuals are not important to most people, even those who read their books and articles. Which brings me to the question of their influence.

The Influence of Public Intellectuals

Public intellectuals are read for information but also for entertainment—educated people enjoy reading the writings of lively minds on current affairs even if they realize that the writers are opinionated, incompletely informed, and basically unreliable—and for buttressing the reader's predispositions, that is, for solidarity, for what in the last chapter I called "rallying." As Charles Sanders Peirce pointed out long ago, people are uncomfortable being in a state of doubt and therefore dislike having their beliefs challenged.[59] Unless compelled by the norms of their calling (the norms of scientific inquiry, for example) to submit their views to challenge, people will seek confirmation and support, including solidarity with like-minded thinkers. Two psychological tendencies related to Peirce's point are confirmation bias[60] and herd instinct, the latter meaning that most people want to feel themselves part of a community of like-minded thinkers because it gives them greater confidence that they are right or at least are not likely to be thought daft for holding the beliefs they do. Dislike of dubiety (Peirce's point) and herd instinct drive people to seek evidence that will confirm rather than disconfirm their priors (confirmation bias), even though searching for disconfirming evidence would be the epistemically more robust procedure, as Mill and later philosophers of science stressed; Mill es-

59. Charles Sanders Peirce, "The Fixation of Belief," in *Collected Papers of Charles Sanders Peirce*, vol. 5: *Pragmatism and Pragmaticism* 223, 231–233 (Charles Hartshorne and Paul Weiss eds., 1934).

60. See Matthew Rabin, "Psychology and Economics," *36 Journal of Economic Literature* 11, 26–29 (1998).

pecially emphasized the danger that conformism poses to intellectual progress.[61] Notwithstanding Mill, nothing is more reassuring, so far as the felt soundness of one's beliefs is concerned, than to find an intelligent, articulate person who shares them and is able to make arguments and marshal evidence for them better than you yourself could do and thus arm you to defend them better if challenged, as well as to still your own doubts.

The psychology of the consumers of public-intellectual work has nothing to do with seeking guidance for action and thus with acting on predictions. If people relied on the predictions of public intellectuals—in the way for example that members of a religious sect sometimes rely on its leader's prediction that the world is about to end by selling all their worldly goods, or that Europeans in 1938 relied on Neville Chamberlain's assurance that the Munich accord would bring a durable peace—then falsification of the public intellectuals' predictions would be noted and the public intellectual, having imposed costs on his readers, would be discredited. That has been the fate of many financial journalists, analysts, and portfolio managers whose erroneous predictions concerning future movements of stock prices were blamed for heavy losses to investors. It is consistent with this point that Paul Ehrlich's mispredictions *have* received considerable publicity (although he has not yet been laughed off the stage): the business community has a large financial stake in fending off extreme proposals for environmental regulation, and so it publicizes environmentalists' pratfalls.

The public intellectual's predictive propensities are related not to truth-seeking and hypothesis-testing but to the competitive and undiscriminating character of the public-intellectual market. The public intellectual's predictions are risky but dramatic bids for the public's attention. In the case of the *academic* public intellectual, they also reflect an academic tendency to take extreme positions. The value that the academy places on novelty, the point noted in Chapter 2, is not the only reason for this tendency. Predisposed to bold ideas and striking models that reveal hidden principles of order beneath the flux of appearances, coming from "difficult" fields of science or social science to the "easy" field of politics dominated by corrupt and mediocre intellects, the academic public intellectual tends to be a radical simplifier of social reality.

61. John Stuart Mill, *On Liberty* 89, 96, 104–106 (1955 [1859]).

Seeing things in black-and-white terms emboldens him to prophesy by obscuring from him the world's intractability to simple causal models.

Yet just to use words like "truth" and "reality" in connection with the political and ideological world, which is the world of the public intellectual as I am defining the term, will grate on the skeptical reader. Is there any knowable truth about politics, any reality behind the flux of political debate? Would anyone but a Platonist entertain such an idea? But the issue is not the inability of public intellectuals, or for that matter of anyone, to discover ultimate or permanent answers to social questions. The issue is the scrupulousness, accuracy, depth, and logicality with which public intellectuals deal with these questions. The questions may or may not be factual or logical at their root; but at least when the religious dimensions of such questions, being undiscussable, are set to one side,[62] fact and logic play a role, sometimes a decisive one, in the answers to social questions. At the very least, people are concerned with the *consequences* of social policy, and determining those consequences requires disinterested inquiry in the manner of a scientist, though even an approximation to the scientist's distinctive and powerful norms and methods of inquiry will often not be possible. The public intellectual's predictions, however, are almost a parody of scientific hypotheses.

The problem afflicts other forecasters too, and for suggestively similar reasons. Despite the financial penalties for erroneous forecasts by finance professionals, such as securities analysts and portfolio managers, there is a documented propensity for extreme forecasts ("scattering") by older finance professionals. Having acquired on whatever basis a good reputation, they can risk making forecasts that are unlikely to be fulfilled but that, by virtue of their boldness, both attract attention to the forecaster and gain him unusual credibility should they turn out (against the odds) to be accurate, while his reputation cushions him against having to pay a high price for a mistake.[63] Similar incentives op-

62. See Richard Rorty, "Religion as Conversation-Stopper," *Common Knowledge*, Spring 1994, pp. 1, 2 (1994). Undiscussable because no modern religion stakes its claim to truth on verifiable or falsifiable factual claims and because it is a strong norm in our society not to question a person's religious beliefs.

63. See Owen A. Lamont, "Macroeconomic Forecasts and Microeconomic Forecasters" (University of Chicago Graduate School of Business, unpublished, Sept. 14, 2000), and references cited there; also David Laster, Paul Bennett, and In Sun Geoum, "Rational Bias in Macroeconomic Forecasts," 114 *Quarterly Journal of Economics* 293 (1999).

erate on public intellectuals, only more strongly because the financial penalties for their errors are milder to the point of being nonexistent. We'll see in the next chapter that the average age of prominent public intellectuals, like prominent business forecasters, is high. Academic public intellectuals tend not to venture daring predictions until they have acquired a reputation, based on solid academic work, that will prevent reputational free-fall if their predictions go awry, as they usually do.

Mistaken prediction goes hand in hand with mistaken assessment of current conditions. The public intellectual who predicts the demise of capitalism is unlikely to have a penetrating insight into the flaws of communism. The number of public intellectuals duped by the Potemkin-village tactics of their communist hosts in tours of the Soviet Union, China, North Vietnam, East Germany, Cuba, and elsewhere in the communist bloc is legion.[64] Paul Hollander quotes a remarkable number of statements by distinguished intellectuals that reveal astonishing ignorance, obtuseness, naïveté, callousness, and wishful thinking. Yet relatively few people have read the small literature of which Hollander's book is an exemplar, and the luster of the deceived fellow travelers (many of them still alive and still speaking on sundry public topics, like John Kenneth Galbraith, Jonathan Kozol, Richard Falk, Staughton Lynd, and Susan Sontag) remains for the most part undimmed by their folly. Similarly, despite professional criticism of Stephen Jay Gould's best-known book, *The Mismeasure of Man* (see Chapter 3), the 1996 paperback second edition is ranked by Amazon.com a highly respectable (considering the age of the book) 9,818th. Amazon.com carries thirty-two editions of Gould's books, and Table 4.1 shows that his media mentions have grown faster in the last decade than that of the average member of the control group.

One reason intellectuals fooled by communism have gotten off so easily is that conservative intellectuals, the natural people to throw stones at the duped fellow travelers, were themselves deceived about the communist system. Not about its cruelty, hypocrisy, and squalor, but about its brittleness. That is why virtually no one on the Right could imagine the system's collapsing of its own weight. In the early

---

64. See Paul Hollander, *Political Pilgrims: Travels of Western Intellectuals to the Soviet Union, China, and Cuba 1928–1978* (1981).

years after the collapse, the Right attributed it to the U.S. arms buildup during the Reagan administration and in particular to the administration's plan to create an antimissile defense that would neutralize the Soviet strategic missile force ("Star Wars"). These developments, supported and indeed inspired by conservative thinkers, were claimed to have driven the Soviet state to the brink of bankruptcy and to have exposed its technological backwardness and impending defenselessness, in turn precipitating efforts at reform under Gorbachev that backfired and brought the system down. This is arguable.[65] But it is equally arguable that the Reagan administration's policies were minor factors and that the communist system, brittle as most authoritarian regimes are, collapsed under the cumulative weight of a series of political and economic failures (the war in Afghanistan, the Chernobyl meltdown, corruption, cronyism, cynicism, and economic stagnation) that owed little to the initiatives of the Reagan administration and that destroyed the morale of the communist leadership.[66] It would not follow that the U.S. arms buildup was a mistake. The Soviet Union was armed to the teeth and bellicose, and its internal weaknesses were not fully understood—even, till near the end, by the Soviet leaders.[67]

Public intellectuals are not unique in operating in an environment of high information costs. Such an environment does not excuse the mistakes that public intellectuals make in assessment and prediction. But to see this we shall have to consider the economics of error.

The optimal number of errors is not zero but is a number derived from minimizing the sum of error costs and error-avoidance costs. The greater the first type of cost, the more of the second type society should be willing to incur, in just the same way that, other things being equal, we would want heavier spending on preventing serious accidents than on preventing trivial ones. Some errors are harmless and so are not worth expending any resources on trying to avoid.

Others are harmful. A medical error, for example, often can do grievous harm. Costly efforts, such as licensing physicians, subsidizing medical research, forbidding the purchase of potentially harmful drugs

65. See, for example, Vladimir Shlapentokh, "A Normal System? False and True Explanations for the Collapse of the USSR," *Times Literary Supplement*, Dec. 15, 2000, p. 11.

66. See Paul Hollander, *Political Will and Personal Belief: The Decline and Fall of Soviet Communism* (1999).

67. Id. at 285

without a doctor's prescription, and creating tort remedies for medical malpractice, are therefore undertaken to minimize medical errors. Erroneous weather forecasts and stock-market forecasts are similar cases of harmful error in prediction. The rise of index funds, which offer diversified portfolios without active trading, is a response to the latter problem of uncertainty; supercomputers are a response to the former. Or consider the uncertainty that is generated by fraudulent representations made by issuers of corporate stock and other securities. Securities laws and common-law fraud doctrines are costly devices employed to minimize this source of investment error, which is thought to impose heavy social costs by undermining investors' confidence in the securities markets. Public inspection of restaurants to prevent food poisoning is another example.

These examples round out the point made in Chapter 2 that government may step in when market incentives and constraints are thought insufficient to dispel high consumer information costs. Actually to justify public regulation, however, it is not enough that a market is failing to produce a product or service of the quality that consumers want and would be willing to pay for. The adverse consequences of the market failure must be grave enough to warrant incurring the costs, which may be considerable, of trying to do something about it. The benefits of the regulation in raising quality must exceed the costs for regulation to be worthwhile, and that is unlikely if either the benefits are slight or the costs great.

A simple model may help to nail down the point. Assuming that belief in true propositions yields greater utility than disbelief in them, and that disbelief in false propositions yields greater utility than belief in *them*, we have

$$U_1(t, b) - U_2(t, d) = Z_1 > 0 \quad \text{and}$$
$$U_3(f, d) - U_4(f, b) = Z_2 > 0,$$

so $Z \equiv Z_1 + Z_2$ is the utility of believing what is true and disbelieving what is false. We must not suppose either that achieving this happy state is costless or that its achievement is necessarily very worthwhile. Take the second point first. The value of Z depends on the utility associated with each of the four possible belief states (believing what is true, disbelieving what is true, disbelieving what is false, and believing what is false). In matters unimportant to the individual, the utility of true knowledge may be slight, in which event Z will be slight and may not exceed the cost of achieving true knowledge. That would be a case of rational ignorance.

Now let K be knowledge, ranging from -1 (false belief) through 0 (no belief) to 1 (true belief—that is, the level of K that generates Z), and let $U(K)$ be the utility generated by each level of knowledge. Assume that K, and therefore $U(K)$, can be raised by buying units of information, denoted by x. But x has a cost; otherwise $U(K)$ would always equal Z. The more x's that are bought, the greater the cost: that is, $C_x > 0$.[68] The rational individual will seek to maximize $U(K)(x) - C(x)$, which is done by buying x's up to the point at which the last unit bought increases the utility of the additional knowledge acquired by an amount just equal to the extra cost: that is, the point at which $K_x = C_x$. Alternatively he seeks to minimize the sum of the error costs (E) resulting from lack of knowledge and the costs (C again) of avoiding mistakes. Both are functions of x. Purchases of x reduce E ($E_x < 0$) but increase C ($C_x > 0$, as before). The sum ($E(x) + C(x)$) is minimized when $C_x = -E_x$, that is, when the last unit of x that is bought reduces the costs of error by an amount just equal to the cost of the unit.

The level of knowledge thus attained will fall far short of full knowledge if the utility of a true belief is small relative to the cost of attaining it. I emphasize that it is the relative, not the absolute, sizes of the competing values that matter. The cost of acquiring knowledge may be so high that it exceeds the utility of the knowledge acquired even if that utility is also high. That is the situation with palm-reading. It would be very nice to be able to obtain accurate knowledge of the future by reading palms (Z would be high), but the cost is prohibitive. Knowing this, you might respond in one of two ways: not bother having your palm read, or discounting the palm reader's prediction steeply and as a result relying on it much less than you would rely on a medical diagnosis or a weather forecast. The harm from disappointed expectations would then be slight. Since knowledge of the infirmities of palm-reading as a predictive methodology is pretty universal, there is no pressure to ban it in order to protect consumers from being fooled to their detriment. They can protect themselves easily.

---

68. C_x denotes the first derivative of C with regard to x. That is, it indicates the effect on C of a small change in x.

So why hasn't palm-reading disappeared? Because it is both a multi-dimensional product and a cheap one. Predicting the future is only one of the benefits that a consumer might obtain from having his palm read; another is the entertainment value of the experience. The entertainment value is not very great, but since the cost is slight some people obtain a net benefit from the experience. And so it is with public intellectuals. They have entertainment and solidarity-building value, and some informational value, even though they are not a reliable source of accurate predictions. Neither value may be very great, but the cost of public-intellectual work to the consumer is not great either.

What would be very costly would be acquiring true beliefs, or rejecting false ones, by sifting and weighing public intellectuals' predictions. That would be almost as costly as obtaining a true prediction from a palm reader. The cost might be bearable if the benefits were very great, but they are not; public intellectuals, unlike palm readers, generally opine about matters that the "customer" can do little about because they require political or other collective action to alter. What profits the ordinary citizen to form a well-founded belief that the nation should, or should not, build a defense against missile attack? He can do very little, to the point of nothing, to influence national policy. The benefits of obtaining accurate information from public intellectuals are so scanty that even inexpensive means of assessing the reliability of public intellectuals, such as by tracking their predictions, are evidently not cost-justified. *Consumer Reports* does not evaluate public intellectuals; nor does any other magazine or information service, except very sporadically.

There is even a vicious cycle at work. The less accurate that public intellectuals are in their assessments or predictions, the less seriously they are taken, which reduces the demand for accuracy, though the cycle is checked by the fact I've been emphasizing that the record of their mistakes is not well known. But neither is the record of their successes. Neither record is carefully compiled and studied because few people take their cues from what public intellectuals say. We can imagine a downward spiral bottoming out in a low value–low cost equilibrium. The educated public spends little time, and incurs few other costs, in consuming public intellectuals' wares and derives correspondingly modest benefits.

Bruce Robbins argues that a calling is not recognized as a profession unless it is important to the general public, and therefore the professionalization of literary criticism implies rather than denies the public relevance of modern literary criticism, esoteric and marginal, though undoubtedly political (and so potentially a public-intellectual genre), as that criticism might otherwise seem.[69] But this is to confuse "profession" with "professionalization." The professionalization of a field implies merely that it has been brought under the discipline of rules and procedures governing hiring, promotion, compensation, prizes, research protocols, and publication that are designed to impart intellectual rigor. It says nothing about the importance of the field to the general public. Egyptology is thoroughly professionalized, but not because a quack Egyptologist could hurt people. In contrast, the occupations traditionally classified as professions, such as law, medicine, architecture, accounting, and military science, are those that require specialized knowledge *and* are of great moment to the public at large, which, along with interest-group pressures, is why many of them are subject to licensure requirements, as Egyptology and other purely intellectual fields are not.[70] Literary criticism is not a profession in this sense, because it is not important to the general public. Robbins does not try to show that the academic critics whom he admires, such as Edward Said and Gayatri Spivak, are influential with regard to any matter in which the general public takes an interest. Even the "profession" is beginning to realize that the increased theorization of literary criticism, a product in part at least of increased professionalization, is contributing to the marginality of literary studies.[71]

Public intellectuals were taken more seriously during the Depression, World War II, the turbulent 1960s, the Cold War, and the stagflation of the 1970s—all periods of perceived political or ideological crisis—when the sorts of issue that the public intellectual likes to address seemed much more consequential than they do today. But more seriously does not mean very seriously, even if the CIA did think it worthwhile at the height of the Cold War to support *Encounter*, a maga-

---

69. Bruce Robbins, *Secular Vocations: Intellectuals, Professionalism, Culture* (1993), esp. ch. 3.

70. Richard A. Posner, *The Problematics of Moral and Legal Theory* 186 (1999).

71. See Ron Rosenbaum, "The Play's the Thing, Again," *New York Times Book Review*, Aug. 6, 2000, p. 12.

zine of and for public intellectuals. Although there was an enormous outpouring of public-intellectual work during the Vietnam War,[72] a detailed study concludes that intellectuals were influential neither in the debate over (or conduct or outcome of) the war, nor in the civil rights crisis that was unfolding at the same time.[73] The study is limited to publication, and does not try to assess the impact of intellectuals' teach-ins and picketing and marches and support of student sit-ins and other demonstrations; but such militancy is rare among intellectuals and frequently backfires—it may well have been a factor in the election of Nixon to the presidency in 1968.

Cutting against the no-influence thesis is the fact that dictatorial regimes often try to stifle public intellectuals. But they do so as part of a general effort to control information rather than out of a special fear of public intellectuals or "the power of ideas." It is hard to think of a dictatorial regime brought down by ideas, other than religious ideas, rather than by material circumstances such as war, political infighting in the governing class, corruption, or economic failure. The proper question to ask in gauging the influence of public intellectuals is whether in a nation with a free press and competitive politics, a nation in which the public therefore has abundant access to information, public intellectuals influence public opinion substantially. Probably they do not, at least not through their writing and public speaking. Their teaching may have a greater effect. The "postcolonialist" school of literary scholars—one of whom, for example, advocates "a decolonizing pedagogy"[74]—has been credited with stirring up some college students to riot against globalization (that is, free trade and free movement of capital).[75] But this Pied Piperism has had little influence on public opinion and behavior,[76] except possibly the perverse one of throwing

72. See Charles Kadushin, *The American Intellectual Elite*, pt. 2 (1974).

73. Id. at 348–356.

74. Joan Pong Linton, *The Romance of the New World: Gender and the Literary Formations of English Colonialism* 189 (1998). See also, in similar vein (and representative of an immense literature), Srinivas Aravamudan, *Tropicopolitans: Colonialism and Agency, 1688–1804* (1999).

75. Chris Hedges, "New Activists Are Nurtured by Politicized Curriculums," *New York Times*, May 27, 2000 (national ed.), p. A17. Incidentally, one of the leaders of the anarchist faction of these rioters has credited Noam Chomsky as one of his inspirers. Roadrunner Krazykatovitch, Letter to the Editors, *New Republic*, June 5, 2000, p. 4. With friends like these, Chomsky does not need enemies.

76. Though not for want of trying. The cultural Left admits to having revolutionary aims.

the 2000 presidential election to Bush by shifting votes from Gore to Nader, who made hostility to globalization the key plank of his platform and appears to have attracted much of his support from college students. The influence of public intellectuals in their role as consultants and officials (one thinks of Henry Kissinger, George Kennan, Conor Cruise O'Brien, Václav Havel, and a number of others) has been greater. But I am interested rather in the activities of public intellectuals in the marketplace of ideas and opinions, their writing and public lectures and other public appearances (including testifying in court or before Congress)—their efforts, in short, to shape public opinion through their public rhetoric.

I am not so thoroughgoing a materialist as to doubt that ideas, even if they are not scientific or otherwise rigorously provable, can influence public opinion and public policy. There is evidence, moreover, of an indirect channel of public-intellectual influence. News commentators and experts have been found to influence public opinion,[77] and these commentators and experts, even if not themselves public intellectuals (they are not identified in the studies I have cited), may in turn be influenced by currents of intellectual thought. Consider the successful effort to deny Robert Bork appointment to the Supreme Court. "People For the American Way, working in coalition with other groups, conducted the classic national op-ed campaign in 1987, combining national media distribution with state-targeted op-eds to build a groundswell against the nomination [*sic*—should be confirmation] of Robert Bork to the U.S. Supreme Court."[78] No doubt the organizers got many of their arguments from public-intellectual law professors, who may for all I know have written some of the op-eds.[79] But one should be wary of the natural tendency of intellectuals to exaggerate the influence

---

"We work in whatever small ways we can toward the end of capitalist patriarchy: not just canon reform or a deconstruction of *Paradise Lost*, but the transformation of society." Richard Ohmann, "On 'PC' and Related Matters," in *PC Wars: Politics and Theory in the Academy* 11, 13 (Jeffrey Williams ed., 1995). This is fodder, of course, for the Right.

77. See Benjamin I. Page, Robert Y. Shapiro, and Glenn R. Dempsey, "What Moves Public Opinion?" 81 *American Political Science Review* 23 (1987); Donald L. Jordan, "Newspaper Effects on Policy Preferences," 57 *Public Opinion Quarterly* 191 (1993).

78. Denice Zeck and Edmund Rennolds, "Op-Eds: A Cost-Effective Strategy for Advocacy" 38 (Benton Foundation 1991).

79. For the opposition of one prominent public-intellectual law professor to Bork's confirmation, Ronald Dworkin, see Chapter 10.

of ideas, especially, if they are academics, of academic ideas, or, what is often not the same thing, ideas propagated by academics. The more stable and complex a society is—also the more complacent it is—the less likely are its public intellectuals to be able to take it by storm.

Any suggestion that academic public intellectuals do not have a significant influence on the formation of public opinion must be qualified, however, by reference to Peter Singer's book advocating what is loosely called "animal rights," though he is a utilitarian rather than a rights theorist and prefers to speak of animal "liberation."[80] The first edition of *Animal Liberation*, published in 1975, sold some half million copies and has been credited with contributing significantly to the worldwide growth of the animal-rights movement.[81] The movement has affected the fur industry, the consumption of meat, and the use of animals in medical experiments.

Singer is an academic philosopher. But his book is written for a popular audience, is not tightly reasoned, and makes no effort to overcome the obvious objections that can be lodged against a version of utilitarianism that expands the community whose aggregate welfare is to be maximized to include animals—objections such as: if there are happier animals than man, we may have a moral duty to shrink the human population to the point at which the maximum number of the happy animals can be supported. Singer's book conveys its message in significant part through gruesome photographs and evades some hard questions, as when he says that "historically . . . the leaders of the animal welfare movement have cared far more about human beings than have other humans who cared nothing for animals."[82] A striking exception is ignored: Adolf Hitler, whom Luc Ferry quotes as saying that "in the new Reich cruelty toward animals should no longer exist."[83] Ferry remarks "the disturbing nature of this alliance between an utterly sincere zoophilia (it was not limited to words but was borne out in law) and the most ruthless hatred of men history has ever known."[84] Singer ignores

---

80. Peter Singer, *Animal Liberation* (2d ed. 1990).

81. See Gary L. Francione, *Rain without Thunder: The Ideology of the Animal Rights Movement* 51–53 (1996); Dale Jamieson, "Singer and the Practical Ethics Movement," in *Singer and His Critics* 1 (Dale Jamieson ed., 1999).

82. Singer, note 80 above, at 221.

83. Luc Ferry, *The New Ecological Order* 91 (1995).

84. Id. at 93.

the affinity between animal protection and the Nazis' celebration of Darwinism and their elevation of instinct over intelligence, barbarism over civilization, cruelty over compassion, struggle over peace, and the natural and the rooted over the humanistic and the cosmopolitan. The Nazis liked to blur the line between the human and animal kingdoms, as when they described the Jews as vermin. The other side of this coin was glorifying the species that had good Nazi virtues, predatory species like the eagle ("Eagle's Nest" was the name of Hitler's summer home in the Bavarian Alps), the tiger, and the panther (both animals gave their names to German tanks). Nietzsche's "blond beast," the opposite pole of degenerate modern man, was the lion. These are examples of how animal-rights thinking can assimilate people to animals rather than just assimilating animals to people.

Singer is forthright in acknowledging some of the morally dubious implications of his philosophical analysis, such as that placing animals on a plane of equality with human beings may make the life of a pig more valuable than the life of a severely retarded human being or that killing an animal painlessly can be completely compensated for by creating a new animal to replace it.[85] The force of the book lies in its description of animal suffering rather than in its arguments, many of which would appall the rank-and-file supporters of animal rights. One of the less academically rigorous philosophical books on animal rights, it is the most influential in the public arena.[86] It has now been complemented by a book by Steven Wise, a practicing lawyer, who argues forcefully, with the aid of history, cognitive science, and affecting anec-

---

85. See Singer, note 80 above, at 17–22, 229. As an *admirer* of Singer has written, "the character of Singer's views can be brought out by saying that generally he thinks that you are more likely to do something wrong by killing a healthy pig rather than your severely handicapped infant; and if you are choosing between an early abortion and killing an adult cow, you should probably have the abortion." Jamieson, note 81 above, at 10. For criticism, see, for example, Peter Berkowitz, "Other People's Mothers: The Utilitarian Horrors of Peter Singer," *New Republic*, Jan. 10, 2000, p. 27.

86. Compare Alasdair MacIntyre, *Dependent Rational Animals: Why Human Beings Need the Virtues*, chs. 2–5 (1999); James Rachels, *Created from Animals: The Moral Implications of Darwinism* (1990); Tom Regan, *The Case for Animal Rights* (1983); Richard Sorabji, *Animal Minds and Human Morals: The Origins of the Western Debate* (1993); Roger Scruton, *Animal Rights and Wrongs* (3d ed. 2000). See also Ian Hacking, "Our Fellow Animals," *New York Review of Books*, June 29, 2000, p. 20. I am told, however, that Regan's book has been influential in the English animal-rights movement.

dotes, for extending legal rights to nonhuman primates.[87] It is not rigorously argued and is as vulnerable to criticism as Singer's book;[88] but it is likely to be influential.

Perhaps it would not be unfair to say of Singer that he *happens* to be an *academic* public intellectual but that he would write in much the same way and have much the same impact if he were a nonacademic one, like Rachel Carson or Betty Friedan.

But to speak only of influence on public opinion and on the laws, policies, and other public actions that public opinion in turn influences is too confining a perspective from which to gauge the influence of the public intellectual on society. To the extent that people are what they read, a steady diet of books and magazine articles by public intellectuals may contribute to the shaping of a person's values and outlook. Public intellectuals in this country do not have a wide readership (we'll look at some magazine circulation figures in the next chapter), but a large fraction of it consists of people who are highly educated and politically active and influential. If public intellectuals vanished, and the only purveyors of political and ideological opinions were academics writing for other academics, classroom teachers, reporters, politicians, the clergy, and policy analysts, the general public—or rather the highly educated fraction of the general public—might be even less interested, informed, and thoughtful about political and ideological issues than it is.

Yet policy and public opinion might not be much different. This is not only because public intellectuals have a small audience and tend by their pronouncements to entrench rather than to resolve differences of opinion; three other factors are also important. The first, and least, is that because most public intellectuals are academics, public-intellectual work subtracts from academic work, which like public-intellectual work and doubtless more so has a diffuse but cumulatively significant effect on public opinion and public policy. If academics stuck to their lasts, and avoided the temptation to engage in public-intellectual work, their influence on society might be greater than it is with the divided focus that defines the academic public intellectual.

But might the chance to become a public intellectual be one of the things that attract able people to an academic career? If so, curtailing

---

87. Steven M. Wise, *Rattling the Cage: Toward Legal Rights for Animals* (2000).
88. See my review of it ("Animal Rights"), 110 *Yale Law Journal* 527 (2000).

that opportunity might reduce the amount or quality of academic work in the long run. Public-intellectual status is, it is true, ordinarily attained only toward the end of an academic's career (we'll see some evidence of this in the next chapter). When its benefits are discounted to present value and further discounted to reflect the large random element involved in becoming a public intellectual, the prospect is unlikely to have a significant effect on the choice of a career. Even so, odd as it may seem, any effort to shut down that prospect could be a significant deterrent to the choice of an academic career. The reason is the difficulty of operationalizing the definition of "public intellectual" and in particular the haziness of the line that separates academic from public-intellectual work. (Much of the work discussed in this book is both—this book itself is both.) As a practical matter, the university might have to forbid its professors to retain *any* outside earned income (that is, income other than investment and other passive income), and this would undoubtedly make an academic career less attractive unless universities raised academic salaries to compensate for the loss of outside income prospects. And that would be hard to do because those prospects vary so across fields and individuals. A uniform raise adequate to compensate faculty members who had the best outside earnings prospects would crush the university. A smaller raise would drive many faculty members out of the university world altogether. A raise tailored to each faculty member's particular opportunities would require too much information to be feasible. The result of any of these approaches would be an increase in the quality-adjusted costs of universities that could well cause a drop in the amount and quality of academic research.

A second reason to doubt that public intellectuals today contribute a great deal to society is that insofar as they are merely translating academic ideas into language that the general educated public can understand, they may be doing nothing more than accelerating slightly the diffusion of academic ideas. They are doing what journalists would do, though perhaps with a lag, as suggested in Chapter 2. The most influential journalists and commentators may be getting their ideas directly from the academic source rather than from public-intellectual translators, in which event the translations may not be accelerating the diffusion of academic ideas. As specialization increases, we can expect more and more of the responsibility for translating academic ideas for the general public to devolve on journalists, as specialists in communication. We have seen this recently in both the Clinton impeachment saga and, even more impressively, the 2000 presidential deadlock, where journalists, some with law degrees, presented generally lucid and accurate explanations of the issues and procedures in the avalanche of litigation precipitated by the closeness of the vote in Florida, even though they were working under great time pressure. As for the "original" work of public intellectuals, the work that is not merely translation or simplification of academic research, it is often, as we have seen, shoddy or even wacky.

Third, a great deal of public-intellectual work is corrective rather than constructive—is negative, though worthily so, rather than positive. The public-intellectual work of the Cold War intellectuals, such as Sidney Hook, George Orwell, Reinhold Niebuhr, Arthur Schlesinger Jr., Robert Conquest, and Raymond Aron, would have been unnecessary had not so many public intellectuals supported communism before and during World War II and afterward opposed U.S. foreign policy toward the communist bloc.[89] Because the characteristic disposition of the intellectual is oppositional and because Marxism was a theory-based creed, it is not surprising that a disproportionate number of intellectuals in the noncommunist world were drawn to Marxism,[90] while intellectuals in the communist world, with a handful of heroic exceptions such as Pasternak and Solzhenitsyn, were too intimidated to play the oppositional role.[91] The result was an imbal-

89. Hollander, note 64 above; Hollander, *Decline and Discontent: Communism and the West Today*, pt. 2 (1992); Hollander, "Intellectuals, Estrangement, and Wish Fulfillment," 35 *Society* 258 (1998); Hollander, "The Berlin Wall Collapses, the Adversary Culture Endures," 34 *Orbis* 565 (1990); Sidney Hook, *Out of Step: An Unquiet Life in the 20th Century* (1987), esp. chs. 11 and 34; Raymond Aron, *The Opium of the Intellectuals* (1957).

90. See, for a biting commentary on this phenomenon, Paul Hollander, "Marxism and Western Intellectuals in the Post-Communist Era," 37 *Society* 22 (2000).

91. A prime example is Georg Lukács, the well-known Hungarian literary critic who lived in the Soviet Union, and after World War II in communist Hungary, during Stalin's reign, faithfully parroting the Communist Party line in all its ugliness and absurdity. See, for example, Georg Lukács, *The Destruction of Reason* (Peter Palmer trans., 1981), and *Essays on Realism* (Rodney Livingstone ed., 1980), esp. "Tribune or Bureaucrat?" in id. at 198 (essay first published in 1940). One quotation will convey the political slant of this distinguished communist public intellectual: "More and more natural scientists are grasping how much dialectical materialism can offer them, especially since this, through its very solution of concrete scientific problems, has raised both science itself and the method of dialectical materialism to a higher

ance of intellectual opinion that the Cold War intellectuals sought to rectify.

It is because many fewer intellectuals supported fascism than supported communism that Orwell is so much better known as an anticommunist than as an antifascist, though he was both. Communist and far-left intellectuals were far more numerous and influential than fascist intellectuals,[92] though there were plenty of the latter as well, particularly in France, Germany, and Italy. Even in the United States, Mussolini had, at least before the Italian invasion of Ethiopia, a number of distinguished intellectual admirers, such as Herbert Croly, George Santayana, and Lincoln Steffens.[93] Both Hitler and Mussolini were public intellectuals prior to their seizure of power, though unlike Lenin and Trotsky they were not taken seriously in intellectual circles, at least as intellectuals.

Homage to Catalonia, Animal Farm, and *Nineteen Eighty-Four,* along with Orwell's numerous left-bashing essays, such as the one from which I quoted his criticism of Auden's poem in the last chapter, were reactions in part to the intellectual Left, to people like Harold Laski, Stephen Spender, and Auden. The Stalinist ideology in *Nineteen Eighty-Four* is called "Ingsoc"—*English* socialism. Similarly, the procapitalist public-intellectual work of a Hayek and a Milton Friedman, as distinct from the scholarly work of these economists, would have been less needful had it not been for the advocacy of collectivist public policies by such left-leaning public intellectuals as Keynes, Galbraith, and Laski. Conservative public intellectuals such as George Gilder, Hilton Kramer, Irving Kristol, Michael Novak, and Norman Podhoretz would not have had so big a role to play in the public life of the nation had it not been for the flock of left-wing public intellectuals—Charles Reich, Herbert Marcuse, C. Wright Mills, Paul Goodman, Mary McCarthy, Norman O. Brown, Adrienne Rich, Catharine MacKinnon, Susan Sontag, and many others. The revolt against post-

---

stage in the Soviet Union. More and more writers are experiencing the same with regard to their art. Hence the Soviet Union's discoveries and achievements are triggering off so sharp a defensive action in reactionary bourgeois science and philosophy (the Lysenko controversy)." "Epilogue" (written in January 1953, two months before Stalin's death), in *The Destruction of Reason,* above, at 765, 847.

92. See, for example, Harvey M. Teres, *Renewing the Left: Politics, Imagination, and the New York Intellectuals,* chs. 1–7 (1996).

93. See John P. Diggins, *Mussolini and Fascism: The View from America,* chs. 3, 9, 10 (1972).

modernism battens on postmodernism. The rise of the conservative public intellectual owes much to the "counterculture" of the 1960s.[94] A culture war requires two sides. My model of the costs and benefits of public-intellectual work implied that dispelling false beliefs can be as important as instilling true ones. But to the extent that public-intellectual work is dominated by the propounding and refuting of false beliefs, its net contribution to policy, even to sanity, may be small. The opposing forces may be playing a zero-sum or even a negative-sum intellectual game.

It is no accident that Catholicism (a traditional target of public intellectuals, beginning with Voltaire), fascism, communism, the 1960s "counterculture," "political correctness," and certain veins of postmodernism, such as radical feminism, are strongly dogmatic, and to nonbelievers both absurd and sinister.[95] Their dogmatic content provides a handhold for the public intellectual's intellectual critique, the absurdity provides the occasion for a polemical engagement with the dogma, and the sinister cast gives the critique the appearance of urgency and a shot at commanding an audience. American society today has many pockets of dogmatism. Yet none of them seems particularly ominous—the silly predominates over the sinister. And so the value of the public intellectual's corrective function is weakening at the same time that the supply of *distinctive* public intellectuals is dwindling for the reasons discussed in Chapter 2.

The apparent ineffectuality of the modern public intellectual to alter public opinion has a paradoxical normative significance that I have now to explain. I have been using the term "market failure" loosely, when what I have meant is closer to "being a disappointment in light of expectations widely held in academic circles." Economists use "market failure" to mean that conditions in a market prevent output from being carried to the point (but no further) at which social marginal product equals social marginal cost, that being the point at which the allocation of resources is optimized. Monopoly can cause market failure by deflecting consumers to products that cost society more to produce than the monopolized product but that, being priced competitively, look

94. See George H. Nash, *The Conservative Intellectual Movement in America since 1945* 277–328 (2d ed. 1996).

95. The link between Catholicism and communism is particularly close, as we'll see in Chapter 7.

cheaper to consumers. A divergence between private and social product or between private and social cost can also be a source of market failure.[96] If some of the benefits of the product (for example, the benefits of an easily copied innovation) are externalized, the product may be underproduced; and if some of the costs are externalized (such as the costs of pollution, unless they are borne by the polluting producer or his customers), the product may be overproduced, relative to the social optimum. Fraud, too, can drive a wedge between private and social benefits and private and social costs, for example by attracting consumers to a product that, if they knew the score, they would avoid.

It is not at all certain that these or other sources of market failure are present to a significant degree in the public-intellectual market.[97] If I am right that the consumers in this market protect themselves by not relying on what the public intellectual says, this implies that they value public-intellectual work for entertainment or solidarity rather than for guidance or direction, and it is not obvious that they aren't getting what they pay for, or that these goods are really social bads, just as it is not obvious that palm-reading is a scene of market failure. The vicious cycle that I mentioned earlier, in which inaccurate predictions by public intellectuals deter their readers from relying on the predictions, thus reducing the penalty for inaccuracy (mistaken predictions, not having induced reliance, are quickly forgotten), does not make the market unravel; it just leads to an equilibrium of low predictive accuracy. Public-intellectual work may even be a superior kind of entertainment, the kind that provokes thought and stimulates curiosity.

The possibility of market failure can't be excluded. For example, luring academics to public-intellectual work (for the next chapter presents evidence that public-intellectual output is indeed a substitute for academic output) could impose costs not borne entirely by the producers and consumers in that market if academics produce value in their teaching and research that they do not capture in their academic in-

96. Actually, the monopoly case is the same: consumers are deflected from the monopolized product to products that cost society more to produce, that is, products whose social costs exceed their private costs.

97. Compare the argument of James T. Hamilton, *Channeling Violence: The Economic Market for Violent Television Programming* (1998), that violent television programs impose external costs because the industry is not able to exclude children from watching them. No similar argument seems available with respect to public-intellectual expression.

come, and if the difference, the external benefit of academic work, exceeds the parallel difference in public-intellectual work.[98] If the analysis in this chapter is correct, public-intellectual work does not generate *net* external benefits, while academic work almost certainly does. Yet we have also seen that trying to stop academics from becoming public intellectuals might well require universities to pay higher faculty salaries; if so, this means that the public-intellectual market is conferring a benefit on the academy. And while the public is sometimes misled by a public intellectual in the interval before an equally effective public intellectual enters the lists against him, this is probably not a serious problem and so the solutions that I propose in the Conclusion are suitably modest. No market is perfectly efficient, but the public-intellectual market may not be worse than most.

The disappointment lingers. A market can be efficient in the economic sense even though what it produces has only a modest value. There is no intrinsic superiority to producing diamonds rather than charcoal. But if someone thought that charcoal was a form of diamond, the error would be worth pointing out and the economic conditions that determine the relative value of these goods elucidated. And similarly the fact that the average quality of a product is falling over time is no reason to infer market failure; if because of falling costs the price falls enough to compensate the consumer fully for the lower quality, there is no market failure. The quality of airline service has declined in recent decades, but the price has declined much more. Much of what I try to do in this book is simply to place the public-intellectual market in perspective by showing that, and why, its average quality is low ("disappointing") and perhaps falling.

98. For more on external benefits, see Chapter 7.

～ 5

More Public, Less Intellectual

> When you can measure what you are speaking about and express it in
> numbers you know something about it; but when you cannot
> measure it, when you cannot express it in numbers, your knowledge
> is of a meagre and unsatisfactory kind.[1]

> The problem with being a public intellectual is you get more and
> more public and less and less intellectual.[2]

$\mathcal{I}$N A STUDY of legal scholars, William Landes and I found
only a weak correlation between scholarly distinction, as proxied by citations to scholarly publications, and public-intellectual status, as proxied by Web "hits" and by mentions in newspapers.[3] We also found
greater inequality in public-intellectual status than in scholarly status.
We explained this by the fact that the public has a more limited interest
in law than the scholarly community does.[4] A handful of legal scholars
can satisfy the public's casual and uncritical demand for information
and opinion about the law. This is some evidence that public intellectuals sell their wares to an undiscriminating consuming public, but it is
evidence confined to a subset of those intellectuals.

The method used in our study can be applied to public intellectuals
in general, and that is what I do in this chapter in an effort to put additional empirical flesh on the theoretical skeleton presented in Chapter
2. Not only the scope but also the method of study and many of the databases used differ from the earlier study. My goals are to present a sta-

1. William Thomson (Lord Kelvin), "Electrical Units of Measurement," in Thomson,
Popular Lectures and Addresses, vol. 1, p. 80 (1891).

2. Jean Bethke Elshtain, as quoted in Karen R. Long, "Ethicist Decries Clinton's 'Cavalier
Disdain' for Rules," *Cleveland Plain Dealer*, Sept. 19, 1998, p. 1F.

3. William M. Landes and Richard A. Posner, "Citations, Age, Fame, and the Web," 29
Journal of Legal Studies 319, 329–341 (2000).

4. Id. at 337.

167

tistical profile of the modern public intellectual and to test hypotheses concerned primarily with the quality issue raised in the previous chapters.

Table 5.1 (the tables in this chapter are collected at the end, following the chapter appendix) compiles from a variety of sources a list of American and (to a much lesser extent) foreign public intellectuals of the twentieth century, both living and dead, academic and nonacademic, male and female, black and white—actually, black and nonblack, as I have not made any further racial distinctions. I have used both Web hits and media mentions (not limited to newspapers, as in Landes's and my study) as proxies for the prominence, as public intellectuals, of the individuals on my list.[5] Media mentions is the better proxy. The Web is a resource for scholars as well as for members of the general public. A search of Web hits on the name of an academic will bring up hits to the academic's own Web page and citations to his academic work in articles posted on the Web along with references to his public-intellectual work. (For a good example of the resulting "contamination," compare in Table 5.1 Noam Chomsky's Web hits and media mentions.) Thus, of the one hundred academics in Table 5.1 who have the most scholarly citations, eighteen are also among the hundred most prominent public intellectuals as measured by media mentions, but thirty-three are among the one hundred individuals who have the most Web hits.

5. I used the Google search engine for the Web hits (see www.google.com), and three Lexis-Nexis databases—Major Newspapers, Magazine Stories (Combined), and Transcripts (of television and radio shows)—for the media mentions. The Major Newspapers database contains the fifty largest U.S. newspapers by circulation plus the major foreign newspapers that are published in English. The Magazine Stories database contains hundreds of English-language (mainly U.S.) magazines. It is a rather miscellaneous collection but does include all the major news magazines plus a large number of more specialized magazines, very few however that are either scholarly or carry much public-intellectual material—but this is good since my purpose is to estimate the standing of public intellectuals in the popular media. The Transcripts database contains transcripts of the major network (including cable) news programs. Because of the rapid expansion of the World Wide Web, the majority of hits picked up by a Web search engine are probably no more than a year or two old and virtually all are within the last five years. I limited my other searches to the last five years. All the databases were visited in a six-week period beginning on July 17, 2000. Online searches of these databases yield many errors, owing mainly to confusion of names. To enable these errors to be corrected, samples of Web hits to and media mentions of all the persons listed in Table 5.1 were examined and the total hits/mentions of each person were adjusted accordingly. Details of the search and estimation methods used are explained in the appendix at the end of this chapter. The methods are imperfect but not, I think, biased in favor of any of my hypotheses.

The table also includes scholarly citations to the academics among those listed.[6] The purpose is to enable a comparison of a public intellectual's academic renown, as proxied by the number of scholarly citations to his writings, to his celebrity as a public intellectual, as proxied by media mentions. The use of scholarly citations as a proxy for scholarly quality or influence is controversial,[7] but it is enough for my purpose that they be accepted as being at least *suggestive* of scholarly distinction or reputation.

The list in Table 5.1 is not exhaustive, despite its length (546 names). There is no census of public intellectuals that could be consulted to make an exhaustive list. Closest, and the only previous quantitative study of public intellectuals that I have found, is Kadushin's list of the seventy most prestigious living American intellectuals in 1970.[8] I have included all seventy in my list; many of them remain prominent.[9] The list that Landes and I used was not afflicted by incompleteness, as it was an exhaustive enumeration of the legal scholars who had received the

6. My data sources for scholarly citations are the *Science Citation Index*, the *Social Sciences Citation Index*, and the *Arts and Humanities Citation Index*, all published by the Institute for Scientific Information (ISI) and all limited to scholarly journals. I used the Dialog search program to count citations (excluding self-citations) for the last five years to each of the academics in Table 5.1. Because the ISI databases (which, incidentally, count citations to coauthored articles as citations to the first named author only) list cited author by last name, last name plus first initial, and last name plus first and middle initial, there is an acute danger, particularly in the case of common last names, of misattributing citations. For example, there are two "D. Bell"'s in Table 5.1, Daniel and Derrick, and the Dialog count will attribute to each of them all citations to either "Bell" or "D. Bell." To enable the disentangling of such overlaps, a sample of the citations to each of the names in Table 5.1 was examined and corrections made accordingly, as with the other data sources; again, see the appendix for details.

7. I defend that use in Richard A. Posner, "An Economic Analysis of the Use of Citations in Law," 2 *American Law and Economics Review* 381 (2000). For evidence that "straight citation counts are highly correlated with virtually every refined measure of quality," see Jonathan Cole and Stephen Cole, "Measuring the Quality of Sociological Research: Problems in the Use of the *Science Citation Index*," 6 *American Sociologist* 23, 28 (1971).

8. Charles Kadushin, *The American Intellectual Elite* 30–31 (1974). He does not use the term "public intellectual," which was not yet in vogue; but his definition of "elite intellectual" is quite similar to my definition of "public intellectual." See id. at 7. His list was compiled essentially by sampling articles published in 1969 in twenty leading intellectual magazines and asking some of the intellectuals identified by this method to rate their peers ("colleague certification"). See id. at 18–19; Julie Hover, "Appendix: Sampling the American Intellectual Elite," in id. at 357. This is not a method well designed for identifying the public intellectuals who are most visible to the general public rather than to each other.

9. The three top-ranked intellectuals on his list were Daniel Bell, Noam Chomsky, and John Kenneth Galbraith, and among the lowest-ranked were Christopher Lasch and James Q. Wilson.

most scholarly citations. We were asking which of these scholars had become public intellectuals, not which public intellectuals also have scholarly reputations, which is what I'm interested in here. Table 5.1 is especially incomplete with respect to foreign intellectuals, but that is because only foreigners whose works are widely read and discussed in the United States are included. A public intellectual might be more important in his native country than anyone on my list, but he is excluded if he has no visibility to the educated general public in this country.

The term "public intellectual" is not yet used with sufficient frequency and consistency for a search of databases that use the term to yield a meaningful list (I tried). So not only is my list incomplete; it is not a random sample of public intellectuals, because there is no census of the population from which such a sample might be drawn. The list may not be representative either. It must therefore be used with the greatest caution as a basis for generalizing about the distribution of public intellectuals across fields, races, sexes, nations, or other classes, though in Table 5.2 I do offer summary statistics of these properties of the sample.

In Table 5.3 I try to correct for the likely nonrepresentativeness of Table 5.1 by creating a subsample consisting of the one hundred most prominent public intellectuals as measured by the number of media mentions they received. Despite the nonrandom and nonrepresentative character of the sample of public intellectuals in Table 5.1, it probably includes most public intellectuals who enjoy prominence today in the United States, and is at least a representative sample of them.[10]

The following qualifications should be noted:

First, "prominent" is not a synonym for "best," or even for "good." In fact, this is one of the major themes of this chapter.

Second, my definition is narrow—a public intellectual is a person who, drawing on his intellectual resources, addresses a broad though educated public on issues with a political or ideological dimension. John Rawls, excluded from my definition of public intellectual for the reason explained in Chapter 1, has a large number both of scholarly citations (3,933) and Web hits (15,825), and even, as I noted there, a respectable though small number of media mentions (374).

---

10. For a somewhat similar method of sample construction, see John P. Heinz et al., *The Hollow Core: Private Interests in National Policy Making* 20 (1993).

Third, it is not always easy to classify a person by field. Some public intellectuals, such as Jane Jacobs, do not work in a field otherwise represented on my list. Jacobs is usually described as an "urbanologist"—I have reclassified her as a sociologist. I have also lumped psychiatry in with psychology; editing in with publishing; and art, music, and film criticism under "literature" because of the similarity of the different areas of cultural criticism and because of a paucity of entries in each of those three fields. Yet even with these consolidations, one finds a number of public intellectuals who are active in more than one field. Robert Maynard Hutchins, Derek Bok, Gerhard Casper, and Edward Levi are all examples of academic lawyers who became university presidents. Should they be classified under law or under education? That would be arbitrary, and I have classified them under both.[11]

Fourth, it is not always easy to classify a public intellectual as academic or nonacademic. I have classified as academics only persons with a full-time academic appointment, and I have excluded a few of these whose full-time academic appointments constituted only an insignificant part of their career.

Fifth, excluded altogether are a number of public intellectuals, such as Theodore Roosevelt, Woodrow Wilson, Richard Nixon (remember all those books on foreign policy that he wrote after leaving office?), Newt Gingrich, and Winston Churchill, whose public-intellectual work was completely overshadowed by other aspects of their careers. But since government service is a frequent springboard to a public intellectual's career—for example, that of Henry Kissinger, a professor before he became national security adviser and later secretary of state, and a prolific author and commentator since—I have noted which public intellectuals on the list had government jobs, excluding internships, clerkships, part-time advisory roles, noncareer military service, and other limited stints.

Public intellectuals whom I have excluded on grounds of overshadowing are not limited to politicians. They include "activists," such as Anthony Amsterdam, Ramsey Clark, William Sloane Coffin, and Tom Hayden (the last also a politician); artists such as Picasso and Leonard Bernstein; scientists such as Albert Einstein; some publishers, such as

11. As a result, in Tables 5.2 and 5.5 the distribution across fields sums to more than 100 percent.

Hugh Hefner; writers such as Hemingway; and businessmen such as George Soros—all persons whose public-intellectual work, though by no means negligible, is slight relative to the work for which they are known and likely to be cited. A borderline case is that of Clinton's last secretary of the treasury, Lawrence Summers (now president of Harvard University). Most of the media mentions of him relate to his government work rather than to his economic ideas (he is a former economics professor) as such, and yet that work is doubtless informed to a considerable extent by his academic views, so I have included him.

Table 5.1 leaves out a number of journalists, writers, and policy analysts who, though they may be very able, are not very "intellectual" in the sense of not bringing the world of ideas, of "culture," into their writings, at least overtly. So Maureen Dowd, Ralph Nader, Studs Terkel, and Woodward and Bernstein are out, along with politically active actors, such as Robert Redford, Warren Beatty, Charlton Heston, and Jane Fonda; but William Safire, Thomas Friedman, and (for a reason explained in Chapter 10) Janet Malcolm are in. I acknowledge the arbitrariness of many of my decisions on whom to classify as a public intellectual. And I repeat that many intellectuals, including interdisciplinary ones, are excluded from my definition of public intellectual, and hence from Table 5.1, either because they don't write for a general audience or because their writings have no discernible political or ideological angle.

Table 5.2, the summary of statistical data concerning the public intellectuals listed in Table 5.1, divides those individuals into two groups, the living (as of mid-2000) and the dead, as a crude but serviceable way of identifying trends in the public-intellectual market. A comparison of the last two columns in Table 5.2 reveals a higher percentage of living public intellectuals who are female, black, or affiliated (that is, employed by either a university or a think tank) than of dead ones. The disparity in the percentage employed by think tanks is especially great, 1.1 percent among the dead versus 9 percent among the living, and is important in explaining the substantial difference in the percentage of dead and of living *independent* public intellectuals.[12] Notice the high average age even of the living public intellectuals (64). This is consistent

---

12. Of Kadushin's 1969 sample of 172 "elite intellectuals" (from which his list of the seventy most prominent ones was derived), only 40 percent were academics. Kadushin, note 8 above, at 20.

with the analysis in Chapter 2 of the likely age profile of the public intellectual.

Looking across fields, we see a marked increase in the percentage of public intellectuals who are either lawyers or economists. In the case of lawyers this reflects the growing importance of law in American society and the growing interdisciplinarity of academic lawyers, and in the case of economics it reflects the strides in breadth and rigor that economics has experienced in recent decades and perhaps the growth of government. The decided drop in the percentage of writers may reflect increased specialization of knowledge, which makes it difficult to write with authority about public issues.[13]

The hiring by the *New York Times* of Paul Krugman (see Chapters 3 and 4) to write a regular column on economics not in the business section of the paper but on the op-ed page is a portent of the growing share of the public-intellectual market held by economists. A number of economists besides Krugman, many of them highly distinguished, are active in this market: for example, Gary Becker, Robert Barro, Martin Feldstein, Milton Friedman, Robert Solow, and Lester Thurow (see Chapter 4). Economics is an improving field, and the improvements in a field should spill over into the public-intellectual work of its practitioners if they stick to their field in their public-intellectual work, as public-intellectual economists have tended to do. Most of their public-intellectual work belongs to the relatively unproblematic genres that I have dubbed "self-popularizing" and "own-field policy proposing." Nevertheless, as we'll see, the media do not appear to make careful quality discriminations among economists.

Table 5.3 lists the top one hundred public intellectuals in Table 5.1 by number of media mentions. Although this list includes a number of deservedly famous public intellectuals, including several discussed in greater detail in subsequent chapters, and excludes several of the false prophets discussed in Chapter 4, such as Paul Ehrlich, Edward

13. Cf. Tony Judt, *The Burden of Responsibility: Blum, Camus, Aron, and the French Twentieth Century* 17 (1998): "In the course of the 1950s the literary intellectual was steadily replaced by the social scientists—historians, sociologists, anthropologists, psychologists—without any obvious gain in the quality of public conversation. Whatever specialized knowledge might have been contributed by the growing prominence of men and women with academic expertise in various disciplines was neutralized by the expectation that, as intellectuals, they should be able to speak about anything."

Luttwak, and Lester Thurow, the inclusions, exclusions, and order-ing reinforce the concern expressed in previous chapters about quality variance in the public-intellectual market. A number of distinguished public intellectuals whom I shall be discussing in subsequent chap-ters do not make the list, such as Daniel Bell, Wayne Booth, Ronald Dworkin, Gertrude Himmelfarb, Martha Nussbaum, Robert Putnam, David Riesman, and Richard Rorty. The absence of Allan Bloom, and the higher percentage of living public intellectuals in this sample than in the next (Table 5.4, which ranks public intellectuals by scholarly cita-tions), are clues to the undiscriminating, short-memory-span character of this market. A number of the persons on the list are not highly re-garded for their contributions to public discussion, and a list in which Camille Paglia outranks Amartya Sen and James Q. Wilson can hardly be considered a reliable index of intellectual quality. Although Thurow is off the map, a glance back at Table 5.1 will reveal that he has more than twice as many media mentions as Gary Becker, though Becker's public-intellectual work (consisting of a regular column in *Business Week*) contains a higher percentage of accurate predictions.[14] To main-tain perspective, I point out that the media celebrity of even celebrated public intellectuals tends to be relatively modest. Only three of the public intellectuals in my samples have more than 10,000 media men-tions, and the highest-ranking one, Henry Kissinger, has fewer than 13,000. Compare Michael Jordan, with 108,000 media mentions, Tony Blair with 138,000, Marilyn Monroe with 33,000, and Colin Powell with 20,000.[15]

Table 5.4 lists the one hundred top public intellectuals in Table 5.1 by number of *scholarly* citations (and thus is limited to the academics in Table 5.1). Although there is a degree of overlap with Table 5.3 (as I noted earlier, eighteen of the top public intellectuals as measured by media mentions are also among the public intellectuals in Table 5.1 who received the most scholarly citations), the difference in ranking is notable. Not that the most prominent academic public intellectuals are negligible scholars; the fifty academics in Table 5.3 account for 16.7 percent of the total number of scholarly citations received by the 354

14. See Gary S. Becker and Guity Nashat Becker, *The Economics of Life: From Baseball to Affirmative Action to Immigration, How Real-World Issues Affect Our Everyday Life* 9–10 (1997).

15. I have rounded these off to the nearest thousand. The list was compiled before Colin Powell became secretary of state.

academics in Table 5.1. This will give a sense of what the cost to scholarship might be if scholars with a thirst for celebrity were denied the
chance to become prominent public intellectuals and as a result were
deflected to a nonacademic career. Yet another way to interpret this figure is that it suggests what is lost to scholarship by the deflection of
scholarly energies to the public-intellectual market, since, as we'll see
later, the most prominent academic public intellectuals would probably
have more citations if they were more focused on scholarship.

Table 5.4 should not be taken to be an authoritative guide to the relative scholarly standing of academic public intellectuals, let alone of all
scholars, since most scholars are not public intellectuals. Many of the
high-ranking public intellectuals in this table are highly controversial
in scholarly circles, and a number of academically distinguished public
intellectuals do not show up at all—which is no surprise, since number of citations in scholarly journals is at best a crude proxy of quality,
influence, or reputation, especially when used to compare scholars in
different fields. Differences across fields in citation practices, in the
number of scholarly journals, and in the size of the relevant scholarly communities may influence rank without regard to merit, though,
as mentioned, these distortions may not be as serious as one might
think.[16]

One problem with interpreting the results in Table 5.3 (top one hundred public intellectuals by media mentions) is that many of the citations may not be to public-intellectual work at all. A good example,
again, is Noam Chomsky, whose scientific work is of some interest to
the general educated public and might therefore be mentioned in the
popular media. But in a random sample of 150 media mentions of
Chomsky, almost 90 percent were of his political rather than his scientific views. As for the writers on the list, since much of their writing has
a political edge, it would not be feasible to apportion their media mentions between the public-intellectual and the purely literary interest in
their work.

Figure 5.1 plots the number of media mentions against the rank of
the public intellectuals in Table 5.3. The highest point on the curve denotes the number of media mentions of Henry Kissinger, the top-

16. As Cole and Cole, note 7 above, at 26, point out, field effects are likely to cancel out.
The larger the field, the more citations there are, but also the more citable books and articles,
so that the average number of citations per scholar may not be any higher.

ranked public intellectual by media mentions, and the bottom the number of media mentions of George Stigler, the bottom-ranked public intellectual in that table. Notice the highly convex shape of the curve. The number of media mentions falls very steeply at first, but beginning at rank number 22 (Gore Vidal) it declines much more gradually. Just the ten top-ranking public intellectuals in Table 5.3 account for 31 percent of all the media mentions of the public intellectuals in that table and for 21 percent of the media mentions of all 546 public intellectuals in Table 5.1, while the bottom ten account for only 5 percent of the total number of media mentions of the public intellectuals in Table 5.3. This pattern implies a highly uneven distribution of celebrity across public intellectuals. Despite the vast range of topics addressed by the public-intellectual community, it seems that a relative handful of public intellectuals can satisfy much of the demand for public-intellectual work. This is a possible sign of an undiscriminating market. The indolent gatekeepers of the public-intellectual market may prefer having a celebrity intellectual opine outside the area of his expertise to searching for the particular expert on the particular topic.

The shape of the curve in Figure 5.1 is consistent with the hypothesis that public intellectuals are valued for confirmation of the audience's biases rather than just as sources of information or insight. The reader confirms his membership in a community of like-minded thinkers by reading the same intellectual that the other members of the community are reading. (Just buying and displaying his books may identify one as a member of a certain ideological community, whether or not one bothers to read any of them.)[17] That intellectual—Kissinger for foreign-policy hardliners, Buckley for conservative Catholics, and so forth—then becomes a focus of discussion, a rallying point, the node of a social network, a personification of the community's position. This pattern requires that each community converge on one or a very small number of intellectuals; otherwise the focal-point purpose of personifying the community would be blurred.

Tyler Cowen, building on earlier work by Moshe Adler,[18] has made a similar point with regard to mass culture. Fans tend to coalesce around

17. For this and other examples of social influences on demand, see Gary S. Becker, "A Note on Restaurant Pricing and Other Examples of Social Influences on Price," in Becker, *Accounting for Tastes* 195 (1996).

18. Moshe Adler, "Stardom and Talent," 75 *American Economic Review* 208 (1985).

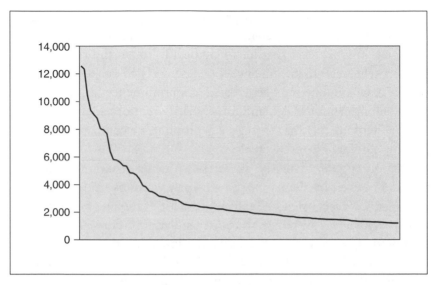

Figure 5.1 Media mentions as a function of rank

a handful of "stars," people who are not necessarily the best in their field (Cowen instances Dennis Rodman, the basketball player) but whose vivid personalities make them apt focal points for like-minded people to organize around.[19] Convergence on a focal point may be the only way of coordinating a group of people too large and dispersed to be coordinated in any other way. "If many fans seek to coordinate around a star performer, the standard for choosing that star must be visible, easy to observe, and easy to evaluate. Mass culture therefore oversimplifies moral and aesthetic issues, even relative to the views of its constituent fans."[20] The same leveling process may be at work in the public-intellectual market.

Another factor in the concentration of public attention on a handful of public intellectuals is rational herd instinct. The information about the actual quality of public intellectuals is poor enough to make it sensible for a member of the public to focus on the prominent ones, that is, the ones to whom most other people are paying attention. The choices made by the others convey some, though slight, information about

19. Tyler Cowen, *What Price Fame?* 16–22 (2000). See also Joshua Gamson, *Claims to Fame: Celebrity in Contemporary America* 132 (1994).

20. Cowen, note 19 above, at 17.

who is worth reading. This factor reinforces the skewness created by the solidarity or "fandom" element in public-intellectual celebrity.

I noted in Chapter 2 that luck may be a factor in the rise of many public intellectuals to prominence. Luck is poorly correlated with quality. Yet once a public intellectual achieves prominence, a snowball effect resulting from the demand for solidarity reinforcement and from rational herd instinct may increase his prominence compared to other, possibly abler public intellectuals.

This interpretation of the skewness of media mentions is undermined, however, by the pattern of scholarly citations to the academic public intellectuals listed in Table 5.4 (the list of the one hundred academics in Table 5.1 who have the most scholarly citations). For it is just as skewed. The ten most-cited academics in Table 5.4 have 29 percent of the total scholarly citations to the individuals in that table and 23 percent of the total scholarly citations to all the academics in Table 5.1, while the ten least-cited individuals in Table 5.4 have only 4 percent of the total number of scholarly citations to the individuals in Table 5.4. These figures are almost identical to those for the distribution of media mentions. But remember that the population from which Table 5.4 is drawn is limited to public intellectuals. A proper comparison of the skewness of media mentions with the skewness of scholarly citations would sample from the scholarly community as a whole rather than just its public-intellectual wing. The skewness of scholarly citations to the individuals in Table 5.4 may signify merely that immensely celebrated academics are likely to have at least slight media recognition and hence to be included in Table 5.1 and thus to be eligible for inclusion in Table 5.4, while most of the academics in Table 5.1 (and hence Table 5.4) might be drawn from a lower tier of academic renown.

Field effects are also a possible distorting factor. In Landes's and my study of public-intellectual lawyers, a study free from field effects and based on a sample selected for scholarly distinction, newspaper mentions were much more skewed than scholarly citations. The top 10 percent in our sample, as measured by scholarly citations, had only 18 percent of the total number of those citations,[21] compared to 29 percent in

21. Landes and Posner, note 3 above, at 336. The figure reported there is actually 22 percent, but it is the share of the top ten of a sample of ninety-four, which is more than 10 percent of the sample; my figure is for the top nine, a little less than 10 percent. I was not able to make a similar adjustment for the bottom 10 percent; the bottom ten had 5.4 percent of the citations.

Table 5.4. In the only comprehensive citations ranking of scholars that I have found—the one hundred authors who received the most citations in the *Social Sciences Citation Index* between 1969 and 1977—the top ten had 24 percent of the total citations and the bottom ten percent,[22] which are, respectively, lower and higher than the corresponding figures computed from Table 5.4 (29 percent and 4 percent).

We can expect skewness in any market in which cost is invariant to output; this is the "superstar" effect discussed in Chapter 2. It costs no more to cite the best scholarly work in a field than the second best, so the best are likely to garner most of the citations even if the quality difference is small. It is only the *incremental* skewness of public-intellectual citations over that of scholarly citations that suggests the presence in the public-intellectual market of additional forces, such as the interrelated factors of luck, herd instinct, and high information costs.

Table 5.5 presents summary statistics on the public intellectuals listed in Table 5.3, and thus bears the same relation to Table 5.3 as Table 5.2 does to Table 5.1. However, because of the small number of dead in the sample in Table 5.4, I did not do a separate tabulation of them. I note, however, that the average age of the sixty-eight living persons in the table is 64, the same as for the larger sample, while the average age of the thirty-two dead is 104, which is just a bit higher than for the larger sample.

The results in Table 5.5 are broadly similar to those in the first column (combining living and dead) of Table 5.2.[23] The most striking difference is the much higher percentage of writers than in Table 5.2—34 percent versus 14.3 percent. This is one reason for the lower percentage of academics in the top one hundred (50 percent versus 64.8 percent), since writers are less likely to have academic appointments than persons in most of the other fields listed in the tables. The fact that academic representation is less in the more select sample of public intellectuals provides some support for the proposition that academization may be inimical to public-intellectual performance. But the support is weak; a disproportionate number of the foreigners in the large sample

---

22. Computed from Eugene Garfield, "The 100 Most-Cited *SSCI* Authors," *Current Comments*, Nov. 6, 1978, p. 5; also published in Garfield, *Essays of an Information Scientist*, vol. 3, p. 675 (1977–1978).

23. The qualification in "broadly" deserves emphasis; a chi-square test indicates that the two samples (the large one of Table 5.1 and the small one of Table 5.2) are not well correlated.

are dead, indicating that they are drawn from a somewhat older age distribution and so belonged to a generation less likely to seek or find academic employment than later generations.

Table 5.5 reports the average number of media mentions for each type of public intellectual.[24] Consistent with my thesis concerning the effects of academization, nonacademics tend to be mentioned more heavily than academics.[25] The heavier media citation rate for living than for dead public intellectuals is a further clue to the presentist—or, less politely, the trendy or ephemeral—character of much public-intellectual work. Of course scholarly work, too, is expected to depreciate.[26] But it is notable that while the thirty-two dead public intellectuals in Table 5.3 receive on average only two-thirds as many media mentions as their living counterparts, the twenty-seven dead academic public intellectuals in Table 5.4 receive *more* scholarly citations on average than the living ones—2,271 versus 2,189. Public-intellectual work is more ephemeral than scholarship.

The strong effect of government service on citations, and the fact that journalism, economics, and political science are the most heavily cited fields, are indicative of the practical nature of the interest that the media take in public-intellectual work. Gary Becker reports that George Stigler (whom we met in Chapter 2) was hired by a business magazine to write a monthly column:

> Stigler was not only an outstanding economist but one of the finest economic writers. George's columns were witty, incisive, and well-written, but they concentrated on analysis and offered few policy recommendations. After a year he quit writing them because he felt that he was writing only for himself since he received essentially no feedback from readers. This was mainly because he did not take a strong stand on policy questions.[27]

24. There is no corresponding column in Table 5.2 because the list of public intellectuals on which that table is based (that is, the list in Table 5.1) is not random and cannot be assumed to be representative, as I argue that the list used in Table 5.4 can be.

25. The high rate of citation to members of think tanks is not meaningful because of the small size of that subsample.

26. See, for example, William M. Landes and Richard A. Posner, "The Influence of Economics on Law: A Quantitative Study," 36 *Journal of Law and Economics* 385, 395–397 (1993).

27. Becker and Becker, note 14 above, at 6.

My guess, however, is that the principal significance of government service is that it makes an intellectual better known to the public. Name recognition is an important asset in a market characterized by significant uncertainty about quality. The fact that you've "heard of" a person is some reason for you to think he might be worth listening to.

Although about two-thirds of the public intellectuals in Table 5.5 are politically to the left, the average number of citations to the left-leaning and to the right-leaning public intellectuals is very close. This pattern is consistent with my conjecture that public intellectuals primarily address people who agree with their stance. In the extreme case in which left-leaning public intellectuals are read only by left-leaning members of the public and right-leaning public intellectuals only by right-leaning ones, we would expect the average public intellectual in each camp to have the same number of citations. The alternative would be for each political position to be occupied by the same number of public intellectuals but with the left-leaning ones having on average twice as many media mentions as the right-leaners. That would be unlikely. People belonging to the right-wing minority presumably have on average the same taste for celebrities as those belonging to the left-wing majority. Therefore each right-wing public intellectual should be as prominent on average as each left-wing one. Each firmament has its own stars, and they shine about as brightly, but one has more stars than the other.

There is another reason to expect this pattern. Assuming that media mentions are correlated with full income, which consists, we recall, of acclaim (for which media mentions are a proxy) as well as other nonpecuniary satisfactions and pecuniary income, we would expect the average number of media mentions to be about the same for right- and left-leaners. For if it were otherwise—say the average left-leaning public intellectual had substantially more media mentions than the average right-leaner—this would imply a higher full income for the former than for the latter. There would then be a tendency for public intellectuals to reposition themselves politically until an equilibrium was restored. It would be like what happens when wages in the same job are higher in one part of the country than in another and relocation costs are small relative to the difference: workers migrate from the low-wage to the high-wage region until the difference in wages (minus relocation costs and any cost-of-living difference) is erased.

In superficial tension with this suggestion, circulation figures for the principal magazines that are heavily devoted to public-intellectual expression (the "Group A" publications in Table 5.6)[28] indicate parity between left-leaning (in the left-hand column) and right-leaning such magazines. But these figures are misleading, because most other major venues for public-intellectual expression are left-leaning; they are not included in Group A because public-intellectual expression is not a principal focus of them, but are listed separately in Group B. When the circulation figures for both groups are combined, 65 percent of the publications weighted by volume are left-leaning. This is consistent with the balance between left- and right-leaning top one hundred public intellectuals and with my hypothesis of parity of celebrity of individual public intellectuals regardless of their political bent.

The two-thirds preponderance of left-leaning public intellectuals suggests that the market for public-intellectual work is primarily a left-wing market, which is consistent with one's general impressions about the political leanings of highly educated people who take an interest in public affairs, a group in which engineers and business executives, many of them at once conservative and highly educated, are underrepresented. But there is no indication that the media are *discriminating* in favor of left-leaning public intellectuals. They would be if right-leaners received more mentions on average than left-leaners, because that would suggest that the media were dipping deeper into the pool of left-leaning public intellectuals than into the pool of right-leaning ones, that is, that they preferred obscure leftists to obscure rightists.

Jewish public intellectuals, however, are mentioned more frequently on average than non-Jewish ones, while, in contrast, black and female public intellectuals are mentioned on average less frequently than white male public intellectuals. This pattern is suggestive, though only weakly so, as we'll see, of discrimination (which need not be invidious, however) against Jews and against white males. As between a relatively more prominent white male or Jewish public intellectual and a relatively less prominent black or female or non-Jewish public intellectual, the media tend to choose the latter. They may be catering to their audience's preferences. Or they may believe that the black or the woman is likely to have a different point of view from that of the white male that

---

28. I omit the *Atlantic Monthly*, as it seems to me to have—remarkably for a public-intellectual venue—no political leaning.

should not be overlooked, or (less plausibly) that many Jews "think alike" and therefore proper diversity requires a limit on how much media attention Jewish public intellectuals should receive.

The heavy overrepresentation of Jews among prominent public intellectuals is no doubt related to their overrepresentation in the media and in academia, and perhaps specifically to the fact that Jews' *verbal* IQ is especially high relative to that of other groups.[29]

Table 5.7 correlates the three measures of reputation (Web hits, media mentions, and scholarly citations) for the fifty academics who are among the one hundred most prominent public intellectuals as measured by number of media mentions within the past five years. Because of the heterogeneous character of the Web—the fact that Web hits are to both academic and nonacademic work (hence the positive, though extremely weak, correlation between Web hits and scholarly citations shown in the table)—the correlation between media mentions and scholarly citations is the most interesting. A positive correlation would imply that public-intellectual status and scholarly achievement are complements and a negative correlation that they are substitutes, while if they are uncorrelated this implies that public-intellectual status and scholarly distinction are unrelated. The correlation is negative, implying that media mentions come at the expense of scholarly citations (and vice versa), which makes sense if we think of public-intellectual work as neither supporting academic work nor as much influenced by scholarly distinction. The correlations shown in Table 5.7 are not statistically significant, however.

Table 5.8 uses multiple-regression analysis to explain the variance in the prominence of academic public intellectuals as disclosed by Table 5.3. The dependent variable is the number of media mentions of the fifty academic public intellectuals in that table. The independent variables are the principal categorizations in Table 5.3 and 5.5 (except for fields) plus number of scholarly citations.[30] In this and the subsequent tables coefficients whose sign is statistically significantly different from

29. Kevin MacDonald, *A People That Shall Dwell Alone: Judaism as a Group Evolutionary Strategy* 189 (1994). Kadushin's sample had an even higher percentage of Jews—50. Kadushin, note 8 above, at 23.

30. All the independent variables except scholarly citations are dummy variables, that is, variables that take a value of either one or zero. The number of observations (indicated by N) is smaller than the sample being tested because of missing data.

I did not use age as a variable, because age and whether living or dead are highly correlated, and the living/dead variable produced the better fit.

zero at the conventional 5 percent level (meaning that there is only a 5 percent probability that the sign of the coefficient is actually zero) are in boldface.[31]

The only two statistically significant coefficients in Table 5.8 are government service and (in the smaller sample only) scholarly citations. Government service has, as expected, a positive effect on media mentions. The negative effect of scholarly citations[32] implies that academic distinction does not contribute to public-intellectual prominence—indeed reduces it, presumably either because scholarly output comes at the expense of public-intellectual work or because of some deeper incompatibility between the scholarly and the public-intellectual careers. An academic who wants to succeed as a public intellectual might be well advised to substitute government service for additional scholarly publications!

The negative correlation between media mentions and scholarly citations is especially striking when one considers the advantage that public intellectuals have in the citations derby. Most public intellectuals write well, which makes their academic work more accessible to academics in other fields, and so they are more likely to pick up citations in journals in other fields than their colleagues who are less gifted writers. Moreover, the prominence they attain as a result of their public-intellectual work makes them more likely to come to the mind of an academic in another field who is doing research out of his field, and hence to be cited. This is the "Matthew effect" (to him who has, more shall be

31. The *t*-statistic must be at least 1.96 (positive or negative) to be statistically significant at the 5 percent level, and somewhat higher when the sample size is below 120, as it is in a number of my regressions. The R^2 is the percentage of the variance in the observations that is accounted for by the regression equation. The adjusted R^2 reduces the R^2 to reflect the fact that as more and more independent variables are added the amount of variance accounted for by the equation will generally increase (and will never decrease) regardless of the explanatory value of those variables: in the limit, if there were as many regressors as observations, the R^2 would equal 1. The *F*-statistic is a measure of whether the equation as a whole has significant explanatory power; stated differently, it is a test of the joint significance of the independent variables. All my regressions "pass" the *F* test at the 3 percent or better significance level, as shown in the "Prob. >" row of each table.

32. A scholarly citation reduces the number of media mentions by only .61 (less than one), while government service adds more than 1,000 media mentions in the larger sample and almost 2,400 in the smaller one. However, the percentage effect of scholarly citations on media mentions is not trivial, as shown more clearly in the next regression.

given) that the sociologist Robert Merton emphasized in a pioneering study of academic reputation.[33]

A spot check indicates, in fact, that well-known public-intellectual academics such as Stephen Jay Gould, Martha Nussbaum, and Richard Rorty receive a sizable percentage of their scholarly citations in journals outside of their scholarly fields. That there is nevertheless a significant negative correlation between media and academic renown suggests that some incompatibility between public-intellectual work and scholarly work is overriding the academic public intellectual's natural advantage in the competition for scholarly citations.

A more direct test of the hypothesis that scholarship and public-intellectual work are substitutes rather than complements would be to correlate the academic output (perhaps weighted by citations) of the academics in Tables 5.1 or 5.3 with their public-intellectual output. That would be a large project, and I leave it for future research.[34]

In the larger sample analyzed in Table 5.8 (the columns under "All"), the negative effect of scholarly citations is replaced by a statistically insignificant positive effect, implying that media and scholarly renown are uncorrelated.[35] The significant negative correlation in the smaller sample is more revealing, however, when one considers the catch-as-catch-can character of the larger sample (and notice its much lower R^2 and adjusted R^2). In any event it is apparent that the media are selecting public intellectuals with little regard for scholarly standing. This is unsurprising in light of the character of the public-intellectual market examined in this and the preceding chapters.

Notice also in Table 5.8 that while the signs on the variables for race, sex, and ethnicity are the same as implied by Table 5.5, they are not statistically significant when the other variables bearing on public-intellectual prominence are taken into account. If there is discrimination of

33. Robert K. Merton, "The Matthew Effect in Science," 159 *Science* 56 (1968).

34. Cf. Harriet Zuckerman, *Scientific Elite: Nobel Laureates in the United States* 222–230 (1977), finding that receipt of a Nobel prize reduces the prize winner's academic productivity, in part because of "requests for advice, speeches, review articles, greater participation in policy decisions, and other public services," id. at 222, which sound like the demands that public-intellectual status makes on an academic's time.

35. In Landes's and my study of public-intellectual lawyers, scholarly citations had a positive effect on newspaper mentions, though the effect was statistically significant in only one of the two regression equations that tested for this effect. Landes and Posner, note 3 above, at 339 (tab. 7).

the sort suggested earlier, it appears to be weak. There is, as I expected, no indication of political discrimination.

Because of the skewness of media mentions and scholarly citations, there is an argument for transforming both of these variables into natural logarithms before performing the regression. Regression analysis assumes linear variables, and a logarithm is a linear transformation of a nonlinear function. Table 5.8a is the same regression as Table 5.8 but with these two variables transformed into natural logarithms.

The higher R^2's, adjusted R^2's, and F-statistics suggest that the logarithmic form does make a better fit with the data. The results for the smaller sample are consistent with the results in Table 5.8, although the negative coefficient on the scholarly citations variable dips below the 5 percent significance level (it is, however, significant at the 6 percent level), presumably because the logarithmic form has the effect of reducing the weight of the larger observations. The most interesting result in the larger sample (given its catch-as-catch-can character, I do not consider the significant positive coefficients of the black and right-leaner variables to be particularly meaningful) is the strongly positive coefficient of the scholarly citations variables, reversing the sign in the small sample. Variables that are expressed in natural logarithms are elasticities, so Table 5.8a indicates that whereas in the small sample a 1-percent increase in scholarly citations is associated with a one-seventh of 1-percent decrease in media mentions, in the large sample a 1-percent increase in scholarly citations is associated with a one-third of 1-percent increase in media mentions.

Can these results be reconciled? I think they can be. Because of the highly skewed distribution of media mentions, the one hundred most prominent public intellectuals have the lion's share (in fact 67.5 percent) of them, with the rest being divided among more than two hundred other public intellectuals. The large sample is therefore dominated by public intellectuals who can fairly be described as obscure to the popular media, especially when correction is made for characteristics such as government service that might propel some of them to public attention. For the others, the *only* thing that might give them *some* public exposure is their scholarly distinction, and so the statistically significant positive correlation between scholarly citations and media mentions in the large sample is not surprising (and again the logarithmic form results in giving less weight to the heavy hitters in this group). Among the most prominent public intellectuals, however, who attract most of the media's attention, other factors determine relative position. To be among the most prominent public intellectuals requires more than scholarly renown. Indeed, scholarly renown may operate as a drag on public prominence by taking time away from public-intellectual work, or may reflect a mindset or intellectual style inimical to communication with a nonspecialist audience.

Tables 5.8 and 5.8a are limited to academic public intellectuals. Table 5.9 expands the analysis first to the full set of the one hundred most prominent public intellectuals and then to the entire sample of 546 public intellectuals. But in place of scholarly citations—for remember that I counted scholarly citations only to academics—I insert a dummy variable that takes a value of one if the individual is an academic and zero if he is not. Table 5.9a reruns the regression using logs for the dependent variable.

The results in these two tables are similar to those in the preceding two. Notice in Table 5.9 the significant negative coefficient on "academic": other things being equal, an academic public intellectual is likely to receive less media attention than a nonacademic one. Also notable is the significant negative coefficient on "dead" in the large sample, and in the small one it misses significance at the conventional 5 percent level by only a whisker. Other things being equal, then, a public intellectual who is dead is less likely to receive media attention than a living public intellectual. This is consistent with the presentist and celebrity emphasis of the media's interest in intellectuals.

The log version of Table 5.9 holds few surprises. In both samples in this table the government-service and academic variables are significant at the 5 percent level and in the same direction as in Table 5.9. Death is also significantly negative in both samples. The effects are large. In the top one hundred sample, being an academic reduces one's media mentions by 37 percent, and being dead by 30 percent, while government service increases them by 57 percent.

In Table 5.10, finally, another regression of media mentions in both the 100 and 546 public-intellectual samples, I substitute the principal fields (as measured by number of occupants in the samples) from Table 5.5 for the academic and think-tank variables. As in the preceding table, the effect of government service on media mentions is strongly positive, while death has a significant negative effect in the large sample and a negative effect significant at the 10 percent level in the small one. What is new is the strong positive effect of being either a journalist or a writer. Both journalists and writers of imaginative literature are specialists in communicating with a lay audience. That is further evidence of the essentially rhetorical character of public-intellectual work. When rerun in logarithmic form (not published), the regression equation of Table 5.10 yields virtually identical results for the small sample, but in the large sample journalism, while still having a positive effect on media mentions, is no longer statistically significant, while humanities, social science, law, and publishing all have statistically significant *negative* coefficients. The humanities and the social sciences are academic fields and most of the lawyers in the sample are academics; these negative coefficients may be picking up the general negative effect of academic employment on media mentions, one of the principal findings in this chapter.

Appendix: Search and Estimation Procedures[36]

Web Hits. Web hits were counted using the Google search engine (www.google.com). Google was chosen over other search engines (such as Yahoo, Excite, and AltaVista) because of its method of recording hits. Most search engines rank hits solely by the number of times the word or phrase in question (for purposes of this book, a name) appears. Google weights hits by the importance of a Web site as measured by its links to other sites.[37]

Each name was first searched for as it appears in Table 5.1, except that, where applicable, the person's first or middle initial (not shown in Table 5.1 unless necessary for identification) was included. The first thirty hits were examined to determine the percentage of correct ones. This percentage was then applied to the total number of hits. The first thirty hits were also examined for other variants of the same name. For example, a search of "Robert H Bork" yielded hits that included "Robert Bork" within a hit that also included "Robert H Bork." When a

36. This appendix was prepared in collaboration with my research assistants Ilisabeth Smith and Bryan Dayton.

37. For more information regarding Google's method of sorting and ranking, consult their Web site. Click on "Everything Else," then under the column entitled "The Search," and then, under "Our Technology," read the document entitled "Why Use Google."

variant was detected, it was searched for separately. Thus we searched for "Robert Bork" – "Robert H Bork" (the minus sign eliminates duplicates). Again the first thirty hits were examined to yield the percentage of correct hits for that search. Finally, the name was searched backward, again eliminating duplicates (no middle initial was used when searching a name backward, because "Bork Robert" also picks up "Bork Robert H"). After a sample was taken from this group as well, the number of correct hits for each search was added and the percentage of correct hits calculated and then applied to the total number of hits that Google records for the individual in question. The errors encountered in this type of search are largely due to finding other people by the same name or, to a lesser degree, finding lists like ". . . Jane Bork, Robert Smith . . ." when searching for "Bork Robert." These errors were corrected by the sampling procedure.

The Web pages that were hit in the Google search included home pages (either created by university or other employers or created by fans), announcements of speaking engagements at various locations, and online publications.

Media Mentions. Media mentions were counted using the three Lexis/Nexis databases—Major Newspapers, Magazine Stories (Combined), and Transcripts—described in note 5 above. The procedure for searching in each database was the same. Because these media include informal materials, nicknames were included in the search protocol. For example, Robert Bork was searched under "sing (Robert or Bob) pre/2 Bork." "Sing" stands for singular, to avoid any hits on "Roberts." ("Bobs" is not as much of a worry.)[38] Using "(Robert or Bob)" brings up mentions of both names. "Pre/2" means that "(Robert or Bob)" must appear no more than two words ahead of "Bork." This allows for middle initials or middle names.

Searches were run for the five years from July/August 1995 to July/August 2000. If the individual had fewer than one thousand mentions (the upper limit that Lexis displays), the first one hundred were examined and the percentage correct was then applied to the total number of hits to produce the estimate of the total used in the tables in this

---

38. One can also use the command "plur" (for "plural"), for example in the case of Patricia Williams, to avoid getting mentions that include "William." Another command, "caps" ("capital letters"), was used for names that double as common words, such as "White" and "Will."

chapter. If he or she had more than one thousand mentions, a sample of one hundred taken from two different periods within the past five years (recent and earlier) was examined to determine the correct percentage of hits. This involved breaking down the years searched from "last 5 years" to smaller increments. Dividing the search into "last 2 years" and then "date, 1995 to date, 1998" was often sufficient, but some searches of individuals having a very large number of mentions had to be broken down into months, weeks, or even days. This illustrates the sensitivity of the media search to time. A and B might have the same number of media mentions for the five-year period, but if A happened to have a "hot" week when his mentions were counted, a misleading impression of his media celebrity relative to B might be created.

Because the Transcripts database consists of transcriptions of the spoken word, spelling was erratic. An effort was made to account for the most likely misspellings by, for example, searching for "Stephen or Steven" and for "Rosenb!rg" (i.e., "Rosenberg" or "Rosenburg"). But some mentions were doubtless not picked up by the search.

Format was also a problem with this search. "Thurman pre/2 Arnold" also brings up mentions of Uma Thurman and Arnold Schwarzeneggar, because they also fit the "Thurman pre/2 Arnold" format. But these errors were corrected by our sampling procedure.

Scholarly Citations. The counts of scholarly citations were performed using the *Science Citation Index*, the *Social Sciences Citation Index*, and the *Arts and Humanities Citation Index*, all compiled by the Institute for Scientific Information (ISI). These three databases were accessed using Dialog (www.dialogclassic.com). Scholarly citations were counted only for those individuals listed in Table 5.1 having full-time academic employment for a significant part of their career. All of these, regardless of field, were searched for in the *Social Sciences Citation Index*, on the theory that any academic who is a public intellectual and thus writing on issues of a political or ideological character might be doing at least some scholarly work as a social scientist or of interest to social scientists. Academics whose fields are anthropology, biology, chemistry, computer science, linguistics, medicine, and/or physics were also searched for in the *Science Citation Index;* those in architecture, classics, literature, philosophy, and/or theology, and writers, were also searched for in the *Arts and Humanities Citation Index*. Persons in borderline fields—education, journalism, politics, publishing, and science writer—were searched for in either the science or the humanities index (or both), as seemed appropriate given the nature of the individual's interests, as well as in the social sciences index. Law was treated as a social science in this search, since the search was limited to academics and thus excluded practicing lawyers.

The Dialog search embraced the publication years 1995 to 2000.[39] The initial search was for each academic in Table 5.1 as a cited author within the subset of these publication years. For example, Robert H. Bork would be searched for under "s s1 and (ca=bork or ca=bork r or ca=bork rh)." The first "s" stands for "search," a Dialog command. "s1" is subset 1, which means "publication year greater than or equal to 1995." "ca" is "cited author" and here we searched by the person's last name only, or last name and first initial, or last name and both initials, to catch all possible permutations of the names as listed in the ISI databases.

The second step in the search was to remove self-citations, which would be performed with the command "s − not (au=bork or au=bork r or au=bork rh)." This command excluded any citations by Bork to his own work. For names searched in more than one citation index, the next step was to remove duplicates ("rd"), since some journals are listed in more than one of the ISI databases.

Dialog has a feature called "postings" that enables the number of citations that fulfill all the search criteria (correct publication year and correct cited author who is not the author of the citing article) to be displayed. Another option is "items," which is the total number of articles citing the author in question. Items is incomplete, because the author may be cited for more than one work in an article. Postings includes the number of times the cited author is cited, but it also includes the number of times the correct publication year appears (which should be once in every article) because "publication year" was one of our search criteria. The number we report, therefore, is postings minus items.[40]

39. Dialog includes in 1995 those journals entered into its system during that year, and so includes some late issues from 1994, while the late issues from 1995 appear in the 1996 category.

40. Usually the list of citations in an article has only one entry (one posting) for each work cited. For example, if an article cites three different pages in a book, that will normally be recorded as one posting, not three. But occasionally, mainly in the case of citations to articles

Once a set of citations to a given individual in Table 5.1 is created with the appropriate parameters (publication years, variations in the spellings of the person's name as cited author, and self-citations and duplicate citations removed), the set is then sampled. The first thirty entries (called "records" by Dialog)—that is, the first thirty citing articles in the set—are brought up by the command "t s_ /9/1–30." "t" stands for "type," the command to display the records. "s_" is again the subset identified after the "remove duplicates" step. "9" designates the type of format we used to view the records. This was the full format, because it is the only one that shows the name of the work by the cited author, thus enabling us to identify whether the record is a correct hit or not. "1–30" means records 1 through 30. Once the thirty records have been sampled, the number that are correct is converted to a percentage and applied to the "Postings minus Items" number to produce the final estimate.

Typographical errors in Dialog or in the ISI databases may have resulted in some legitimate hits being missed. Those errors, however, are likely to be very small. Of course, sampling error is possible in all the corrective searches. Because sampling was limited to a recent five-year period, public intellectuals whose academic and public-intellectual careers did not coincide might come up misleadingly short on either media mentions or scholarly citations, depending on the rate at which citations depreciate. For example, a prominent scholar in a field in which scholarly citations depreciate rapidly (perhaps because it is a highly progressive field, such as physics) who switched into public-intellectual work might have few scholarly citations yet be highly renowned as a scholar—that renown might have been what enabled him to make the switch! However, it is unclear that errors such as these are biased in favor of any of the hypotheses tested in this chapter.

(particularly articles published in law journals and in scientific journals) rather than to books, there will be a separate posting for each *page* cited. A spot check suggests that the count of scholarly citations is inflated for some of the academics in Table 5.1 by anywhere from 5 percent (in the case of one legal academic whose cited work consists mainly of books) to 36 percent (in the case of another legal academic most of whose cited work consists of articles), though most such cases appear to fall between 20 and 30 percent. No thorough check was conducted and none of the totals was adjusted. The problem is not limited to legal and scientific academics, because law journals are voracious citers and many of the social scientists in Table 5.1 are cited frequently in law journals and so are also subject to the inflationary effect explained in this note.

After completing the study reported in this chapter, I expanded my list of public intellectuals from 546 to 607, by adding names that occurred to or were suggested to me, and I replicated the study on the expanded list. Although there were some different results, the differences are insufficient to warrant encumbering the book with the longer study. Also, a weakness of that study is that the search for scholarly citations to and media mentions of the additional sixty-one names, being conducted roughly two months after the search on the original 546 names, is not strictly comparable; number of media mentions in particular is highly sensitive to the time searched.

All the data used in both studies, that of the list of 546 and that of the list of 607, and all the tables (including regressions) for both studies, are available on the Web to anyone who wants to check the accuracy of my findings or to use my data in further studies.[41]

41. The Web site is http://home.uchicago.edu/~rposner/publicintellect. It is accessible either directly or through my academic Web site, which is http://home.uchicago.edu/~rposner.

Table 5.1 Public intellectuals: media mentions, Web hits, and scholarly citations (1995–2000)

Name	Media	Web	Scholarly
Abrams, Floyd	1,285	1,295	N.A.
Ackerman, Bruce	457	1,367	1,400
Adler, Mortimer	130	3,931	92
Adler, Renata	127	387	N.A.
Adorno, Theodor	230	7,240	2,776
Amar, Akhil	357	1,094	1,704
Anderson, Kenneth	63	361	374
Appiah, Anthony	269	2,302	487
Arendt, Hannah	1,062	14,182	1,122
Arnold, Thurman	30	401	171
Aron, Raymond	158	3,084	414
Ash, Timothy Garton	392	2,711	186
Auden, W. H.	2,364	12,795	N.A.
Baldwin, James	2,019	22,592	N.A.
Banfield, Edward	70	467	278
Barber, Benjamin	282	3,140	238
Barnet, Richard	45	1,067	N.A.
Barnett, Randy	47	934	316
Barrett, William	49	896	33
Barthes, Roland	568	14,886	3,552
Barzun, Jacques	249	2,367	143
Bauer, Peter	27	1,522	139
Bayles, Martha	54	313	N.A.
Beauvoir, Simone de	1,156	226	N.A.
Becker, Gary	494	5,329	5,028
Begley, Louis	33	881	N.A.
Bell, Daniel	349	4,003	1,045
Bell, Derrick	243	1,779	654
Bellah, Robert	194	2,609	1,060
Bellow, Saul	2,356	9,950	186
Benedict, Ruth	98	2,772	256
Bennett, William	9,070	978	N.A.
Berkowitz, Peter	55	556	22
Berlin, Isaiah	1,306	5,271	904
Berube, Michael	60	746	126
Bhabha, Homi	81	3,828	1,732
Bickel, Alexander	57	385	574
Billington, James	586	3,044	60
Black, Charles, Jr.	231	72	441
Bloom, Allan	386	3,588	398
Bloom, Harold	1,114	9,950	393
Blumenthal, Sidney	8,044	7,612	N.A.
Bok, Derek	421	3,299	282
Bok, Sissela	216	1,400	274

Table 5.1 (continued)

Name	Media	Web	Scholarly
Boorstin, Daniel	559	4,471	399
Booth, Wayne	51	2,510	231
Bork, Robert	3,130	8,039	881
Boskin, Michael	910	1,505	299
Botstein, Leon	437	1,062	61
Boulding, Kenneth	69	2,212	974
Bourdieu, Pierre	124	12,270	7,472
Bourne, Randolph	163	863	N.A.
Bowles, Samuel	29	594	749
Brandeis, Louis	1,022	6,589	N.A.
Brecht, Bertold	2,240	4,898	N.A.
Brewster, Kingman	29	8,123	11
Breyer, Stephen	3,350	370	751
Brinkley, Alan	418	2,066	175
Brock, Dan	53	996	366
Brooks, David	1,375	4,431	N.A.
Broun, Heywood	36	499	N.A.
Brown, Norman O.	118	778	37
Bruner, Jerome	50	3,623	3,253
Brzezinsky, Zbigniew	1,430	6,344	225
Buchanan, James	161	6,146	1,275
Buckley, William F., Jr.	3,938	12,231	N.A.
Bundy, McGeorge	628	2,831	90
Bundy, William	137	1,092	N.A.
Bunzel, John	30	248	21
Burnham, James	101	588	24
Buruma, Ian	242	1,105	N.A.
Butler, Judith	184	6,989	2,559
Calabresi, Guido	97	1,021	917
Camus, Albert	1,494	32,370	N.A.
Carothers, Thomas	70	492	N.A.
Carson, Rachel	1,845	31,447	N.A.
Carter, Stephen	254	4,365	437
Casper, Gerhard	349	2,165	52
Castañeda, Jorge	504	55	115
Céline, Louis	108	997	N.A.
Chayes, Abram	43	435	390
Cheney, Lynne	674	1,211	N.A.
Chomsky, Noam	1,300	46,860	5,628
Cockburn, Alexander	619	4,277	N.A.
Cohen, Joshua	31	735	745
Coleman, James	250	1,495	3,029
Coles, Robert	617	6,393	365
Collier, Peter	214	870	3
Commager, Henry Steele	136	1,785	99

Table 5.1 (continued)

Name	Media	Web	Scholarly
Conant, James	183	3,506	248
Conquest, Robert	274	2,053	118
Coulter, Ann	1,530	13,701	N.A.
Cox, Archibald	1,459	2,435	221
Craig, Gordon	120	1,701	54
Croly, Herbert	112	490	N.A.
Crouch, Stanley	1,057	2,695	N.A.
D'Souza, Dinesh	763	2,926	N.A.
Daniels, Norman	61	438	354
Davis, Angela	462	7,694	265
Dawkins, Richard	1,765	16,890	1,922
Decter, Midge	139	564	N.A.
Derrida, Jacques	535	15,510	6,902
Dershowitz, Alan	5,778	5,040	163
Devlin, Patrick	23	58	N.A.
Dewey, John	957	28,104	3,644
Diamond, Jared	713	4,560	2,268
Dickstein, Morris	73	521	69
Didion, Joan	1,140	4,435	N.A.
DiIulio, John	201	243	137
Dionne, E. J.	2,894	5,503	N.A.
Djilas, Milovan	104	1,342	N.A.
Doctorow, E. L.	1,822	6,306	N.A.
Dorsen, Norman	44	519	40
Douglas, William	796	4,785	185
Draper, Theodore	67	423	N.A.
Duberman, Martin	159	1,583	93
Du Bois, W. E. B.	1,469	13,081	N.A.
Dworkin, Andrea	560	5,043	N.A.
Dworkin, Ronald	287	3,209	2,392
Easterbrook, Gregg	338	1,763	N.A.
Eco, Umberto	1,193	34,950	1,877
Ehrenreich, Barbara	534	4,841	N.A.
Ehrlich, Paul	601	13,445	2,422
Eisner, Robert	211	1,094	262
Ellison, Ralph	1,588	10,925	N.A.
Ellsberg, Daniel	524	2,306	N.A.
Elon, Amos	98	551	N.A.
Elshtain, Jean	310	2,167	435
Epstein, Barbara	50	708	N.A.
Epstein, Cynthia Fuchs	13	323	271
Epstein, Jason	130	619	N.A.
Epstein, Joseph	269	1,029	N.A.
Epstein, Richard	321	3,610	1,974
Erikson, Erik	255	268	3,358

Table 5.1 (continued)

Name	Media	Web	Scholarly
Eskridge, William, Jr.	70	561	1,858
Estrich, Susan	1,876	1,686	344
Etzioni, Amitai	546	3,387	1,483
Fadiman, Clifton	170	1,966	N.A.
Fairbank, John	115	1,775	130
Falk, Richard	64	2,121	328
Fallows, James	1,097	3,545	N.A.
Faludi, Susan	903	4,804	N.A.
Fanon, Franz	293	5,743	N.A.
Fast, Howard	212	4,957	N.A.
Feldstein, Martin	887	3,803	1,406
Fiedler, Leslie	194	1,164	204
Finn, Chester	719	2,447	142
Finn, James	73	127	N.A.
Finnis, John	37	708	385
Fish, Stanley	224	3,103	1,267
Fiss, Owen	41	591	878
Fitzgerald, Frances	474	987	N.A.
Fogel, Robert William	69	1,676	528
Foner, Eric	348	3,017	300
Forster, E. M.	1,940	11,106	N.A.
Foucault, Michel	731	28,934	13,238
Frank, Jerome	40	487	N.A.
Frank, Robert	428	897	872
Frank, Waldo	19	561	N.A.
Frankfurter, Felix	593	2,783	450
Franklin, John Hope	1,285	4,194	253
Freedman, James	116	473	96
Fried, Charles	447	607	540
Friedan, Betty	2,099	8,354	N.A.
Friedenberg, Edgar	4	222	18
Friedman, Milton	2,534	22,850	2,706
Friedman, Thomas	2,962	6,961	N.A.
Fromm, Erich	159	10,520	971
Frum, David	1,234	1,918	N.A.
Fukuyama, Francis	1,104	12,950	1,058
Fuller, R. Buckminster	973	6,246	54
Fussell, Paul	347	2,294	285
Galbraith, John Kenneth	1,595	9,639	773
Galston, William	396	1,179	300
Gardner, Howard	683	13,178	1,585
Gardner, John	590	3,931	197
Gardner, Richard	47	472	92
Gates, Henry Louis, Jr.	1,901	8,485	941
Gay, Peter	277	2,884	708

Table 5.1 (continued)

Name	Media	Web	Scholarly
Gelernter, David	643	3,903	163
Gellner, Ernest	52	105	1,043
Genovese, Eugene	126	1,359	244
George, Robert	204	809	127
Giddens, Anthony	514	7,700	4,910
Gide, Andre	497	4,428	N.A.
Gilder, George	775	8,675	N.A.
Gillers, Stephen	633	685	166
Gilligan, Carol	424	4,282	2,799
Ginsburg, Allen	1,466	1,550	N.A.
Gitlin, Todd	490	2,868	548
Glazer, Nathan	370	1,885	523
Glendon, Mary Ann	329	1,610	664
Goodman, Paul	272	2,768	N.A.
Goodwin, Doris Kearns	2,491	3,836	38
Goodwin, Richard	280	157	N.A.
Gould, Stephen Jay	1,890	17,975	4,891
Graff, Gerald	54	1,161	269
Gramsci, Antonio	186	7,159	N.A.
Grass, Gunter	787	9,944	N.A.
Gray, John	176	0	558
Greeley, Andrew	1,003	4,432	545
Greenberg, Clement	427	2,300	N.A.
Gregorian, Vartan	319	1,795	13
Guinier, Lani	1,205	2,867	438
Gunther, Gerald	39	388	550
Gutmann, Amy	102	1,410	52
Habermas, Jürgen	199	3,938	7,052
Hacker, Andrew	287	1,139	291
Hackney, Sheldon	189	813	54
Halberstam, David	2,124	4,968	N.A.
Hand, Learned	470	3,174	N.A.
Handlin, Oscar	46	1,007	241
Hardwick, Elizabeth	178	551	N.A.
Harrington, Michael	425	1,658	N.A.
Hart, H. L. A.	27	1,375	1,154
Hartman, Geoffrey	33	1,307	320
Havel, Václav	4,701	33,949	N.A.
Hayek, Friedrich	609	10,056	1,655
Hearne, Vicki	30	284	19
Heilbroner, Robert	135	2,315	258
Heilbrun, Carolyn	144	961	218
Hellman, Lillian	1,537	5,361	N.A.
Hentoff, Nat	1,086	11,041	N.A.
Herrnstein, Richard	304	1,872	1,581

Table 5.1 (continued)

Name	Media	Web	Scholarly
Hesburgh, Theodore	281	2,023	9
Higginbotham, A. Leon	473	963	161
Himmelfarb, Gertrude	395	1,631	335
Hirsch, E. D., Jr.	516	3,982	599
Hirschman, Albert	69	1,556	1,776
Hobsbawm, E. J.	632	5,812	1,309
Hoffman, Stanley	206	415	48
Hofstadter, Richard	334	2,187	657
Holmes, Oliver Wendell	1,675	9,345	N.A.
Holmes, Stephen	63	842	382
Hook, Sidney	153	1,379	106
hooks, bell	360	10,190	N.A.
Horowitz, David	1,501	10,400	N.A.
Howe, Irving	368	2,125	277
Huber, Peter	422	5,532	N.A.
Hughes, H. Stuart	24	323	83
Huntington, Samuel	831	6,238	2,038
Hutchins, Robert Maynard	153	1,556	77
Huxley, Aldous	2,060	29,206	N.A.
Huxtable, Ada Louise	203	691	N.A.
Iannone, Carol	13	127	N.A.
Ilych, Ivan	82	0	N.A.
Jackson, Robert	319	3,010	N.A.
Jacobs, Jane	744	4,760	N.A.
Jacoby, Russell	66	684	142
James, William	866	60,480	3,291
Jencks, Christopher	191	1,233	958
Johnson, Paul	1,317	10,339	173
Judis, John	352	1,094	N.A.
Kael, Pauline	1,334	4,297	N.A.
Kagan, Donald	108	1,039	39
Kahn, Herman	160	1,716	N.A.
Kass, Leon	177	990	346
Kaysen, Carl	34	203	59
Kazin, Alfred	434	1,961	142
Kempton, Murray	397	1,029	N.A.
Kennan, George	899	5,241	N.A.
Kennedy, Duncan	54	650	923
Kennedy, Paul	196	3,133	230
Kennedy, Randall	293	1,348	276
Kernan, Alvin	48	628	147
Kerr, Clark	185	3,010	N.A.
Keynes, John Maynard	1,705	13,420	1,667
Kimball, Roger	139	959	N.A.
Kinsey, Alfred	522	3,774	777

Table 5.1 (continued)

Name	Media	Web	Scholarly
Kissinger, Henry	12,570	39,976	323
Koestler, Arthur	705	6,440	N.A.
Kolakowski, Leszek	51	1,211	235
Kolko, Gabriel	38	1,072	168
Kopkind, Andrew	26	128	N.A.
Kozol, Jonathan	578	4,808	N.A.
Kramer, Hilton	273	1,264	N.A.
Kramer, Larry	614	4,388	N.A.
Kristol, Irving	570	2,028	N.A.
Kristol, William	4,389	4,843	N.A.
Kronman, Anthony	78	469	597
Krugman, Paul	2,076	13,707	3,011
Laffer, Arthur	218	898	10
Lapham, Lews	369	1,673	N.A.
Laqueur, Walter	96	1,669	127
Lasch, Christopher	328	2,260	760
Laski, Harold	217	1,038	93
Lasky, Melvin	43	150	N.A.
Laumann, Edward	207	693	735
Leary, Timothy	2,982	27,040	228
Leavis, F. R.	420	1,271	218
Lefkowitz, Mary	124	1,329	203
Lemann, Nicholas	414	1,770	N.A.
Leonard, John	672	4,540	N.A.
Lerner, Max	68	804	104
Lerner, Michael	621	2,388	N.A.
Lessig, Lawrence	655	6,111	859
Lester, Julius	308	3,500	63
Levi, Edward	143	785	108
Lévi-Strauss, Claude	267	3,749	2,283
Lewis, Anthony	2,032	3,065	N.A.
Lewis, C. S.	2,891	61,736	411
Lewontin, Richard	142	1,870	1,996
Lichtheim, George	3	171	N.A.
Lifton, Robert Jay	240	2,549	507
Lilla, Mark	32	224	68
Liman, Arthur	170	322	N.A.
Lind, Michael	574	1,827	N.A.
Lippman, Walter	881	4,755	N.A.
Lipset, Seymour Martin	299	2,229	1,675
Loury, Glenn C.	500	1,153	239
Lovejoy, Arthur O.	15	528	114
Lowell, Robert	844	5,670	N.A.
Luce, Henry	1,358	6,246	N.A.
Lukács, Georg	59	1,230	980

Table 5.1 (continued)

Name	Media	Web	Scholarly
Luttwak, Edward	398	1,619	N.A.
MacDonald, Dwight	273	867	N.A.
Macedo, Stephen	28	374	82
MacKinnon, Catharine	426	3,432	1,192
Magnet, Myron	103	245	N.A.
Mailer, Norman	4,860	17,106	N.A.
Malcolm, Janet	317	994	N.A.
Malreaux, Andre	125	26	N.A.
Mann, Thomas	2,043	36,100	N.A.
Manne, Henry G.	12	259	207
Mansfield, Harvey	157	713	83
Marcuse, Herbert	285	5,759	680
Marquez, Gabriel Garcia	2,156	11,327	N.A.
Maurois, Andre	91	1,045	N.A.
Maurras, Charles	48	976	N.A.
McCarthy, Mary	943	3,130	N.A.
McCloskey, Deirdre (Donald)	70	1,341	734
McConnell, Michael	200	530	864
McLuhan, Marshall	1,446	19,991	699
McWilliams, Carey	122	1,024	178
Mead, Margaret	1,272	18,371	498
Meiklejohn, Alexander	33	380	218
Menand, Louis	76	506	90
Mencken, H. L.	2,462	16,871	N.A.
Merton, Robert K.	283	1,846	2,133
Miller, Arthur	7,955	28,798	N.A.
Miller, James	317	970	474
Miller, William Ian	49	175	120
Mills, C. Wright	181	4,119	950
Minow, Martha	83	1,033	756
Mitford, Jessica	489	1,420	N.A.
Montagu, Ashley	99	2,225	N.A.
Moore, Barrington, Jr.	28	973	534
Morgenthau, Hans	76	1,219	450
Morris, Willie	669	2,961	N.A.
Morrison, Toni	5,633	43,891	N.A.
Moyers, Bill	2,496	12,214	N.A.
Moynihan, Daniel Patrick	12,344	19,495	394
Mumford, Lewis	413	5,048	N.A.
Murray, Charles	688	3,530	N.A.
Myrdal, Gunnar	277	2,588	852
Nagel, Thomas	102	2,927	1,058
Navasky, Victor	344	1,026	N.A.
Neibuhr, Reinhold	506	4,390	N.A.
Neuhaus, Richard John	360	2,840	N.A.

Table 5.1 (continued)

Name	Media	Web	Scholarly
Newfield, Jack	527	773	N.A.
Nisbet, Robert	68	961	N.A.
Noonan, John	110	842	254
Novak, Michael	478	3,291	N.A.
Nozick, Robert	107	2,944	1,086
Nussbaum, Martha	186	3,563	1,463
O'Brien, Conor Cruise	886	1,313	66
Oates, Joyce Carol	2,298	11,613	144
Odets, Clifford	693	1,917	N.A.
Olasky, Marvin	517	4,438	55
Olson, Walter	275	1,119	N.A.
Ortega y Gassett, Jose	87	1,818	34
Orwell, George	5,818	48,874	N.A.
Ozick, Cynthia	737	2,734	N.A.
Packer, Herbert	7	136	177
Paglia, Camille	1,676	15,412	180
Paton, Alan	415	3,019	N.A.
Patterson, Orlando	350	1,308	207
Paz, Octavio	971	15,192	N.A.
Peretz, Martin	429	955	N.A.
Phillips, William	49	413	N.A.
Pipes, Richard	313	1,827	138
Podhoretz, Norman	507	1,477	N.A.
Polsby, Nelson	86	789	201
Posner, Richard	1,592	7,808	4,321
Pound, Ezra	1,839	17,704	N.A.
Presser, Stephen	288	298	130
Prose, Francine	527	1,936	N.A.
Putnam, Hilary	32	2,815	1,860
Putnam, Robert	807	4,700	2,162
Radosh, Ronald	150	522	26
Rahv, Philip	72	285	N.A.
Rakove, Jack	127	760	253
Rand, Ayn	2,227	45,441	N.A.
Raskin, Marcus	59	394	11
Ravitch, Diane	549	2,471	292
Reed, Adolph, Jr.	75	769	82
Regan, Tom	192	1,585	193
Reich, Charles	70	435	179
Reich, Robert	8,795	12,480	931
Reich, Wilhelm	152	9,134	491
Reston, James	549	1,963	N.A.
Rhodes, Richard	530	3,100	N.A.
Rich, Adrienne	534	9,001	N.A.
Ridley, Matt	689	2,380	N.A.

Table 5.1 (continued)

Name	Media	Web	Scholarly
Riesman, David	154	1,262	198
Rifkin, Jeremy	998	8,639	N.A.
Roberts, Paul Craig	409	1,710	156
Rodriguez, Richard	622	3,414	94
Rorty, Richard	339	7,096	3,336
Rosen, Jeffrey	565	1,022	407
Rosenbaum, Ron	273	1,323	N.A.
Rosenberg, Harold	142	1,018	38
Rosenfeld, Isaac	8	89	2
Ross, Andrew	1,626	7,851	362
Rostow, Eugene	42	463	119
Rostow, Walt	102	1,016	334
Roth, Philip	2,727	8,965	N.A.
Rovere, Richard	46	226	N.A.
Rushdie, Salman	7,688	33,714	N.A.
Rustin, Bayard	275	1,733	N.A.
Sachs, Jeffrey	1,450	7,410	783
Safire, William	6,408	8,282	N.A.
Said, Edward	982	16,410	2,958
Samuelson, Paul	597	4,473	1,943
Sandel, Michael	338	1,558	929
Santayana, George	496	6,254	226
Sartre, Jean-Paul	1,712	26,174	2,217
Scalia, Antonin	5,381	11,707	827
Scarry, Elaine	118	1,004	411
Schell, Jonathan	194	1,636	30
Schelling, Thomas	88	1,588	1,225
Schlesinger, Arthur, Jr.	2,305	4,892	542
Schmitt, Carl	28	3,135	237
Schultz, George	674	545	22
Schurmann, Franz	15	298	38
Scruton, Roger	782	2,124	265
Sedgwick, Eve Kosofsky	59	1,716	989
Sen, Amartya	1,100	10,289	3,526
Sennett, Richard	177	2,343	416
Shattuck, Roger	133	863	88
Shaw, George Bernard	4,835	41,091	N.A.
Shaw, Peter	116	265	N.A.
Shawn, William	477	525	N.A.
Sheed, Wilfrid	85	136	N.A.
Sherman, Nancy	64	240	54
Shils, Edward	61	1,033	339
Shklar, Judith	59	419	276
Showalter, Elaine	330	2,528	720
Shulman, Marshall	18	109	5

Table 5.1 (continued)

Name	Media	Web	Scholarly
Siegler, Mark	127	284	202
Silber, John	2,584	1,988	16
Silone, Ignazio	86	1,493	N.A.
Silvers, Robert	198	236	N.A.
Simon, Herbert	398	6,308	1,275
Simon, John	422	1,146	5
Simon, Julian	336	5,380	536
Singer, Peter	560	11,100	423
Skocpol, Theda	177	2,126	1,327
Snow, C. P.	522	3,672	N.A.
Sokal, Alan	240	3,748	464
Solotaroff, Theodore	42	156	N.A.
Solow, Robert	418	3,139	1,359
Solzhenitsyn, Aleksandr	1,579	7,628	N.A.
Sommers, Christina Hoff	1,476	8,703	113
Sontag, Susan	1,857	12,033	N.A.
Sovern, Michael	102	357	11
Sowell, Thomas	900	2,678	414
Spender, Stephen	124	2,388	N.A.
Spengler, Oswald	141	1,602	228
Spock, Benjamin	2,226	4,570	N.A.
Staples, Brent	379	785	N.A.
Starr, Paul	36	283	729
Starr, Roger	185	652	N.A.
Steel, Ronald	393	1,689	44
Steele, Shelby	491	1,169	103
Stein, Herbert	3,093	13,123	N.A.
Steinbeck, John	3,477	30,410	N.A.
Steinem, Gloria	1,795	3,777	N.A.
Steiner, George	223	2,335	682
Stigler, George J.	1,200	6,221	2,056
Stiglitz, Joseph	698	2,303	2,050
Stone, I. F.	957	2,039	N.A.
Strachey, Lytton	130	2,301	N.A.
Strauss, Leo	1,048	6,171	604
Sullivan, Andrew	515	921	N.A.
Sullivan, Kathleen	393	89	688
Summers, Lawrence	9,369	16,276	449
Sunstein, Cass	514	1,677	3,594
Talese, Gay	649	1,606	N.A.
Tate, Allen	185	1,318	N.A.
Tawney, R.H.	164	964	155
Taylor, Charles	351	7,509	2,264
Teller, Edward	563	4,657	249
Thernstrom, Abigail	918	1,091	106

Table 5.1 (continued)

Name	Media	Web	Scholarly
Thernstrom, Stephan	372	138	182
Thompson, E.P.	330	3,389	874
Thurow, Lester	1,024	5,395	585
Tiger, Lionel	148	712	94
Toffler, Alvin	916	10,600	N.A.
Tribe, Laurence	1,421	3,204	1,532
Trilling, Diana	220	508	N.A.
Trilling, Lionel	522	2,145	312
Trotsky, Leon	755	8,117	N.A.
Tuchman, Barbara	88	3,241	N.A.
Tucker, Robert	93	860	70
Turley, Jonathan	2,393	846	43
Unger, Roberto	39	645	258
Van den Haag, Ernest	37	404	63
vanden Heuvel, Katrina	408	447	N.A.
Vidal, Gore	3,175	11,947	N.A.
Vonnegut, Kurt	3,837	33,850	N.A.
Wald, George	66	1,132	278
Walzer, Michael	212	2,919	1,505
Wanniski, Jude	452	1,809	N.A.
Warner, Michael	126	982	390
Warshow, Robert	25	165	N.A.
Weber, Eugen	108	1,150	170
Weber, Max	850	24,300	5,463
Wechsler, Herbert	39	245	140
Wells, H. G.	3,525	40,521	N.A.
West, Cornel	842	6,376	1,022
West, Rebecca	626	3,265	N.A.
White, James Boyd	6	358	261
White, Morton	2	265	126
Whyte, William H.	271	800	165
Wieseltier, Leon	300	730	N.A.
Wilentz, Sean	393	1,037	107
Will, George	10,425	31,100	N.A.
Williams, Patricia	336	2,513	762
Williams, Raymond	253	4,620	1,794
Williams, Walter	460	6,032	133
Wills, Garry	1,314	10,480	396
Wilson, Edmund	1,008	3,885	N.A.
Wilson, Edward O.	692	6,549	2,984
Wilson, James Q.	1,257	3,875	2,048
Wilson, William Julius	670	3,577	2,560
Wohlstetter, Albert	66	353	48
Wohlstetter, Roberta	21	124	N.A.
Wolf, Naomi	1,028	1,275	N.A.

Table 5.1 (continued)

Name	Media	Web	Scholarly
Wolfe, Alan	1,208	382	229
Wolfe, Tom	5,342	15,840	N.A.
Woodward, C. Vann	184	1,743	414
Wouk, Herman	566	3,612	N.A.
Wrong, Dennis	9	198	189
Yeats, William Butler	1,221	218,503	N.A.
Zinn, Howard	356	6,857	84

Table 5.2 Public-intellectual summary statistics

	Living and dead		Living		Dead	
Total	546	(100%)	368	(67.4%)	178	(32%)
Male	475	(87.0%)	310	(84.2%)	165	(92.7%)
Female	072[a]	(13.2%)	59[a]	(15.8%)	13	(7.3%)
Academic	354	(64.8%)	255	(69.3%)	99	(55.6%)
Nonacademic	192	(35.2%)	113	(30.7%)	79	(44.4%)
Black	26	(4.8%)	21		5	(2.8%)
Nonblack	520	(95.2%)	347	(5.7%)	173	(97.2%)
Foreign	88	(16.1%)	29	(7.9%)	59	(33.1%)
U.S.	458	(83.9%)	339	(92.1%)	119	(66.9%)
Govt. service	80	(14.7%)	54	(14.7%)	26	(14.6%)
No govt. service	466	(85.3%)	314	(85.3%)	152	(85.4%)
Think tank	35	(6.4%)	33	(9.0%)	2	(1.1%)
Non–think tank	511	(93.6%)	335	(91.0%)	176	(98.9%)
Affiliated[b]	374	(68.5%)	274	(74.5%)	100	(56.2%)
Nonaffiliated	172	(31.5%)	94	(25.5%)	78	(43.8%)
Right-leaning	140	(25.6%)	101	(27.4%)	39	(21.9%)
Left-leaning	362	(66.3%)	232	(63.0%)	130	(73.0%)
Unknown or neither	44	(8.1%)	35	(9.5%)	9	(5.1%)
Jewish	235	(43.0%)	171	(46.2%)	64	(36.4%)
Non-Jewish	311	(57.0%)	299	(53.8%)	112	(63.6%)
Age[c]	74		64		97	
	Fields					
Humanities	116	21.2%	77	20.9%	42	23.6%
Classics	2	(0.4%)	2	(0.5%)	0	(0.0%)
Literature	57	(10.4%)	39	(10.6%)	18	(10.1%)
Philosophy	54	(9.9%)	31	(8.4%)	23	(12.9%)
Theology	6	(1.1%)	5	(1.4%)	1	(0.6%)
Social science	200	36.6%	144	39.1%	61	34.3%
Anthropology	5	(0.9%)	1	(0.3%)	4	(2.2%)
Economics	45	(8.2%)	36	(9.8%)	9	(5.1%)
History	57	(10.4%)	39	(10.6%)	18	(10.1%)
Political science	46	(8.4%)	35	(9.5%)	11	(6.2%)
Psychology	15	(2.7%)	6	(1.6%)	9	(5.1%)
Sociology	37	(6.8%)	27	(7.3%)	10	(5.6%)
Science	14	2.6%	9	2.4%	5	2.8%
Biology	8	(1.5%)	6	(1.6%)	2	(1.1%)
Chemistry	1	(0.2%)	0	(0.0%)	1	(0.6%)

Table 5.2 (continued)

	Living and dead		Living		Dead	
Computer science	1	(0.2%)	1	(0.3%)	0	(0.0%)
Linguistics	1	(0.2%)	1	(0.3%)	0	(0.0%)
Physics	3	(0.5%)	1	(0.3%)	2	(1.1%)
Other	270	49.5%	192	52.2%	97	54.5%
Architecture	2	(0.4%)	0	(0.0%)	2	(1.1%)
Education	26	(4.8%)	20	(5.4%)	6	(3.4%)
Journalism	63	(11.5%)	47	(12.8%)	16	(9.0%)
Law	87	(15.9%)	65	(17.7%)	22	(12.4%)
Medicine	4	(0.7%)	2	(0.5%)	2	(1.1%)
Politics	2	(0.4%)	0	(0.0%)	2	(1.1%)
Publishing	23	(4.2%)	18	(4.9%)	5	(2.8%)
Science writer	4	(0.7%)	3	(0.8%)	1	(0.6%)
Writer	78	(14.3%)	37	(10.1%)	41	(23.0%)
One field only	469	(85.9%)	317	(86.1%)	152	(85.4%)
More than one field	77	(14.1%)	51	(13.9%)	26	(14.6%)

a. Deirdre McCloskey also counted as Donald McCloskey.
b. Either an academic or a member of the research staff of a think tank.
c. Number of years from date of birth to 2001.

Table 5.3 Top 100 public intellectuals by media mentions

Name	Media mentions (1995–2000)
Kissinger, Henry	12,570
Moynihan, Daniel Patrick	12,344
Will, George	10,425
Summers, Lawrence	9,369
Bennett, William J.	9,070
Reich, Robert	8,795
Blumenthal, Sidney	8,044
Miller, Arthur	7,955
Rushdie, Salman	7,688
Safire, William	6,408
Orwell, George	5,818
Dershowitz, Alan	5,778
Morrison, Toni	5,633
Scalia, Antonin	5,381
Wolfe, Tom	5,342
Mailer, Norman	4,860
Shaw, George Bernard	4,835
Havel, Václav	4,701
Kristol, William	4,389
Buckley, William F., Jr.	3,938
Vonnegut, Kurt	3,837
Wells, H. G.	3,525
Steinbeck, John	3,477
Breyer, Stephen G.	3,350
Vidal, Gore	3,175
Bork, Robert	3,130
Stein, Herbert	3,093
Leary, Timothy	2,982
Friedman, Thomas	2,962
Dionne, E. J.	2,894
Lewis, C. S.	2,891
Roth, Philip	2,727
Silber, John	2,584
Friedman, Milton	2,534
Moyers, Bill	2,496
Goodwin, Doris Kearns	2,491
Mencken, H. L.	2,462
Turley, Jonathan	2,393
Auden, W. H.	2,364
Bellow, Saul	2,356
Schlesinger, Arthur Jr.	2,305
Oates, Joyce Carol	2,298
Brecht, Bertold	2,240
Rand, Ayn	2,227

Table 5.3 (continued)

Name	Media mentions (1995–2000)
Spock, Benjamin	2,226
Marquez, Gabriel Garcia	2,156
Halberstam, David	2,124
Friedan, Betty	2,099
Krugman, Paul	2,076
Huxley, Aldous	2,060
Mann, Thomas	2,043
Lewis, Anthony	2,032
Baldwin, James	2,019
Forster, E. M.	1,940
Gates, Henry Louis, Jr.	1,901
Gould, Stephen Jay	1,890
Estrich, Susan	1,876
Sontag, Susan	1,857
Carson, Rachel	1,845
Pound, Ezra	1,839
Doctorow, E. L.	1,822
Steinem, Gloria	1,795
Dawkins, Richard	1,765
Sartre, Jean-Paul	1,712
Keynes, John Maynard	1,705
Paglia, Camille	1,676
Holmes, Oliver Wendell	1,675
Ross, Andrew	1,626
Galbraith, John Kenneth	1,595
Posner, Richard	1,592
Ellison, Ralph	1,588
Solzhenitsyn, Aleksandr	1,579
Hellman, Lillian	1,537
Coulter, Ann	1,530
Horowitz, David	1,501
Camus, Albert	1,494
Sommers, Christina Hoff	1,476
Du Bois, W. E. B.	1,469
Ginsburg, Allen	1,466
Cox, Archibald	1,459
Sachs, Jeffrey	1,450
McLuhan, Marshall	1,446
Brzezinsky, Zbigniew	1,430
Tribe, Laurence	1,421
Brooks, David	1,375
Luce, Henry	1,358
Kael, Pauline	1,334
Johnson, Paul	1,317

Table 5.3 (continued)

Name	Media mentions (1995–2000)
Wills, Garry	1,314
Berlin, Isaiah	1,306
Chomsky, Noam	1,300
Abrams, Floyd	1,285
Franklin, John Hope	1,285
Mead, Margaret	1,272
Wilson, James Q.	1,257
Frum, David	1,234
Yeats, William Butler	1,221
Wolfe, Alan	1,208
Guinier, Lani	1,205
Stigler, George	1,200

Table 5.4 Top 100 public intellectuals by scholarly citations (1995–2000)

Name	Scholarly citations
Foucault, Michel	13,238
Bourdieu, Pierre	7,472
Habermas, Jürgen	7,052
Derrida, Jacques	6,902
Chomsky, Noam	5,628
Weber, Max	5,463
Becker, Gary	5,028
Giddens, Anthony	4,910
Gould, Stephen Jay	4,891
Posner, Richard	4,321
Dewey, John	3,644
Sunstein, Cass	3,594
Barthes, Roland	3,552
Sen, Amartya	3,526
Erikson, Erik	3,358
Rorty, Richard	3,336
James, William	3,291
Bruner, Jerome	3,253
Coleman, James	3,029
Krugman, Paul	3,011
Wilson, Edward	2,984
Said, Edward	2,958
Gilligan, Carol	2,799
Adorno, Theodor	2,776
Friedman, Milton	2,706
Wilson, William Julius	2,560
Butler, Judith	2,559
Ehrlich, Paul	2,422
Dworkin, Ronald	2,392
Lévi-Strauss, Claude	2,283
Diamond, Jared	2,268
Taylor, Charles	2,264
Sartre, Jean-Paul	2,217
Putnam, Robert	2,162
Merton, Robert	2,133
Stigler, George	2,056
Stiglitz, Joseph	2,050
Wilson, James Q.	2,048
Huntington, Samuel	2,038
Lewontin, Richard	1,996
Epstein, Richard	1,974
Samuelson, Paul	1,943
Dawkins, Richard	1,922
Eco, Umberto	1,877
Putnam, Hilary	1,860

Table 5.4 (continued)

Name	Scholarly citations
Eskridge, William, Jr.	1,858
Williams, Raymond	1,794
Hirschman, Albert	1,776
Bhabha, Homi	1,732
Amar, Akhil	1,704
Lipset, Seymour Martin	1,675
Keynes, John Maynard	1,667
Hayek, Friedrich	1,655
Gardner, Howard	1,585
Herrnstein, Richard	1,581
Tribe, Laurence	1,532
Walzer, Michael	1,505
Etzioni, Amitai	1,483
Nussbaum, Martha	1,463
Feldstein, Martin	1,406
Ackerman, Bruce	1,400
Solow, Robert	1,359
Skocpol, Theda	1,327
Hobsbawm, E. J.	1,309
Simon, Herbert	1,275
Buchanan, James	1,275
Fish, Stanley	1,267
Schelling, Thomas	1,225
MacKinnon, Catharine	1,192
Hart, H. L. A.	1,154
Arendt, Hannah	1,122
Nozick, Robert	1,086
Bellah, Robert	1,060
Fukuyama, Francis	1,058
Nagel, Thomas	1,058
Bell, Daniel	1,045
Gellner, Ernest	1,043
West, Cornel	1,022
Sedgwick, Eve Kosofsky	989
Lukacs, Georg	980
Boulding, Kenneth	974
Fromm, Erich	971
Jencks, Christopher	958
Mills, C. Wright	950
Gates, Henry Louis, Jr.	941
Reich, Robert	931
Sandel, Michael	929
Kennedy, Duncan	923
Calabresi, Guido	917
Berlin, Isaiah	904

Table 5.4 (continued)

Name	Scholarly citations
Bork, Robert	881
Fiss, Owen	878
Thompson, E. P.	874
Frank, Robert	872
McConnell, Michael	864
Lessig, Lawrence	859
Myrdal, Gunnar	852
Scalia, Antonin	827
Sachs, Jeffrey	783
Kinsey, Alfred	777

Table 5.5 Summary statistics for top 100 public intellectuals by media mentions

Category	No. (%)	Mentions (avg. no.)
Male	84	3,193
Female	16	2,009
Academic	50	2,728
Nonacademic	50	3,280
Black	7	2,157
Nonblack	93	3,068
Deceased	32	2,198
Living	68	3,383
Foreign	21	2,657
U.S.	79	3,096
Govt. service	23	4,731
No govt. service	77	2,488
Think tank	4	3,734
Non–think tank	96	2,974
Affiliated (*a* and/or *t*)	53	2,797
Nonaffiliated	47	3,238
Right-leaning	35	3,113
Left-leaning	63	2,991
Unknown or neither	2	1,519
Jewish	36	3,331
Non-Jewish	64	2,820
Age	78	
Fields		
Humanities	12	2,407
Classics	0	—
Literature	7	1,819
Philosophy	5	3,230
Theology	0	—
Social science	24	3,377
Anthropology	1	1,272
Economics	10	3,341
History	5	1,742
Political science	5	6,398
Psychology	1	2,982
Sociology	2	1,339

Table 5.5 (continued)

Category	No. (%)	Mentions (avg. no.)
Science	3	1,652
Biology	2	1,827
Chemistry	0	—
Computer science	0	—
Linguistics	1	1,300
Physics	0	—
Other	70	3,265
Architecture	0	—
Education	1	2,584
Journalism	15	4,243
Law	16	3,198
Medicine	1	2,226
Politics	0	—
Publishing	2	1,429
Science writer	1	1,845
Writer	34	3,065
One field only	92	2,896
More than one field	8	4,245

Table 5.6 Circulation data

Group A			
American Prospect	28,000	*American Spectator*	109,455
Boston Review	41,600	*Commentary*	30,000
Dissent	10,490	*First Things*	26,525
Monthly Review	4,879	*Lingua Franca*	20,000
Nation	102,271	*National Interest*	18,000
New Republic	104,841	*National Review*	150,480
		New Criterion	7,800
New York Review	115,000	*Public Interest*	36,800
Partisan Review	8,000	*Reason*	55,000
		Weekly Standard	50,000
Subtotal	414,801		457,865
Group B			
New Yorker	858,175		
New York Times (Sunday)	1,668,100		
Washington Post (Sunday)	1,219,059		
Harper's	216,630	*Wall Street Journal*	1,925,622
Subtotal	3,961,964		1,925,622
Grand total	4,376,765		2,383,487

Table 5.7 Correlation of Web hits, media mentions, and scholarly citations for academics among top 100 public intellectuals, 1995–2000

	Web hits	Media mentions	Scholarly citations
Web hits	1.000		
Media mentions	0.017	1.000	
Scholarly citations	0.081	−0.169	1.000

Table 5.8 Regression of media mentions of academic public intellectuals

	(a) Top 50		(b) All	
Independent variable	Coefficient	t-statistic	Coefficient	t-statistic
Black	−217.63	−0.133	90.77	0.279
Dead	24.30	0.021	−259.89	−1.523
Female	−957.08	−0.863	21.21	0.088
Foreign	−385.54	−0.318	187.17	0.793
Govt.	**2369.06**	2.763	**1081.51**	5.422
Jewish	1311.66	1.461	65.22	0.427
Right-leaner	121.18	0.160	134.10	0.082
Scholarly citations	**−0.61**	−2.050	0.06	1.100
Constant	2334.42	2.243	391.50	2.516

$R^2 = .34$
Adj. $R^2 = .21$
$F = 2.49$
Prob. $> F = .0282$
$N = 47$

$R^2 = .10$
Adj. $R^2 = .08$
$F = 4.31$
Prob. $> F = .0001$
$N = 326$

Table 5.8a Regression of media mentions of academic public intellectuals (natural-log version)

	(a) Top 50		(b) All	
Independent variable	Coefficient	t-statistic	Coefficient	t-statistic
Black	−0.083	−0.223	**0.623**	2.016
Dead	0.040	0.143	−0.310	−1.902
Female	−0.259	−1.006	0.114	0.495
Foreign	−0.046	−0.157	0.248	1.116
Govt.	**0.591**	3.038	**0.828**	4.345
Jewish	0.287	1.435	−0.194	−1.328
Right-leaner	0.030	0.173	**0.379**	2.432
Scholarly citations	−0.143	−1.994	**0.331**	6.150
Constant	8.318	16.664	3.583	10.815

$R^2 = .37$
Adj. $R^2 = .23$
$F = 2.69$
Prob. $> F = .0195$
$N = 46$

$R^2 = .19$
Adj. $R^2 = .17$
$F = 8.93$
Prob. $> F = .0000$
$N = 322$

Table 5.9 Regression of media mentions of public intellectuals, both academic and nonacademic

Independent variable	(a) Top 100		(b) All	
	Coefficient	t-statistic	Coefficient	t-statistic
Academic	**−1125.34**	−2.317	**−707.60**	−4.951
Black	−270.13	−0.273	288.97	0.742
Dead	−1146.08	−1.950	**−481.11**	−3.179
Female	−1135.21	−1.734	−204.04	−1.044
Foreign	125.37	0.174	287.42	1.455
Govt.	**2305.59**	3.893	**1063.55**	5.671
Jewish	−201.13	−0.360	−57.78	−0.412
Right-leaner	77.39	0.143	174.29	1.120
Think tank	−839.54	−0.674	−546.46	−1.895
Constant	3725.24	6.050	1292.60	7.636

$R^2 = .26$
Adj. $R^2 = .18$
$F = 3.31$
Prob. $> F = .0017$
$N = 95$

$R^2 = .11$
Adj. $R^2 = .10$
$F = 7.00$
Prob. $> F = .0000$
$N = 501$

Table 5.9a Regression of media mentions of public intellectuals, both academic and nonacademic (natural-log version)

Independent variable	(a) Top 100		(b) All	
	Coefficient	t-statistic	Coefficient	t-statistic
Academic	**−0.374**	−3.194	**−0.700**	−5.312
Black	−0.133	−0.560	**0.676**	2.367
Dead	**−0.301**	−2.118	**−0.472**	−3.364
Female	−0.297	−1.887	−0.049	−0.269
Foreign	0.068	0.392	**0.443**	2.425
Govt.	**0.573**	4.013	**0.622**	3.582
Jewish	−0.068	−0.508	−0.230	−1.772
Right-leaner	−0.009	−0.067	0.124	0.859
Think tank	−0.289	−0.967	−0.070	−0.261
Constant	8.037	54.428	6.267	40.261

$R^2 = .29$
Adj. $R^2 = .21$
$F = 3.85$
Prob. $> F = .0004$
$N = 95$

$R^2 = .11$
Adj. $R^2 = .10$
$F = 7.03$
Prob. $> F = .0000$
$N = 501$

Table 5.10 Regression coefficients for public intellectuals, by field

Independent variable	(a) Top 100		(b) All	
	Coefficient	t-statistic	Coefficient	t-statistic
Black	−211.97	−0.213	142.59	0.471
Dead	−1026.28	−1.676	**−461.95**	−3.166
Female	−808.47	−1.191	−294.00	−1.522
Foreign	−481.15	−0.589	87.02	0.430
Govt.	**2460.06**	3.583	**1146.92**	6.121
Jewish	−113.83	−0.201	23.23	0.169
Right-leaner	−159.68	−0.296	124.86	0.862
Humanities	718.60	0.800	−128.88	−0.593
Law	456.22	0.501	−217.13	−0.909
Journalism	**2325.85**	2.556	**810.52**	3.086
Science	552.51	0.295	−196.89	−0.435
Social Science	914.95	0.955	−166.85	−0.762
Writer	**2236.59**	2.459	**1145.55**	4.607
Education	486.70	0.201	−397.18	−1.231
Publishing	−655.93	−0.375	−566.08	−1.661
Constant	1,652.22	1.814	723.90	3.059

$R^2 = .32$	$R^2 = .17$
Adj. $R^2 = .19$	Adj. $R^2 = .15$
$F = 2.51$	$F = 6.74$
Prob. $> F = .0045$	Prob. $> F = .0000$
$N = 95$	$N = 501$

～ II
Genre Studies

~ 6

The Literary Critic as
Public Intellectual

There are kinds of beauty before which the moral imagination ought
to withdraw.[1]

The humanities do not humanise.[2]

Society tends to exert a pressure, such that every poet is either
accepted or rejected, according to his fitness to the set of social values
of the time . . . The artist, being always alone, being heterodox when
everyone else is orthodox, and orthodox when everyone else is
heterodox, is the perpetual upsetter of conventional values.[3]

*T*HIS CHAPTER begins the examination in depth of se-
lected public-intellectual expressive genres. I start with literary criticism, which for three reasons has long been a medium for public-intellectual work. First, the general educated public, which is the audience
for that work, is also the audience for works of literature, and it takes
some interest in what experts have to say about them. Second, many
works of literature deal with political, social, or economic questions;
there is a clue to this in the number of writers among the most prominent public intellectuals (see Tables 5.3 and 5.5). Third, the cultural
significance of literature—in education, in relation to other subjects,
particularly of a scientific or social-scientific cast, and in relation to
popular culture—is itself an ideological issue. For these reasons, commentary on literature or on particular works of literature is one way
of commenting on political or ideological questions to a general audi-

1. Irving Howe, *A Margin of Hope: An Intellectual Biography* 336 (1982), quoted in Richard
Rorty, *Achieving Our Country: Leftist Thought in Twentieth-Century America* 116 (1998).

2. George Steiner, *Errata: An Examined Life* 117 (1997).

3. T. S. Eliot, *Turnbull Lectures: The Varieties of Metaphysical Poetry*, in Eliot, *The Varieties of
Metaphysical Poetry* 231, 288 (Ronald Schuchard ed., 1993).

ence. Many prominent public intellectuals have been part-time or full-time literary critics, such as T. S. Eliot, C. S. Lewis, Edmund Wilson, George Orwell, Lionel Trilling, and Irving Howe. Some of the most distinctive twentieth-century criticism, that of the New Critics in the United States and of T. S. Eliot and F. R. Leavis in England, is, even when nominally "formal" or aestheticist, as in the case of the New Criticism, marked by a Heideggerian despair at the increasingly technocratic organization of society.[4] We'll encounter that theme, a public-intellectual staple, in the next two chapters.

The academization of literary studies, a process well in hand at the outset of the twentieth century[5] but accelerating in recent decades, together with a declining interest in literature, has thinned the ranks of public-intellectual literary critics. This is a paradox, because that academization has been accompanied by an unprecedented politicization of literary studies. The overlapping theoretical approaches that dominate these studies today, such as new historicism, postcolonial and subaltern studies, queer theory, multiculturalism, radical feminism, de-

---

4. On Eliot, and on the Southern New Critics (such as Ransom and Tate), see, respectively, Louis Menand, "T. S. Eliot," in *The Cambridge History of Literary Criticism*, vol. 7: *Modernism and the New Criticism* 17 (A. Walton Litz, Louis Menand, and Lawrence Rainey eds., 2000), and Mark Jancovich, "The Southern New Critics," in id., vol. 2, p. 200. For especially clear statements of the political slant of the Southern New Critics, see Stark Young, "Not in Memoriam, But in Defense," in *I'll Take My Stand: The South and the Agrarian Tradition, by Twelve Southerners* 328 (1930), and John Crowe Ransom, "Reconstructed but Unregenerate," in id. at 1. On Leavis, see in particular F. R. Leavis, *Two Cultures? The Significance of C. P. Snow* (1962), a fierce polemic against C. P. Snow, *The Two Cultures and the Scientific Revolution* (1959). Snow, scientist and civil servant turned novelist, and Leavis, England's leading literary critic, were among England's preeminent public intellectuals of the middle years of the twentieth century. Snow took the modern "science will save us" position, Leavis (like the Southern Agrarians) the "science (and industry, and technology—in short, modernity) will destroy us" position. See *Cultures in Conflict: Perspectives on the Snow–Leavis Controversy* (David K. Cornelius and Edwin St. Vincent eds., 1964). The "two cultures" debate has resurfaced in the contemporary "law and literature" movement. Compare, for example, Peter Read Teachout, "Worlds beyond Theory: Toward the Expression of an Integrative Ethic for Self and Culture," 83 *Michigan Law Review* 849, 881 (1985), and James Boyd White, "Economics and Law: Two Cultures in Tension," 54 *Tennessee Law Review* 161 (1987), with Richard A. Posner, *Law and Literature* 295–302 (revised and enlarged ed. 1998), cited in this chapter as *Law and Literature*.

5. Josephine M. Guy and Ian Small, "The British 'Man of Letters' and the Rise of the Professional," in *The Cambridge History of Literary Criticism*, vol. 7: *Modernism and the New Criticism*, note 4 above, at 377, 378, points out that "the removal of literary criticism from the arena of educated public debate to that of academic institutions began in the late nineteenth century" and was largely complete by the late 1930s.

construction, reception theory, and poststructuralism, are all outposts of the cultural Left. But they are characterized by a forbidding jargon and an unappetizing selection of works to study (in reaction to the traditional canon dominated by the works of dead white males) that in combination largely disable the practitioners in these fields from communicating outside their immediate circle.[6] It is no accident, therefore, that the public-intellectual literary critics whom I shall be discussing in this chapter, Wayne Booth and Martha Nussbaum,[7] are not in the mainstream of contemporary literary studies, Booth because he belongs to an earlier generation and Nussbaum because she comes to literature from philosophy—and also from classics, which encompasses literary criticism of ancient Greek and Roman literature, but her approach to classics is philosophical. She is explicit in relating her interest in literary criticism to her work as a public intellectual, believing that "the literary imagination is a part of public rationality" and is indeed essential to political and other public discourse.[8]

Whether making literary criticism a public-intellectual venue is consistent with a rewarding conception of literature pivots on the age-old debate between aestheticists, such as Oscar Wilde, Benedetto Croce, George Steiner, Helen Vendler, and the young James Baldwin,[9] and moralists, such as Plato, Tolstoy, Samuel Johnson, Matthew Arnold, and Georg Lukács.[10] Booth, and even more emphatically Nussbaum, are in the moralist camp. The public-intellectual literary critics I men-

6. As they are now beginning to realize. See Ron Rosenbaum, "The Play's the Thing, Again," *New York Times Book Review*, Aug. 6, 2000, p. 12. A number of them, such as Judith Butler, Stanley Fish, and Edward Said, are listed in Table 5.1 but their media mentions range from modest to negligible. "[Literary] theory has had a bad effect. The higher the level of discourse, the fewer who can understand it. Scholarship is conducted on a more sophisticated plane (in the anglophone academy, at least). In the process, the larger extramural audience has been lost." John Sutherland, "Tales of the Tenured," *Times Literary Supplement*, Oct. 27, 2000, p. 22.

7. I take as the jumping-off points of my discussion two papers: Wayne Booth, "Why Banning Ethical Criticism Is a Serious Mistake," 22 *Philosophy and Literature* 366 (1998), and Martha C. Nussbaum, "Exactly and Responsibly: A Defense of Ethical Criticism," 22 *Philosophy and Literature* 343 (1998). I cite the latter paper in this chapter as "Exactly and Responsibly."

8. Martha C. Nussbaum, *Poetic Justice: The Literary Imagination and Public Life* xiii, xvi (1995), cited in this chapter as *Poetic Justice*.

9. See the discussions of *Uncle Tom's Cabin* and *Native Son* in James Baldwin, *Notes of a Native Son* 13–45 (1955).

10. See, for example, William K. Wimsatt Jr. and Cleanth Brooks, *Literary Criticism: A Short History*, chs. 20–22 (1957).

tioned at the outset, such as Eliot, Wilson, and Trilling, actually strad-
dle the divide.[11] But all wrote some public-intellectual literary criticism, and such criticism is perforce moralistic. Purely aesthetic
criticism, even if written for a general audience, does not fit my definition of public-intellectual work, as it does not contribute to public discourse on political or ideological matters. This is true even if the work
analyzed by the critic is a didactic novel; a critic interested only in the
formal properties of the work would not be doing public-intellectual
work. I illustrate such criticism with my closing discussion of *Nineteen
Eighty-Four* in the next chapter.

The moralistic critic thinks that the most important thing about literature is its moral or political message or impact.[12] The aesthetist
thinks that the moral or political content of a work of literature or of
art has little or nothing to do with either the value of the work or the
pleasure to be derived from it. The aestheticist's slogan is Wilde's dictum, in the preface to *The Picture of Dorian Gray*, that "there is no such
thing as a moral or an immoral book. Books are well written, or badly
written. That is all." In other words, immersion in literature does not
make us better citizens or better people. Some works of literature may
be edifying, but if so they are a small and skewed sample of the great
literary works. Conversely, a work of literature is not maimed or even
marred by expressing odious moral views, and by the same token a mediocre work of literature is not redeemed by expressing moral views of
which we approve. The author's moral qualities or opinions should not
affect our valuation of the work either (*Law and Literature* 306–307).

Mention of Oscar Wilde may evoke in some readers a sense of preci-
osity and *fin de siècle* decadence that leaves no room for such titans of
literature as Shakespeare and Tolstoy. To describe their works merely
as "well written" would misleadingly suggest an art of surfaces, a literary counterpart to the drawings of Aubrey Beardsley and the other
masters of art nouveau, contemporaries of Wilde. But in contrasting
the aesthetic with the moralistic I mean only to distinguish the conception of the work of art as an artifact from its conception as a set of precepts. The artifact may be radiant with emotional power, a source of
insight into human nature and social interactions, a source even of con-

11. Eliot most strikingly. See Menand, note 4 above, at 18.
12. Message and impact are not necessarily the same thing. I return to this point in Chapter 9 in discussing the difference between Nussbaum's brand of ethical criticism and that of
Richard Rorty.

solation and of strength, and a stimulus to reflection, including self-reflection and self-criticism. But these things are distinct from moral or political guidance. We should not be fooled into thinking that because there is no completely abstract verbal art, corresponding to abstract painting and abstract instrumental music, literature must be "humanistic" in a sense continuous with discursive writing, with history or philosophy or sociology, and that the best way to approach a work of literature is by asking how can it help the reader to conduct his life.

A work of literature founded on a moral system unintelligible to most readers, for example a system founded on a belief in the beauty and goodness of torturing children, would not be widely enjoyed however great its surface beauties. But that is a far cry from a work whose moral system we can understand a sane person's holding, even if we reject it—a moral system for example that includes antisemitism and other types of prejudice now generally condemned. It takes no great imagination, provided we know something of the social and intellectual history of the West, to understand how writers who were both sane and brilliant, writers like Shakespeare, Dickens, Henry James, and T. S. Eliot, could nevertheless be antisemitic. As Orwell said in reference to *Gulliver's Travels*,

> none of this [the power and simplicity of Swift's prose, his imaginative ability to make impossible worlds credible, and his other literary gifts] would enable us to enjoy Swift if his world-view were truly wounding or shocking. Millions of people, in many countries, must have enjoyed *Gulliver's Travels* while more or less seeing its anti-human implications . . . The explanation must be that Swift's world-view is felt to be *not* altogether false—or it would probably be more accurate to say, not false all the time . . . The views that a writer holds must be compatible with sanity, in the medical sense, and with the power of continuous thought: beyond that what we ask of him is talent, which is probably another name for conviction . . . The durability of *Gulliver's Travels* goes to show that, if the force of belief is behind it, a world-view which only just passes the test of sanity is sufficient to produce a great work of art.[13]

13. George Orwell, "Politics vs. Literature: An Examination of *Gulliver's Travels*," in *The Collected Essays, Journalism and Letters of George Orwell*, vol. 4: *In Front of Your Nose, 1945–1950*, pp. 205, 221–223 (Sonia Orwell and Ian Angus eds., 1968).

If the aesthetic approach, as qualified by Orwell, is the most fruitful one to take to literature, then literary critics may not, at least qua literary critics, belong in the ranks of the public intellectuals at all. The aesthetic approach implies that they have no *professional* competence to address moral issues, because literature, when best understood and appreciated, is seen not to be "about" those issues. I have considerable sympathy with this position. I go so far as to argue in the next chapter that even a political satire, such as *Nineteen Eighty-Four*, written by one of the leading public intellectuals of the twentieth century, may not be political *au fond*, that the proper mode of understanding it may be aesthetic, and that the role of the public intellectual in relation to it may therefore be a limited one.

Mention of didactic literature, such as political satire, requires distinguishing between contemporary and classic works of literature. Many works of literature have a didactic element; again I instance the writers in Table 5.3. But that element tends to date quickly as the specific political or social situations that concerned the writer mutate or expire. When a work of literature is read many years, often centuries, after it was written, the didactic element in it is likely to be anachronistic, and sometimes unrecognizable without a good deal of literary archeology to uncover the topical references, as in such works as the *Faerie Queen, Gulliver's Travels*, and the *Dunciad*. We'll see examples in the next chapter involving much more recent works. Moralistic criticism insists that the classics be understood and valued as didactic works *today*. There isn't much point in a critic's pointing out that Saul Bellow's novels are conservative and Toni Morrison's liberal, as these terms are used today; these things are obvious. What the moralistic critic undertakes is the more challenging task of quarrying old works of literature for implications for current political or ideological issues.

Responding to a fuller elaboration and defense of the aesthetic approach than I have space for here,[14] Nussbaum argues in "Exactly and Responsibly" that distaste for moralistic criticism is politically motivated: one who is not an egalitarian will not be moved by works of literature that stir compassion for the poor in readers such as herself. The assumption that a reader's reaction to a work of literature is inevitably

---

14. See Richard A. Posner, "Against Ethical Criticism," 21 *Philosophy and Literature* 1 (1997), reprinted in revised form as chapter 9 of *Law and Literature*.

colored by his politics begs the question of the relation between literature and politics by taking for granted that aesthetic responses are at
root political. Nussbaum also ascribes rejection of moralistic criticism
to insensitivity to the difference between the novel and lyric poetry,
which gives readers a pleasure that indeed "is closest to the pleasure
that we get from the visual arts, especially abstract art, and from music,
especially instrumental music" (*Law and Literature* 331). But none of us
aesthetes considers that the only pleasure that literature yields or even
the only *aesthetic* pleasure; it is merely the pleasure *most* remote from
the moral realm. Most of the works of literature discussed not only in
Law and Literature but in this book as well are novels, plays, and epic
poems, rather than lyric poems.[15] And I have emphasized not the "mu-
sical" pleasures that these longer works generate, though there are
some, but rather their "vicarious living" and "echo chamber" pleasures
(*Law and Literature* 326–331).[16] I am merely skeptical that they are
fruitfully regarded as works of political or moral instruction. I deny
that even "Dickens is an author who demands to be read ethically, and
ethically in a very specific sense, with attention to . . . the misery caused
human beings by unique social institutions" ("Exactly and Responsibly" 360). An author can't "demand" anything of his readers, least of all
that they value his works for its political content whether or not important to him. The social criticism in Dickens's novels—dated, frequently
superficial, and sentimental—is no longer their most valuable aspect, if
it ever was.

Because novels and plays present human characters whose motivations, values, personality, decisions, and intelligence constitute a focus
of interest for the reader or viewer (remember the contrast I drew earlier between literature on the one hand and abstract painting and music
on the other), it is natural to think that we might take a judgmental
stance toward them, just as we do to the real people with whom we interact. Just the fact that works of literature so often contain both "vil-

---

15. These are not mere "mention[s]," deficient in "detailed analysis," as Nussbaum con-
tends ("Exactly and Responsibly" 345). *Law and Literature* discusses in considerable detail
novels and novellas by Dostoevsky, Manzoni, Melville, Kafka, Camus, Richard Wright, and
others—and in great detail works of literature that while not novels are not lyric poems either, including the Homeric epics and a number of plays by Greek and Elizabethan drama-
tists. I discuss novels and a play in this chapter and two novels in the next.

16. See also Peter Caws, "Moral Certainty in Tolstoy," 24 *Philosophy and Literature* 49
(2000).

lains" and "heroes" shows that we're meant to make value judgments about characters in literature. The vicarious life to which literature beckons has, like real life, a moral dimension. But the moral evaluation of a fictional character takes place within a framework created by the work of literature, which may have little to do with our social world. Who is a hero and who a villain is relative to the values of the character's fictional world rather than to our values. This point defeats any project of comparing the characters (or their implied authors) in different works of literature along a moral dimension. We cannot, without seeming ridiculous, say that Pip is a better man than Achilles, or Leopold Bloom than Odysseus. To make such comparisons would require ripping the characters out of their context and so destroying the aesthetic structure of which they are components. We can say that Shylock is a more interesting character because more realistic than his counterpart, the diabolical Barabas, in Marlowe's "Jewish" play. But to say that *The Merchant of Venice* is a better play than *The Jew of Malta* not because its Jew is more interesting and lifelike (and so perhaps to the original audience *more* sinister),[17] but because he is a little closer to the modern conception of the Jew than Barabas, is to confuse the aesthetic with the political and moral realms.

Nussbaum claims that a particular philosophical position, which she associates with Aristotle, "requires literary works of a very specific type, primarily exemplified by the late novels of James, for its complete investigation" ("Exactly and Responsibly" 348). The philosophical position that she describes involves moral particularism and an emphasis on the cognitive (especially the evaluative) role of the emotions and on human vulnerability, in contrast to the Stoics' emphasis on self-sufficiency; she sees this mixture as conducing to an egalitarian outlook. The relation of this point to James's late novels is obscure, however, and anyway what does it mean for a philosophical position to "require" works of literature?

Elsewhere Nussbaum has said something simpler—that James is to be our moral guide: "in the war against moral obtuseness, the artist is our fellow fighter, frequently our guide."[18] The particular guidance

17. Shakespeare's play, like Marlowe's, vividly parades all the traditional scary stereotypes about Jews, see James Shapiro, *Shakespeare and the Jews* (1996), but with greater realism.

18. Martha C. Nussbaum, *Love's Knowledge: Essays on Philosophy and Literature* 164 (1990), cited in this chapter as *Love's Knowledge*. The quoted passage could serve as the motto of moralistic criticism.

that she finds in *The Golden Bowl* is that the dishonored wife should get rid of her husband's lover without rage, without indignation, and without ruffling the smooth surface of sociability on which the four persons involved in the adulterous liaison, either as participants or as victims, floated. She should "grow up" and accept her husband's adultery. "To be a woman, to give herself to her husband, Maggie will need to come to see herself as something cracked, imperfect" (*Love's Knowledge* 133–134). If this is how Aristotle's approach resolves moral issues, it is banal, unedifying, trivializing, and untrue to James.[19] Nor does Nussbaum's choice of this approach seem to owe anything to philosophical argument or moral theory. She "might say that the reactions [to James] she admires are adult, whereas the others are childish, but that would be a moral judgment on her part. What she has not shown, and could not show, is that such a distinction is demanded by philosophical reflection—but that is her claim."[20]

In a discussion of *The Ambassadors*, Nussbaum casts Mrs. Newsome as Kant and Lambert Strether as Aristotle (*Love's Knowledge*, ch. 6). I would prefer to call Mrs. Newsome a Calvinist and Strether a Calvinist shaken in his beliefs by his encounter with French worldliness and sensuality. But I accept Nussbaum's point that literary characters can sometimes be recast as spokesmen for rival philosophical positions, even in a less overtly "philosophical" novel than *La Nausée* or *The Magic Mountain*. Can be, but should they be? They are less interesting when they are made the poster children of philosophical doctrines.

One of James's late novels that Nussbaum does not discuss—it would be particularly difficult to fit to her thesis—is the penultimate one, *The Wings of the Dove*. Kate Croy, the novel's central character, is a monster. But she is a monster for whom the novel engenders in the reader a deep sympathy because of her strength, purposefulness, beauty, charm, in-

---

19. "To focus on the moral issues in *The Golden Bowl* is to risk losing sight of the prurient and Gothic vein of James's imagination—his fascination with the lurid, the unnatural, the quasi-incestuous . . . and the voyeuristic: the wife committing adultery with her stepson-in-law . . . the father and daughter aware of and managing the adultery, the whole weird ménage seen through the eyes of the shocked and fascinated squares . . . James was not a moralist, but something stranger and more interesting." *Law and Literature* 318. See also Camille Paglia, *Sexual Personae: Art and Decadence from Nefertiti to Emily Dickinson* 607–622 (1990) ("Henry James, normally considered a social novelist, is a Decadent Late Romantic, which gives his writing its unique and aggravating character," id. at 607); notes 21 and 22 below. One of James's finest novels, *The Tragic Muse*, is a celebration of the artist's moral *ir*responsibility.

20. D. Z. Phillips, *Philosophy's Cool Place* 135 (1999).

telligence, boldness, and ambition. She stands for life, in contrast not only to Millie Theale, the ostensible heroine of the novel, sickly and dying, but also to Merton Densher, Kate's fiancé, who like most men in James's novels is weak.[21] It is also and critically the case that Kate lacks money, as does Charlotte in *The Golden Bowl*, a Kate-like character whom I am not alone in finding more endearing than Maggie, the ostensible, and to Nussbaum the actual, heroine.[22] But Kate and Charlotte are not poor, and it would be odd to describe Henry James as an egalitarian and even odder to describe Aristotle so.

Granted, if the "moral" issue in literature is taken to be, in a manner more Greek than modern, not "How can we be good?" but "How should one live?" (*Love's Knowledge* 173), there may be a sense in which literature can provide "moral" guidance. The bookish may identify with characters in literature, or with the values of the implied author, and that identification may produce a change in the reader's outlook. But this, the vicarious-living aspect of literature, the possibility of "trying on" a character or a suite of values that one encounters in a work of literature to see whether it fits, is unrelated to any concept of moral betterment or political enlightenment. Nothing in the nature of literature or any of its genres, including the realistic novel, tends to produce models of modern moral behavior. The classic works of literature were produced in a variety of moral climates by people who for the most part were not moralists or political theorists, or, if they were, had values alien to ours. It is not surprising, in view of this provenance, that the moral values reflected in these works cover a huge range with no tendency to converge on our values. The morality play, moreover, has not been a genre popular with the greatest writers. Kate Croy is one of countless charming immoralists who populate the literary canon. Insofar as the values reflected in works of literature influence the moral beliefs of some readers, there is no tendency to reinforce any *particular* school of morality, and thus, for example, to make these readers more egalitarian. You must pick and choose to find the edifying works.

Nussbaum concedes this point with respect to what she describes as "a different task" (different, that is, from the Aristotle–James project)—

21. James "invests a great deal of space convincing us that she [Kate] is likely the most complex, socially capable, and intelligent character in the novel." Robert B. Pippin, *Henry James and Modern Moral Life* 6 (2000). See also id. at 21 n. 6.

22. See id. at 78–80, 87 n. 18.

that of "commending *certain* works of literature to citizens and public officials, as a valuable source of deliberative enrichment" ("Exactly and Responsibly" 349–350).[23] These are works that promote sympathy for "the poor and excluded" (id. at 351). The difference between the moral value of such works and that of the late novels of Henry James is the difference between sympathy (or compassion) and empathy.[24] James's novels, like great literature generally, stimulate in their small readership empathy in its sense of capacity and inclination to enter imaginatively into other ways of life, good *or* bad, but leave it to the reader to decide whom to sympathize with, Kate or Milly, Charlotte or Maggie.

Nussbaum's critical approach can be summarized as follows: interpret the work of literature to make it as edifying as possible (her technique with James); rap the knuckles of the generally edifying author when he lapses into moral obtuseness (as with antisemitism in James's novels); bring into the canon works that are edifying even if they are deficient in aesthetic merit of the usual kinds; and discard literature that has a "bad influence" ("Exactly and Responsibly" 353). Nussbaum places Nietzsche and Wagner in the last category; if these are examples, the list is endless. They are to be excluded because "literature needs ethical assessment and . . . not all works will prove valuable in my imaginary curriculum for citizenship" (id. at 355). "Localized patches of obtuseness" can be forgiven, though they must, as I have noted, be pointed out. But if a work viewed as a whole flunks the moral test—that of conformity to Nussbaum's liberal political and social views—then it can be read only "for historical interest or for rhetorical and grammatical interest" (id. at 356).

Such mediocre novels as Richard Wright's *Native Son* and E. M. Forster's *Maurice* become for Nussbaum exemplary works of literature because of their compassionate regard for blacks and homosexuals, respectively. The literary imagination is equated to the possession of a social conscience. No body of literature is exempt from her censorious gaze. Her emphasis may be on the "realist Anglo-American novel[s] . . . with [their] social and political themes" (*Poetic Justice* 10), but of Sophocles too she says that "it is impossible to see what it could mean to

23. It *seems* a very different task, yet she soon brings James back into the discussion, bracketing him with Dickens.

24. In short, to know is *not* necessarily to love. Michael Stocker with Elizabeth Hegeman, *Valuing Emotions* 214–217 (1996).

read" his plays "in the detached"—that is, aesthetic or formalistic—
"way."[25] She claims without qualification that the novel—the genre, not
the subgenre constituted by the Anglo-American realist novel—"con-
structs empathy and compassion in ways highly relevant to citizenship"
(*Poetic Justice* 10). Again without qualification she expresses agreement
with the view that "the novel as genre is committed to liberalism in its
very form"[26] and that "in a genre such as the novel, a turning away from
traditional political concerns to private concerns and formal experimentation is awfully likely to express a wish to avoid some unpleasant
social reality."[27] Nussbaum has even made her writ run to lyric poetry,
though the only poet mentioned is Walt Whitman, as well as to Greek
and Renaissance tragedy (*Poetic Justice* 6–7). She derives "joy" from the
egalitarian sentiments in Dickens's novels ("Exactly and Responsibly"
362), in particular *Hard Times,* which most readers of Dickens don't
consider among his best. She even insists on bracketing James with
Dickens.

Nussbaum's approach is commended, though in a fashion that seems
equivocal, in a review of her book *Poetic Justice* by another public intellectual, Morris Dickstein. He is well aware that Nussbaum is exaggerating the edifying content of literature—that she is mistaken to think
that literary quality is correlated with social-democratic politics:

> Are novels really this virtuous and high-minded [as Nussbaum be-
> lieves]? They can also seduce us in illicit and unexpected ways.
> There are novels in which we identify with the rich and successful,
> not the "disadvantaged"; novels that turn people into butts of sat-
> ire, even hatred; novels manipulating our fantasies rather than en-
> larging our sympathies . . . Nussbaum's argument depends too
> much on novels up-to-date in their politics but strictly 19th-cen-
> tury in their storytelling conventions.

But that, he thinks, is just what we need: "Nussbaum's appeal to the
outlook of fiction as a model for judicial and social policy is bracingly

25. Martha C. Nussbaum, *Cultivating Humanity: A Classical Defense of Reform in Liberal Education* 104 (1997).

26. Id. at 105.

27. Martha C. Nussbaum, "Invisibility and Recognition: Sophocles' *Philoctetes* and
Ellison's *Invisible Man*," 23 *Philosophy and Literature* 257, 280 (1999).

utopian and immensely heartening . . . *Poetic Justice* is less a study of literature than a lay sermon for beleaguered liberals."[28] Exactly.

With Nussbaum's conception of literature's value compare that of George Steiner. Although his overwhelming erudition, which is not worn lightly, and the solemnity and portentousness of his prose, rather grate on the Anglo-American sensibility, no one will deny him the title of a lover of literature and the arts. He is also a social democrat, and a noted public intellectual to boot. Yet when Steiner asks himself whether public encouragement of high culture (and there is none higher than Henry James) is consistent with "the ideals and the institutions of democracy" or can be justified "on any pragmatic-democratic basis" or on the basis of "social justice," he answers no.[29] Steiner is well aware that few people nowadays are interested in works of high culture and that there is no evidence that force-feeding the populace, even the educated populace, with such works would yield any social, political, or moral dividends. But these points, Steiner argues, are impertinent in the literal sense—that is, not pertinent to his love of works of high culture—because, for him, these works are "the excuse for life."[30] This is a little grand; but it captures the essential attitude of the lover of literature toward literature, which is one of love rather than of use.

Or even of friendship. Nussbaum follows Wayne Booth in employing the metaphor of friendship to describe the relation between the reader of a work of literature on the one hand, and on the other the characters in the work and its implied author (for neither Booth nor Nussbaum believes that the moral beliefs or behavior of the actual author are relevant to the evaluation of the work). In Nussbaum's version more than in Booth's, it is a cold and calculating friendship. "Just as we may criticize our friends while still remaining friends, so too we may criticize James for having prejudices that were a little retrograde in his time, without utterly condemning him . . . But the question will always be, what are we offered that makes us want to maintain the friendship despite what we criticize?" ("Exactly and Responsibly" 355–356). Nussbaum's implicit answer is—political support.

"We see in Nussbaum's work a sort of 'Take two Flaubert and call me

---

28. Morris Dickstein, "Moral Fiction: A Case for the Novel as a Source of Truth in the Information Society," *New York Times Book Review*, April 7, 1996, p. 19.

29. The quotations are from Steiner, note 2 above, at 117–118.

30. Id. at 119.

in the morning' approach to all kinds of moral deficiencies."[31] It is not an approach likely to change many minds. Values are not changed by making people (presumably as students) read literary works of edifying content, or by doctoring that content to make it conform to our current prejudices. Literature has too feeble a grip on the modern mind; students sense when they are being propagandized;[32] and the specific values of cosmopolitan egalitarianism that Nussbaum propagates are too rigorist to be effectively inculcated. She cites no case of a nation, a community, or even a single person edified by the novels of Dickens, James, Wright, or Forster, or any other work of literature. And while she is right that the Nazi leaders were not great readers and so could not have been saved by Dickens, her observation misses the essential point—that the cultural sophistication of the *Gymnasium*-educated upper and upper-middle class of Germany, including the judiciary and the professoriat, did not inoculate the members of that class against participating, often with passionate enthusiasm, in the Nazi system. To *that* point she has no reply, provoking Simon Stow's quip that all her claim for reading amounts to is that "reading will only engender compassion in those who already have it."[33]

Henry James's most socially engaged—and also, and relatedly, most Dickensian—novel is *The Princess Casamassima*, and naturally it has drawn Nussbaum's attention (*Love's Knowledge*, ch. 7), just as it had Lionel Trilling's. Conceived in political terms, *The Princess Casamassima* is, as Trilling pointed out, in the tradition of distinguished literary warnings against revolutionary terrorism;[34] in this respect it is perhaps closest to Conrad's *The Secret Agent*. Nussbaum tries to make *The Princess Casamassima* a work of advocacy for her own political position, which is approximately that of the British Labour Party before Tony

31. Simon Stow, "Unbecoming Virulence: The Politics of the Ethical Criticism Debate," 24 *Philosophy and Literature* 185, 194 (2000).

32. One should be "suspicious of attempts to require courses that will shape students' sociopolitical attitudes, the sort of courses students at Berkeley now refer to as 'compulsory chapel.'" Richard Rorty, "John Searle on Realism and Relativism," in Rorty, *Truth and Progress* 63, 67 (1998).

33. Stow, note 31 above, at 193–194.

34. Lionel Trilling, "The Princess Casamassima," in Trilling, *The Liberal Imagination: Essays on Literature and Society* 59, 69–74 (1976). It is ironic that Nussbaum wrote her essay on *The Princess Casamassima* in honor of Hilary Putnam, who once advocated revolutionary violence. *Love's Knowledge* 195–196, 217.

Blair and comprises socialist economic and social policies, political liberty, and the preservation and encouragement of art and other cultural activities.[35] She believes that these three sets of policies are mutually supporting. For example, the alleviation of poverty is necessary to enable people to enjoy art, yet the cultivation of an artistic sensibility is equally important to foster a temperament that will resist political fanaticism. The last point is a central plank in the platform of the ethical critic yet is actually refuted (so far as novels may ever be said to "refute") by *The Princess Casamassima* in the person of Millicent Henning, who is at once philistine and impervious to radical politics.

Whatever the merits of the program of Old Labour, they are not commended in James's novel. Nussbaum quotes a passage to show that James rejects any notion of hereditary aristocracy "by insisting repeatedly that it is material conditions, conditions that can be changed, that make the difference in thought."[36] In fact the passage ("centuries of poverty, of ill-paid toil, of bad, insufficient food and wretched homes, had not a favourable effect upon the higher faculties . . . In his own low walk of life people had really not the faculty of thought; their minds had been simplified") is a Lamarckian or Social Darwinian commonplace about the inheritance of acquired characteristics—and Hyacinth Robinson himself, the shining exception, whose mind has not been simplified despite his low walk of life, is the son of a nobleman. The novel insists repeatedly on Hyacinth's French characteristics, such as facility with the French language, even though he had never known his French mother. James's emphasis (actually overemphasis) on inherited characteristics implies that alleviating poverty would have no immediate effect on character and taste—generations of affluence would be necessary to "recomplexify" those "simplified" minds. That is not Nussbaum's view. She thinks that Hyacinth owes his remarkable sensitivity and culture (but his knowledge of French? where did that come from?) to his stable, loving upbringing. Yet the most unrealistic feature of the novel, because intelligible only in terms of the inheritance of acquired characteristics (the French mother and noble father, neither of whom Hyacinth ever knew), is that although Hyacinth is ap-

---

35. For a compendious summary expressly invoking the "Britain of the pre-Thatcher years," see *Love's Knowledge* 205–206. I discuss Nussbaum's politics further in Chapter 9.

36. *Love's Knowledge* 201, quoting Henry James, *The Princess Casamassima* 217–218 (Penguin ed. 1987). The text reprinted by Penguin is the original (1886) text of the novel.

prenticed as an artisan at the age of fifteen, after having had virtually no education, he is cultivated, well read, fluent, grammatical, gentlemanly. None of these things can be produced simply by a warm and stable home.

Much is said in the novel about wealth and poverty but none of the characters is actually poor by nineteenth-century standards (although some live in straitened circumstances) and the real drama and interest lie far from social questions. Hyacinth Robinson, who is short, delicate, hypersensitive, ineffectual, and asexual, forms with Paul Muniment— robust, callous, the ruthless man of action who gets the girl Hyacinth has been pining for (the Princess)—a "twinned hero."[37] By himself nei- ther twin is a satisfactory human being. Cultured but incomplete, ob- serving but inert, Hyacinth is the type of the artist, and his suicide marks the artist's incapacity for full participation in the world—and reveals *The Princess Casamassima* as belonging to the same genre as Mann's *Tonio Kröger* and Kafka's *The Hunger Artist*. It is secondarily a novel of betrayal, and Millicent is one of the betrayers (in fact, the ulti- mate betrayer), as Nussbaum, who describes Millicent as "generous and compassionate and loving . . . her genuine kindness of heart sus- tain[s] him in a very essential way" (*Love's Knowledge* 216), neglects to mention. We are far from the platform of Harold Wilson's Labour Party.

Nussbaum is entitled to take an interest in literature whose "sub- ject matter is not aesthetic, but ethical or political (as is the case with many realist novels)" ("Exactly and Responsibly" 359). But *The Princess Casamassima* is not such a novel. Nussbaum has mistaken background, the *mise-en-scène*, for subject.

There is a superficial primness to Henry James, a function of a per- sonal and a prose style easily misunderstood. But he was a great art- ist, and his vision was aesthetic rather than ethical. Of another great modernist it has been said, in words equally applicable to James, that "intuitions of splendour cut across his existence with a strength which ethical discourse could not compass."[38] To this aspect of literature Nussbaum is blind.

37. Derek Brewer, "Introduction," in id. at 7, 19.
38. A. D. Nuttall, "Two Political Poems: Marvell's 'Horatian Ode' and Yeats's 'No Second Troy,'" in 105 *Proceedings of the British Academy* 115, 128 (2000).

By seeking to make literature safe for politics, the literary critic as public intellectual not only devalues literature but may actually endanger it (though only slightly, since the power of public intellectuals is slight) in three closely related ways. First, if literature is a branch of political advocacy, it has no *distinctive* value; it is interchangeable with a political speech or advertisement. Second, when political criteria are imposed on literature, the list of canonical works that emerges (*Maurice, Native Son, Uncle Tom's Cabin*, and so forth) is mediocre (preachy, dreary, banal, sentimental, implausible, poorly written), making readers wonder—if this is the "best" literature, why bother with literature at all? Many a student has been turned off to literature by the emphasis of college English departments on edifying works. Third, if literature has political significance, it invites censorship; it is better protected when it is thought harmless.[39] Poetry makes nothing happen, as Auden said in his threnody to William Butler Yeats—and he was right, as well as trying to ward off the censors.

These are, no doubt, themselves political or ideological points. Simon Stow is wrong to argue, however, that a political defense of the aesthetic approach to literature must be ironic, if not self-contradictory.[40] He has committed the genetic fallacy. One might prefer the aesthetic approach because one thought it truer to the "nature" of literature than the alternatives, or because one thought it gave more pleasure, or because one thought the alternatives politically undesirable, or for a combination of these and other reasons. None of the reasons would alter the *character* of the approach. The practitioner would still resist the politicization of works of literature, though that would sometimes involve him in another activity that seems to Stow to contradict the aesthetic approach—that of correcting the political interpretations placed on a work of literature by didactic critics. One way to try to shake Nussbaum's commitment to didactic criticism is to show that the interpretation she places on a work such as *The Princess Casamassima* is implausible. James is not the ally she thinks. To point that out is not to claim him as an ally of someone else or to commend the search for political allies among writers.

39. As shown in Peter D. McDonald, "'Not Undesirable': How J. M. Coetzee Escaped the Censor," *Times Literary Supplement*, May 19, 2000, p. 14.

40. Stow, note 31 above, at 188.

〜 "DESPITE HER repeated affirmation that the autonomy of literary art must be recognized and respected by the interested moral
philosopher, say, or legal theorist, Nussbaum fails to persuade, here as
in her previous work, that her concern with literature is a concern with
something more than drawing a moral lesson from it."[41] She does not
deny the possibility of formalistic criticism, but for her it is another
form of ethical criticism: "The New Critics' decision *not* to concern
themselves with the social and historical dimensions of literary works
was itself a political act, an act of a quietistic sort."[42] Wayne Booth seeks
to deflect charges that ethical criticism is insensitive to literary values
by balancing the purely aesthetic, or formal, values of literature against
the ethical conceived in the very broadest "How should one live?"
sense. He argues that as between two works of literature—both beautiful, exciting, memorable but one implicitly commending virtue in either the moral or the broader ethical sense *(ethos, virtu)* or criticizing
vice, and the other reversing these valences—the one that is ethically
superior should be considered the finer work of literature. And so we
might, if "liberal," prefer Euripides to Sophocles, Dreiser to Hemingway, Steinbeck to Fitzgerald, Auden to Pound, Naipaul to Nabokov. If
we are "conservative," we may want to reverse these orderings. We
may wish to say with Irving Kristol that "Jane Austen is a greater novelist than Proust or Joyce" and that "T. S. Eliot's later, Christian poetry is
much superior to his earlier."[43] Ethical criticism is not a monopoly of
the Left.

From statements culled from my writings—for example, that "we are
. . . made to understand [by Homer] that revenge ought to have some
limits—that Achilles goes too far in mutilating Hector and that the return of Hector's body to Priam is necessary to prevent the Greeks from

41. David Gorman, Book Review [of *Poetic Justice*], 21 *Philosophy and Literature* 196, 198
(1997).

42. Nussbaum, note 25 above, at 106.

43. Irving Kristol, "Reflections of a Neoconservative," 51 *Partisan Review* 856, 859 (1984).
The word "much" raises a question whether Kristol is a serious reader of modern poetry. It is
possible to prefer *Ash-Wednesday* and *Four Quartets* (and Eliot's other Christian poetry) to *The
Love Song of J. Alfred Prufrock* and *The Waste Land* (and the other secular poems of his youth),
but to regard the former as "much superior" to the latter is an eccentric judgment that Kristol
might have been expected, if serious, to try to defend. Kristol's entire attitude toward Christianity is peculiar, as we'll see in Chapter 8.

crossing the line that separates lawful revenge from barbarism"[44]—
Booth argues that even I must agree deep down that ethical criticism of
literature is inescapable. The *Iliad,* like *Hamlet* and many other works
of literature, cocks a critical eye at revenge. This enabled me to press
these works into service as jurisprudential texts, as others have used
them as historical or anthropological documents. It does not follow
that the value of these works as literature depends to even an infini-
tesimal degree on whether we agree with the position they take on revenge; or that, culturally remote from us as they are and barren of systematic argument or evidence, they should alter our views about the
proper role of revenge in the criminal justice system, global politics, or
everyday life. They illustrate jurisprudential possibilities but they do
not supply the arguments or the evidence that we would need to be
able to choose intelligently among them.

What Booth should have said is that a work can be both a work of literature and a contribution to political thought, a public-intellectual
work. This combination is particularly common in satire; we'll consider important examples in the next chapter. I should say "other" important examples, because *Hard Times* is a satire, a satire of Jeremy
Bentham's version of utilitarianism. A didactic writer with strong political convictions, Dickens was a major nineteenth-century public intellectual, and we can if we want treat *Hard Times* as a public-intellectual
work. But if we do so we shall diminish it because of my earlier point
that the political content of a work of literature usually dates very
quickly. The deficiencies of utilitarianism are by now so well known
that reading *Hard Times* as an anti-utilitarian tract becomes an occasion
for beating a dead horse. Nor will defenders of utilitarianism be shaken
by Dickens's novel; they've had a century and a half to hone their arguments. It is almost a detail that *Hard Times* is a crude satire that
does not do justice to the variety of utilitarian thought, or even to
Bentham.[45] *Hard Times* lives on not as social commentary but as literature.

To prove the inescapability of the ethical in any final aesthetic judgment on a work of literature, even when it is a brief lyric, Booth does

44. Booth, note 7 above, at 368, quoting *Law and Literature* 72–73.

45. See Donald Winch, "Mr Gradgrind and Jerusalem," in *Economy, Polity, and Society:
British Intellectual History 1750–1950* 243, 257–265 (Stefan Collini, Richard Whatmore, and
Brian Young eds., 2000).

something very strange—I am tempted to say desperate: he changes the end of the second stanza of Keats's "Ode on Melancholy" so that feeding on peerless eyes[46] becomes stroking peerless thighs. But this is *aesthetic* butchery. The imagery of devouring (mostly poison) is pervasive in the poem, and this gives the image of feeding on the peerless eyes a resonance and hint of menace that Booth's image of stroking thighs lacks. The substitution changes an image of great emotional power—because of the fusion of devouring with seeing—that is integral to the poem's pattern of imagery into an irruption of soft-core porn that breaks the spell created by the poet. Not that pornography can't be literature; but the "Ode on Melancholy" is not improved by being made risqué, just as a pig is not enhanced by wearing lipstick. Everything in its place. Booth must value lyric poetry *solely* for its music, so that as long as the substitution of one word for another preserves rhyme and meter, the substitution cannot damage the poem.

His *pièce de résistance* is a rewriting of *The Merchant of Venice* as a play in which Shylock is painted in the blackest hues and the Christians in the whitest; he also offers a version in which the hues are reversed. Booth claims that from a purely aesthetic standpoint his fiercely antisemitic version is just as good as Shakespeare's original, which goes to show the inadequacy of that standpoint, since his version is loathsome. But we already have *that* play—*The Jew of Malta*. It's a splendid play, and no doubt Shakespeare could have out-Marlowed Marlowe in presenting the Jew as monster—for look what he did with Iago, Regan, and Goneril. Wayne Booth isn't as good a playwright as either Marlowe or Shakespeare, so his revised *Merchant* falls flat. And speaking of Iago, I note that Booth doesn't argue that *Othello* is marred by Shakespeare's not having portrayed Iago with the empathy with which he portrays Shylock. The "flat" Iago is "right" for the kind of play that *Othello* is, and the more rounded figure of Shylock is right for the kind of play that *The Merchant of Venice* is. Booth must know this, because his philosemitic rewriting of the play is *just as awful* as his semitophobic rewriting; its ethical superiority doesn't tip the evaluative balance a millimeter.

---

46. Or if thy mistress some rich anger shows,
    Emprison her soft hand, and let her rave,
    And feed deep, deep upon her peerless eyes.

The Merchant of Venice is a comedy, and in almost every comedy young lovers are initially thwarted by an older person, sometimes a buffoon but sometimes an ogre, and the plot is the overcoming of this obstacle by the lovers and ends with their marriage. Shakespeare was notably defiant of literary convention, so *The Merchant of Venice* cracks the mold. The marriage takes place before the end of the play, and the ogre—Shylock—actually facilitates the marriage by financing Bassanio's courtship of Portia, though he then becomes an obstacle to their felicity by his threat against Antonio, to whom Bassanio owes a lot.

To say that Shylock is an ogre grates on modern sensibilities. But to an Englishman of Shakespeare's time a Jew was almost a mythical being. The Jews had been expelled from England by Richard the Lionheart in the thirteenth century, and though there were a few Jews in London in Shakespeare's time, they were hardly a regular part of the city's life; for all we know Shakespeare never met one. Strange rumors were abroad about Jews, including that they drank the blood of Christian children on Passover; this rumor is echoed in the pound-of-flesh pact in the play. The ogreish character of Jews is a given in the play, and if you want to understand and enjoy a work of literature you must grant the author his givens. That is precisely what the moralistic critic refuses to do. Anthony Julius, though deeply offended by the antisemitic passages in T. S. Eliot's poems and essays and insistent that Eliot was a serious antisemite, rightly argues that the antisemitic passages are organic to the poems, that the antisemitic poems are organic to Eliot's poetic *oeuvre*, and that the *oeuvre* has great artistic value. "One can teach anti-Semitism from such texts; one can also teach poetry. One reads them, appalled, and impressed."[47]

Shylock is a fantasy Jew, and there is much else in the play, as in so many comedies (and for that matter many tragedies), that is also fantasy. The sixteenth-century English legal system would not have enforced a penalty clause of the kind contained in Antonio's bond, involving the killing of the debtor, especially when the debtor offers to repay the creditor's loan with extravagant interest. The riddling method that

47. Anthony Julius, *T. S. Eliot, Anti-Semitism, and Literary Form* 40 (1995). See also Christopher Ricks, *T. S. Eliot and Prejudice* 28–33 (1988). Julius, however, exaggerates Eliot's antisemitism. See Christopher Hitchens, "How Unpleasant to Meet Mr Eliot," in Hitchens, *Unacknowledged Legislation: Writers in the Public Sphere* 184 (2000).

Portia is constrained to employ for choosing a husband is another fantasy element, echoing the tales of medieval chivalry in which the fair maid is won by the hero who risks all, as Bassanio does. The element of fantasy in the play should make it easier for a modern audience to suspend its disbelief in the inherent wickedness of Jews.

Shakespeare was an actor as well as a playwright, and there is an actor's adage that no man is a villain in his own eyes. To play a villain convincingly, the actor must play him from the inside, must make him appear to us as he appears to himself. It is much easier to do this if the playwright has given the villain self-exculpatory speeches. Think of Edmund in *King Lear* defending the claims of bastards to equal treatment with legitimate children, or Macbeth's introspective soliloquies, or even Claudius (in *Hamlet*) trying to pray. So Shakespeare has Shylock state the case for himself eloquently, referring to his abuse by Christians and asserting his common humanity with them and movingly recalling his love for his dead wife. Today, when the status of Jews has changed greatly since Shakespeare's time, these lines seem self-evident rather than merely plausible or ingenious, and a skillful director and cast can redirect the audience's sympathy from the other characters to Shylock.

It is all the easier to do because Shakespeare has made the Christians less than fully attractive. Even Portia, that icon of women lawyers today, is a trickster. It is not so much that she impersonates a doctor of laws—a very small sin, in the world of the play, to save a man's life. It is that she betrays her father by giving Bassanio, her choice for husband, the hint that helps him solve the riddle and that she conceals from the Venetian court her financial interest in Shylock's case—for it is out of her pocket that Bassanio proposes to repay Shylock's loan, and Portia arranges things so that Shylock won't have to be repaid anything. Bassanio himself is a classic gold digger, borrowing money to give himself a good appearance so he can win the hand of the rich girl. Jessica is a thief and Lorenzo her accomplice. And Antonio not only is a rather depressed and depressing bachelor, but also has definite affinities with Shylock. Both are modeled on the Puritans, whom Shakespeare must have disliked since they wanted to close down the theater (and succeeded in doing so a quarter of a century after Shakespeare's death). The last scene of the play opens ominously with Lorenzo and Jessica invoking four classical examples of doomed romances—Troilus and Cressida, Dido and Aeneas, Pyramus and Thisbe, and Jason and Medea. Three of the four romances (all but that of Pyramus and Thisbe) involved a betrayal by one of the lovers.

But it would be a mistake to try to turn the tables and make Shylock the hero and the Christians the villains. *The Merchant of Venice* is a comedy, with young lovers and an old ogre; and if the young lovers are not entirely pure, if there is a distinctly mercenary element to their relationship, and if the ogre is not entirely without a claim to the audience's sympathy, still there can be little doubt that we are meant to enjoy, and even admire, Bassanio's debonair charm (in sharp contrast to the dourness of both Antonio and Shylock), his risk-taking, his aristocratic indifference to commerce, and Portia's beauty and cleverness, and to see their marriage, once Shylock is vanquished, as the achievement of a true felicity, the defeat of bad by good, age by youth, commercial by aristocratic values, gloom by joy. There is a certain naïveté in the idea that a person can't be a real villain unless he's 100 percent a villain. It is an aspect of the fallacy that I mentioned in Chapter 2 of exaggerating the degree to which an individual is a unity. We should not be surprised that Hitler loved children and animals, or Shylock his wife.

The Merchant of Venice is sufficiently plastic that it can be pressed into public-intellectual harness to work on either side of the political divide. It was one of the Nazis' favorite plays but it has also been performed in Yiddish theaters (once with Shylock speaking German and the Christian characters Yiddish!).[48] People obsessed with politics, with what they think is social justice, with contemporary social problems generally, or with historical injustices (such as the mistreatment of Jews by Christians or blacks by whites) are incapable of divorcing the experience of reading literature from their nonliterary concerns and can't resist making *The Merchant of Venice* a political football. Not for them the possibility of stepping from time to time outside of the quotidian world with its political and religio-ethical obsessions and its professional preoccupations and into a world of morally and politically indifferent enchantment.

I do not argue that there is *no* role for political critique of literature. Some literature fairly begs to be evaluated in political terms. We saw an example in Chapter 3—Auden's poem "Spain 1937." Orwell's criti-

---

48. John Gross, *Shylock: A Legend and Its Legacy* 241, 276–282, 319–322 (1992).

cism of it exemplifies worthwhile public-intellectual literary criticism. There are many other good examples as well, such as *Patriotic Gore*, Edmund Wilson's study of the literature of the American Civil War. But it is noteworthy that Orwell was criticizing a *contemporary* work of literature and that most of the texts discussed in *Patriotic Gore* are not literary texts. The fact that great literature is almost by definition separable from the social context of its creation does not eradicate that context, but neither does it suggest that injecting great literature into modern political debates is a fruitful way to treat that literature. Doing so is more likely to diminish the literature than to improve the debates. And, by the way, the change that Auden made in "Spain 1937" in response to Orwell's criticism—the change from "necessary murder" to "fact of murder"—weakened the poem.

~ 7

Political Satire

$\mathcal{P}$UBLISHED a half century ago, in a political, economic, and social milieu now felt to be rapidly receding, *Nineteen Eighty-Four* has yet managed to retain a certain topicality. Originally celebrated as a warning against the totalitarian actuality of the Soviet Union and like tendencies that Orwell discerned in the West, it is nowadays more often viewed as a warning against the dangers that technocratic modernism poses to privacy and freedom, which is the light in which I'll be mainly considering it. We glimpsed in Chapter 4 how popular a theme technology is for public intellectuals of the eco-catastrophic and overproduction schools; we shall discover that Orwell belonged to the latter.

It might seem obvious that the most famous work by one of the greatest public intellectuals of the twentieth century would be a gourmet meal for public intellectuals. I am going to challenge this idea with some help from another famous English satiric novel, by another great public intellectual, from the era that produced *Nineteen Eighty-Four*. Aldous Huxley's *Brave New World* was published in 1932 and has many parallels to Orwell's novel, published in 1949, yet it is far more technology intensive.

Both novels are pessimistic about the technological future. Some economic concepts can help us see that there is indeed a downside to technological change and can at the same time reveal some of the limitations of these novels as contributions to public discourse. The concepts are externality, marginality, rent seeking, interaction effects, and economies of scale and scope. These may sound formidable, but are easily and simply explained.

Externality. A seller may fail to take account of the full costs of a new technology, in which event the technology may be introduced even though its net social benefits are negative. For some of the costs may be *external* to the seller's decisionmaking. Supersonic transcontinental airline service would reduce travel time but it would also generate sonic booms, annoying people and breaking windows beneath the flight path. These harms would be costs of supersonic travel but not costs borne by the airline unless the law made it liable for them.

The external effects of a new technology can be positive as well as negative. Because most technological innovations are imitable and patent laws provide only limited protection against imitation, the benefits to consumers of technologically advanced products, ranging from pharmaceuticals to color television, greatly exceed the profits of the manufacturers; the difference is the external benefits of the technology. And workers benefit from increases in productivity brought about by technological advances, because competition by employers for workers enables the workers to capture much of the gain from their increased productivity in the form of higher wages.

The idea that technological progress leads to overproduction and underemployment, eventually bringing on an economic crisis that can be resolved only by war or some kind of collectivism, or in optimistic versions ushering in a utopia that enables all material incentives and resulting inequalities to be eliminated, is at once a public-intellectual staple[1] and an economic fallacy. It is true that by increasing worker productivity, technological progress enables the same output to be produced with fewer workers. But workers made redundant by technological advances in their industry find employment at comparable wages

---

1. Besides the references in Chapter 4, see, for example, Lewis Mumford, *Technics and Civilization* 355 (1934): "the machine has achieved potentially a new collective economy, in which the possession of goods is a meaningless distinction, since the machine can produce all our essential goods in unparallelled quantities." See also id. at 390–406—and Kurt Vonnegut's novel *Player Piano* (1952). For a much more perceptive public-intellectual treatment of the social effects of technological change, see Marshall McLuhan, *Understanding Media: The Extensions of Man* (1964).

in other industries. The enhanced productivity reduces the cost of producing the output of technologically advanced industries, releasing consumers' resources for the purchase of other products, which require workers to produce. Wages have risen and unemployment has fallen in recent years despite a rate of technological advance and economic change far more rapid than foreseen by doomsters who thought that technological progress would wreak economic havoc. It is true, though, that wages have risen faster for educated workers because the particular technologies introduced on a large scale in recent years have enabled the substitution of machines operated by highly skilled workers, notably computers, for the labor of less skilled workers.[2]

Marginality. The output of a competitive market is determined by the intersection of price and marginal cost (the cost of increasing output slightly, as we saw in Chapter 4). This implies that the marginal purchaser—the purchaser willing to pay a price no higher than marginal cost—is the sovereign consumer and drives economic change. A technological innovation attractive to him may thus be introduced even though it lowers consumer welfare overall because it reduces the welfare of the intramarginal consumers more than it increases that of the marginal one. This is a kind of negative externality. It is well illustrated today by the crowding of airplanes due to low fares. The low fares attract the marginal customer; the crowding distresses the intramarginal ones (mainly business travelers).

Rent Seeking. Economic "rents" are gains not offset by costs. A pop singer who has a net income of $500,000 a year but who in her next best job would be a waitress earning $20,000 obtains an economic rent of $480,000 if the only cost she incurs to obtain this income is the forgone income from the waitress's job. This ignores, however, her investment in acquiring the skills that enabled her to become a successful singer. The prospect of large rents is a magnet drawing resources into efforts to obtain the rents. And unlike the example of investing in performing skills, not all costs incurred in rent-seeking increase society's overall wealth. A more lethal gun has value both to criminals—classic rent seekers, because their efforts do not increase the social product but

2. See, for example, Chinhui Juhn, Kevin M. Murphy, and Brooks Pierce, "Wage Inequality and the Rise in Returns to Skill," 101 *Journal of Political Economy* 410 (1993); Kevin M. Murphy and Finis Welch, "The Structure of Wages," 107 *Quarterly Journal of Economics* 285 (1992).

merely shift a portion of it to them—and to the police. After both sides in the war against crime are equipped with the new gun, the innovation's only effect will have been to increase the costs both of crime and of crime control. Likewise with munitions. Indeed, the arms race is the classic example of wasteful competition. The costs incurred in trying to obtain an advantage by developing a new military technology are wasted from the standpoint of overall social welfare except to the extent that the technology can be beneficially adapted to law-abiding civilian use—a spillover analogous to the informational or entertainment quality of advertising that may have been intended purely to wrest business from a competitor.

A form of arms race that is relevant to the two novels under discussion is the struggle on the one hand to invade and on the other hand to protect privacy. Advances in electronics have both increased the efficiency of surveillance and, through such devices as electronic encryption and untraceable e-mail addresses, made some types of communication more private than was possible for users of earlier technologies, such as the telephone.

Interaction Effects. Technological innovations can interact with each other or with the social structure to produce unforeseeable long-run consequences, good or bad. This possibility was dramatized by World War I, which revealed the unexpected destructiveness of warfare in a technologically progressive era. The problem of technology's unanticipated consequences—the subject of a vast literature in history, sociology, and cultural studies[3] and, as we glimpsed in Chapter 4, a prime subject for public intellectuals' speculation—is the problem of externalities writ large. For I am speaking now of external effects that cannot be predicted;[4] often they cannot be evaluated even after they have come to pass. Consider such innovations of the last half century as improved contraceptive and labor-saving devices, fast food, and the automation of many tasks formerly requiring substantial upper-body strength. Their interaction may be a good deal more responsible for women's emancipation from their formerly constrained role in society than *The Second Sex* or *The Feminine Mystique*. And women's technol-

---

3. See, for example, *The Intellectual Appropriation of Technology: Discourses on Modernity, 1900–1939* (Mikael Hård and Andrew Jamison eds., 1998), and references cited there.

4. See the fascinating story of the effect of the invention of the stirrup on medieval society in Lynn White Jr., *Medieval Technology and Social Change*, ch. 1 (1962).

ogy-driven emancipation has brought in its train a high divorce rate, a low marriage rate and high age of first marriage, a high rate of abortion and of birth out of wedlock, a low birth rate, an increase in fertility problems that has contributed in turn to an increased rate of innovation in reproductive technology, and a profound change in sexual morality, including greatly increased tolerance of homosexuality.[5]

None of these consequences was foreseen and the net impact on social welfare is unclear, or at least unmeasurable, though I am inclined to think it positive. Others disagree—and not all on ecological or overproduction grounds. Public intellectual Leon Kass has said that "technology is not problem but tragedy," and that "homogenization, mediocrity, pacification, drug-induced contentment, debasement of taste, souls without loves and longings—these are the inevitable results of making the essence of human nature the last project for technical mastery."[6]

Economies of Scale and Scope. The points made thus far should help us understand the sense that many people have that scientific and technological progress is out of control and leading us into a future that may not be a net improvement on the present. But none of them figures in either *Brave New World* or *Nineteen Eighty-Four.* What worried the authors was that technology, and technocratic methods and attitudes more generally, might destroy both economic competition (the market) and political competition (democracy). Like many of their contemporaries, Huxley and Orwell believed that engineering methods, applied both to production and to people ("social engineering"), epitomized rationality, entailed central planning and centralized control, were more efficient than the free market, and implied political as well as economic rule by experts. In the language of economics, the concern was that technology was bringing about radically increased economies of scale and scope—was making the efficient size and scope of enterprises so large that eventually all activity would be conducted on a monopoly basis.

The relation between monopoly and technology is more compli-

5. See Richard A. Posner, *Sex and Reason* (1992).

6. Leon R. Kass, "Introduction: The Problem of Technology," in *Technology in the Western Political Tradition* 1, 20 (Arthur M. Melzer, Jerry Weinberger, and M. Richard Zinman eds., 1993). On our modern "technology anxiety" generally, see Arthur M. Melzer, "The Problem with the 'Problem of Technology,'" in id. at 287.

cated than this. Technological innovation is costly and commercially risky. If competitors can appropriate the benefits of a successful innovation without having to compensate the innovator, too little innovation may be undertaken. This is the reason for giving innovators patent protection, which is a form of monopoly. So technology may invite monopoly, after all; and at the same time it may lower the costs of monopoly to the would-be monopolist, perhaps by reducing the cost of controlling a large enterprise. Computers were once expected to facilitate central planning of a nation's entire economy—monopoly writ large. Lately they have been substituting for middle management, and this is another way of reducing the costs of internal control of enterprises and so presumably increasing the span of effective control and thus, once again, the optimum size of enterprises. Equally, however, technology can foster decentralization, as by reducing transaction costs among independent firms.[7] And if new and hence small firms happen to be better at technological innovation than large ones,[8] technological progress will favor the small and thus will favor competition over monopoly. It is an empirical question whether technological progress on balance favors monopoly or competition. As of now it appears, contrary to widespread fears in the 1930s and 1940s, not only that competition is a more efficient method of organizing production than central planning but that the more technologically advanced the economy, the greater the advantages of competition.

Nor has technological progress imperiled democracy; rather the opposite. It has brought about an increase in average incomes, and the average income in a society not only is positively correlated with political freedom but also appears to play a causal role in that freedom.[9] But may not technology threaten freedom indirectly, through its effect on privacy? That is difficult to say. When distinguished from autonomy (for which "privacy" has become a common synonym in constitutional law, where rights of sexual and reproductive freedom are described as aspects of the "right of privacy"), privacy has two aspects—solitude and

7. This effect is emphasized in Larry Downes and Chunka Mui, *Unleashing the Killer App: Digital Strategies for Market Dominance* (1998).

8. As argued in Clayton M. Christensen, *The Innovator's Dilemma: When New Technologies Cause Great Firms to Fail* (1997).

9. Richard A. Posner, "Equality, Wealth, and Political Stability," 13 *Journal of Law, Economics, and Organization* 344 (1997).

secrecy. Solitude—not complete isolation, but enough private space to enable a person to think for himself—fosters individualistic attitudes, while conversely the constant presence of other people, or sense of being under constant surveillance, enforces decorum and conformity. Secrecy, in the sense of concealment of what one is thinking, or writing, or saying to friends or other intimates, enables subversive thinking and planning to be hidden from the authorities.

Secrecy has both a private and a social dimension. Being able to hide one's thoughts is important, but it is not enough to protect one from succumbing to conformism; privacy of communication is indispensable. Not only is the planning of concerted activity impossible without communication, but serious independent thinking is hardly possible without having someone to bounce ideas off. And few people are sufficiently independent-minded to persist in holding an unorthodox opinion if they don't know that others share it. We want to be part of a herd even if it is a very small one. So while solitude is a necessary condition of independent thought, secrecy is a necessary condition of the persistence, refinement, propagation, and implementation of that thought.

To a totalitarian regime, the social costs of both solitude and secrecy are great; and in both *Brave New World* and *Nineteen Eighty-Four* a consequence of this fact, conjoined with technological advances that make it cheap to invade but costly to maintain privacy, is that privacy has virtually disappeared.

The cost of maintaining privacy in our society seems to be growing. The culprit is again technology, specifically the "information revolution"—now the "cyberspace revolution."[10] This point will become vivid when we see how labor intensive are the means of surveillance employed in *Nineteen Eighty-Four*. Yet the net amount of privacy seems not to have declined. Privacy is what economists call a "superior good," meaning that a larger quantity is demanded as people's incomes rise. When the demand for a good increases, the amount supplied will rise unless the net cost of supplying the good increases faster than the demand, which seems not to have happened in the case of privacy; technological progress has fostered the protection as well as the invasion of

10. See, for example, Lawrence Lessig, *Code—and Other Laws of Cyberspace* 142–156 (1999).

privacy. If privacy has, on balance, increased rather than decreased, we would expect people to be more independent, individualistic, and self-assertive today than they were in Huxley's and Orwell's time—and they are. But as Huxley intuited, they are also becoming less diverse, and the reason, we'll see, is technology, though not privacy-invading technology.

Privacy as secrecy is not an unalloyed good. Charismatic political leadership—the most dangerous kind—depends on the leader's ability to control public information about himself. If he loses that ability—if he loses his "privacy"—his mystique, and with it his power, erodes. The same technological advances that have made it costly for private persons to protect their privacy have also, by making government more transparent, made it harder for public officials to conceal bad acts—including snooping into the private affairs of the citizenry. This is another reason why on balance technology seems to have increased rather than diminished popular control of government, contrary to the fears of the technology pessimists.

No doubt in examining issues of technology from the standpoint of economics I will be thought to be instantiating the problem as well as analyzing it. Modern economics is a form of "technocratic" thought closely allied to such other technocratic fields as statistics, engineering, computer science, and operations research. Max Weber would have thought that modern economic thinking illustrates the culmination of the trend, which for him defined modernity, toward bringing more and more areas of human activity under the reign of rational methods. This theory, which as we'll see influenced both Huxley and (under the rubric of "managerialism") Orwell, is indeed worth considering in a discussion of the relation of *Brave New World* and *Nineteen Eighty-Four* to issues of technology. We shall see the disenchantment of the world predicted by Weber to be a by-product of the triumph of rational methods popping up in Orwell's novel as a nostalgia for Romantic values. We saw in earlier chapters that it is technocracy, in the form of an increasing specialization and professionalization of knowledge, that is obsolescing the traditional public intellectual.

We need to think about the genre, satire,[11] to which both novels be-

11. Superbly discussed in Alvin Kernan, *The Cankered Muse: Satire of the English Renaissance*, ch. 1 (1959).

long, *Brave New World* more obviously. Satire is a genre of fiction that invites the reader's attention to the flaws in his society, or in society or humanity generally. Often, as in such classics of the genre as *Gulliver's Travels*, it is set in a fantastic world, seemingly remote in time, place, or culture from the satirist's world. Thus the fact that *Brave New World* and *Nineteen Eighty-Four* are set in the future (six hundred years and thirty five years, respectively) need not imply that they are efforts at prophecy, rather than critiques of, or warnings against, tendencies visible in the writer's own society. The futuristic technology in both novels is a straightforward extrapolation from well-known technologies of the authors' time.

Satire is the public-intellectual genre *par excellence*. It conveys social criticism with enchanting, seductive obliquity, avoiding drab social science, heavy-handed didacticism, and explicit and therefore quickly dated prophecy. Yet the enduring interest of the best satire lies elsewhere than in the political concerns that may have motivated it, as I'll try to show with respect to both novels. An equally important point is that satire is the public-intellectual genre to which only the *independent* public intellectual can contribute. It is a literary rather than an academic genre. This is another reason to regret the increasing displacement of the independent by the academic public intellectual. The classic satires are not enough; their social criticism is dated. We need new satires to keep alive the satire as a public-intellectual genre and we are unlikely to get them from the academy except insofar as universities may be willing to employ writers on terms that do not academize the writer to the point of crippling his literary talent.

Most satires have a satirist *character*—a denouncer of the flaws to which the author wishes to invite the reader's attention, but not necessarily the author's alter ego. Often he is a gloomier, shriller figure than the author and sometimes he embodies many of the flaws that he denounces. *Brave New World* has two such characters—the Savage, who like Gulliver is an outsider to the world being satirized, and Bernard Marx, the insider, a classic satiric misfit.[12] In *Nineteen Eighty-Four* the

12. Marx is bitter, marginal, overintelligent, insecure, timid, boastful, nerdish, socially inept—all apparently stemming from his being short. "'They say somebody made a mistake when he was still in the bottle—thought he was a Gamma and put alcohol into his blood-surrogate. That's why he's so stunted.'" Aldous Huxley, *Brave New World* 46 (1932). (All my quotations are from the 1998 HarperCollins Perennial Classics edition, and subsequent page ref-

satirist character is also an insider, Winston Smith. He is something of
a misfit, too, though in keeping with the different tone of Orwell's
novel he is not ridiculous, as Bernard becomes. Also like Bernard,
Winston has the taste for solitude that both novels deem a precondition for independent thinking, and so is able to see through the lies that
undergird his society. In both novels the satirist figures come to a bad
end—death, "unpersonhood," or, in the case of Bernard Marx, exile to
Iceland—which is also typical of the genre. Likewise the fact that both
novels provide an anchor to the real world of the present by dwelling
on certain familiar objects, such as the Savage's copy of Shakespeare's
complete works, or, in Orwell's novel, the paperweight, thrush, statue
of Oliver Cromwell, real coffee, silver-foil-wrapped chocolate, and
other objects left over from before the revolution. Characters in satires
tend to be cardboard figures, "humors" rather than three-dimensional
human beings. Winston and Julia, in *Nineteen Eighty-Four*, are the only
richly human characters in either novel, and some readers doubt that
even they are that. Satire tends, finally, to be topical. This makes it perilous to try to understand a satire without some knowledge of social
conditions in the time and place in which it was written.

Identifying the genre of the two novels may help us resist jumping
to certain conclusions that may bear on interpreting them as public-
intellectual works, such as that the authors were trying to predict the
future, that they were pessimists (as they would have to be regarded if
they thought they *were* predicting the future), and that Huxley identifies with the Savage (or, less plausibly, with Bernard) and Orwell with
Winston Smith. To decide to write in a particular genre is to adopt the
conventions of that genre—the decision need reveal nothing of the
character, emotions, or even beliefs of the author. From all we know
about Orwell, as well as from many references in his novel, it is apparent that *Nineteen Eighty-Four* is a warning, now no longer needed,
about communism, specifically its Stalinist variant.[13] But that is not

erences to it appear in the text of this chapter.) He is probably meant to remind the reader of a
Jew, though there are no Jews in the society depicted in the novel. Orwell's satirist character,
Winston Smith, is physically challenged as well, as we shall see.

13. It can, however, be argued, from the meeting in O'Brien's apartment at which the tactics of the Brotherhood, led by Emmanuel Goldstein, the Trotsky figure, are laid out and
Winston pledges his willingness to throw sulphuric acid in a child's face if that will advance
the Brotherhood's cause, that Orwell believed that a Trotskyite version of communism would
have been no better than the Stalinist.

necessarily the most important thing about it. Among other things, Orwell was warning about tendencies that he believed latent in capitalism—and I shall argue later that the heart of the novel is not a warning at all. Also, the novel is more pessimistic than Orwell the person was,[14] which is both relevant to evaluating him as a public intellectual and a clue to understanding his novel.

Huxley's novel is much more high-tech than Orwell's. Futuristic technology permeates the society depicted in it and is meticulously described and explained. It is of three types. There is mind- and body-altering technology, including hypnopaedia (hypnosis during sleep), Pavlovian conditioning, elaborate cosmetic surgery, happiness pills (*soma*, similar to our Prozac, but nonprescription and taken continually by everyone), and, for the elderly, "gonadal hormones" and "transfusion of young blood" (p. 54). There is happiness-inducing entertainment technology, including television, synthetic music, movies that gratify the five senses (the "Feelies"), and, for the Alphas, personal helicopters for vacations. Above all, there is reproductive technology. Contraception has been made foolproof yet does not interfere with sexual pleasure—sex has been separated reliably from procreation at last. At the same time, procreation has been separated from sex. Ova extracted from ovaries are mixed in the laboratory with sperm, and once fertilized are brought to term in incubators. The procedure has enabled the perfection of eugenic breeding, yielding five genetically differentiated castes, ranging from high-IQ Alphas to moronic Epsilons, to enable a perfect matching of genetic endowment with society's task needs.

Huxley was neither the first nor the last public intellectual to explore the closely related themes of eugenic breeding of human beings and reproductive technology. A few years earlier Bertrand Russell had argued that since (he believed) black people were inferior to whites, there was an argument for forbidding blacks to reproduce, though he rejected it on the ground that blacks make better workers in tropical climes.[15] More recently, public intellectual George Gilder has expressed concern that, just as Huxley predicted, the divorcing of reproduction from

14. See, for example, George Orwell, "Burnham's View of the Contemporary World Struggle," in *The Collected Essays, Journalism and Letters of George Orwell*, vol. 4: *In Front of Your Nose, 1945–1950*, p. 313 (Sonia Orwell and Ian Angus eds., 1968), an essay first published in 1947. I return to this point later.

15. Bertrand Russell, *Marriage and Morals*, ch. 18 (1929).

sex would "demote" sex from its procreative to a merely hedonistic role.[16] Gilder's deeper concern, again one prefigured by Huxley, is that the severing of sex from reproduction will destroy the family. And "individuals no longer so closely tied to mother, family, and sexuality become more open to a totalitarian state" because—here Gilder departs from Huxley—men who are no longer dependent on women for offspring will be liberated "to celebrate, like the ancient Spartans, a violent, misogynistic, and narcissistic eroticism" epitomized by a Marine Corps boot camp.[17] Playing variations on the same basic theme, Leon Kass argues that should the cloning of human beings ever become technologically feasible, we shall be "faced with having to decide nothing less than whether human procreation is going to remain human, whether children are going to be made rather than begotten, whether it is a good thing, humanly speaking, to say yes in principle to the road which leads (at best) to the dehumanized rationality of *Brave New World.*"[18]

The technological advances depicted in Huxley's novel are represented as having profound social effects, just as Gilder and Kass would expect. They induce unreflective contentment, guiltless promiscuous sex, intellectual and cultural vacuity, and complete political passivity. Marriage, the family, and parenthood—all conceived of as sources of misery and tension—have gone by the board. "Mother" has become a dirty word. But none of these consequences is presented as an *unintended* consequence of technological innovation, which is our fear of technology and a fear for which the economics of technology offers some ground. Technology in *Brave New World* is slave, not master; it is the slave of a utilitarian ideology. A send-up of utilitarianism, Huxley's novel is a more *philosophical* novel than any that Martha Nussbaum has discussed except *Hard Times.* "The higher castes . . . [must not] lose their faith in happiness as the Sovereign Good and take to believing, instead, that the goal was somewhere beyond, somewhere outside the present human sphere; that the purpose of life was not the maintenance of well-being, but some intensification and refining of consciousness,

16. George F. Gilder, *Sexual Suicide* 255 (1973).
17. Id. at 257–258.
18. Leon Kass, "The Wisdom of Repugnance: Why We Should Ban the Cloning of Humans," *New Republic*, June 2, 1997, pp. 17, 18.

some enlargement of knowledge" (p. 177). Technology has enabled happiness to be maximized at the cost of everything that makes human beings interesting. The Savage is unhappy but vital; the "civilized" people are fatuous, empty. Technology has created the conditions in which a tiny elite can fuse control over social, political, and economic life with the attainment of material abundance. This is an expression of the 1930s belief in the efficacy of central planning.

Huxley's critique of utilitarianism cuts deeper than that of Dickens, who in *Hard Times* was not attacking utilitarianism so much as commodification, the idea that everything can be given a money value and traded in a market. His point, which Nussbaum echoes, is that commodification does not maximize happiness. Huxley's point is that maximizing happiness is not a goal worthy of human beings.

The topicality of satire, well illustrated in Huxley's novel by the caste system that is transparently a parody of the English class system, and by the exhibition of the Savage and his mother to the shocked Londoners as exotic specimens of New World savagery (though the two actually are English), invites us to consider conditions in England when *Brave New World* was written. It was during a world depression which Keynes was teaching had been caused or exacerbated by a deficiency in consumer demand and could be cured only by aggressive government intervention to stimulate demand. Capitalism was believed to have failed for lack of sufficient coordination or rationalization, resulting in excessive production (supply outrunning demand) that had caused destructive competition, widespread business failures, and massive unemployment. There was also great anxiety about falling birth rates and the quality of the gene pool.

All these concerns are mirrored in *Brave New World*. One of the salient features of the society depicted in it is consumerism, which encompasses planned obsolescence and a "throwaway" mentality ("ending is better than mending" [p. 49]). People are brainwashed to want ever more, ever newer consumer goods, lest consumer demand flag. (Recall from Chapter 3 the concern that David Riesman expressed in 1950 that consumers might soon become satiated.) Everything down to the smallest detail of culture, technology, and consumption is planned and directed from the center. Eugenic breeding solves the population and gene-pool problems. The society of *Brave New World* is the logical outcome of reform measures advocated by advanced thinkers in England and other countries during the depression. The book is a satire of the public-intellectual thought of the time.

That thought is dated; what makes *Brave New World* still a good read is the fact, which should place Huxley in the pantheon of twentieth-century public intellectuals, that so many of its predictions of futuristic technology and morality have come or are coming to pass. Sex has been made largely safe for pleasure by the invention of methods of contraception that at once are reliable and do not interfere with sexual enjoyment. A variety of other technological advances, ranging from better care of pregnant women and of infants to household labor-saving devices and advances in the medical treatment of infertility and the automation of the workplace, have (along with the contraceptive advances and safe abortion on demand) freed women from the traditional restrictions on their sexual freedom.[19] The result is a climate of sexual freedom, and of public obsession with sex and sexual pleasure, much like that depicted in Huxley's novel, though "mother" is not yet a dirty word and marriage has not yet been abolished, although the marriage rate has fallen considerably.

The society of happy, thoughtless philistines depicted by Huxley seems merely an exaggeration of today's America. We too are awash in happiness pills, of both the legal and illegal variety, augmented by increasingly ambitious cosmetic surgery to make us happier about our appearance. We are enveloped by entertainment technology to a degree that even Huxley could not imagine. In our society too "cleanliness is next to fordliness" (p. 110). We have a horror of physical aging and even cultivate infantilism—adults dressing and talking like children. "Alphas are so conditioned that they do not *have* to be infantile in their emotional behaviour. But that is all the more reason for their making a special effort to conform. It is their duty to be infantile, even against their inclination" (p. 98). We live in the present; our slogan, too, might be, "Never put off till to-morrow the fun you can have today" (p. 93). Popular culture has everywhere triumphed over high cul-

19. In some areas, "despite its being a dystopia, *Brave New World* offers women a better deal than the contemporary British society of the 1930s. There is no housework, no wifely subjugation, no need to balance children and a career." June Deery, "Technology and Gender in Aldous Huxley's Alternative (?) Worlds," in *Critical Essays on Aldous Huxley* 103, 105 (Jerome Meckier ed., 1996).

ture; the past has been largely forgotten. We consider it our duty as well as our right to pursue happiness right to the edge of the grave. In the "Park Lane Hospital for the Dying . . . we try to create a thoroughly pleasant atmosphere . . . , something between a first-class hotel and a feely-palace" (pp. 198–199). Shopping is the national pastime. Although not entirely passive politically, Americans are largely content with the status quo, largely free from envy and resentment; the major political parties are centrist, agree on fundamentals (while wrestling fiercely over personalities and symbolic issues), and freely borrow policies from each other. A 1930s-style depression is to most of us unimaginable. Depression in both its senses is becoming unimaginable.

There is even a tendency, though as yet nascent, toward a technology-driven conformism. The inhabitants of Huxley's imagined world are conformists, their conformism being both fostered and symbolized by the physical uniformity of each caste. Bernard is not deformed, but he is several inches shorter, and correspondingly thinner, than the Alpha norm, probably as a result of an accident in the baby hatchery, and his physical peculiarities are cause as well as symbol of his social misfitness.[20] In our society, heroic measures are taken with increasing success to erase all physical and mental deviations from an idealized norm through medical and psychological interventions—including the administration of growth hormone to short children. The latest triumph of our therapeutic culture is the classification of people who are shy and socially awkward as social phobics, candidates for psychiatric treatment. We can look forward to a time when almost everyone is "normal," free from all hang-ups resulting from deformity, disfigurement, handicap, ugliness, neurosis, hyperactivity, and sexual deviance. This will be a gain in happiness for the "normalized" and their families but it will involve a social loss, because "abnormals" are an important source of diversity and creativity. One place the loss will be felt is the public-intellectual market. The outsider's perspective, the gadfly role, comes more easily to misfits of one sort or another than to normals; think only of Socrates with his famous ugliness or Nietzsche with his severe psychosomatic illnesses. The repulsive Thersites of Homer and

20. "Too little bone and brawn had isolated Bernard from his fellow men, and the sense of this apartness, being, by all the current standards, a mental excess, became in its turn a cause of wider separation" (p. 67).

Shakespeare is the abiding symbol of the obnoxiously intelligent outsider.

But all that I have described is coming about without foresight or direction, contrary to the implication of Huxley's novel. A society, it
turns out, does not need centralization in order to attain "Fordism"[21]—
the rationalization, the systematization, of production, or more
broadly the normalization of human beings (people as "cogs" in the social machine), originally symbolized by the assembly line. Our society
has no utilitarian master plan and no utilitarian master planner. Huxley
seems to have had no inkling that technology might merely evolve, un-
planned, to a level that would make the regimented, trivial society depicted in the novel a realistic possibility. Technology in *Brave New
World* plays a supporting rather than initiating role, as the tool of a
philosophical and economic vision. No law of unintended consequences is operating. This is where Huxley's prophetic powers faltered.
Nothing in our own brave new world corresponds to Huxley's "Controllers," the successors to Dostoyevsky's Grand Inquisitor: "Happiness is a hard master—particularly other people's happiness" (p. 227).
And despite its resemblance to Huxley's dystopia, what we have seems
to most people, even the thinking people, rather closer to Utopia. Not
to all, though; we shall encounter dissenters in the next chapter.

By 1948, the year Orwell completed *Nineteen Eighty-Four* (he had
begun writing it two years earlier), the depression of the 1930s was
over and concern with rationalizing production and simulating consumption had diminished. The thought of politically conscious people
was dominated instead by vivid recent memories of World War II and
by the menace of the Soviet Union, and these gloomy, foreboding
thoughts are everywhere reflected in the novel. The dinginess of London in 1984 is recognizably the dinginess of that city during and immediately after the war, a time of shortages, rationing, and a prevailing
grayness of life; and rocket bombs are falling on London in 1984 just as
they did in the last year of World War II. The novel dwells obsessively
on these features of life in Orwell's imagined dystopia, making a stark
contrast to *Brave New World*'s consumers' heaven. Orwell portrayed the
future London as he did less, I suspect, because he was prescient about

---

21. Henry Ford is the Jesus Christ or Karl Marx of the society depicted in *Brave New
World*. Instead of making the sign of the cross, the denizens of the world make a "T," which
stands for Ford's Model T.

the incapacity of socialist central planning to bring about abundance— a loyal member of the Labour Party to the end of his life, he never relinquished his belief in democratic socialism—but because he was extremely sensitive to squalor, and to the sights and sounds and texture of lower-class life in London. Orwell's ambivalence about the lower class (the "proles," in *Nineteen Eighty-Four*), which he seems to have found at once repellent and appealing, is strongly marked.

The novel's take on technology is a curious one. On the one hand, *The Theory and Practice of Oligarchic Collectivism*—the treatise ostensibly written by the Trotsky figure in the novel but actually forged by the Inner Party—describes the world of 1984 as technologically retrogressive. The world is divided into three totalitarian superstates that have tacitly agreed to impose rigid thought control on their populations, stifling the scientific and inventive spirit. On the other hand, this development is depicted as having been fated by technology, which in the form of machine production enables—in effect, decrees—an almost effortless creation of wealth. (Shades of Huxley, Arendt, Mumford, Riesman, Sennett, and a host of other public intellectuals, past and present.) When wealth is abundant, people cease believing in the necessity of a hierarchical society with marked inequalities. To stave off equality, the ruling classes channel the overproduction stimulated by technology into warfare, which has the further advantage that in times of war people are readier to submit to collective control. So technology leads to totalitarianism, though by a more indirect route than fostering centralization at all levels because of the greater efficiency of technocratic methods—which Orwell also believed, however, as we're about to see.

Orwell was right that the conditions of a totalitarian society, in particular its suppression of freedom of thought and expression, retard scientific and technological progress. This, another reason to doubt that technology conduces to the elimination of political freedom, is one of the lessons of the fall of communism. The technological successes that the Soviet Union achieved, mainly in nuclear weaponry and space travel, were due, we now know, in significant part to the Soviet conquest of the eastern part of Germany in World War II, which brought some of Germany's rocket facilities and personnel under Soviet control, and to espionage. The other half of the novel's technology thesis, however, is wrong. The great increase in material wealth in the developed countries of the world since Orwell wrote has led to an increase in both economic inequality *and* political stability.

In an afterword to a 1961 republication of *Nineteen Eighty-Four,* Erich Fromm, another noted public intellectual, attributes to the novel the view (with which Fromm makes clear that he agrees, with less excuse than Orwell since he was writing more than a decade later) that "the danger [of the Orwellian nightmare is] inherent in the modern mode of production and organization, and relatively independent of the various ideologies [that is, capitalist and communist]" (p. 267). The view is wrong but the attribution of it to Orwell seems approximately correct. One clue is that the currency of Oceania is the dollar, not the pound. And among the sources of Orwell's novel was the concept much touted in his day of "managerialism," which predicted incorrectly that capitalism would evolve into a *dirigiste,* bureaucratized, centralized economic system virtually indistinguishable from Soviet communism.[22] The superior efficiency of competitive markets for coordinating production was not widely understood.

But here we must distinguish between the novel and its author. The guru of managerialism was the prominent public intellectual James Burnham. Orwell borrowed not only Burnham's managerialist vision for *Nineteen Eighty-Four* but also his prediction that World War II (which had not yet ended when Burnham made his prediction) would result in a division of the world into three indistinguishable superstates.[23] But although fascinated by Burnham, Orwell was not captivated by him, and in fact pointed out that Burnham's predictions, to the extent verifiable (like the predicted emergence of the three superstates), were consistently wrong.[24] We of course are not surprised to find a public intellectual's predictions falsified.

The only technological innovation that figures largely in *Nineteen Eighty-Four* is two-way television (the "telescreen") by which the securities services keep watch over the members of the Party. The technol-

---

22. See, for example, James Burnham, *The Managerial Revolution: What Is Happening in the World* (1941). And recall the similar convergence thesis of John Kenneth Galbraith, mentioned in Chapter 4.

23. See, for example, Burnham, note 22 above, at 264–265.

24. George Orwell, "James Burnham and the Managerial Revolution," in *The Collected Essays, Journalism and Letters of George Orwell,* note 14 above, vol. 4: *In Front of Your Nose, 1945–1950,* pp. 160, 172. The essay was first published in 1946.

ogy is that of modern videoconferencing. Though a powerful meta-phor for the loss of privacy in a totalitarian state, the telescreen is not essential to the novel's political theme. That theme is the feasibility of thought control through propaganda, education, psychology (including behavioral modification), informers (including children), censorship, lobotomizing, stirring up war fever, terror, and, above all, the manipulation of historical records and of language. The novel's most interesting invention is Newspeak, a parody of Basic English as well as of Nazi and Soviet rhetoric, designed to make dangerous thoughts un-thinkable by eliminating the words for them.[25] None of the instru-ments of thought control described in the novel, except the telescreen and possibly the machine that eliminates portions of Winston's mem-ory, involves any technological advance over Orwell's time. All but the telescreen and the lobotomy machine were in use in the Soviet Union during the 1930s and 1940s, though in a less thoroughgoing form than in Orwell's imagined world. *Nineteen Eighty-Four* would be less vivid and suspenseful, but not different in essentials, without telescreens.

Because there is so little futurism in Orwell's novel, he had no rea-son to set it in the *remote* future. He was extrapolating only modestly from contemporary conditions—one can imagine Soviet leaders read-ing *Nineteen Eighty-Four* for ideas.[26] Yet it is Huxley's far-futuristic ex-travaganza that comes closer to describing our world. The reason is not that Huxley could foresee the future but that science is the story of our time, and Huxley, who came from a distinguished scientific family and trained to be a doctor, was genuinely interested in science. Until re-cently, moreover, there was a long lead time between scientific discov-ery and widespread practical application. Helicopters, television, mind-altering drugs, eugenic breeding, and large-screen color movies with wraparound sound were all known in the 1930s to be technologically feasible, but it was decades before any of them became an important part of our culture. The longer the lead time between invention and

---

25. For a comprehensive discussion, see John Wesley Young, *Totalitarian Language: Or-well's Newspeak and Its Nazi and Communist Antecedents* (1991). Cf. Victor Klemperer, *The Lan-guage of the Third Reich: LTI—Lingua Tertii Imperii: A Philologist's Notebook* (2000).

26. A defector from the Polish Communist Party, the distinguished writer and public in-tellectual Czeslaw Milosz, claimed that members of the "Inner Party," who alone could easily obtain copies of *Nineteen Eighty-Four,* were fascinated by Orwell's "insight into details they know well." Milosz, *The Captive Mind* 42 (1990).

application, the easier it is to foresee the future technological structure of society. That lead time has shrunk—another reason the scope for public-intellectual work has contracted; it is hard to warn against a future that is unknowable even in hazy outline.

Although Soviet-style brainwashing undoubtedly had an effect on the minds of the people of the communist countries,[27] the rapidity and completeness with which the communist regimes collapsed demonstrated its ultimate ineffectuality. *Nineteen Eighty-Four* reckons without the fact—which, we recall, David Riesman saw very early—that the secrecy and lack of accountability of communist oligarchs would breed corruption that would make the oligarchs look weak (and become weak, or at least soft) and cause the public, and even many of the leaders, to become disillusioned with the regime. That the combination of surveillance and control techniques described in *Nineteen Eighty-Four* is frighteningly plausible is a tribute to Orwell's artistic imagination; the system the novel describes is not realistic. To see this, one need only ask who is to man all the telescreens. There are several in every apartment and office occupied by members of the Party—of whom there are a total of about 45 million, for we are told that 15 percent of the population belongs to the Party and that Oceania's total population is 300 million—and it is implied (this is critical to my calculations) that all the telescreens are manned all the time. Suppose there are 100 million telescreens; that would probably require 10 million watchers. I am assuming two shifts, so that each watcher would be responsible for monitoring 20 telescreens.

Minus telescreen surveillance, the system of thought control depicted by Orwell is essentially the Soviet system under Stalin, which began eroding shortly after Stalin died,[28] four years after *Nineteen Eighty-Four* was published. Even in the Stalin era, the Communist Party's control of people's minds was spotty.[29] The novel hints at the

27. See Timur Kuran, *Private Truths, Public Lies: The Social Consequences of Preference Falsification*, ch. 13 (1995).

28. See, for example, Abbott Gleason, "'Totalitarianism' in 1984," 43 *Russian Review* 145 (1984). This would not have surprised Orwell, who thought it entirely possible that the Soviet regime would eventually become more liberal and less dangerous. Orwell, note 14 above, at 325. Indeed, he went further and predicted that "the Russian régime will either democratise itself, or it will perish." Orwell, note 24 above, at 180.

29. Sheila Fitzpatrick, *Everyday Stalinism: Ordinary Life in Extraordinary Times: Soviet Russia in the 1930s* 222 (1999).

fragility of thought control. Eighty-five percent of the population of Oceania consists of the proles, who are much like Huxley's lower castes except that the proles' stupidity is not genetic—and, potentially, is redemptive. For, having no "brains," the proles are immune to being brainwashed, as is Julia, who is not "clever," though she can be broken by torture. Most brainwashing is directed at Party members, and it is not completely successful; Winston and Julia, we discover late in the novel, are not the only imperfectly socialized Party members.[30] Hence the large number of "vaporizings" (liquidations), though, just as in Stalin's Soviet Union, many of those liquidated are in fact loyal Party members, notably the lexicographer Syme.

Most important, the Inner Party—the directing mechanism, 2 percent of the population—necessarily comprises people who see through the lies they are trying to foist on the rest of the society. Like the rulers of the Soviet Union, the members of the Inner Party have their own shops, which stock otherwise unobtainable luxury goods of traditional bourgeois character. The novel denies that the fanaticism of the Inner Party has been undermined by comfort or hypocrisy, arguing that through the mental technique of "doublethink" the members both know and don't know that their ideology is false. This was indeed a characteristic of thought under communism,[31] but the novel exaggerates its effectiveness and tenacity.

Orwell realized that a system of thought control would be unstable if major nations, knowledge of the conditions in which could not be wholly masked from the subject population, remained outside the totalitarian sphere. The novel emphasizes that there are no such nations in 1984, the three totalitarian superstates having tacitly agreed to refrain from competing in military research. Without such an agreement the totalitarian oligopoly would be unstable. Each superstate would have a compelling incentive to seek a military advantage by relaxing its thought control sufficiently to foster scientific and technological innovation. We now know that liberal nations, like the United States, tend to be politically and militarily more formidable than authoritarian or

30. Consider the egregious Parsons, a Party zealot turned in by his seven-year-old daughter who overhears him saying in his sleep, "Down with Big Brother!" (p. 193). Maybe, though, his real sin is being proud of his daughter for turning him in; it shows that he continues, contrary to Party doctrine, to attach great importance to family.

31. Kuran, note 27 above, at 218.

totalitarian ones, because they create better preconditions for rapid social and economic development (in part by generating a fuller and
more accurate information flow), more than offsetting the loss of centralized direction and control.[32] A particular weakness of totalitarian
states is the tendency to "subjectivism,"[33] the view much emphasized in
Nineteen Eighty-Four that truth is what the Party or Leader says is true.
Subjectivism led to such disastrous totalitarian misadventures as the
Nazi rejection of "Jewish physics," the Soviet embrace of Lysenko's
crackpot genetic theories, and Maoist China's "Great Leap Forward."

The Orwellian nightmare is unstable in a second sense as well. Neither Stalin nor Mao, the greatest practitioners of the kind of thought
control depicted in Orwell's novel, was able to *institutionalize* the system of thought control. It disintegrated rapidly after their deaths.
Their tyrannies were personal, while that depicted in *Nineteen Eighty-
Four* is collective. Big Brother is not a living person but a symbolic fab-
rication. The collective leaderships that succeeded Stalin and Mao in
their respective nations were authoritarian, but they were unable to
maintain the degree of control that Stalin and Mao had achieved and
that *Nineteen Eighty-Four* parodies. The novel does not explain how the
Party, and its counterparts in the novel's other totalitarian superstates,
manage this trick.

Orwell was famously contemptuous of intellectuals. He liked to say
such things as "the more intelligent, the less sane" (p. 177) and "one
has to belong to the intelligentsia to believe things like that: no ordinary man could be such a fool."[34] His hostility to intellectuals may seem
surprising in light of his own status as one of the twentieth century's
leading public intellectuals (not that he would have thought of himself
in those terms). But his contempt was directed at university (particularly Oxbridge) intellectuals, and he never attended a university. And
remember that public intellectuals tend to be counterpunchers, and the
punchers are other intellectuals. O'Brien—the villain of the novel, the

32. Orwell was well aware of this, although the awareness does not surface in the novel.
See, for example, Orwell, note 14 above, at 324; Orwell, note 24 above, at 179–180.

33. For an excellent discussion, see George Watson, "Orwell's Nazi Renegade," 94
Sewanee Review 486 (1986).

34. George Orwell, "Notes on Nationalism," in *The Collected Essays, Journalism and Letters
of George Orwell*, note 14 above, vol. 3: *As I Please, 1943–1945*, pp. 361, 379. The "that" was
that American troops had come to England during World War II not to fight the Germans
but to crush an English revolution.

torturer, the Orwellian Grand Inquisitor—is an intellectual of the most sinister kind: the ideologist of a totalitarian regime. He is a parody of the English communist intellectuals who so infuriated Orwell.

But Orwell was himself an intellectual and this shows in *Nineteen Eight-Four*. It is natural for intellectuals to exaggerate, as the novel does, the efficacy of attempts at brainwashing, since, loosely speaking, intellectuals are in the business of brainwashing as well as being principal targets of it. (The same exaggeration is visible in another notable novel about Stalinism, Arthur Koestler's *Darkness at Noon*.)[35] It is noteworthy that Oceania has no counterpart to the Gulag, a central institution of the Soviet regime but not one as interesting to an intellectual as brainwashing. Winston, Julia, and the other targets of thought control and intimidation in *Nineteen Eighty-Four* are all engaged in "political work"; such people—the stratum that includes the intellectuals—pose the greatest political threat to a totalitarian regime and so must be watched the most closely.

The intellectual's bias may explain why *Nineteen Eighty-Four* gets the political significance of television backwards, conceiving of it as a medium of surveillance (the telescreen) and indoctrination (the "Two Minutes Hate") when instead it has proved to be a medium of subversion, vastly increasing people's access to information about society and politics. It played a role not only in the fall of communism but also, long before that, in the thwarting of Lyndon Johnson's attempt to conduct a war in Vietnam without the informed consent of the American people. This surprised intellectuals. They tend to despise television as a potent underminer of book-based culture.

Orwell's most recent biographer takes the "message" of *Nineteen Eighty-Four* to be that

> there must be a place in the modern world for things that have no power associated with them, things that are not meant to advance someone's cause, or to make someone's fortune, or to assert someone's will over someone else. There must be room, in other words, for paperweights and fishing rods and penny sweets and leather hammers used as children's toys. And there must be time for wandering among old churchyards and making the perfect cup of tea

35. See Richard A. Posner, *Law and Literature* 138 (revised and enlarged ed. 1998).

and balancing caterpillars on a stick and falling in love. All these things are derided as sentimental and trivial by intellectuals who have no time for them, but they are the things that form the real texture of a life.[36]

This is a bit mawkish, but I agree that *Nineteen Eighty-Four* is trying to tell us that if political freedom is to be preserved, "there must be time for . . . falling in love." The Party is emphatic in teaching that the sole legitimate function of sex is procreation and in discouraging sexual pleasure among its members. Think what other "party" of "thought controllers" takes this line on sex. Orwell would have said that it was the Roman Catholic Church.[37] He compares the "adoptive" (as distinct from a hereditary) oligarchy of the Church with that of the Party. And the Church preaches love, but in its heyday tortured and burned people—the junction symbolized by Oceania's Ministry of Love, which is the torture and liquidation bureau. There are other parallels. In the final scenes of the novel, "there is a parody of the atonement . . . when the hero is tortured into urging that the torments be inflicted on the heroine instead. The assumption is made [in *Nineteen Eighty-Four*] that the lust for sadistic power on the part of the ruling class is strong enough to last indefinitely, which is precisely the assumption one has to make about devils in order to accept the orthodox picture of hell."[38]

Christianity and communism both began as revolutionary movements preaching radical equality and an end to history (the Sermon on the Mount is a distant ancestor of the *Communist Manifesto*), and both ossified into corrupt and often cruel bureaucracies that paralleled and influenced (in the Soviet case, controlled) the formal organs of government and tried to control the minds of the population.[39] I am painting with a broad brush, and overlooking many differences; still, there are suggestive parallels. The Catholic practice of confession dramatizes

36. Michael Shelden, *Orwell: The Authorized Biography* 436–437 (1991).

37. He was thinking of course of traditional Roman Catholicism, not of modern American Catholicism. On the differences, see James D. Davidson and Andrea S. Williams, "Megatrends in 20th-century American Catholicism," 44 *Social Compass* 507 (1997).

38. Northrop Frye, *Anatomy of Criticism: Four Essays* 238 (1957).

39. And both received their comeuppance in Germany—the Church from Luther, the communists from the East Germans' surge to freedom in 1989.

Christianity's concern with people's thoughts—it is a mode of surveillance, though also of absolution, and there are elements of that, too, in Winston's ordeal—and its placing of thought on a moral par with action. Another name for concern with thoughts even when they are divorced from action is thought control—Catholic priests correspond to the Thought Police of Orwell's novel. The traditional Church often seemed preoccupied with people's sex lives, and hostile to or at least suspicious of sex itself; the Party likewise. In both cases concern with private thoughts is linked to hostility to sex through the fact that sexual pleasure involves thoughts that are in the control very largely of our animal nature rather than of a priestly caste that tells us what we ought to be thinking about. "Not merely the love of one person, but the animal instinct, the simple undifferentiated desire: that was the force that would tear the Party to pieces" (p. 105). In this respect *Nineteen Eighty-Four* is the opposite of *Brave New World*, where promiscuous sex is obligatory for good citizens. "Orgy-porgy, Ford and fun, / Kiss the girls and make them One. / Boys at one with girls at peace; / Orgy-porgy gives release" (p. 84).

The contrast between the two novels' views of the political significance of a society's sexual mores suggests that there may not be a unique totalitarian position on sexual freedom.[40] This is true even if intimacy, and hence the family, is a threat to a totalitarian society, which seeks to mobilize the population for selfless communal projects. The societies depicted in both novels are indeed hostile to the family. In *Brave New World* it has been abolished, while in *Nineteen Eighty-Four* its abolition is one of the Party's long-term goals, to be achieved in part by perfecting the system under which children are encouraged to report thought crime by their parents. But it is unclear what policy toward sex weakens the family by discouraging intimacy. If promiscuity can undermine the family, so can a degree of puritanism that weakens the sexual bonding of married people. Maybe that's why some communes encourage free love and others celibacy, or why the Soviet Union veered from sexual liberalism in the 1920s to puritanism in the 1930s. Notice that if Huxley is right, the U.S. Supreme Court is wrong to think that contraception and abortion protect privacy viewed as a precondition of intimate relationships, while if Orwell is right, those things do protect pri-

40. See Posner, note 5 above, at 239.

vacy in that sense. Either extreme may be inimical to intimacy. Maybe, then, they are both right.

But maybe they are both wrong. The premise that totalitarianism is inherently hostile to the family and intimacy is dubious. Radical Islamic nations are both authoritarian and strongly pro-family. They are hostile to nonmarital sex, but not to marital sex; marriage is *obligatory* for Islamic clergy. Hitler, Stalin, Franco, and Mussolini were all strongly pro-family, as is the Roman Catholic Church, despite its prohibiting sex and marriage to its clergy. The dictators wanted to increase the birth rate and believed that encouraging family formation was an effective way of doing this. Pronatalism to one side, the traditional patriarchal family might be thought to echo and reinforce an authoritarian political regime.

Sex is thus rather a side issue in the analysis of totalitarianism, and perhaps in political governance generally. But the idea that one is *always* under surveillance, no matter how alone one thinks one is, is central both to totalitarian practices and to most forms of Christianity. The Christian is under surveillance by God, and the inhabitants of Oceania by Big Brother, who, like the Christian God, is

> infallible and all-powerful . . . Nobody has ever seen Big Brother. He is a face on the hoardings, a voice on the telescreen. We may be reasonably sure that he will never die, and there is already considerable uncertainty as to when he was born. Big Brother is the guise in which the Party chooses to exhibit itself to the world. His function is to act as a focusing point for love, fear, and reverence, emotions more easily felt toward an individual than toward an organization. (p. 171)

The Inquisition, which is perfected in the Ministry of Love, was merely the pathological extreme of the Christian concern with what Orwell calls "crimethink." As O'Brien explains,

> We do not destroy the heretic because he resists us; so long as he resists us we never destroy him. We convert him, we capture his inner mind, we reshape him. We burn all evil and all illusion out of him; we bring him over to our side, not in appearance, but genuinely, heart and soul. We make him one of ourselves before we kill

him . . . By the time we had finished with them [three notorious traitors] they were only the shells of men. There was nothing left in them except sorrow for what they had done, and love of Big Brother . . . They begged to be shot quickly, so that they could die while their minds were still clean. (pp. 210–211)[41]

My point in bringing out the parallels between the practice of totalitarianism in *Nineteen Eighty-Four* and the usages of the Roman Catholic Church is not to be gratuitously offensive,[42] or to obscure the role of Catholicism post-Orwell, notably in Poland and Hungary, in opposing totalitarianism. It is to bolster my earlier statement that brainwashing is not the story of today. The Catholic Church has lost most of its control over people's minds, at least in the developed world. Gone are the Inquisition and the *index purgatorius*. Italy has a very high abortion rate and a very low birth rate. Ireland has legalized divorce and abortion. Freethinking among even deeply religious people is the order of the day, not everywhere (in particular, not in all Muslim nations), but in most quarters of the wealthy nations and many of the nonwealthy ones as well.

With 1984 receding into the past, and the memory of Stalinism and Maoism dimming in our rapidly changing world—with *Nineteen Eighty-Four* proved "wrong," and *Brave New World* "right," or at least more right, by history—how to explain the fact that Orwell's novel is, I believe (without having been able to obtain proof), far more popular than Huxley's? The part of the answer that interests me is that Orwell's may be the "better" novel (my use of scare quotes acknowledging the inherently subjective character of such a judgment). As the political relevance of *Nineteen Eighty-Four* fades, its literary quality becomes more perspicuous. We can see it better today for what it is—a wonderfully vivid, suspenseful, atmospheric, and horrifying (in the sense, not meant

41. "Orwell plays brilliantly upon traditional religious language." Joseph Adelson, "The Self and Memory in *Nineteen Eighty-Four*," in *The Future of Nineteen Eighty-Four* 111, 116–117 (Ejner J. Jensen ed., 1984). To get the point, just substitute "God" for "Big Brother" and "burned at the stake" for "shot" in the passage quoted in the text.

42. The parallels have been noted before, moreover. See, for example, William Steinhoff, *George Orwell and the Origins of 1984* 184–185 (1975); Jaroslav Krejci, "Religion and Anti-Religion: Experience of a Transition," 36 *Sociological Analysis* 108, 120–122 (1975). Orwell used O'Brien's name "to suggest the absolute power of the Catholic Church." Jeffrey Meyers, *Orwell: Wintry Conscience of a Nation* 281 (2000).

pejoratively, that much of Henry James is horrifying, even Gothic) romantic adventure story. In places it is even a melodrama, even a boy's adventure story, as when the villains, O'Brien and Charrington, recite nursery rhymes, or Charrington is seen without the disguise that had made him look old. The scenes in Charrington's shop bear the stamp of *The Secret Agent*, while the visit of Winston and Julia to O'Brien's apartment for induction into the nonexistent Brotherhood could be a scene in a John Buchan novel. The fairy-tale note is sounded in the very first sentence of Orwell's novel: "It was a bright cold day in April, and the clocks were striking thirteen" (p. 5). We soon discover that there is nothing uncanny about a clock's striking 13 in Oceania, because Oceania numbers the hours one to twenty-four, a clearer method of keeping time than the A.M.-P.M. system, just as it uses the dollar rather than the nondecimal English currency of Orwell's day and just as it uses the metric system in place of English weights and measures. Yet these simple, "rationalizing" measures turn out to be sinister in their own right. They illustrate the Party's effort to empty the culture of its historical residues, to make the present discontinuous with the past.

The *literary* significance of the telescreen has less to do with technology or privacy than with enhancing the perilousness of Winston's affair with Julia, the need for their elaborate rituals of concealment, and the inevitability of eventual detection and punishment. The suspense is so intense, right up to the dramatic arrest scene, that inevitably the third of the book that remains is anticlimactic. Except for the scene in which Winston confronts in the mirror the damage that torture and starvation have done to his body, and the final meeting and parting of Winston and Julia, the last third is inferior as literature to the first two-thirds of the novel. This is not because it is "didactic," however. The most didactic portion of the book is the long selection from *The Theory and Practice of Oligarchic Collectivism* that Winston reads (to us, as it were) just before he and Julia are arrested. The reading has enormous dramatic impact. The problem with the last third of the book is that it is not well crafted. The first post-arrest scene, with Winston in a holding cell with other political prisoners, is intended to be horrifying but succeeds only in being disgusting—and with the entry of Parsons, who expresses pride in his seven-year-old daughter for her having turned him in for thought crime, even a bit ridiculous. That is also my reaction to the famous scene in which Winston is threatened with the rats and screams "Do it to Julia! Do it to Julia!" (p. 236).

Oddly, given Orwell's political aims, the last part of the book undermines the satire of communism (and to no literary purpose) by making the totalitarian dictators seem almost benign compared to O'Brien, who is, at least so far as the reader is given to understand him (for we see him only through Winston's eyes), a sadistic lunatic. Hitler and Stalin were cruel and paranoid. But they would hardly have said, or, probably, even thought, that "progress in our world will be progress toward more pain" or that "we shall abolish the orgasm" (p. 220).[43] This is overdone to the point of being ridiculous, though it echoes and parodies the ascetic strain in Christianity, and so is further evidence for the link that the novel forges between Catholicism and totalitarianism. Also bordering on the ridiculous is O'Brien's insistence on getting Winston to accept that if the Party says that $2 + 2 = 5$, then it is so. That scene, a too deeply buried allusion to the Soviet Union's five-year plans,[44] and so again an error of literary craft, makes O'Brien seem more like a bullying schoolmaster trying to drum the rules of arithmetic into the head of a slow student than like a torturer.

The deeper problem with the last third of the book, so far as verisimilitude is concerned, is that no *political* purpose is served by the elaborate cat-and-mouse game that O'Brien plays with Winston and Julia. Neither has valuable information about the "Brotherhood" (which probably does not exist) or is important enough to have to be brainwashed into making a public recantation of heresies. Neither is a member of the Inner Party, let alone an "old revolutionary" whose taming is important to the Party's image of omnipotence and infallibility. No one of O'Brien's eminence would waste so much time on such nobodies.

Also implausible is the characterization of O'Brien as having no fear. It is because he is without fear that his treatment of Winston seems sadistic and insane. To suppose the "Inner Party" of a totalitarian state composed primarily of lunatics and sadists is unrealistic. A state so governed would be unstable. Members of the ruling clique of such a state

43. "The worst Nazi lived on something besides cruelty." George Kateb, "The Road to *1984*," in *Twentieth Century Interpretations of 1984* 73, 75 (Samuel Hynes ed. 1971).

44. The slogan "2 + 2 = 5" was popular in the Soviet Union during the first five-year plan; it expressed the aspiration to complete the plan in four years. Steinhoff, note 42 above, at 172.

are cruel in order to maintain their positions. They fear their superiors, their rivals, and even a rising of the people. O'Brien has none of these fears. The only hint that he too is under surveillance is the suggestion that members of the Inner Party, although allowed to turn off the telescreens in their apartments, would be ill advised to do so for more than a half hour at a stretch.

These are details. The important point is that we can read Orwell's novel as we read Kafka, or *The Waste Land,* with which *Nineteen Eighty-Four* has some curious affinities[45]—for the vividness of its nightmare vision relieved by the occasional poignant glimpse of redemptive possibilities. Reading it as literature (and cognizant of its literary imperfections), we resist, as Orwell sought to resist, the politicization of everything, a trend that has debilitated university English departments of late.[46] A rich understanding of social context may be necessary to appreciate the wit and bite of a satire, an example being O'Brien's effort to get Winston to believe that two and two are five. But it is one thing for an understanding of political and other social issues to be a precondition to fully appreciating a work of literature, and another thing to suppose that the significance of that work lies in its relation to those issues.

When we approach these two novels with as much freedom from nonliterary preconceptions as we can muster, we discover in both that "Romantic" dissatisfaction with everyday life sometimes referred to as "Bovarism," after Madame Bovary. *Brave New World* has the more brilliant surface, and a sparkling wit that links it to the great British comic tradition. But it is not a happy book. It has no characters who engage the reader's sympathy and no emotional depth. The conquest by science of the tragic realities of human life is shown as destroying the possibility of romance. Conversely, the love affair that is the emotional core of *Nineteen Eighty-Four* is exalted by the proximity of terror and death. Julia is neither beautiful nor clever, is in fact rather shallow; and

45. Both works, for example, are nostalgic about the London of the past and associate modernity with sterility and "bad sex."

46. "'On every campus . . . there is one department whose name need only be mentioned to make people laugh' . . . Everyone knows that if you want to locate the laughingstock on your local campus these days, your best bet is to stop by the English department." Andrew Delbanco, "The Decline and Fall of Literature," *New York Review of Books,* Nov. 4, 1999, p. 32.

Winston, at thirty-nine, with his varicose veins, his five false teeth, his "pale and meager body" (p. 118), is already middle-aged.[47] Their relationship—like that of Jordan and Maria in *For Whom the Bell Tolls* or Frederick Henry and Catherine Barkley in *A Farewell to Arms*, Andrei and Natasha in *War and Peace*, Julien Sorel and Madame de Rênal in *The Red and the Black*, or Tristan and Isolde, Radames and Aïda—would lack savor were it not for the background of terror and danger and the certainty of doom. His love for Julia is the last thing that Winston relinquishes under torture. The world of today, made so comfortable and safe by the technology foreseen by Huxley, has no place for Romanticism. The world has become disenchanted. That Julia is rather commonplace is not, as some feminists believe, a sign of Orwell's alleged misogyny; it is part of the point of the novel. (They also overlook her courage.)

From this perspective we see that the significance of the paperweight that Winston buys in Mr. Charrington's shop is not as a symbol of the charm of the ordinary. It is to show how even the most commonplace object can become luminous when it is bracketed with danger; one is put in mind of how some people get a greater kick out of sex when there is a risk of discovery.

A Weberian perspective can also help us see that people who think that *Nineteen Eighty-Four* is "about" technology in some deep sense are confusing technology with technocracy. Technology is the application of rational methods to material production and technocracy their application throughout the whole of life.[48] Weber's vision of human life so completely rationalized that all enchantment would be squeezed out of the world[49] is antiromantic and therefore dismaying to persons of Ro-

47. Julia is twenty-six years old, so thirteen years separate them (and both their ages are divisible by thirteen)—another sinister touch. As writers so often do, Orwell borrowed heavily from his personal life. Winston is closely modeled on Orwell himself, and Julia on Sonia Brownell, Orwell's second wife. Meyers, note 42 above, at 282–283, 300–301.

48. "'Technocracy' . . . signifies a social order organized on principles established by technical experts." W. H. G. Armytage, "The Rise of the Technocratic Class," in *Meaning and Control: Essays in Social Aspects of Science and Technology* 65 (D. O. Edge and J. N. Wolfe eds., 1973).

49. See, for example, Max Weber, "Science as a Vocation," in *From Max Weber: Essays in Sociology* 129, 144 (H. H. Gerth and C. Wright Mills ed. and trans., 1946). The dehumanizing effects of a technocratic organization of society remain a popular theme for intellectual speculation. See, for example, Andrew Feenberg, *Alternative Modernity: The Technical Turn in Phi-*

mantic temperament. It is also an accurate prediction of the transformation of the modern university and resulting decline in the independent intellectual.

To attribute to Orwell a Romantic fascination with the theme of love
braided with cruelty and death will seem perverse to anyone who ex-
pects a work of imaginative literature to be continuous with the author's public persona and conscious self-understanding. Orwell, as everyone knows, because he told us again and again (and because it was
largely true), stood for honesty, simple decency, plain talking, common
sense, abhorrence of cruelty, delight in the texture of ordinary life,
and the other conventional English virtues. But to write imaginative
literature one must have an imagination, and imagination draws on
the unconscious. The author of *Nineteen Eighty-Four*, who objected to
the publisher's blurb for the book because "it makes the book sound
as though it were a thriller mixed up with a love story,"[50] was a more interesting person than we think, and perhaps than he knew. The life,
moreover, was a Romantic one—from service in the Imperial police to
"down and out" in Paris and London to fighting in Spain to tuberculo-
sis and early death. And I have noted discrepancies between the political views expressed in the novel and the views actually held by Orwell;
the novel is more than the recasting in literary form Orwell's views as a
public intellectual.

It would be a mistake to deny political, even philosophical, significance, let alone purpose, to either novel; and that is not my aim. (But
the economics in both novels is terrible—and another sign of the diminishing scope for public intellectuality: no longer is economics an
appropriate subject for amateurs' speculations.) These two novels lend
themselves to political analysis, and thus to the attention of the public
intellectual, better than the novels of Henry James do. Huxley's novel is
a powerful satire of utilitarianism. Orwell's satire of communism has
lost its urgency, but its topical significance should not be forgotten.

---

losophy and Social Theory (1995). Weber's concern is echoed by Leon Kass, who in arguing
against permitting the cloning of human beings remarks that if it is permitted, "human nature
becomes merely the last part of nature to succumb to the technological project, which turns
all of nature into raw material at human disposal, to be homogenized by our rationalized
technique according to the subjective prejudices of the day." Kass, note 18 above, at 23.

50. George Orwell, Letter to Roger Senhouse, Dec. 26, 1948, in *The Collected Essays, Journalism and Letters of George Orwell*, note 14 above, vol. 4: *In Front of Your Nose, 1945–1950*,
p. 460.

Written by a self-proclaimed democratic socialist at a time when many left-wing intellectuals were Stalinists, it strengthened the anticommunist Left. And its reminder of the political importance of truth,[51] the malleability and hence vulnerability of historical records, and the dependence of complex thought on a rich vocabulary (that is, that language is a medium of thought as well as of expression) remains both philosophically interesting[52] and timely—especially when history textbooks are being rewritten to comply with the dictates of political correctness. That truth shall make us free, and that ignorance is weakness (to reverse one of the slogans of the Party), have rarely been so powerfully shown as in *Nineteen Eighty-Four*. And while Orwell was not much interested in technology, it is easy to see how recent advances in photographic simulation and computer data manipulation may facilitate a project of rewriting history—easy to imagine Winston's work station as a computer terminal in which he edits "history" conveniently stored online.

I am not, in short, trying to undermine Orwell's standing as one of the premier public intellectuals of the twentieth century, or to deny the centrality of *Nineteen Eighty-Four* to Orwell's career and significance as a public intellectual. I thus have no objection to a philosopher's drawing on Orwell's expository writings—indeed treating *Nineteen Eighty-Four* as continuous with those writings—for help in arguing, in the words of James Conant, that "what his novel aims to make manifest is that if reality control and doublethink were ever to be practiced on a systematic scale, the possibility of an individual speaking the truth and the possibility of an individual controlling her own mind would begin simultaneously to fade out of the world."[53] I have no objection, in short, to Orwell's novel being used as a shuttlecock in a game of philosophical badminton.

But we must be careful not to lose sight of *Nineteen Eighty-Four* as a work of literature, rather than just as social commentary; for social commentary is bound to be superseded sooner or later, and usually

51. In the sense of factuality—truth with a lower-case "t," not the Truth of religious or political dogmatism, or the scientific dogmatism of a Steven Weinberg or a Stephen Gould.

52. Young, note 25 above, at 11–18; cf. Peter Carruthers, *Language, Thought and Consciousness: An Essay in Philosophical Psychology* 51–52 (1996).

53. James Conant, "Freedom, Cruelty, and Truth: Rorty versus Orwell," in *Rorty and His Critics* 268, 310 (Robert B. Brandom ed., 2000).

sooner. This is happening to *Nineteen Eighty-Four*, so conceived. As prophecy, it is discredited. Even as a depiction of Soviet reality, it is flawed, as we have seen, though more perceptive than most such depictions at the time Orwell was writing. Its take on technology is wrong. It is imperceptive about television. It overintellectualizes the totalitarian system of social control. To some extent these are not *mistakes* by Orwell at all, but deliberate displacements of reality made for literary effect, a distinction likely to be missed by readers who treat Orwell's novel as a political tract. The aesthetic approach advocated in the preceding chapter should guard us against such a confusion. It should make us alert to the danger that in studying yesterday's literature from a political, philosophical, or moralistic perspective we may become distracted by what from that perspective, though not from the literary perspective, are anachronisms, such as Henry James's antisemitism or *Nineteen Eighty-Four*'s pessimism. James Conant's civic-minded take on the novel, quoted in the preceding paragraph, strikes me as a little flat; but I am not much taken by his rival Rorty's claim that the real focus of the book is not on Winston's pain but on O'Brien's pleasure.[54] Public intellectuals who treat the novels of yesterday as political tracts are merely demonstrating the ephemeral character of public-intellectual work, their own and their subjects'. Public intellectuals date; artists need not.

54. See Richard Rorty, *Contingency, Irony, and Solidarity*, ch. 8 (1989).

~ 8

The Jeremiah School

If that nation, against whom I have pronounced, turn from their evil,
I will repent of the evil that I thought to do unto them.[1]

This is the supreme instant, the turning point in history at
which man either vanquishes the processes of change or vanishes,
at which, from being the unconscious puppet of evolution
he becomes either its victim or its master.[2]

Nostalgia . . . is the unthinking man's way of
coming to terms with history.[3]

$\mathcal{G}$ERTRUDE HIMMELFARB is a well-known intellectual
historian, social conservative, and public intellectual. In her book *One
Nation, Two Cultures* (1999) she argues that the "counterculture" of the
1960s, with its unbridled sexuality, its flight from tradition and personal responsibility, its flouting of authority, and its cultural relativism,
has become the dominant culture of today's United States, while the
culture of the 1950s—the culmination of an era, stretching back to
the founding of the nation, when strong family values, a belief in absolute standards of truth and morality, and respect for religion and authority were the cornerstones of the national culture—has become a
dissident culture, though with signs of renewed vitality. Americans live,
she thinks, in a period of moral decay, but there is growing resistance
to the cultural revolution engineered in the sixties. This resistance is
manifested in increased religiosity and in the recent improvement in
such social indicators as the number of abortions, births out of wedlock, persons on welfare, and crimes.

1. Jeremiah 18:8.
2. Alvin Toffler, *Future Shock* 416 (1970).
3. Werner J. Dannhauser, "Nietzsche and Spengler on Progress and Decline," in *History and the Idea of Progress* 117, 118 (Arthur M. Melzer, Jerry Weinberger, and M. Richard Zinman eds., 1995).

281

Himmelfarb's book belongs to a genre, that of cultural pessimism[4] or national decline, that has a remarkable uniformity, at least in its American version. The remote origins are the prophetic books of the Old Testament. The more proximate origins and major examples are mainly European, like Spengler's *Decline of the West*,[5] though *The Education of Henry Adams* could be adduced as an American precursor. I will come back to Himmelfarb's book, but I want first to describe and illustrate the genre. There is the obligatory depiction of the 1950s as the last echo of an American golden age, the 1960s as the descent into barbarism, the present as the era of decadence, the future as bleak. There is the indictment of "modern liberalism," including radical feminism and a pervasive atmosphere of permissiveness—all traceable to John Stuart Mill's *On Liberty*—which has brought us to this pass.[6] There is proof by telling anecdote and selective statistic. Declinist works get much of their rhetorical force from contrasting an idealized past, its vices overlooked, with a demonized presence, its virtues overlooked. This is a marked characteristic of the public-intellectual literature on the alleged decline of the legal profession since the supposedly halcyon 1950s.[7]

The genre's most distinctive feature is the assumption of cultural unity—the mutual dependence of the various departments of culture in

4. As distinct from ecological pessimism, which is, however, another thriving genre of doom prophecy by public intellectuals, such as Paul Ehrlich.

5. See Arthur Herman, *The Idea of Decline in Western History* (1997). With specific reference to cultural pessimism, see Tyler Cowen, *In Praise of Commercial Culture*, ch. 5 (1998).

6. To the same effect, see Gertrude Himmelfarb, *On Liberty and Liberalism: The Case of John Stuart Mill* 309–328 (1974). As one judge put it, dissenting from a decision invalidating a state law against consensual homosexual sodomy, "the entire discussion and rationale of the majority opinion is rooted in legalistic language based in large part on the discredited and irresponsible philosophy of John Stuart Mill." Commonwealth v. Wasson, 842 S.W.2d 487, 519 (Ky. 1992). And in the words of public intellectual Russell Kirk, in his introduction to a 1955 reprinting of *On Liberty*, what Mill in his advocacy of individualism failed to foresee was that "in actuality, a century later, the real danger is that custom and tradition and prescription will be overthrown utterly by neoterism, the lust after novelty, and that men will be no better than the flies of a summer, oblivious to the wisdom of their ancestors, and forming every opinion solely under the influence of the passion of the hour" (p. xiv). See also Roger Kimball, "Mill, Stephen, and the Nature of Freedom," in *The Betrayal of Liberalism: How the Disciples of Freedom and Equality Helped Foster the Illiberal Politics of Coercion and Control* 43 (Hilton Kramer and Roger Kimball eds., 1999).

7. See, for notable examples, Mary Ann Glendon, *A Nation under Lawyers: How the Crisis in the Legal Profession Is Transforming American Society* (1994), and Anthony T. Kronman, *The Lost Lawyer: Failing Ideals of the Legal Profession* (1993), discussed, respectively, in my books *The Problematics of Moral and Legal Theory* 194–200 (1999), and *Overcoming Law* 93–94 (1995).

its broadest sense, the sense in which we might speak of a political culture, a popular culture, a legal culture, a regional culture, a work ethic,
a morality, and so forth. So the vulgarization of popular culture has significance not only for popular culture but also for crime, politics, the
family, and morals generally, as does the loosening grip of belief in a
strict, judgmental God, the entrenchment of affirmative action, and the
decision to allow women to serve in combat. The public and the private
are one; recall how during the Clinton impeachment controversy Robert Bork wrote that if Clinton was not removed from office, "it will be a
clear sign that we have turned a corner, that American morality, including *but not limited to* our political morality, is in free fall."[8] The fabric of
civilization is woven of law, popular and elite culture, religion, family
structure, even etiquette; pull on any of these threads and the entire
fabric unravels.

Criticism of dumb left-wing ideas and their cultural manifestations is
not my target. I applaud such criticism. It need not be declinist.[9] And
"declinist" literature is not inherently right-wing. At the end of this
chapter I discuss Robert Putnam's *Bowling Alone*, the left counterpart to
Himmelfarb's book, and in the next we'll see left-liberal Richard Rorty
describe the United States as a nation in decline. (We shall encounter
some of his other gloomy forebodings in this chapter as well.) Environmental and natural-resource doomsayers, such as Paul Ehrlich and
Jeremy Rifkin,[10] are invariably leftists. And consider the slew of books
by the quasi-leftist historian Christopher Lasch, all aimed at the general public and marking him as a public intellectual. In his last book,
published in 1995, we read the usual soon-to-be-dated indictment of
American society: "The decline of manufacturing and the consequent
loss of jobs; the shrinkage of the middle class; the growing number of
the poor; the rising crime rate; the flourishing traffic in drugs; the decay of the cities—the bad news goes on and on."[11] Lasch blames the

---

8. Robert H. Bork, "Counting the Costs of Clintonism," *American Spectator,* Nov. 1998,
p. 55 (emphasis added).

9. See, for example, William J. Bennett, *The De-Valuing of America: The Fight for Our Culture and Our Children* (1992); also Myron Magnet, *The Dream and the Nightmare: The Sixties'
Legacy to the Underclass* (1993), which despite its alarming title is a generally sober criticism of
the "political correctness" movement and other features of current left-liberal ideology.

10. See, for example, Jeremy Rifkin with Ted Howard, *Entropy: A New World View* (1980).

11. Christopher Lasch, *The Revolt of the Elites and the Betrayal of Democracy* 3 (1995). An
even gloomier assessment, complete with predictions of ecological disaster, appears in an essay by Lasch published the same year: "The Age of Limits," in *History and the Idea of Progress,*

sorry state of the nation mediately on the decline of judgmental religion and the debasement of public discourse but ultimately on prosperity. "A moral condemnation of great wealth must inform any defense
of the free market, and that moral condemnation must be backed up
with effective political action."[12] "A cultural conservative cloaked in a
leftish fleece," Lasch "struggles to distance himself from his conservative look-alikes . . . by uncovering the capitalist roots of most modern
ills. What American rightwingers typically fail to see, he asserts, is the
all-corrosive power of a free-market economy."[13]

Although not a right-wing monopoly, the literature of national decline does have a right-wing bias. Conventional conservatives, as distinct from libertarians, use the past as the benchmark for judging the
present, while liberals tend to be utopian and thus to compare the present against an imagined future. (Lasch was no liberal—was in fact an
antiliberal, as Stephen Holmes explains.)[14] The liberal paints a roseate
future, the conservative a roseate past, and both a dismal present, so
that the curve is downward for the conservative but potentially upward
for the liberal. But whatever the author's politics, the genre is tailor-
made for public intellectuals and largely monopolized by them. In an
age of academic specialization, a work of scholarship devoted to tracing
the decline of the United States in every sphere of culture and behavior, and to establishing the interrelations of the spheres and the impli-

---

note 3 above, at 227, esp. 230–231. Robert Bellah's books, which I mentioned in Chapter 4,
are gentler, more liberal, but otherwise Lasch-like jeremiads, and, in their emphasis on loss of
community, precursors to Putnam's *Bowling Alone*. Another example of recent liberal declinist
literature is Morris Berman, *The Twilight of American Culture* (2000). The title epitomizes the
genre.

12. Lasch, *The Revolt of the Elites and the Betrayal of Democracy*, note 11 above, at 22. Derek
Bok, the former president of Harvard University, gives a curious twist to Lasch's thesis by arguing that our problem is that professionals and business executives are overpaid. Writing in
the early 1990s, he expressed doubt that "the acquisitive, self-centered goals reflected in our
compensation practices are truly what our society needs." Derek Bok, *The Cost of Talent: How
Executives and Professionals Are Paid and How It Affects America* 297 (1993). He suggested, incorrectly as it turned out, that we could not shake off "the principal failures of the past two
decades—lagging productivity, shrinking savings, mounting deficits, growing poverty" unless
we placed "less emphasis on personal gain and a greater stress on common sacrifice and sharing." Id.

13. Stephen Holmes, *The Anatomy of Antiliberalism* 125–126 (1993).

14. Id., ch. 5. See also Louis Menand, "Christopher Lasch's Quarrel with Liberalism," in
The Liberal Persuasion: Arthur Schlesinger, Jr., and the Challenge of the American Past 233 (John
Patrick Diggins ed., 1997).

cations of the decline, invites dismissal as academic charlatanry. Nor would the methodology of anecdote and selective statistic—a systematic slanting in favor of the decline thesis—be considered respectable.

Robert Bork's book *Slouching towards Gomorrah*[15] exemplifies the genre. The title comes from the last two lines of Yeats's poem "The Second Coming": "And what rough beast, its hour come round at last, / Slouches towards Bethlehem to be born?" Bork's use of the poem will not commend itself to lovers of poetry and language—this in a book that deplores the degradation of culture. Yeats's "rough beast" is the messiah—not the Jewish or Christian messiah, to be sure, but a redeemer all the same; the title of the poem is not ironic. Bork's rough beast is decadence, which is not redemptive, which is a gradual process rather than a sudden event like a birth, and which Bork believes to be already far advanced rather than something we're merely slouching toward. The seeds were sown, he believes, in the eighteenth century, by the draftsmen of the Declaration of Independence. *On Liberty* was one of the fruits. The 1960s merely punctuated the long decay that the 1950s had somehow masked. Bork states that soldiers sang as they went off to fight in World War I, while in World War II they wisecracked their way into combat. That was a sign of our decay, our loss of romance and *gravitas*, as was the fact that our World War II soldiers liked Eisenhower, with his "informality" and "regular-guy manner," more than they liked MacArthur, with his "grand manner," though the latter, Bork asserts, was the abler general—a questionable judgment[16] that Bork does not defend.

These curious examples, undeveloped and undefended, typify the casualness with which declinists handle evidence. It is a casualness Bork would not have tolerated in his former roles as a law professor, as solicitor general and acting attorney general of the United States, and as a federal court of appeals judge. The declinist genre is not strong on logic or consistency either, as Bork's handling of Yeats's poem reveals. Or consider that after describing attacks on science and technology as symptomatic of our decadence, Bork joins the attack by claiming that

15. Robert H. Bork, *Slouching towards Gomorrah: Modern Liberalism and American Decline* (1996).

16. See Williamson Murray and Allan R. Millett, *A War to Be Won: Fighting the Second World War* 181–182 (2000); Stanley Weintraub, *MacArthur's War: Korea and the Undoing of an American Hero* (2000).

scientific evidence is shifting against the theory that man evolved from lower animals and that life is the result of random forces in nature rather than the gift of God. He presents this thesis as a shift within science rather than as a rejection of science. But given his lack of scientific credentials and his insistence that religious belief is essential to a civilized future, his questioning of evolution and of the natural origins of life allies him with those who raise religious objections to the teaching of evolution. The science he defends elsewhere in the book is science that demonstrates ineradicable inequalities among people.

Yet it is important to note that this picking and choosing among scientific theories by people who have no scientific competence is characteristic of public-intellectual work, and political debate more generally, rather than anything peculiar to Bork or to the Right. The Left believes steadfastly in evolution and in the statistical evidence linking cigarette smoking to lung cancer and other diseases, but turns skeptical when confronted with the application of the theory of evolution to differences between the sexes and to homosexual orientation, or with statistical evidence indicating racial differences in intelligence.

Bork's handling of the issue of abortion rights illustrates the carelessness of so much public-intellectual work even when it is the work of a highly able, well-trained person. He divides the issue into two questions: whether abortion is always the killing of a human being; if so, whether that killing is motivated only by considerations of convenience. But he refuses to "address instances where most people, however they might ultimately decide the issue, would feel genuine moral anguish; cases, for example, where it is known that the child will be born with severe deformities" (p. 174). That is a cop-out. Whether we consider the fetus a fully entitled human being, a child in other words, is inseparable from how we judge aborting a severely deformed fetus, as we do not consider it proper to kill severely deformed children. Bork's refusal to consider the case of the deformed fetus also implies a negative answer to the first question, whether abortion is always the killing of a human being. The refusal implies that it is an entirely respectable position, one he won't even attempt to refute, that it is morally permissible to abort, that is, to kill, the deformed fetus—but if so, how can abortion *always* be the killing of a human being? Bork would not countenance the killing of a human being.

In fact and inconsistently Bork deems the question whether abortion is always the killing of a human being a simple one to answer in the affirmative because as a matter of biology the fertilized egg is continuous with the child that emerges from the mother's womb if the fetus is carried to term, and with the adult that the child grows into. But this is equally true if the fetus is deformed, unless it is so deformed that it won't survive the birth trauma. And Bork does not discuss whether, in any event, biology should be normative. Nor does he ponder the significance of the fact that in all likelihood a majority of fertilized human ova are spontaneously aborted[17]—are these deaths of human beings?

Having satisfied himself that all fetuses are human beings, Bork uses a survey of the reasons women give for abortions to argue that the overwhelming majority of abortions are done for the mother's convenience. But what he means by convenience is anything unrelated to her health or that of the fetus (except rape, although he does not explain why a victim of rape who has an abortion is not doing it for her convenience), so that, for example, the fact that the woman is too young to be a competent mother, or that having a baby now will prevent her from getting an education or supporting her future children, counts only as a convenience factor.

Bork is right that most abortions are not health related. But it is remarkable in light of his emphasis on that fact that he should turn immediately to the issue of "partial birth abortion," which he regards as monstrous, a form of "infanticide [that] underscore[s] the casual brutality born of nihilism that is an ever more prominent feature of our culture" (p. 183). The term "partial birth abortion" refers to a late-term abortion procedure in which the physician, instead of crushing the fetus's skull, and dismembering the fetus, while the fetus is entirely inside the mother's womb, turns the fetus around before beginning the abortion, so that the lower portion of the fetus is in the mother's vagina

17. The usual estimates of the frequency of spontaneous abortion (miscarriage) run from 13 to 19 percent. See, for example, Charles R. Hammerslough, "Estimating the Probability of Spontaneous Abortion in the Presence of Induced Abortion and Vice Versa," 107 *Public Health Reports* 269 (1992); Allen J. Wilcox, Alan E. Treloar, and Dale P. Sandler, "Spontaneous Abortion over Time: Comparing Occurrence in Two Cohorts of Women a Generation Apart," 114 *American Journal of Epidemiology* 548 (1981). But these figures are limited to spontaneous abortions that occur after the woman is sure she is pregnant, and it appears that most spontaneous abortions occur earlier. Timothy F. Murphy, "The Moral Significance of Spontaneous Abortion," 11 *Journal of Medical Ethics* 79, 80 (1985). Murphy cites one study that estimates that three-fourths of all pregnancies spontaneously abort. Id.

and part of it (the feet, even the legs) may actually be outside her body. The medical rationale for the procedure is that the risk of cutting the uterus with sharp instruments or inducing infection by failing to remove all the fetal parts is increased when the fetus is dismembered inside the womb. The procedure is ugly and its medical rationale has been questioned.[18] But Bork's denunciation misses several important points. First, in singling out partial birth abortion for particular condemnation he fails to consider the alternative methods of late-term abortion. They are just as ugly; *all* late-term abortions involve crushing the fetus's skull, so that the mother doesn't have to go into labor in order to expel the fetus. The right to life movement knows this, of course. The reason for the emphasis it has placed on partial birth abortion is political: to educate the public in the realities of late-term abortion while seeming only to condemn a single, medically controversial procedure.

Second, having earlier distinguished between abortions for convenience and abortions for reasons of fetal or maternal life or health, Bork unaccountably fails to consider which a partial birth abortion, or other late-term abortion, is likely to be. The mortality risk to the woman of a late-term abortion is many times greater than that of an early abortion.[19] This makes it less likely that she would decide on a late-term abortion (having earlier decided not to have an abortion when it would have been safer) for trivial reasons, such as sex selection, rather than for substantial reasons, such as the woman's health or the fetus's being profoundly deformed. Bork ignores this point completely. I would not myself put too much weight on it, though zero weight is too little. Although I have not been able to find statistics on how often the decision to have a late-term abortion is motivated by the discovery of fetal deformities or by concern for the woman's health, it appears that other, less compelling, though not necessarily trivial, reasons figure more prominently, such as failure to have discovered the pregnancy earlier, indecision about whether to abort, and difficulty in arranging for an abortion.[20]

18. These issues are fully canvassed in the opinions in Stenberg v. Carhart, 530 U.S. 914 (2000), where the Supreme Court invalidated state laws prohibiting partial-birth abortion.

19. Stanley K. Henshaw, "Unintended Pregnancy and Abortion: A Public Health Perspective," in *A Clinician's Guide to Medical and Surgical Abortion* 11, 20 (Maureen Paul et al. eds., 1999).

20. Anne Baker et al., "Informed Consent, Counseling, and Patient Preparation," in id. at

Bork also ignores the fact that because the Supreme Court's abortion doctrine permits states to limit abortions of viable fetuses (that is, fetuses that can survive outside the uterus), whatever the abortion method used, to cases in which there is a medical need for the abortion,[21] states are not required to permit partial-birth abortions for mere reasons of convenience. The partial-birth abortion statutes that the Court invalidated made no exception for cases in which the woman's health (rather than life) was at risk, and were not limited to the killing of viable fetuses.

The fact that late-term abortions are indeed particularly horrible creates a dilemma for the opponents of abortion. The more that early-term abortions are discouraged by parental-notification requirements, lack of subsidization, picketing of abortion clinics, and scarcity of abortion providers, the more late-term abortions there will be simply as a consequence of unavoidable delay in arranging for an abortion. Discouraging late-term abortion could actually raise the abortion rate. Testing for fetal abnormalities presupposes the availability of late-term abortion. The less feasible such an abortion is, the less benefit there is from testing; and women who believe themselves at risk of having an abnormal fetus may therefore abort, when if they had been tested they would in all likelihood have been reassured that the fetus was normal.[22]

Bork says that "the systematic killing of unborn children in huge numbers is a part of a general disregard for human life that has been growing for some time" (p. 192). The word "systematic" is misplaced; government is not compelling or encouraging abortion, but merely permitting it. And Bork does not attempt to square the proposition that there is a growing disregard for human life with the growing emphasis that public policy places on human safety and health, and the reduction in the death rate from accidents and disease that has resulted, in part anyway, from that emphasis.

Given his concern for the disregard of human life, Bork might have been expected to discuss America's continued employment of capital punishment at a time when almost all the nations that we consider our peers in civilization have abolished it. Reserved as it is in our society for

---

25, 31–32; Janet E. Gans Epner, Harry S. Jonas, and Daniel L. Seckinger, "Late-Term Abortion," 280 *JAMA (Journal of the American Medical Association)* 724, 725 (1998).

21. Planned Parenthood of Southeastern Pennsylvania v. Casey, 505 U.S. 833, 879 (1992).

22. David A. Grimes, "The Continuing Need for Late Abortions," 280 *JAMA (Journal of the American Medical Association)* 747, 749 (1998).

murder, capital punishment could be thought a tribute to the emphasis we place on the value of human life or it could be thought a sign of the very callousness that concerns Bork in regard to abortion and assisted suicide. Bork drops hints that he approves of capital punishment (pp. 165, 172)—more precisely, that he disapproves of its opponents—but he does not discuss it. He does not mention, for example, that the Catholic Church, whose doctrines on abortion and sex he appears to accept, opposes capital punishment. The Church thinks it reflects the same callousness toward human life as abortion.

Although Bork's subject is a process of decay that he thinks has been going on for centuries ("current liberalism's rot and decadence is merely what liberalism has been moving towards for better than two centuries" [p. 63]), and presumably therefore at a glacial pace since civilization has not yet collapsed, the tone is apocalyptic. "In the 1980s, it seemed, at last, that the Sixties were over. They were not. It was a malignant decade that, after a fifteen-year remission, returned in the 1980s [*sic*—he means the 1990s] to metastasize more devastatingly throughout our culture than it had in the Sixties . . . The Sixties radicals are still with us, but now they do not paralyze the universities; they run the universities" (p. 53). "Modern liberalism, the descendant and spiritual heir of the New Left, is what fascism looks like when it has captured significant institutions, most notably the universities" (p. 85).[23] Bork endorses a comparison of "the rampant anti-Semitism among the educated classes even in pre-Hitler Germany to the assault in American universities on white males" (p. 235). There is considerable hyperbole here, which is entirely consistent with the genre.[24] The situation of white males in American universities is not comparable to that of Jews in Weimar Germany. Radicals do not run any major American universities, though quite a number have faculty positions in them. And fascism of both the German and the Italian varieties did capture

23. Although here he qualifies "liberalism" with "modern," he is hostile to classical liberalism, the liberalism for example of Mill's *On Liberty*, as well.

24. Compare Roger Kimball, *The Long March: How the Cultural Revolution of the 1960s Changed America* (2000). The allusion to Maoism in the terms "Long March" and "Cultural Revolution" is intended, for Kimball quotes with approval the claim that the social and cultural changes in the United States initiated in the 1960s constitute "a cultural revolution, comparable to the one in China *if not worse.*" Id. at 6 (emphasis added). See also id. at 15. Bork's claim that we are "slouching towards Gomorrah" is endorsed in id. at 14.

the significant institutions of their societies, including the universities, yet did not look like modern liberalism.

Extreme problems require extreme solutions. So rather than merely urging that our obscenity laws be strengthened or that the existing laws be enforced more vigorously, Bork wants censorship reinstituted in order that violence and indecency may be banned from the theater, the media, and the other outlets for expression. He might even welcome a "deep economic depression,"[25] maybe even a "cataclysmic war." For these are two of only four developments "that could produce a moral and spiritual regeneration" (p. 336), and the other two—"a religious revival" and "the revival of public discourse about morality"—seem unpromising; we are in the *midst* of a religious revival, which has not saved us, and there are few signs of a revival of public discourse about morality. Aligning himself with Christopher Lasch, Bork tells us that while liberalism is the enemy, it is the growth of affluence that has enabled liberalism to weaken the grip of old-time religion, which worshipped "a demanding God, a God who dictates how one should live and puts a great many bodily and psychological pleasures off limits" (p. 281). Yet if affluence powers modern liberalism, it is surprising that Bork should criticize progressive taxation and affirmative action because they reduce economic growth and therefore national wealth by distorting incentives. Bork endorses the remarkable claim that affirmative action has cost the nation *trillions* of dollars.

Bork's "hard God" puts one in mind of the description by James Fitzjames Stephen, one of Bork's predecessors in the tradition of social conservatism, of the Sermon on the Mount as "a pathetic overstatement of duties."[26] Mill's *On Liberty* was Stephen's *bête noire*,[27] as it is Bork's (see pp. 59–61, 64) and Himmelfarb's. And here is what one of Bork's neoconservative confrères, Irving Kristol (who happens to be

---

25. Compare one of the dwindling band of left-leaning Jeremiahs, Richard Rorty: "I think nothing is going to happen until you can get the masses to stop thinking of the bureaucrats as the enemy, and start thinking of the bosses as the enemy. I suspect this will only happen if there's a great, huge recession." *Against Bosses, against Oligarchies: A Conversation with Richard Rorty* 33 (Derek Nystrom and Kent Puckett eds., 1998). See also Rorty, "Intellectuals in Politics: Too Far In? Too Far Out?" *Dissent*, Fall 1991, pp. 483, 484.

26. James Fitzjames Stephen, *Liberty, Equality, Fraternity* 259 (1992 [1874]).

27. *Liberty, Equality, Fraternity* is an attack on *On Liberty*. See Richard A. Posner, *Overcoming Law*, ch. 10 (1995).

Gertrude Himmelfarb's husband) has to say on the subject of a religion of fire and brimstone:

> If I may speak bluntly about the Catholic church, for which I have enormous respect, it is traumatic for someone who wishes that church well to see it modernize itself at this moment. Young people do not want to hear that the church is becoming modern. Go tell the young people that the message of the church is to wear sackcloth and ashes and to walk on nails to Rome, and they would do it. The church turned the wrong way.[28]

Setting to one side the oddity of Kristol's giving advice to the Catholic Church on how to keep up its membership (Kristol is Jewish), I think he's on to something.[29] A religion that does not require any sacrifices of its votaries is unlikely to have much influence on people's behavior. The religiosity of Americans, so surprising to European observers, is by this standard behaviorally rather meaningless and social conservatives are right therefore to be dissatisfied with it. Apart from Mormons, Christian Scientists, Jehovah's Witnesses, Orthodox Jews, and members of a few other sects, religious Americans do not differ greatly in their outlook and behavior from nonreligious ones. And only Christian Scientists, Jehovah's Witnesses, and some Pentecostals actually reject science in matters vital to their personal welfare. If the economist's concept of "revealed preference" is substituted for professed preference, the preference of most Americans is to live a secular life.

Should this be a cause for regret? Do we really want our young people to be willing to walk on nails to Rome, or Jerusalem, or Mecca? In commending religious zealotry, isn't Kristol playing with fire, just as Auden was when he commended political fanaticism (see Chapter 3)? Religious zealotry has an intimate historical association with violence, bigotry, censorship, ignorance, and repression. The association persists today in many parts of the world, and we see it operating in a small way in this country in the violent attacks on abortion providers and abortion clinics and in the persistent efforts to discourage the teaching of

---

28. Irving Kristol, *Reflections of a Neoconservative: Looking Back, Looking Ahead* 326 (1983).

29. See also Roger Finke and Rodney Stark, *The Churching of America, 1776–1990: Winners and Losers in Our Religious Economy* 238, 265–275 (1992).

evolution in the public schools. In light of such experience, a revival of the old-time religion may not be something devoutly to be wished.

Behind Bork, behind Himmelfarb and Kristol, stalks the ghost of Mill's great antagonist, James Fitzjames Stephen. Against Mill and Mill's modern avatars, Stephen thought that people could not be kept in line unless government supported religion; specifically, law had to be founded on the moral doctrines of no-nonsense Christianity (recall his comment on the Sermon on the Mount). Against believers in equality, he argued that the result of giving women equal rights with men would be

> that women would become men's slaves and drudges, that they would be made to feel their weakness and to accept its consequences to the very utmost. Submission and protection are correlative. Withdraw the one and the other is lost, and force will assert itself a hundred times more harshly through the law of contract than ever it did through the law of status.[30]

He also thought it "a question . . . whether the enormous development of equality in America, the rapid production of an immense multitude of commonplace, self-satisfied, and essentially slight people is an exploit which the whole world need fall down [before] and worship."[31]

He was wrong in all these respects. Americans are not an "essentially slight people." Equal rights for women have not made women slaves and drudges compared to what they were before, although it has made some of them worse off. The old-time religion has not proved necessary to maintain social order. Europe has lost religion but retained order; America has lost the old-time religion and retained order—though less so than the irreligious Europeans.

∼ IN A BOOK ominously entitled *The Coming Anarchy*,[32] Robert Kaplan takes the Bork–Lasch story of a nation gone soft through affluence—and Kaplan adds, through peace—to its logical conclusion. Our wealth has made us passive and apathetic. "Material possessions not

30. Stephen, note 26 above, at 209.

31. Id. at 220.

32. Robert D. Kaplan, *The Coming Anarchy: Shattering the Dreams of the Post Cold War* (2000).

only focus people toward private and away from communal life but also encourage docility. The more possessions one has, the more compromises one will make to protect them" (p. 89). Having rejected repeated warnings that "material prosperity would breed servility and withdrawal" (id.), we have allowed faceless, cosmopolitan international corporations to take over the effective governance of the society. We will go the way of Rome; in fact, there are many affinities between the United States of today and Rome in its decline. A new Dark Ages loom. For Kaplan, as for Edward Luttwak (see Chapter 4), "The future of the Third World may finally be our own" (p. 98).

Where Bork merely intimates the possibility of salvation through war, Kaplan is refreshingly explicit. "Universal peace is something to be feared" (p. 169).[33] Since war is, Kaplan acknowledges, a bloody business, "the Cold War may have been as close to utopia as we are ever likely to get" (p. 171), despite the nasty wars in Korea and Vietnam. "Whereas war leads to a respect for large, progressive government, peace creates an institutional void filled by, among other things, entertainment-oriented corporations" (p. 175). "A more concretely frightening prospect of peacetime," Kaplan explains, "is the reduction of standing armies" (id.). Standing armies serve to discipline unruly youth; without them we can foresee "an increase in gang activity and other forms of violent behavior" (id.). He argues that "because morality is unachievable without amoral force, the re-authorization of assassinations by the U.S. Congress might do much more to contain evil than enlarging the Security Council to include nations such as India and Brazil" (pp. 178–179). "We think we know what *political correctness* is: we have no idea how intensely suffocating public discourse could become in a truly unified and peaceful world" (p. 180).

The similarities between Bork and Kaplan on the one hand and Lasch on the other, that is, between the right-wing declinists and the left-wing declinists, are noteworthy. Both wings are antiliberal, seeking a more bracing concept of national purpose than liberalism, with its pluralism and tolerance, its materialism and antimilitarism, affords. Also noteworthy is how skinny is the public-intellectual body to

33. I am put in mind of the prayer of John Mitchel (a nineteenth-century Irish nationalist), quoted approvingly by Yeats in his great poem "Under Ben Bulben": "Send war in our time, O Lord!" For Kaplan, however, the benefits of war or threat of war are utilitarian; for Yeats they were spiritual.

which the wings are attached. There is only a small center in public-intellectual land, because public intellectuals have difficulty differentiating themselves without taking extreme positions and because the demand for public intellectuals is to a significant effect a demand for creating solidarity within groups that feel in jeopardy by virtue of their own marginality. The imbalance between wings and body creates a false impression of a divided nation.

There is a symbiotic relation, not merely a resemblance, between the wings. Without the crazy radicals of the 1960s and today's smaller, less disruptive, though equally zany radical fringe, Bork would quickly run out of fuel for his jeremiad. He could still talk about high rates of divorce, abortion, teenage pregnancy, births out of wedlock, and crime, and about pornography and about violent lyrics in popular songs, but he would have difficulty describing these as by-products of a cultural revolution that in its virulence and lunacy was bringing on a new Dark Ages. He would be writing as a sociologist rather than as a prophet. It is the elaborate dogmatic structure of Christianity and of communism that makes these ideologies so enticing to intellectuals, and it is the *intellectual* defenders of cultural radicalism—postmodernists, radical feminists, deconstructionists, queer theorists, cultural relativists, crits, Afrocentrists, and the rest—who provide a manageable target for the cultural warrior who is not a social scientist.

But if Bork thus battens on the intellectual Left, the intellectual Left battens on him. It is as if Bork perversely wanted to vindicate those public intellectuals such as Ronald Dworkin who diabolized him during his fight to get on the Supreme Court. In his advocacy of censorship, his proposal to amend the Constitution to allow Congress to overrule the Supreme Court's constitutional decisions, and his call for a return to Victorian morality and the old-time religion, Bork became a pretext for the Left to embrace and defend President Clinton—who is not a leftist and was in many ways the conservator of the Reagan (counter)revolution[34]—as a defender of modernity against a scary band of reactionaries. Bork says that "the intellectual class, then, is composed of people whose mindset is very like that of the student radicals of the Sixties: hostility to this culture and society coupled with millenarian

---

34. As recognized by some on the Left. See, for example, William Greider, "Unfinished Business: Clinton's Lost Presidency," in *The Best of the Nation: Selections from the Independent Magazine of Politics and Culture* 583 (Victor Navasky and Katrina vanden Heuvel eds., 2000).

dreams" (p. 84). Yes; and if you substitute "nightmares" for "dreams," you have Bork as well.

Either end of the public-intellectual political spectrum provides a big target for the other end, but not a target worth the expenditure of the ordnance necessary to destroy it. The United States is not an unstable nation vulnerable to being taken over by extremists of the Left or the Right. It is true that radicals have undue influence in many college and university humanities and social-science departments; true also that as I noted in Chapter 4 they have, Pied Piper–like, stirred up a few silly students to campaign and even riot against "globalization"; and true that their awful take on literature is ruining many high-school as well as college English classes.[35] But radicals do not control the colleges and universities, which increasingly are managed as the big businesses they have become, or any other stratum of the educational system for that matter. Nor, of course, do Bork and his allies occupy the "commanding heights" of culture or politics. They're a fringe too. Each fringe has three symmetrical effects, all unintended: to discredit its side of the political spectrum (that is, the radical Left is an embarrassment to the liberal side and the radical Right to the conservative side), to dissipate the energies of potential revolutionaries or counterrevolutionaries in battles over symbols and cultural institutions,[36] and to provide a *raison d'être* for the polemics of the opposite fringe. Equal and opposite radical wings of the body politic thus can actually stabilize, rather than, as they wish to do, destabilize, centrist politics.

Another feature of Bork's book, besides its extremism, that has general significance for appraising today's public intellectuals is the rapidity with which it has dated. It was published in 1996 and so probably was completed in 1995, at the nadir of Clinton's fortunes, when few thought he would be reelected, and on the heels of the Republican takeover of Congress following the 1984 congressional elections. If we nevertheless were in 1995 trembling on the edge of a new Dark Age, how awful our situation should be today (2001), after Clinton's second term, after his survival of an impeachment brought upon himself by just the sort of immoralism that a Bork would expect of someone who

35. See Francine Prose, "I Know Why the Caged Bird Cannot Read: How American High School Students Learn to Loathe Literature," *Harper's Magazine*, Sept. 1999, p. 76.

36. Imagine if the *only* things that had bothered Hitler about Weimar Germany had been German expressionism and the Berlin nightclub scene.

grew up during the 1960s, after the disarray in the conservative movement resulting from the failure of the impeachment, after the election of a Republican president who despite running a centrist campaign lost the popular vote to an opponent who campaigned on strident populist themes, and above all after years of dizzying U.S. economic expansion that by making us wealthier should have further sapped our moral fiber and worsened our social problems. Bork cannot be criticized for not having foreseen these events. But it was implicit in his book that if they came to pass, the bad things he describes in his book would be worse: there would be more crime, more abortions, more divorce, a higher rate of births out of wedlock, a more callous attitude toward human life, a decline in civility and religion, a more aggressive feminism, more people on welfare, more black anger, more hostility to business. All these social pathologies have declined, some of them dramatically (such as the murder rate and the number of people on welfare), since Bork wrote.[37] They have declined even though, if his analysis were correct, they would have grown. In effect, though less recklessly than a Luttwak or an Ehrlich, he made predictions that have been falsified by events.

Topicality and datedness go hand in hand, of course. But the prophetic character of declinist literature exacerbates the problem of datedness. The Hebrew prophets, who made this a respectable genre, had the advantage of being published long after the events they prophesied. Our modern prophets have no similarly convenient way to avoid a reality check. Again the problem is not limited to right-wing Jeremiahs. There are striking examples of quickly falsified prophecy from the

---

37. The murder rate has fallen by about a third since the early 1990s, and is now at the level it was in the mid-1960s, though still considerably above that in the 1950s. See U.S. Dept. of Justice, Bureau of Justice Statistics, "Crime Data Brief" (March 2000 NCF 179767). On the improvement in the other social indicators, see U.S. Census Bureau, *Statistical Abstract of the United States 1999* 75 (tabs. 91–92), 76 (tab. 94), 91 (tab. 124), 214 (tab. 342) (119th ed. 1999); Karl Zinsmeister, Stephen Moore, and Karlyn Bowman, "Is America Turning a Corner?" *American Enterprise*, Jan./Feb. 1999, p. 36; also Gregg Easterbrook, "America the O.K.," *New Republic*, Jan. 4 and 11, 1999, p. 19. *American Enterprise* is published by the American Enterprise Institute—the conservative Washington think tank of which Bork is a senior research fellow. Another AEI study, Daniel T. Slesnick, "Living Standards in the United States: A Consumption-Based Approach" (American Enterprise Institute 2000), finds that since the 1970s, contrary to the widespread impression that indicators of U.S. economic welfare were stagnant or declining until the 1990s, there has been a substantial improvement in living standards, a large decline in poverty, and no increase in inequality when consumption is substituted for money income as the measure of economic welfare.

other end of the political spectrum—for example Richard Rorty saying in 1987, two years before the Berlin Wall came down and four years before the Soviet Union dissolved, that "time seems to be on the Soviet side";[38] a year later that "if there is hope, it lies in the Third World";[39] in 1992 that America "could slide into fascism at any time";[40] in 1995 that "America now seems to be having a nervous breakdown: the country is exhausted, dispirited, frightened, irresolute, and utterly unable to contribute to the resolution of international problems."[41]

There is a lesson the modern public intellectual should have taken from the Hebrew prophets: if your prophecy is published after the events prophesied, be sure to conform the prophecy to the events. Hilary Putnam, a distinguished philosopher with strong political and religious views that he wishes to communicate to the educated public at large, in 1990 published a book that contains a chapter that had first been delivered as a lecture in 1983. Chomsky-like, the lecture accuses the Reagan administration of foisting dictatorship on Latin American nations.[42] Maybe that was a plausible accusation in 1983. It was not in 1990, by which time every junta and dictator in Latin America, except Castro, had been kicked out and been replaced by some approximation to a democratic government.[43] (Later there was some backsliding—under the Clinton administration!) But Putnam made no attempt to update his lecture, or to remark on any of the changes in Latin America since 1983.

38. Richard Rorty, "Thugs and Theorists: A Reply to Bernstein," 15 *Political Theory* 564, 566 (1987).

39. Richard Rorty, "Unger, Castoriadis, and the Romance of a National Future," 82 *Northwestern University Law Review* 335, 340 (1988).

40. Richard Rorty, "Trotsky and the Wild Orchids," 1 *Common Knowledge* 140, 151 (1992). Rorty reprinted this essay, including the quoted passage, in 1999. Rorty, *Philosophy and Social Hope* 3, 17 (1999).

41. Richard Rorty, "Half a Million Blue Helmets?" *Common Knowledge*, Winter 1995, pp. 10, 13.

42. Hilary Putnam, *Realism with a Human Face* 186 (James Conant ed., 1990). There are other anachronisms, such as a reference to U.S. unemployment rates in excess of 10 percent. Id. at 187. Although acknowledging that he is not an economist, Putnam is not shy about making pronouncements on economic policy. See id. at 187–192.

43. This is not to deny that the Reagan administration supported right-wing governments in Chile and El Salvador, or that it worked to bring down the Sandinista government of Nicaragua. But that is not the same thing as imposing dictatorship, as Putnam alleged.

❧ By 1999, when *One Nation, Two Cultures* was published, the alleviation of our social problems to which I have referred was too conspicuous to be ignored. Himmelfarb's book is a chastened version of Bork's. Version it is; the genre I am discussing imprisons its contributors in rigid conventions. Most of her book, like Bork's, is devoted to describing our current fallen moral state and contrasting it with our former Edenic one. She is particularly troubled by "the loss of respect for authorities and institutions" (p. 20) but does not pause to ask whether the authorities and institutions in question (they are not specified) deserve respect. Like Bork, she wants a deferential society, in which the common people are cosseted by religious, moral, and customary norms. She doesn't consider whether such a society could rise to the challenges of modernity. Her book is more moderate in tone than Bork's, buttressed by statistics, and cognizant of the recent improvements in our social indicators, but ultimately no more convincing.

Its major shortcoming, which it shares with Bork's book, Lasch's books, and the declinist genre as a whole, is its uncritical conflation of social phenomena that have different causes, are differently amenable to correction, and differ in gravity. They are thrown together and the resulting stew is labeled a morally sick society. One set of phenomena consists of social pathologies for which government is primarily responsible and which can be cured or at least greatly alleviated by governmental reform. These include a welfare system that encourages dependency and irresponsible reproduction and an excessive lenity toward criminals that encourages crime. Both these pathologies have been addressed effectively in recent years—for which, needless to say, Himmelfarb gives Clinton no credit. The fact that they are susceptible of being reformed even in the "permissive" climate resulting from our fall from grace suggests that they are not deeply rooted in "the culture."

Next are those social pathologies that seem the inevitable by-products of modernity. Here we probably must take the bad (as social conservatives conceive it to be) with the good. As I noted in the preceding chapter, the advent of safe and effective contraception and of household labor-saving devices, advances in reproductive technology, the reduction in infant mortality to near zero, and the transformation of the economy into a service economy where most work does not require masculine strength are developments that in combination were bound to free (or, if you prefer, eject) women from their traditional role and by doing so bring about profound changes in sexual behavior and family structure. Unless the United States wants to go the way of Iran and Saudi Arabia, we shall not be able to return to the era of premarital chastity, low divorce, stay-at-home moms, pornography-free media, and the closeting of homosexuals and adulterers.

It is not even clear how much of the sexual activity that social conservatives like Bork and Himmelfarb deplore is actually pathological rather than merely offensive to people who hold conservative views of sex. As we saw in discussing Orwell's and Huxley's novels, the relation between sex and family structure on the one hand and social and political structure on the other is uncertain. In precisely what sense, then, is the divorce rate "too high"? As women become more independent, they demand more of marriage; they are less dependent on their husbands and so will not put up with as much. This has reduced the stability of marriage, but it has not destabilized the society and it does not even necessarily imply that the average happiness of married people is less than it was in the 1950s, since unhappy marriages are now more easily dissolved.

It is true that spouses in rocky marriages who decide to tough it out often find that their marriage improves.[44] But that does not imply that spouses who do decide to divorce are mistaken in doubting that *their* marriage will improve if they stick it out. Even in a no-fault era, divorce is sufficiently costly, both financially and emotionally, to discourage impulsive divorce. Rational people will consider the possibility of a future improvement in a bad situation in deciding what to do about that situation. And while the more difficult it is to divorce the more carefully people will search for a suitable marital partner and the more assiduously they will seek to make marriage a success, the very ease of divorce, given that divorce remains costly, will make for more careful premarital search too. The expected cost of divorce depends on the likelihood of divorce as well as on the cost if it occurs; given the increased likelihood of divorce, the expected cost of divorce may not

44. Linda J. Waite and Maggie Gallagher, *The Case for Marriage: Why Married People Are Happier, Healthier, and Better Off Financially* 75, 148–149 (2000).

have fallen. It may actually have risen.[45] This is suggested by the rising age of marriage, which may be indicative of more thorough premarital search.

What is true and important is that divorce often harms children.[46] But fewer married couples have children, or have many children. Himmelfarb deplores America's low birth rate, which she attributes to selfishness and hedonism, neglecting to consider the possibility that parents are investing more care and affection in each child than is possible in large families—in other words, that there has been a shift in parents' emphasis from quantity to quality of children. As divorce has become more common, moreover, its stigma has lessened and with it the harm to children. That harm, plus the financial and psychological harm that many divorced persons suffer from divorce, may nonetheless exceed the benefits of easy divorce. But this cannot be taken for granted. And although divorce may be particularly destructive for lower-income people, Himmelfarb evinces no interest in so concrete and localized a consequence of the moral trend that she deplores.

But it is not only that the divorce rate is higher; the marriage rate is lower.[47] And marriage is a source of substantial benefits: it civilizes young males, confers economies of scale and of joint consumption,

45. Consider the following simplistic but illustrative example. Let the cost of divorce to each spouse if divorce occurs be 100 and let the probability of divorce be .2. Then, for a spouse who is risk neutral (that is, who is indifferent between a sum certain and its actuarial equivalent), the expected cost of divorce—the cost of, as it were, of the divorce lottery ticket that he or she receives upon marriage—is 20. Now let the cost of divorce if it occurs fall to 50 but the probability of divorce rise to .6. Even though divorce is now a much less costly outcome of marriage, the *expected* cost of divorce is greater (30), and this should incite more careful premarital search.

46. Margaret F. Brinig, *From Contract to Covenant: Beyond the Law and Economics of the Family* 174–176 (2000); Theda Skocpol, *The Missing Middle: Working Families and the Future of American Social Policy* 115–118 (2000); David Popenoe, *Life without Father: Compelling New Evidence That Fatherhood and Marriage Are Indispensable for the Good of Children and Society* 30–34, 57–59 (1996); Paul R. Amato and Bruce Keith, "Parental Divorce and the Well-Being of Children: A Meta-Analysis," 110 *Psychological Bulletin* 26 (1991); Judith A. Seltzer, "Consequences of Marriage Dissolution for Children," 20 *Annual Review of Sociology* 235 (1994); Judith S. Wallerstein, "Children of Divorce: A Society in Search of Policy," in *All Our Families: New Policies for a New Century* 66 (Mary Ann Mason, Arlene Skolnick, and Stephen D. Sugarman eds., 1998).

47. This is a little misleading. It is lower in part because people are marrying later, and they are marrying later in part because improvements in treatments for infertility are enabling women to have children at a more advanced age. This is a good example of the indirect social effects of technology, in this case medical technology.

minimizes sexually transmitted disease, and provides a stable environment for childrearing. But these are private as well as social benefits,[48] in the sense that they are reaped by the married couple as well as by society as a whole. Given these considerable private benefits,[49] the private costs of marriage must have risen considerably for the marriage rate to have fallen. And they have. I have mentioned the growing independence of women, which has increased their opportunity costs of marriage at the same time that it has reduced the benefits of marriage to them—and to men as well insofar as women demand more from marriage. As people become more individualistic, hence less like other people, they find it harder to mesh their life with the life of another person. Even so, as in the case of easy divorce, the *net* social benefits of the falling marriage rate may be negative; the social benefits of marriage may exceed the private benefits, large as they are, and also the costs.[50] But the implications for policy are obscure. Making divorce more difficult won't do the trick; it might even reduce the marriage rate further, since marriage is a bigger gamble the more difficult it is to get out of. Like the higher divorce rate, the lower marriage rate is probably an unavoidable consequence of social changes that cannot be reversed. Conservatives are supposed to be realistic, not like those starry-eyed liberals; and part of realism is recognizing that certain problems cannot be solved, just as certain chronic diseases cannot be cured but can only be lived with.

And what purpose is served by keeping homosexuals out of sight, unless you believe, and Himmelfarb does not suggest she does, that homosexual orientation is contagious? Many people are distressed or even revolted by the flaunting of homosexuality, the easy availability of pornography, the proliferation of four-letter words in movies, and the distribution of condoms by high schools—in short, by a societywide decline in reticence about sexual matters. But that the decline matters

48. I emphasized the distinction between private and social benefits and costs in discussing technology at the outset of Chapter 7.

49. Particularly emphasized in Waite and Gallagher, note 44 above. The authors are not able to explain convincingly why, if even unhappy marriages confer the psychiatric, emotional, medical, sexual, financial, and parenting benefits that the authors suppose, the marriage rate is so low and the divorce rate so high.

50. To illustrate, if the social benefits of some privately undertaken practice are 10, the private benefits 5, the private costs 7, and the social costs 8, the practice will be abandoned (because the private costs exceed the private benefits) even though the net social benefits are positive $(10 - 8)$.

from the larger social standpoint is assumed rather than demonstrated by the declinist literature of the Right. It is another example of the symbiosis of the political extremes. The 1960s radicals, here taking their cue from Herbert Marcuse, claimed that sexual promiscuity would undermine capitalism.[51] We now know they were wrong, for by the end of the century there was more promiscuity and more capitalism. Divorce and deregulation had gone hand in hand; easy divorce *is* a form of deregulation, as it tends to transform marriage from a state-defined status relationship into a contractual relationship. As we saw in the discussion of *Brave New World* and *Nineteen Eighty-Four,* sex and politics run on different tracks. The Right has yet to grasp that fact. Still fighting those sixties brats, it believes that capitalism depends on monogamous sexuality.

Himmelfarb might respond that there can be too much of a good thing; that free markets should be confined to economic relations, while sex should be channeled by law and custom into marriage, a defined legal status, rather than be left to be regulated by whatever explicit or implicit contract the participants would prefer. There is nothing illogical about wanting to have different regulatory regimes for different types of activity. What is untenable is to argue that we need to adopt *dirigiste* family policies in order to protect freedom in economic markets.

One might have thought that the last entry in Himmelfarb's enumeration of cultural offenses, the distribution of condoms in schools, would recommended itself to her given the concerns she has about AIDS and about teenage pregnancy. Not at all. She wants to make premarital sex dangerous in order to discourage it, and believes that withholding condoms from teenagers will do just that by increasing both the pregnancy risk and the disease risk of sex. She deplores the fact that "public schools have displaced parents in instructing the young in sex education" (p. 35), which has also made sex safer because parents are notoriously bashful about instructing their children in "the facts of life."

Himmelfarb is on to something: the more dangerous sex is, the less of it there will be. But reducing the amount of teenage sex may not reduce the amount of personal and social harm that it causes if the reduction is brought about by making sex more dangerous. Without con-

51. Herbert Marcuse, *Eros and Civilization: A Philosophical Inquiry into Freud* (1955).

doms, a higher fraction of the reduced number of sexual encounters will result in an unwanted pregnancy or the transmission of a sexually transmitted disease, so that the total *number* of such misfortunes may be no lower, or even higher. These are possibilities that she does not address.

Like Bork, though less stridently, Himmelfarb reads the signs of moral decay in "the degradation of popular culture" (p. 20), as evidenced by "vulgarity on TV" (p. 25), by "confessional memoirs," and by those television talk shows in which the "participants proudly flaunt the most sordid details of their lives" (p. 27). These are offenses against good taste rather than, as Himmelfarb believes, "diseases, moral and cultural" (p. 20). Her belief is an aspect of the totalizing view I mentioned in connection with Bork, where every dimension of social behavior is assumed to be interlocked with every other. Popular culture has always offended the fastidious. Whether today's popular culture is more depraved than that of yesterday may be doubted. The popular culture of the 1950s was not as raunchy as today's, but today's popular culture does not ridicule obese people, ethnic minorities, stammerers, retarded people, and effeminate men, as the popular culture of the 1950s did.

Himmelfarb's implicit taste in popular culture runs to square dances, Glenn Miller, and *South Pacific*. But there has always been a subversive streak in American popular culture. Think only of the Marx brothers comedies, such as *A Night at the Opera* (1935), which confronts a WASP establishment of top-hatted officials, first-night opera goers, wealthy widows, grasping capitalists, the first-class passengers and captain of an ocean liner, and a supporting cast of thick-necked plainsclothesmen and other capitalist lackeys with a trio of vulgar, lawless, destructive, ostentatiously non-WASP scalawags led by a Leon Trotsky look-alike. Yet this disorderly trio (portrayed in the film as a loudmouth, doubtless Jewish schemer, a thickly-accented lower-class Italian, and a simple-minded clownish mute of indefinite foreign origin) not only runs circles around the establishment but also vindicates artistic values and unites the romantic leads. Yet not even in 1935 were the Marx brothers perceived as a threat to capitalism and decency.[52] And

---

52. *A Night at the Opera* was praised in reviews by both the *New York Times* and *Newsweek*. Wes D. Gehring, *The Marx Brothers: A Bio-Bibliography* 168 (1987).

one would have to be completely humorless, if not paranoid, to be troubled today by the film's subversive implications. It is only intellectuals who even *notice* these things.

The final ingredient in Himmelfarb's goulash is the lunatic postmodernist Left, represented by a play in which Jesus Christ is a homosexual and has sexual relations with the apostles, a sitcom in which Abraham Lincoln and his wife make sexual overtures to the same black man, and "'whiteness studies' (which celebrate 'white trash' and expose the inherent racism in being white)" (p. 132). That a fringe group of bohemians, as they used to be called, poses a threat to the nation's values is preposterous. Once again we see the symbiotic relationship between the political extremes. A paranoiac might think that the cultural Left is being subsidized by Opus Dei in order to galvanize the Religious Right, at the same time that it is inducing political quietism within the Left itself. "Lately we [leftists in the American academy] have been concentrating on cultural politics and trying to persuade ourselves that cultural, and especially academic, politics are continuous with real politics. We have been trying to believe that upsetting our students' parents will sooner or later help upset unjust institutions."[53] Because postmodernist professors of cultural studies "no longer think of themselves as citizens of a functioning democracy, they are producing a generation of radical students who think of 'the system' as irredeemable, and who therefore can think of nothing better to do with their sense of moral outrage than to fling themselves into curricular change."[54]

---

53. Richard Rorty, "The End of Leninism and History as Comic Frame," in *History and the Idea of Progress*, note 3 above, at 211, 222.

54. Rorty, "Intellectuals in Politics," note 25 above, at 489–490. Elsewhere Rorty has remarked the "political uselessness, relative illiteracy, and tiresomely self-congratulatory enthusiasm" of the "Academic Left." Richard Rorty, "Response to Jacques Bouveresse," in *Rorty and His Critics* 146, 153 (Robert B. Brandom ed., 2000). See also John Patrick Diggins, *The Rise and Fall of the American Left*, chs. 7–9 (1992). For typical mainstream media ridicule of academic radicals, see Walter Goodman, "Sociologists to the Barricades: Thinkers Who Would Be Doers See Social Injustice Wherever They Turn," *New York Times* (national ed.), Aug. 19, 2000, p. A17. And recall from Chapter 4 what one of those postmodernist professors, Richard Ohmann, said about them: "We work in whatever small ways we can toward the end of capitalist patriarchy: not just canon reform or a deconstruction of *Paradise Lost*, but the transformation of society." Notice that "end" can mean "goal" as well as "termination." Ohmann and his fellow radicals may inadvertently be working toward the goal of "capitalist patriarchy" by energizing the Right.

We can see in Himmelfarb's and Bork's preoccupation with culture, in Bork's worry about universities' being taken over by leftists, and in the leftists' desire to politicize university curricula, that tendency of intellectuals that I remarked in connection with Orwell to exaggerate their influence and that of their products (including cultural artifacts both elite and popular) on the larger society. It is the tendency that leads people to attribute Nazism to Nietzsche, and the current worldwide enthusiasm for free markets to Hayek. The tendency is given plausibility by famous historical examples—think only of the influence of Augustine, Montesquieu, and Marx on beliefs and social structures. The exaggeration lies in ascribing great menace to tiny slivers of intellectual opinion. It is true that Nazism and communism started small too. But they would have remained small had it not been for the extraordinary demoralization—which has no counterpart in the temper of modern America or that of the other wealthy countries—of the societies in which they took root. Should such demoralization someday overtake us (for we cannot know what the future holds), creating a demand for crazy ideas, there will be no dearth of suppliers. Stamping out "whiteness studies" today will not protect us from the rise of a Hitler tomorrow should some disaster create a nourishing bed for him. By the same token, the barely concealed yearning of some rightists, though not Himmelfarb, for war or depression would if fulfilled be more likely to bring upon us a more dangerous version of the ideas that they abhor than to restore us to an earlier state of grace.

It is easy enough with anecdotes and a few statistics to create an impression of a nation on its moral uppers. But it would be more accurate to speak not of a cultural revolution but of a change in morals and manners resulting from diverse material factors that include changes in the nature of work, growing prosperity, advances in reproductive technology, increasing ethnic diversity, and a communications revolution that has created a better-informed population. One of the social changes these developments have brought about is increased tolerance for people different from the norm whether in race, religion, gender, sexual orientation, or even physical and mental health (no more "moron" jokes). This will strike most people, including I assume Himmelfarb, as moral progress since the 1950s, though probably not Bork, who says "it would be difficult to contend that, the end of racial segregation aside,

American culture today is as healthy as the culture of the 1950s."[55] He does not remark the decline that has also occurred in racial *discrimination* (as distinguished from the ending of official *segregation* by Supreme Court decree) and in discrimination against Jews, Catholics, disabled persons, and other groups

The more relaxed attitude toward sex—what Himmelfarb refers to disapprovingly as the "Europeanization" of American sexual attitudes (p. 120)—seems on the whole a healthy development as well, though it has had some bad side effects. In any event it poses no greater threat to the nation's basic soundness than the sexual "laxity" (as it seems to many Americans) of countries like Denmark and Japan poses to those nations' basic health. The idea that America's success depends on its being more prudish than Europe—Himmelfarb proudly contrasts the "relatively reserved . . . bohemianism" of Greenwich Village with Bloomsbury, which was "flagrantly promiscuous" (p. 10)—is an old story, but Himmelfarb presents no evidence that it is a true one. (It is, by the way, a story that not all American conservatives accept. There is a genuinely libertarian wing of American conservatives, and even a small public-intellectual literature defending it.)[56] We don't have to emulate Europeans in all things in order to recognize that a society can be civilized without being religious, puritanical, intolerant, nostalgic, elitist, and censorious. Shall we regret that Europeans rarely fight any more, and that when they do they don't enter battle singing? The refusal to learn anything positive from European experience is the equally fallacious converse of seeking to model the United States on the Scandinavian societies without taking account of differences in the size, homogeneity, and cultural heritage of their respective populations.

I mentioned the *de haut en bas* character of Himmelfarb's prescriptions. It points back to a problem I emphasized in Part One of this book—the difficulty the modern public intellectual has in demonstrating commitment. Both Bork and Himmelfarb express concern with the decline of "judgmental" religion. But neither of them, despite Bork's flirtation with "creationism," which after all does not necessarily im-

55. Bork, note 15 above, at 342.

56. See, for example, Charles Murray, *What It Means to Be a Libertarian: A Personal Interpretation* (1997).

ply a personal God, gives the impression of being religious people, or indeed of being anything different from what they are, which is sophisticated urban intellectuals. Bork had a substantial though truncated academic career; Himmelfarb was an academic historian until her retirement. They want to put the lid on, but they don't want to be in the pot. Irving Kristol wants the Catholic Church to be militant and severe;[57] he doesn't want to *be* a Catholic.

Much fun is made by conservatives, and rightly too, of "limousine liberals," left-leaning intellectuals whose motto is "think Left, live Right." But we should not overlook their counterparts on the Right, such as Bork and Himmelfarb and Kristol—call them "Grand Inquisitor conservatives," after the Grand Inquisitor in *The Brothers Karamazov*, who, we recall from the preceding chapter, takes it to be the prime task of the state to instill in its citizens a belief—which he does not himself hold—in the afterlife. The deviousness of these conservatives is taken to an extreme by the Straussians, whom we shall meet in the person of Allan Bloom in the next chapter.

Discordance between life and work is more common than otherwise and does not invalidate a person's ideas. But in areas of uncertainty we cast a wide net for evidence of credibility and when we see people advocating practices or beliefs that they themselves would find irksome, or even intolerable, it makes us doubt the soundness of their advocacy. The modern public intellectual may think Right or think Left, but he or she lives Center, and this fact has made it difficult for either extreme to capture the public imagination.

Another denouncer of modern America as a decadent society, one who nicely complements Bork and Himmelfarb, is the cultural historian Jacques Barzun.[58] He sounds their lugubrious chords, except the religious, and combines them in a dirge that he calls the "demotic style." This involves "act[ing] as if nothing stood in the way of every wish" (p. 781) and is typified by the movement—the ominous significance of which Bork and Himmelfarb had inexplicably missed—toward an ever greater casualness in dress. "To appear unkempt, undressed, and for perfection unwashed, is the key signature of the whole age" (id.). This is absurd, and not only because Americans, however

57. See note 28 above.

58. Jacques Barzun, *From Dawn to Decadence: 500 Years of Western Cultural Life: 1500 to the Present* 773–802 (2000).

casually they dress, remain fanatical about hygiene. It is absurd in its insistence that every change in culture, even so mutable an aspect of culture as the dress code, is fraught with menace. It is characteristically declinist in its failure even to consider an innocent, let alone an optimistic, interpretation of the change.

What the movement to casual dress may signify is a recession of theatricality as a mode of organizing social interactions, together with a rising cost of time (it takes longer to select, dress in, and undress from formal dress). Especially but not only when worn in the workplace, formal dress is a method of signaling wealth, authority, and other dimensions of hierarchical status. It is "dressing up" to "act" a part in the social game.[59] It is related to charismatic authority and opposed to rational authority. If positions of authority were always assigned on the basis of merit alone, and if the performance of the people occupying those positions were perfectly transparent or perfectly monitored, no one would care how they dressed or how they looked. A person in a position of authority would not have to dress differently from his underlings in order to cement his authority, and no premium would be placed on height or a commanding presence or a distinguished name in choosing leaders. We would then expect a movement to casual dress because formal dress is less comfortable and generally more expensive, especially when time costs are figured in.

In the fiercely competitive setting of the American Civil War, a shabby, stubby, taciturn man wholly lacking in personal presence and always badly dressed, namely Ulysses S. Grant, became the commanding general of the Northern armies and led them to victory. Leaders in the fiercely competitive computer industry are, like Grant, notably lacking in "front," because their leadership is assessed by rational criteria, without need to add even a dollop of mystification. The trend to casual dress may be a sign not of decadence but instead of modernity conceived in Weberian terms as the movement toward governance by rational methods in place of charisma and other forms of "enchantment." This is not to deny the occasional resort to casual dress as a method of social aggression, not only by hippies and other rebels but, at the other end of the social spectrum, by the multimillionaires who

59. See Erving Goffman, *The Presentation of Self in Everyday Life* (1959); Posner, note 27 above, at 532.

dress down from their subordinates as a way of exhibiting power by defying convention with impunity.

Barzun's concern with the movement to casual dress raises a general
question about declinist literature—the question of what, or when, the
declinist wants to return to. Nietzsche and Heidegger thought we had
gone off the tracks with Socrates. A teacher of mine in college thought
that literature had been going downhill since Homer. Hesiod, Homer's
contemporary, thought the golden age was long past, and the Homeric
epics themselves depict a heroic age in dissolution. T. S. Eliot thought
society was last in good shape in Dante's time. Himmelfarb hankers for
the restoration of the Victorian era. Bork, more moderate in this respect, seems content to go back to the 1950s, though he thinks the rot
began in the eighteenth century. None of these restorations, whether
to thirty-five hundred years ago or to fifty, is feasible, so that, as far as
rational hope is concerned, the declinists are the intellectual equivalent
of the Orléanist or Romanoff pretenders. Still, most declinists at least
specify a benchmark. But it is difficult even to identify the golden age
of formal dress. Barzun scatters no clues. Are coat and tie formality
enough? Or must the soft collar give way to the stiff detachable collar,
or perhaps to the ruff? Must women wear corsets, and must men dress
(that is, put on a tuxedo) for dinner?

But maybe restoration is not the point. The hidden message of much
though not all declinist literature is one of hopelessness. We can be
saved only if we go back, but we cannot go back. Some of the literature,
however, as we are about to see, holds out a hope of redemption.

∽ I TURN LAST, and left, to Robert Putnam's *Bowling Alone*.[60] It
and *One Nation, Two Cultures* make a nice pair of bookends. Published
within a year of each other, both are written for a general audience and
warn that American society is in decline as a consequence of an excess
of individualism. There are even affinities with Bork's book, as we're
about to see. Yet Putnam is emphatically a liberal—another example of
the convergence between left and right declinists.

The most important difference between Putnam's book and the
books by Himmelfarb and Bork, or for that matter by Lasch and Rorty,

---

60. Robert D. Putnam, *Bowling Alone: The Collapse and Revival of American Community*
(2000).

is that it is a work of massive social-scientific scholarship, rich in statistical and survey data that the author marshaled and analyzed with the aid of an immense research team (see p. 507). Ordinarily such a book would be published by an academic press for an academic audience. But as Putnam explains, an earlier article with the same title as the book had made him a celebrity.[61] It was natural for him, therefore, as well as lucrative, to publish with a commercial press that saw bestseller potential.[62] Without fatal compromise of its scholarly character, the book was packaged for a general audience, its voluminous references exiled to endnotes of unreadably minute type and disagreements with other scholars sidetracked.[63] The heavy diet of tables and graphs is periodically relieved by anecdotes. The style in which the book is written is very simple and free of jargon, though (to a sourpuss like me, at any rate) irritatingly folksy, breezy, cute, and *faux* modest.[64] There are

61. "I was invited to Camp David, lionized by talk-show hosts, and (the secular equivalent of canonization in contemporary America) pictured with my wife, Rosemary, on the pages of *People*" (p. 506).

62. In light of the huge advance that he received from the publisher, one is startled to read in a review of the book that "Putnam's research is itself a fine illustration of civic engagement. Not the least of its achievements is that it teaches by example." Paul Starr, "The Public Vanishes," *New Republic*, Aug. 14, 2000, pp. 35, 37.

63. In particular there is no serious engagement with Everett Carll Ladd, *The Ladd Report* (1999), published a year earlier by the same publisher, addressing the same issue (the alleged decline of community in America), criticizing the earlier work by Putnam on which *Bowling Alone* is based (see the index references to Putnam in Ladd's book), and reaching the opposite conclusion from Putnam. Putnam's book contains no index reference to Ladd, though there is a dismissive endnote (p. 503 n. 6) referring to an article in which Ladd had criticized an earlier version of Putnam's thesis. Ladd's book is much shorter than Putnam's, but it is a work of genuine scholarship and deserves more attention than Putnam gave it, which was none.

Additional criticisms of some of Putnam's findings are made in Robert E. Lane, *The Loss of Happiness in Market Democracies* 334 (2000). Lane agrees with Putnam that the United States is excessively individualistic, but he perceives and laments a decline not in civic involvement but in companionship. He attributes the decline to the market, but does not explain, to my satisfaction at any rate, why if people would be happier with more companionship and less income, they don't choose less demanding, and therefore lower-paying, jobs. But that is a debate for another day.

64. Through the relentless use of the pronoun "we" to denote the people about whom he's writing, as in "Americans are spending a lot less time breaking bread with friends than we did twenty or thirty years ago" (p. 100), or "one reason that some of us are harried is precisely that we are civically engaged" (p. 191), Putnam tries to create an impression that he's your typical, average American, something I very much doubt. This rhetorical device attains absurdity when he, a royalty-rich Harvard professor with two homes (we learn from the dust-

even thoughtful (some might say condescending) assists for the culturally challenged reader (for example, "Alexis de Tocqueville, a perceptive French visitor to early-nineteenth-century America" [p. 48]). The
alarming subtitle—"The Collapse and Revival of American Community"—is a clear bid for bestsellerdom, with its clever combined appeal
to fear and hope. Clever, but also misleading; Putnam argues neither
that American community has "collapsed" nor (if it has) that it has "re-
vived" or that it will revive.

The central concept in the book is that of "social capital," a term
used by sociologists and, increasingly, by economists[65] to indicate that
people can derive benefits from being "connected" through repeated,
usually face-to-face interactions with one another in networks of
friends, relatives, neighbors, coworkers, coreligionists, and social and
business acquaintances generally. The interactions take place in the
home, at work, in churches, in clubs, in union meetings, in neighborhood and civic associations, in reading groups, in card games, in bowling leagues (of course), on the boards of charities, and so forth. They
forge mutual trust, which in turns facilitates productive cooperative effort. Putnam presents statistics to show that since the 1960s participation in virtually all activities that build or draw on social capital has declined. He blames this trend for the rise in political apathy as measured
by a decline in voter turnout and newspaper reading, for the fall in sur-
vey-reported happiness indicators, and for the increases in crime, ille-
gitimacy, depression, and suicides.

Putnam's analysis of the data is not entirely convincing, quite apart
from his brush off of Ladd.[66] Some of his statistics *must* be wrong, such
as that "road rage" is implicated in twenty-eight thousand deaths a year
(p. 143)—that would be about two-thirds of the entire death toll from
automobile accidents—or that "federal domestic spending" is only 2.2
percent of GNP (pp. 281–282 and fig. 78). Putnam's conjecture that it
is easier to unmask lies if one is face to face with the liar (hence the im-

---

jacket), says, "As my economic situation becomes more dire, my focus narrows to personal
and family survival" (p. 193).

65. See, for example, James S. Coleman, *Foundations of Social Theory* (1990); Gary S.
Becker and Kevin M. Murphy, *Social Economics: Market Behavior in a Social Environment*
(2000). Putnam himself is a political scientist, but the boundaries separating the social sciences have virtually ceased to exist—and a very good thing, too.

66. See note 63 above.

portance of face-to-face interactions, which are in decline as part of the general decline in sociality) rather than reading the lies is probably wrong.[67] His analysis of the causes of crime mysteriously omits deterrence and incapacitation variables, such as arrest and conviction rates and length of imprisonment (see ch. 18 and pp. 489–490 nn. 3–7). He unduly disparages the substitutability of electronic for face-to-face interaction. And the recent improvements in social indicators are inconsistent with his causal hypothesis, as is the extraordinary economic boom of the 1990s—for he believes that social capital is essential to economic efficiency. The book's lack of a significant comparative dimension is telling here; Japan and Germany have more social capital per capita than the United States but have been lagging behind us economically for many years.

Putnam thinks cooperation more productive than competition, but again the evidence is against him. It is false that the very successful entrepreneurs of Silicon Valley are only "nominally competitors" (p. 324). Putnam's sole source (see p. 492 nn. 25, 27) for this characterization is AnnaLee Saxenian's book *Regional Advantage*,[68] which compares high-tech firms located along Route 128 outside of Boston with similar firms in Silicon Valley. Saxenian presents evidence that the Silicon Valley firms cooperate more with each other than the Route 128 companies, but says that "these cooperative arrangements seem unusual in part because of the intensity of competition in Silicon Valley ... Intense peer pressure among an ambitious and talented professional community forced engineers to work extraordinarily long hours and contributed to high rates of drug use, divorce, and burnout in the region"[69]—not the sort of thing recommended by Putnam!

But let me now assume that he is correct both that social capital has eroded in America and that such erosion is having a number of ill effects. The causes of this erosion, he argues, are, in order of importance, generational change (the biggest single factor, he believes, accounting for as much as half the total erosion), television, suburbanization, and—but here Putnam treads very gently, to avoid the wrath of femi-

67. Michael J. Saks, "Enhancing and Restraining Accuracy in Adjudication," 51 *Law and Contemporary Problems*, Autumn 1988, pp. 243, 263–264.

68. AnnaLee Saxenian, *Regional Advantage: Culture and Competition in Silicon Valley and Route 128* (1994).

69. Id. at 46.

nists—increased female participation in the workforce. I take up these points in reverse order. Putnam notes that most women say they work because of economic necessity rather than a preference for work over home, and so he argues that women are not at fault in spending less time in social interactions that build social capital. But he overlooks the fact that more women work nowadays than in the past because fewer are married, because the divorce rate is so high that married women must hedge against the risk of divorce by establishing themselves in the work force, and because women have better job opportunities. This is not to ascribe "fault" to anyone but merely to shift the emphasis away from economic necessity. The idea that the middle class is being squeezed economically is no more convincing than the idea of Bork and Lasch that Americans are too rich for their own good.

Putnam's discussions of the impact of suburbanization and television on social capital are right on, however. Suburbanization entails commuting to work, to shopping, to schools, to meetings, ordinarily by car. Americans are spending more time in their cars—alone. Watching television also tends to be a solitary, and in any event rather unsociable, activity, and like driving is consuming a growing amount of people's time. The combined effect of women working, of driving, and of television has been to cut deeply into the time available for communal activities that build social capital.

By "generational change" Putnam means the diminishing relative size of the generation that was shaped by the depression and World War II.[70] He thinks these events—the war in particular—stimulated an unusual sense of community that has now regressed to the historical mean.[71] Here is an interesting convergence with Bork, and even with Kaplan. Although Putnam claims not to want to romanticize war, his description of the social solidarity that World War II fostered—its contribution to civic and economic equality, its other "powerfully positive enduring consequences" (pp. 275–276)—and his characterization of the war period as one of "heightened civic obligation" (p. 272) are apt to induce nostalgia for that "great mid-century global cataclysm" (p. 275). Very Bork-like, Putnam says that "creating (or re-creating) so-

70. He calls this the "long civic generation" (pp. 254–255).

71. He was anticipated in this by an earlier and gloomier declinist. See Robert Nisbet, *Twilight of Authority* 161–162 (1975). Nisbet referred to "the twentieth century in the West" as "a twilight age." Id. at vi.

cial capital is no simple task. It would be eased by a palpable national crisis, like war or depression or natural disaster, but for better *and* for worse, America at the dawn of the new century faces no such galvanizing crisis" (p. 402). The emphasis is his.

This is to look on the glum side, in standard declinist manner. All that Putnam is really saying is that poverty and fear fuel a sense of community. People circle the wagons; strong ties of mutual dependence develop for purposes basically of self-defense—in short, "external conflict increases internal cohesion" (p. 267). Rather than being a good thing in itself, let alone something important to encourage in a peaceful and prosperous society, social solidarity is a means of coping with economic and geopolitical insecurity. It need have no more value in itself than a suit of armor or a nuclear arsenal.

We might be inclined to congratulate ourselves that, living in an era in which we feel safe, we can throw off, or at least loosen, the often irksome ties of family and other forms of belongingness and stand forth as individuals. Rather than wringing our hands as Putnam does at the increase in the number of lawyers, we might note that law is supplanting the family and custom as the essential cement of society because it is the method by which the interactions of free individuals, as distinct from those of cells in larger social organisms, are regulated. Putnam's call for a "revival of American community" is both quixotic and retrograde. Americans don't want to live cossetted in a web of "intermediate" organizations unless they have to, and they don't have to, and they won't be persuaded by Putnam to want to. He may be right that they would be happier in such a web even though they don't know it. He may even be right that "regular . . . church attendance is the happiness equivalent of getting a college degree or more than doubling your income" (p. 333). (Another point of convergence with Bork; but Putnam expresses no interest in the *content* of religious belief and likewise none in sexual morality.) But they would also be happier if the government laced the water supply with Prozac. And then the direction of causation, at least, would be clear, as it is not in the example of religious attendance. People who believe in a benevolent deity are more likely both to attend church *and* to be happy, rather than to be happy *because* they attend church. In any event we have learned from *Brave New World* that a society is not to be judged by its success in maximizing the happiness of its citizens. Putnam's contention that we would be more

prosperous if economic activity were more cooperative and less competitive is particularly unconvincing.

He realizes there have been improvements in American society since
the golden 1950s—being a liberal, he emphasizes the growth in tolerance and, despite his concern about the effects of women working, the
feminist revolution. But he argues that these improvements did not *depend* on the diminution of social capital that took place over the same
period. He notes, for example, that the generation born during World
War II was more tolerant than the preceding generation had been and
is today as tolerant as the succeeding ones, yet unlike the latter it has
preserved a high degree of civic engagement. He also reports that,
other things being equal, people who are active in civic and other asso-
ciational activities tend to be more rather than less tolerant than social
isolates.

Putnam's attempt to reconcile acknowledged social improvement
with the continued decline of social capital suggests a possible strategy
for right-wing declinists such as Bork and Himmelfarb to use in trying
to explain—or rather to explain away—the recent uptick in the social
indicators. That is to investigate the causes of the uptick. The declinists
might discover that it has causes that would not falsify their gloomy
prognoses. If for example the causes are just more effective repression
(such as longer prison sentences), a change in age composition away
from riotous youth, fear of AIDS, a long economic boom likely to turn
to bust at some point, or the placing of time limits on entitlement to
public welfare, the improvement in the social indicators could be improvements merely in outward conduct, consistent with a continued
rot in character and morality. They would be improvements, quite possibly temporarily, in symptoms, but not in moral health.

There is an amusing tension between Putnam's praise for what he
calls the "long civic generation" and a book by David Kaiser published
the same year in which the mistakes that led us into the disastrous
quagmire of the Vietnam War are blamed in significant part on the
"GI generation."[72] This is the generation that was shaped by the experience of World War II, and it largely overlaps Putnam's favorite generation.

---

72. See David Kaiser, *American Tragedy: Kennedy, Johnson, and the Origins of the Vietnam
War* (2000).

> Their strengths included an exemplary willingness to tackle difficult and costly tasks, a faith in the institutions of the government of the United States, a great capacity for teamwork and consensus, and a relentless optimism. Their weaknesses, alas, included an unwillingness to question basic assumptions, or to even admit the possibility of failure, or to understand that the rest of the American population was less inclined to favor struggle and sacrifice for their own sake.[73]

They were particularly good at keeping secrets and at lying for the greater good, tactics of solidarity which boomeranged when the war turned sour. Their whimpy successors, the "Silent Generation," turned out to have deeper insights into the war.

If Putnam argued that war and material deprivation are bracing, that they add savor to life, that it is better to live in a great imperial power than in Sweden or Denmark, it would be easier to understand why he regrets the decline of the community spirit that war and struggle foment. But he is not a Romantic, so when he says "we desperately need an era of civic inventiveness to create a renewed set of institutions and channels for a reinvigorated civic life that will fit the way we have come to live" (p. 401), he needs to explain why the nation requires war's by-product when there is no war. Happiness is not a good answer. Prosperity is not an answer at all. And he presents scant evidence that any of the acknowledged improvements in American life would have come faster had the amount of social capital remained constant.

A proper jeremiad, as the quotation from the original Jeremiah at the head of this chapter suggests, holds out a hope of salvation for those who, stung by the prophet's words, repent. The last section of Putnam's book ("What Is to Be Done?") is the call to repentance. He says that we live in a new "Gilded Age" (p. 367), the term for the last third of the nineteenth century, a byword for the excesses of capitalism and a veritable "'Saturnalia' of political corruption" (p. 368).[74] But the Gilded

---

73. Id. at 8.

74. Recall from Chapter 3 Sean Wilentz's invocation of the Gilded Age. The Gilded Age could also be regarded as having been the indispensable transition to modernity, the link between the Civil War era and the twentieth century, and even a kind of golden age of American energy and nation-building, not to mention of immigration. It is possible to argue that the Civil War and the Gilded Age *made* the United States.

Age gave way to the Progressive Era (the first decade and a half of the twentieth century), an era of social-capital building; there is hope for us too. The hope lies, oddly, in Putnam himself, the natural leader of a new Progressive Era because of his "experience in spearheading in recent years a concerted nationwide conversation" called the "Saguaro Seminar: Civic Engagement in America" (p. 403). His other proposals seem, to this cynic, equally marginal, and even whimsical, such as "bestow[ing] an annual Jane Addams Award on the Gen X'er or Gen Y'er who comes up with the best idea" for restoring social capital (p. 406). He would like employers to provide their employees with time and space for "civic discussion groups and service clubs" (p. 407) and real estate developers to create more "pedestrian-friendly areas" (p. 408). He wants a religious revival, but also potluck dinners, community gardens, and flea markets.

He wants, in fact, what a more famous public intellectual, David Riesman, deplored in *The Lonely Crowd*, which the dustjacket of Putnam's book tells us is one of the precursors of *Bowling Alone*. (Notice how "lone" is a key component of both titles.) He wants the fifties.[75] Riesman thought that fifties groupiness, the substitution of cooperation (albeit a covertly rivalrous cooperation) for competition, the heightened sensitivity to the opinion of one's peers, the displacement of the highly individualized "inner-directed man" (the man who embodied Weber's concept of the Protestant ethic) by men who were "socialized, passive, and cooperative"[76]—all these things except passivity that Putnam tells us are essential to prosperity and happiness—were producing a society of anxious conformists, what another public intellectual of the period, William Whyte, called "organization men." Riesman's rather pathetic other-directed man is Putnam's hero, busy playing poker once a week with his cronies, gabbing around the water cooler at the office, attending church socials, participating in the local chapter of the Elks or the Masons, going to square dances, bowling in a league, hobnobbing with the neighbors, rarely alone.

I am exaggerating. The other-directed man as conceived by Riesman is not so much a joiner as he is a person highly sensitized to the sig-

75. *The Lonely Crowd* was first published in 1950, but I am using the term "the fifties" loosely to refer to the entire period from the end of World War II to the inauguration of President Kennedy.

76. David Riesman with Reuel Denney and Nathan Glazer, *The Lonely Crowd: A Study of the Changing American Character* 190 (1950).

nals emitted by the members of his peer group. And he lacks the civic virtues so prized by Putnam. In striking contrast to Putnam's take on the generation forged during World War II, Riesman says that "the veterans of World War II bring scarcely a trace of moral righteousness into their *scant political participation.*"[77] The very thing most salient to Putnam about that generation—its high degree of civic engagement—was invisible to Riesman.

One of them must be wrong—could both be? Quite possibly. By now we expect a high error rate in the writings of public intellectuals. After fifty years *The Lonely Crowd* is so dated as to be unreadable. Riesman (and we recall this also from the essay of his that I cited in Chapter 3) thought that the United States was entering a period in which the economy would be so effortlessly productive that there would be little meaningful work and virtually the only asset needed to get ahead would be social competence, the sort of thing to which other-directed man is habituated. There would be no place for individualists. (There is a distinct echo of *Brave New World*.) That era has never arrived. Fifty years on we have Putnam worrying about our social problems and the efficiency of our industry and wanting to restore the small-town virtues. These are not discussed in Riesman's book, though Putnam thinks they suffused Riesman's own generation. In Riesman's taxonomy the small-town virtues belong to a stage intermediate between "tradition-directed" (premodern) man, whom Riesman discusses only briefly, and inner-directed man; they were thus passé in 1950—when Putnam thought them at their height.

The virtues that Putnam stresses are real. But a number of us who grew up in the fifties do not regret the displacement of many of those virtues, and of the culture they formed, by the freer, more individualistic, faster-paced, richer, more varied, and more exciting, if also more vertiginous, society of the present. Yet no public intellectual worth his salt will agree. For what in the end unites Riesman, Putnam, Bork, Himmelfarb, Kaplan, Barzun, and Lasch is deep misgivings about the present, whether it is the late 1940s, for Riesman, or the 1990s for the others. Jeremiah looks backward to a golden age and sometimes forward to the possibility of redemption, but the present is for him, at best, a trough.

77. Id. at 198 (emphasis added).

~ 9

The Public Philosopher

$\mathcal{M}$ARTHA NUSSBAUM and Richard Rorty are philosophers not content to write for an audience exclusively of professional philosophers on the issues that standardly engage such persons' interest, for example the problem of free will, the ontology of numbers, the possibility of accurate knowledge of the external world, and the existence of moral absolutes. They are the latest in a long line of academic philosophers who also wrote as public intellectuals—among many others Bertrand Russell, Jean-Paul Sartre, Michel Foucault, and, perhaps the most notable American examples, William James and John Dewey. With philosophy increasingly professionalized, jargonized, hermetic, this tradition is in decline. Nussbaum and Rorty are among the most prominent of those few living American public intellectuals (others include Ronald Dworkin and Thomas Nagel) who are drawn from the front ranks of academic philosophy.[1] Peter Singer, the "animal liberationist," is a more influential public intellectual, but is not I think as well regarded by most other academic philosophers as Nussbaum and Rorty, and particularly Dworkin and Nagel, are. (Singer actually is Australian, though he now lives in America.)

1. See Robert S. Boynton, "Who Needs Philosophy?" *New York Times*, Nov. 21, 1999, § 6, p. 66; Russell Jacoby, "Introduction to the 2000 Edition," in Jacoby, *The Last Intellectuals: American Culture in the Age of Academe* xix (2000); James Ryerson, "The Quest for Uncertainty: Richard Rorty's Pragmatic Pilgrimage," *Lingua Franca*, Dec. 2000/Jan. 2001, pp. 42, 44.

320

"American" is an important qualification here, and also that the public-intellectual philosopher ("public philosopher" for short) express himself in a way accessible to the nonspecialist. Jürgen Habermas is a model European public philosopher. Amartya Sen, though he lives in England after having taught in the U.S. for a number of years, is a model Asian one, whose public-intellectual work concerns such problems of the Third World as famine and the neglect of female children; but his main discipline is economics rather than philosophy. John Rawls is America's foremost political philosopher, but he writes a dense academic prose in books published by academic presses and in articles for academic journals; he writes nothing for the popular media and does not appear on radio or television talk shows, though, as I noted in the Introduction, he is mentioned occasionally in these media (more so in fact than Nussbaum or Rorty). Several English academic philosophers, such as Alan Ryan and Bernard Williams, are prominent public intellectuals, though Ryan mainly, and Williams only, in England rather than in the United States. Hilary Putnam and Robert Nozick are examples of the "attempting" public philosopher. They want to reach beyond an academic audience, but most of their writing (the principal but only partial exception is Nozick's first book, *Anarchy, State, and Utopia*) is too difficult and technical for nonacademics to understand; and they do not have the special charisma of the obscure that Allan Bloom, almost uniquely in the English-speaking world, mysteriously achieved. Both Nussbaum and Rorty write primarily for an academic audience but both have also written for intellectual magazines and even for newspapers.[2]

The model for their careers is John Stuart Mill. Although he was not an academic, he turned to public-intellectual work, most notably in *On Liberty* and *The Subjection of Women*, after establishing a sterling scholarly reputation with his treatises on logic and on economics. Successfully porting this reputation to his public-intellectual work, Mill received a respectful though critical hearing for views that were radical and even heretical at the time and might have been dismissed as crackpot had he not been so respected for his scholarly contributions.[3] Simi-

2. See, for example, Richard Rorty, "Give My Check to a More Deserving 68-Year-Old," *New York Times*, March 6, 2000 (late ed.), p. A23; Martha Nussbaum, "Hope, Fear, Suspense: A Chance to Focus on What Democracy Means," *Newsday*, Nov. 12, 2000, p. B4.

3. See Peter Nicholson, "The Reception and Early Reputation of Mill's Political

larly, Nussbaum and Rorty, who have strong opinions on issues of social justice and public policy, such as homosexual rights, multicultural
education, and the plight of women in the Third World, in the case
of Nussbaum, and redistributive policies and trade unionism, in the
case of Rorty, began writing for a general audience on political and social questions after establishing their academic reputations by writing
scholarly books published by academic presses.

In focusing on the work of these public philosophers, I hope I will
not be thought to be denigrating technical philosophy. That much of it
is arid does not distinguish it from other fields of scholarship. I discuss
public philosophy in this book not because I prefer it to technical philosophy (in fact my preference runs the other way), but because it is a
branch of public-intellectual work, as technical philosophy is not.

Although the specific issues of social justice and public policy that
Nussbaum and Rorty write about differ, their politics and social philosophy are the same. They are social democrats, well to the left of the
center of the modern Democratic Party, as we glimpsed in Nussbaum's
case in Chapter 6. They are welfare liberals, social liberals, *cosmopolitan*
liberals—for both are greatly concerned with the income gap between
the rich and the poor countries, though Rorty lacks Nussbaum's special
interest in the status of women in poor countries. And both deplore the
frivolity of the cultural Left. Yet juxtaposing these two philosophers
who write as social democrats on issues of social justice and public policy, one discovers a curious split. Nussbaum believes that the central
philosophical tradition of the West, the tradition that begins with Plato
and Aristotle and runs through the Stoics to Locke, Hume, Kant, Mill,
and Rawls, is (with some help from literature, as we know from Chapter 6) the key to formulating, justifying, and moving society to adopt
the social democratic policies she advocates in common with Rorty;
for his part, Rorty believes that this tradition is at best a distraction
from the quest for social justice and at worst an obstacle to achieving it.
Like Nussbaum, he looks to literature for help. But he also seeks help
in a heterodox philosophical tradition in which the central figures are
Nietzsche, James, and Dewey.

Thought," in *The Cambridge Companion to Mill* 464 (John Skorupski ed., 1998). Mill was a
strong believer in the "higher journalism," which is close to my conception of "public-intellectual work." See Eldon J. Eisenach, "Self-Reform as Political Reform in the Writings of
John Stuart Mill," 1 *Utilitas* 242, 250–251, 256–257 (1989).

The joinder of philosophy with public intellectuality has a certain logic to it. It is no accident that the founding public intellectuals—Socrates, Plato, Cicero, and Seneca—were illustrious philosophers, as were many later public intellectuals. The public intellectual is a generalist, but so, traditionally at least, was the philosopher. The philosopher in the Socratic tradition asks uncomfortable questions, challenging his society's conventional certitudes—this is what, in the view of Straussians, makes philosophy a dangerous occupation. The philosopher is, in short, a social gadfly—as is the public intellectual. But in an age of specialization, both arenas for generalists are shrinking. Not only has area after area of intellectual endeavor been hived off from philosophy and made the subject of its own specialized field (such as natural science, psychology, sociology, theology, and economics), but philosophy itself has become an academic specialty divided up into a host of subspecialties. Neither the typical career nor the typical interests of the modern academic philosopher intersect the activities and interests of nonacademic people. With signal exceptions he is an intellectual recluse. Nussbaum is well aware of this. Rorty-like, she has criticized "the academicization and professionalization of philosophy."[4] She has acknowledged the narrowness of academic philosophers' experience of life, implied that they should try not to spend their whole lives in the university, conceded that "too often, our insularity is evident in the way we write," and acknowledged that philosophers have difficulty communicating with a broader audience than their fellow academics and that "the journals in which one must publish to get tenure discourage a more flexible use of style . . . The jargon-laden nonwriting of the philosophical journals is a good style for persuading no human being."[5] But whereas Rorty has given up on academic philosophy, Nussbaum is fighting a rearguard action in its defense.

4. Martha C. Nussbaum, *Love's Knowledge: Essays on Philosophy and Literature* 20 (1990).

5. Martha C. Nussbaum, "Still Worthy of Praise," 111 *Harvard Law Review* 1776, 1794–1795 (1998). She is echoed by the lawyer-philosopher Brian Leiter, who points out that "analytic philosophers generally become unbearably trite and superficial once they venture beyond the technical problems and methods to which their specialized training best suits them, and try to assume the mantle of 'public intellectual' so often associated with figures on the Continent." Brian Leiter, "A Note on 'Analytic' and 'Continental' Philosophy," *http://www.blackwellpublishers.co.uk/gourmet/methods.htm*, visited January 28, 2001. (And he does not admire Continental philosophers!) See also Peter Edidin, "I Have Tenure, Therefore I Am: Philosophy in Hiding," *New York Times*, Jan. 28, 2001, § 4, p. 4.

She has appealed to the philosophical tradition as a guide to social reform in two quite different ways, corresponding to her interests in homosexual rights and Third World women's rights, respectively. She has also defended the current emphasis of American universities on multicultural education by reference to the tradition of Socratic inquiry.[6] But her use of philosophy in that endeavor (or for that matter in her literary criticism) is not distinctive; her essential argument is that multicultural education can be at once broadening and rigorous.

With regard to homosexual rights, she invokes the philosophers of Greece and Rome more as exemplars of her preferred position, which is that of treating homosexuality as a morally indifferent characteristic, than as reasoners to that position.[7] She does, however, claim that they "provide us with some valuable concrete arguments concerning the important human goods a sexual relationship of this sort [that is, a homosexual relationship] may promote" (*Sex and Social Justice* 301). Let us examine that claim.

The overall view of the classical world toward homosexuality is not easy to characterize. Undoubtedly it was more tolerant than the Christian view which displaced it. Indeed, it contained pockets and perhaps more than pockets of downright enthusiasm for homosexuality. But only for male homosexuality and with considerable reservations concerning the role of the passive partner, concerning specific practices (notably fellatio), and sometimes concerning *any* physical manifestation of homosexual love. A tolerant view of homosexuality is common among Greek and Roman philosophers—not a surprise, since philosophers generally reflect the values of their time and place. But there is no uniformity of view, sometimes even within the writings of the same philosopher. That is one of the things, along with a paucity of evidence, that makes it difficult to ascribe an overall view of homosexuality to the classical world. If Plato's *Symposium* (also *Phaedrus*) is pro-homosexual, *Laws* is anti, though exegetes have tried to paper over the tensions.

Apart from the eloquence of the *Symposium*, just the fact that a world historical genius such as Plato should have endorsed homosexual love

---

6. Martha C. Nussbaum, *Cultivating Humanity: A Classical Defense of Reform in Liberal Education* (1997), cited in this chapter as *Cultivating Humanity*.

7. See Martha C. Nussbaum, "Platonic Love and Colorado Law: The Relevance of Ancient Greek Norms to Modern Sexual Controversies," in Nussbaum, *Sex and Social Justice* 299, 309–328 (1999), cited in this chapter as *Sex and Social Justice*.

becomes a kind of "argument" for tolerance of homosexuality; and it has been Nussbaum's endeavor to demonstrate the consistency with which the Greek and Roman philosophers line up with the position defended in the *Symposium*. But this endeavor is better described as cultural history than as philosophy. If it's true that these philosophers were pro- or at least not anti-homosexual, this is a fact that, rightly or wrongly, may weigh heavily with some modern people, though I think very few, especially in the United States, where the Greek classics have little cachet. But it is a fact that stands apart from any philosophical argument that might be made in favor of tolerance for homosexuality.

The argument of the *Symposium*, insofar as it bears on the issue of homosexuality, is that all men long for immortality but inferior men seek to achieve it through procreation while superior ones seek to achieve it through the propagation of great ideas.[8] Hence the superior man seeks love, viewed as a road to philosophical knowledge, with other men rather than with women, who have no philosophical capacity. Since ideas are more important (to Plato anyway) than babies, love between two men is potentially more valuable than love between a man and a woman, and *a fortiori* between two women, a coupling procreative in neither a biological nor, given Plato's opinion of women's intellectual capabilities, a philosophical sense.

Despite Nussbaum's reference to "valuable concrete arguments" (plural), the argument that I have just sketched is the only one I can find in her summary of what the Greek philosophers said on the subject (see *Sex and Social Justice* 326, 328). It is concrete, but it is not valuable. It is a misogynistic argument, reflecting the dominant Greek view of women. And given Plato's preference for "Platonic" over carnal love, and his evident approval of Socrates' refusal to yield to Alcibiades' sexual importunings, it is really an argument for male bonding rather than for homosexuality. It is in any event an argument that Nussbaum herself does not accept and that undermines her effort to use the Greek philosophers in defense of homosexual rights for Americans today, since the argument of those philosophers for condoning or even encouraging homosexuality rests on a view of women that is unacceptable in today's America and so makes homosexuality itself seem misogynistic. This may be one reason (though doubtless a very minor one) why,

8. See Bruce S. Thornton, *Eros: The Myth of Ancient Greek Sexuality* 210–212 (1997).

as we shall see in the next chapter, courts inclined to provide legal protection for homosexuals do not appeal to the ancient Greek attitude.

Nussbaum argues that whatever the Greeks themselves thought, "we can also think for ourselves and see that the Greeks' defense of same-sex relationships as containing important human goods is in fact completely independent of misogyny, both logically and empirically" (p. 330). But stripped of its misogyny, the Greek philosophers' "defense" is, as I have said, a defense not of homosexuality but of friendship. If men and women are equal, a heterosexual relationship, which enables physical as well as mental procreation, is, by the logic of the *Symposium*, superior to a homosexual one, which enables only the latter form. It is only the presumed superiority of men that in works like the *Symposium* gives an aura to homosexual relationships. So, yes, the ancient Greeks, including distinguished philosophers such as Plato, were more tolerant of homosexuality than our society is. But for a reason we don't accept—their contempt for women's intellectual capacity.

Nussbaum's effort to use philosophy in the distinct role of promoting social reform in Third World societies sets as its goal improving the often miserable lot of women in those societies relative to the also but less miserable lot of the men. She has been emphatic, notably in her book *Women and Human Development*,[9] that philosophy is not an optional, but an essential, means to this end. She believes that cultural relativism, by denying the possibility of objective moral judgments on the practices of other societies (such practices as infibulation)[10] is retarding efforts to improve women's lot in those societies. She also believes that many of the leaders of Third World countries, and their most influential advisers in the West, are in the grip of a type of economic thinking that both retards social reform and rests on an ignorance of philosophy. By demonstrating the rottenness of the implicit philosophical premises of this economic thinking, sound philosophical reasoning can clear away a major obstacle to reform.

9. Martha C. Nussbaum, *Women and Human Development: The Capabilities Approach* (2000), cited in this chapter as *Women and Human Development*. See also the introduction and first four chapters of *Sex and Social Justice*.

10. Actually clitoridectomy and infibulation, but I'll use "infibulation" to cover both procedures. They used to be called "female circumcision" and are now more commonly called "female genital mutilation." The former term normalizes the practice by assimilating it to the far less controversial procedure of male circumcision, while the latter term is pejorative. The neutral term "infibulation" is therefore preferable in a scholarly discussion.

This project is not completely unrelated to Nussbaum's invocation of the classical philosophers in defense of homosexual rights. To appeal to ancient Greek attitudes as guides to our own thinking about sex is implicitly to deny the form of cultural relativism that commands us to withhold judgment about the morals of other societies. And part of her argument against the development economists is simply that they, like the homophobes, are ignorant of the philosophical tradition. Most economists, to the extent that they propose reforms and thus use economics as a normative rather than purely positive tool of analysis, are, she argues, unreflective utilitarians. They are ignorant not only of their own philosophical tradition but also of the criticisms of utilitarianism that philosophers have made and of alternative conceptions of the good life and the good society to those propounded in the utilitarian tradition. Economists take preferences as given and conceive it to be the function of government to create and protect free-market institutions that will allow those preferences to be gratified to the maximum extent possible. They assume that all preferences can be monetized and that measures of strictly economic welfare, such as gross national product (GNP), are reasonable proxies for the total preference satisfaction achieved in the society. So as between two societies the one that has the higher GNP per capita is "better" in the economic sense of having maximized utility or economic welfare (treated as synonyms) more successfully than the other society.

Nussbaum considers this a deeply flawed approach to development. She thinks that it is unrealistic, for example in ignoring the role of adaptive and otherwise inauthentic preferences, and that it rests on an impoverished conception of human welfare. People's preferences don't always reflect what a neutral observer would think good for them or what they would think good for themselves if they lived in a different kind of society or just if they knew more about alternative ways of living. A person who, having been born into a low caste, cannot aspire to rise beyond the rank of a ditch digger is ill advised to bewail his fate. He will be happier if he accepts the system and sees his place in it as dictated by a higher law or power from which he may expect to receive posthumous justice. Having scaled down his preferences to his condition, he may be content with the status quo and resist change. Slaves may develop a slave mentality. The servile may come to internalize the values of servility. Women confined by caste-like restrictions to household production may adapt to that condition by embracing it as their natural state. They may be happy to play the role to which their parents, reflecting the values of their society, have predestined them.

Economists do not think of themselves as cultural relativists, and cultural relativists do not think of themselves as development economists. But they are similar in tending to take at face value the preferences revealed by the attitudes and behavior of the society they are studying. The idea that there is some universal conception of the good life that is criterial of the practices of particular societies, that enables us to applaud the ancient Greek tolerance of homosexuality and condemn Third World practices of infibulation, female infanticide, sex-selective abortion, and denial of equal educational and job opportunities to women, is anathema to strict cultural relativists and foreign to the thinking of most economists. The utilitarian has a universal moral criterion, that of happiness or preference satisfaction. But as we saw in discussing *Brave New World* in Chapter 7, it is not a criterion that enables such questions to be asked as whether people should be considered happy when they live an "objectively" degraded life.

Nussbaum has gone to the philosophical tradition, in particular to Aristotle and Kant, and come back with a universalist notion of human fulfillment or flourishing which she has codified in the "capabilities approach" that provides the subtitle of *Women and Human Development*. Rather than focusing on a society's per capita income, a figure that might conceal enormous inequality, or on how contented the people are with their lot in life, the capabilities approach looks at what people "objectively" require in order to enjoy a rich, fully human life. These requirements include reasonable longevity, good health, freedom to travel, freedom from unreasonable fear or want, political freedom, sexual and reproductive freedom (within limits)—in fact the full menu of human rights as they are understood in liberal circles in the wealthy countries.

Nussbaum believes that to establish these as rights requires philosophical arguments. There are two senses in which this might be true. First, those who either actively oppose or simply do not employ the capabilities approach—the cultural relativists and the development economists—might be basing their opposition or indifference on a philosophical theory, such as relativism in its philosophical sense or utilitarianism. In that case, a philosophical critique of their premises would certainly be appropriate. Second, philosophical arguments might be available to show that the capabilities approach is the correct one to take to issues of development. Philosophy might in other words have a constructive rather than purely critical role to play in establishing the approach and perhaps also in convincing people to adopt it.

Regarding the first point, I do not think that either cultural relativists or development economists resist the capabilities approach because they are wedded to a philosophical theory. The idea that every person is dancing to some philosopher's tune is flattering to philosophers, but not very plausible, at least in the present setting. A philosophical relativist is someone who believes that no proposition can be shown to be always and everywhere true. He thinks that "truth" is relative to the perspective of the person uttering the proposition; what is true for me is therefore not necessarily true for you. Relativism in this extreme sense is vulnerable to serious criticisms, such as that the relativist is disabled from arguing that relativism is true; he can say only that it is true for him. But the cultural relativists whom Nussbaum attacks would not be bothered by this point. Their relativism is political rather than epistemological. They like to remind us that the colonial powers of a former day thought they could make "correct" judgments about the morality of the native civilizations they had conquered, that such cultural imperialism breeds discrimination and oppression and has been discredited by history, that the use of a capabilities approach that in effect codifies the aspirations of the comfortable citizens of wealthy secular societies is a revival of the old cultural imperialism, and that the attempt to impose our values on other societies that we barely understand—what Dickens in *David Copperfield* called "telescopic philanthropy"—may have unforeseeable adverse consequences. These are not philosophical points. Nor are they points that a philosopher is well equipped by training or experience to evaluate.

Likewise, while most development economists may be utilitarians, they do not offer a *philosophical* defense of their views. Nor need they, because their normative aspirations are modest. A watch repairer doesn't need philosophy to justify his saying that a broken watch ought to be fixed, and an economist doesn't need philosophy to justify advocating measures for increasing a nation's rate of economic growth or reducing inflation or unemployment. The economist must be careful not to neglect unwanted side effects of the measures he proposes; but then the watch repairer has to consider the cost of repairing the watch.

Economists' hesitancy to explore the implications of adaptive prefer-

ences, to penetrate beneath the surface indications of preference that
they call "revealed preference" (that is, preference revealed by behavior), or to deal with nonmonetizable phenomena (though this is changing), is not the product of philosophical commitment or confusion either. It is a consequence of the character of economics as a discipline.
The assumptions that preferences are stable and are reliably revealed
by behavior (by "putting your money where your mouth is"), and that
money values, express or imputed, are a meaningful index to a meaningful concept of human welfare, enable economists to formulate testable hypotheses about behavior. Economists may cling too tightly to
these assumptions, but if so it is for methodological rather than philosophical reasons. It is a commitment not to utilitarianism, but to a certain model of inquiry—what economists regard as scientific and their
critics as scientistic—that leads many economists to slight the features
of Third World societies to which Nussbaum wishes to draw attention. Actually, we'll see that development economists are not as blink-
ered as Nussbaum suggests. There is a long tradition in economics of
distinguishing between monetary and real phenomena; indeed, from
Adam Smith's advocacy of fair trade onward, an important function of
the economist has been to remind people of the difference. I mentioned in the last chapter an economic study of a consumption-based
approach to U.S. living standards; although the study was commissioned by a conservative think tank (the American Enterprise Institute)
and reaches "conservative" results, it does so by denying, just like
Nussbaum, that money income is an accurate measure of economic
welfare.

Turning to the second arguable contribution of philosophy to development, the constructive, I am skeptical that philosophy can demonstrate that the capabilities approach is correct or, what is a separate
point, can motivate anyone to adopt it. Ethical argument is notoriously
inconclusive. The argument for the capabilities approach comes down
to saying, "This is what we like; if you're as much like us as we think,
even though you live in the Third World, you'll like it too." This is not
much of an argument; and its inescapable air of condescension may
make it a hard sell in the Third World.

Nussbaum's belief that the capabilities approach can be made more
palatable by being given a philosophical foundation (or patina) is part
of her more general belief that social reform must be grounded in the-

ory to be effective. She believes for example that Cicero, Seneca, Grotius, and Kant have importantly influenced how war and international relations are conducted.[11] It is difficult to imagine a sphere of human activity more ruled by politics and passion. To credit Kant with the United Nations is like blaming Max Weber for Hitler—and that has been done too, as we'll see when we come to Allan Bloom. Nussbaum has also argued that

> had Catharine MacKinnon made a series of concrete critical judgments, rather than articulating a theory that offered a systematic, explicit, and abstract account of the structure of sex relations, the very concept of sexual harassment would not have been forged. Women would have gone on having experiences of it, but without an abstract and systematic conceptual structure we would not have been able fully to name what we were experiencing.[12]

This misconceives MacKinnon's contribution to the campaign against sexual harassment. An able lawyer, fierce polemicist, tireless activist, and "martyr" (see Chapter 2), she did much to alert the legal community to the need for legal remedies for sexual harassment. She did this by pointing to the problem and suggesting specific, concrete legal remedies for its solution. Her book on sexual harassment, her first and most influential book, is not in the least philosophical.[13] Her later-articulated feminist theory, a mixture of Marx and hostility to men,[14] does not appear in that book and has played no role in the acceptance by judges, legislators, and the public at large of the arguments for effective

11. Martha C. Nussbaum, "Why Practice Needs Ethical Theory: Particularism, Principle, and Bad Behavior," in *"The Path of the Law" and Its Influence: The Legacy of Oliver Wendell Holmes, Jr.* 50, 62, 77–78 (Steven J. Burton ed., 2000).

12. Id. at 78.

13. Catharine A. MacKinnon, *Sexual Harassment of Working Women: A Case of Sex Discrimination* (1979).

14. As in such famous dicta as "no pornography, no male sexuality," and "the major distinction between intercourse (normal) and rape (abnormal) is that the normal happens so often that one cannot get anyone to see anything wrong with it." Catharine A. MacKinnon, *Toward a Feminist Theory of the State* 139, 146 (1989). In her book *Only Words* 1 (1993), we read that "you grow up with your father holding you down and covering your mouth so another man can make a horrible searing pain between your legs. When you are older, your husband ties you to the bed and drops hot wax on your nipples and brings in other men to watch and makes you smile through it."

legal remedies against sexual harassment. Its only practical significance has been to provide a target for opponents of feminism. It has been an impediment to the adoption of the reforms that she advocates.

Practical reformers can do without MacKinnon's theories, or, for that matter, Aristotle's. He is Nussbaum's favorite philosopher.[15] Yet his writings approve of slavery and deem women inherently inferior to men. His philosophy supplied much of the intellectual foundation of the medieval Church, which in its preachments as well as its practices was, at least from a modern standpoint, a notably undemocratic, misogynistic, and illiberal institution. It is true that Aristotle had and articulated a concept of human flourishing that was distinctly worldly (or we might say secular) yet richer than utilitarianism, entailing as it did that people be *capable* of employing the variety of powers that we think of as distinctively human. This emphasis on capability, which places Aristotle in the ancestral line of Nussbaum's capabilities approach, might be thought to imply (is thought by Nussbaum to imply) some duty of material support of the needy, and so to have redistributive implications. But these were not implications that Aristotle himself drew. And just as he held a concept of human nature and potential that was compatible with a political and social world view opposite to Nussbaum's,[16] so Acquinas and other scholastics, including such modern disciples of theirs as Alasdair MacIntyre and John Finnis, have (approvingly) considered Aristotle's political and moral philosophy illiberal, inegalitarian, patriarchal, and hierarchical. For Nussbaum to attempt to enlist Aristotle in her social-democratic program is to grasp the blade of a two-edged sword.

Nussbaum is not uncritical of Aristotle. She treats him as a point of departure rather than as the terminus of inquiry. She starts with him only because she finds some of his ideas illuminating. But why is pedigree important? Why can't the ideas stand on their own, without being tied back to an illustrious progenitor who would have disagreed with the uses to which Nussbaum wants to put them? A scholar writing for a strictly academic audience may feel obliged to acknowledge the provenance of his or her ideas. But Nussbaum wishes to reach a wider audi-

15. See Martha C. Nussbaum, "Aristotle, Politics, and Human Capabilities: A Response to Antony, Arneson, Charlesworth, and Mulgan," 111 *Ethics* 102 (2000).

16. See, for example, Richard Mulgan, "Was Aristotle an 'Aristotelian Social Democrat'?" 111 *Ethics* 79 (2000).

ence, to which her intellectual debts are of no interest. Suspicion arises that when philosophers conjure for the general public with the great names of intellectual history, it is to lend authority to the conjurer rather than to illuminate the conjurer's ideas or to fend off charges of plagiarism. It is to seek allies among the famous dead.[17]

This is a constant feature of Nussbaum's public-intellectual writings and suggests anxiety that the arguments she makes—that any normative philosopher makes—are not compelling in themselves without regard to their provenance, just as anxiety about being able to judge the "true" value of a work of art leads to a catastrophic decline in the market value of a painting formerly attributed to Rembrandt when it is discovered to have been painted by someone else. But the Greeks are unreliable allies of a modern social democrat because most of what they thought about political and social issues, such as slavery, the rights of women and children, equality, and liberty, are reactionary by our lights. Nussbaum is assiduous in mining the Greeks for foreshadowings of modern views (among the Stoics, in particular); but considered as a whole, ancient Greek political and philosophical thought is not social democratic. Recall how Greek tolerance for homosexuality was bound up with misogyny. This is not surprising. It is more likely that a tolerant view of homosexuality would be a projection of the same underlying values that generated other characteristic features of ancient Greek ideology (slavery, infanticide, misogyny, militarism, and the rest) than that it would be an island of modernity. So in seeking to use the Greek view of homosexuality to support gay rights Nussbaum may be guilty of anachronism. Her alliance with Aristotle may be as fragile and opportunistic as Catharine MacKinnon's alliance with Edwin Meese in the war against pornography.

Even if the giants of the Western philosophical tradition not easily assimilated to Nussbaum's political agenda could be yoked without undue violence to the capabilities plow, there is no method for demonstrating that they are worthier of being heeded than rival founts of

17. As Nussbaum acknowledges, stating in the preface to the second edition of her book *The Fragility of Goodness: Luck and Goodness in Greek Tragedy and Philosophy* xvi (rev. ed. 2001) that she "aims to appropriate the Greeks as allies of an expanded version of Enlightenment liberalism." Elsewhere in the preface she says, "We could, of course, set ourselves right without returning to Greek thought at all." Id at xxiv. She does not explain why that would not indeed be the preferable course.

wisdom—Nietzsche, for example, or Jesus, or Confucius, or Mohammed, or Tolstoy, or Gandhi. The model society implied by the capabilities approach resembles the modern-day Scandinavian societies— wealthy, peaceful, prosperous, socially liberal societies with generous social safety nets. That is not every great thinker's idea of utopia, and there is no intellectual procedure for arguing someone who would prefer a society dedicated to martial glory or aesthetic or spiritual perfection or radical egalitarianism out of his preference. Only a lack of imagination makes us unshakably convinced that our values are really the best and that we can prove this.

The significance of Nussbaum's invocation of the Western philosophical tradition in support of her capabilities approach is, as I have been hinting, rhetorical rather than philosophical. At that level it converges with her approach to homosexual rights. The great philosophers are cultural icons and to drag them to your side of the cultural debate gives your arguments a heft and panache they would lack if you admitted that all you really had to say was that we like our values and think you would too if only you'd try them; or if you said, just a little more elaborately, that if you want to be like us, here is what you ought to do with respect to matters such as infibulation, the education of women, the social role of religion, and the regulation of the press.

It is a little to one side of my present purposes to consider whether it is an *effective* rhetoric, this invocation of the great philosophers; but I will venture to suggest that it is not. The philosophers whom Nussbaum likes to invoke have little resonance for modern Americans, even of the educated class. To invoke those philosophers, to argue over what they meant or what they should mean to us, is to write for a coterie; it is the wrong strategy for an aspiring public intellectual. "Over the past thirty years, political philosophy has become a self-referential discourse, one of whose defining features is its non-existence as far as the real political world is concerned."[18] It is doubtful that even Rawls's *A Theory of Justice*, first published in 1971, the most celebrated work of political philosophy of the twentieth century, has had a significant impact on public policy. (Rawls is one of the philosophers whom John Gray was talking about in the passage that I just quoted.) One reason is its austerely academic style. Another and deeper reason—because the

18. John Gray, "John Stuart Mill's Neglected Insights; His Understanding of Human Variety and His Plea for the Wilderness," *Times Literary Supplement*, Feb. 11, 2000, p. 12.

want of an accessible style could be supplied by Rawls's public-intellectual acolytes, of whom there are many—is that its most novel and arresting thesis, that justice requires the government to redistribute all wealth beyond what is necessary to "incentivize" the workers of the society to be productive, is equivocal. This thesis (the "difference principle") is applauded by liberals as giving philosophical sanction to redistribution and by conservatives as giving philosophical sanction to incentive-compatible public policies. To put it crudely, the difference principle sanctions greed,[19] but only up to a point—a point that no one can ascertain—and so either side of the policy debate can render homage to the principle itself.[20] What has guided the evolution of public policy in the three decades since *A Theory of Justice* was published has not been a book; it has been the failure of certain social experiments, notably but not only communism, highlighted by the success of (partially) deregulated capitalism in producing unimagined prosperity in much of the world. The empirical triumph of capitalism has removed redistributive policies from the policy agenda in most countries and thus made Rawls's book seem—academic.

To note the limited impact of social theory on the real world is not to take a dig at John Rawls but to make the general point that real-world events have a much greater impact on public opinion than academic theories do. Milton Friedman acknowledged this point in refusing to credit his book *Capitalism and Freedom* with the increased popularity of free-market thinking.[21] That popularity is due to the same events that have beached Rawls's theory of justice. But in retrospect we see that Friedman was prescient. If false prophets are not dishonored, at least the true ones are honored; this must modify my claim that no one is keeping score in the debates between public intellectuals. Rawls is not given to prophecy, and has not been refuted; he has been bypassed.

But if I am underestimating Rawls's influence, this would not undermine my reservations about the influence of public intellectuals. For

19. See G. A. Cohen, *If You're an Egalitarian, How Come You're So Rich?* chs. 8–10 (2000).

20. "Justice as fairness leaves open the question whether its principles are best realized by some form of property-owning democracy or by a liberal socialist regime. The question is left to be settled by historical conditions and the traditions, institutions, and social forces of each country." John Rawls, "Preface for the Revised Edition," in Rawls, *A Theory of Justice* xi, xv–xvi (rev. ed. 1999).

21. Milton Friedman, "Preface, 1982," in *Capitalism and Freedom* vi (1960; reissued 1982).

Rawls has not taken the public-intellectual path; and if he is more influential than the political philosophers who have, it suggests that the academic who sticks to his last may have the better prospects for moving
the world.

~ THE ALTERNATIVE WAY of doing public philosophy to
Nussbaum's is that of Rorty, which involves bracketing deep normative issues. He studiously avoids appealing to the central Western
philosophical tradition, the tradition to which Nussbaum appeals. We
must consider why he thinks the appeal to that tradition misguided
from the standpoint of advancing the reformist goals that he shares
with Nussbaum. One reason is that her way is ineffectual and therefore a distraction, a waste of time. "We [leftist intellectuals] can no
longer function as an avant-garde."[22] To be of any practical use, we
must "giv[e] up the claim that philosophical or literary sophistication is
important because it prepares us for the crucial, socially indispensable
role that history has allotted to us—the role of 'critic of ideology.'"[23]
Rorty may also believe that the tradition to which Nussbaum appeals
is antipathetic to his and her reformist goals. There are hints of such
a belief in his work,[24] though the argument is difficult to make out.
Clearly he thinks the center of the tradition is the notion of objective truth, whether scientific, moral, or political. Nussbaum would no
doubt agree. She regards as "pernicious" the postmodernist attacks on
the possibility of attaining truth and objectivity. She believes that "we
can establish claims as true by arguments that rightly claim objectivity
and freedom from bias" (*Cultivating Humanity* 39; see also id. at 40–
41). Almost her whole point is that the capabilities approach *is* such
a claim—is therefore true for everyone and not just for the wealthy
North Atlantic nations. One can see why Rorty, as a pragmatist, an
antifoundationalist, might disagree with her truth claims. But why
might he think that resolving the disagreement her way could retard
the achievement of their shared political goals?

22. Richard Rorty, "The End of Leninism and History as Comic Frame," in *History and the
Idea of Progress* 211, 219 (Arthur M. Melzer, Jerry Weinberger, and M. Richard Zinman eds.,
1995).
    23. Id. at 223.
    24. Notably in the essays collected in Richard Rorty, *Philosophy and Social Hope* (1999),
cited in this chapter as *Philosophy and Social Hope*.

Three answers can be inferred from Rorty's writings. First, with its claim to be in search of fundamental or ultimate truths, traditional philosophizing resembles theology in fostering a mindset inimical to compromise and tolerance and therefore to democracy, whereas "philosophical superficiality and light-mindedness helps . . . make the world's inhabitants more pragmatic, more tolerant, more liberal, more receptive to the appeal of instrumental rationality."[25] Second, social reform will be slowed down if "judgment must remain suspended on the legitimacy of cultural novelties until we philosophers have pronounced them authentically rational."[26] And third, building philosophical foundations for political programs saps enthusiasm for social experimentation. Experiments are intended to test hypotheses, which by definition are tentative; otherwise there would be no point in testing them. You don't do an experiment to verify that two plus two equals four. The capabilities approach is not advanced as a set of hypotheses to be tested, but as a set of established truths. A social program that does not square with it—for example, that denies equal rights to women—is false and must be rejected.

Rorty puts experimentation front and center in the quest for social justice and does not want to see it impeded by a conviction that we know what social justice is and just have to work out the details of implementation. He wants to help "free mankind from Nietzsche's 'longest lie,' the notion that outside the haphazard and perilous experiments we perform there lies something (God, Science, Knowledge, Rationality, or Truth) which will, if only we perform the correct rituals, step in to save us."[27] He wants us to "get rid of the conviction common to Plato and Marx . . . that there just *must* be large theoretical ways of finding out how to end injustice, as opposed to small experimental ways."[28] In this Rorty is faithful not only to Dewey but to Mill, who also taught the importance of experimentation. The premise of *On Lib-*

25. Richard Rorty, "The Priority of Democracy to Philosophy," in *Reading Rorty: Critical Responses to Philosophy and the Mirror of Nature (and Beyond)* 279, 293 (Alan R. Malachowski ed., 1990). Elsewhere Rorty has said that he thinks "a world of pragmatic atheists . . . would be a better, happier world than our present one." Rorty, "Response to Farrell," in *Rorty and Pragmatism: The Philosopher Responds to His Critics* 189, 195 (Herman J. Saatkamp Jr. ed., 1995).

26. Richard Rorty, "Philosophy and the Future," in id. at 197, 201.

27. Richard Rorty, *Consequences of Pragmatism (Essays: 1972–1980)* 208 (1982).

28. Rorty, note 26 above, at 211 (emphasis in original).

erty is that "we cannot know a priori, and custom cannot tell us, what is good for us: the only way we can find out is by trying and seeing."[29] In its lack of goal orientation and its emphasis on diversity of approaches,[30] Mill's theory is alien to the spirit of Nussbaum's public-intellectual writings, which is teleological: we know where we are going and we must bend every effort to get there.

John Dewey, Rorty's favorite philosopher, thought the central Western philosophical tradition, the tradition that runs from Plato to Kant, too rationalistic, too abstract, too metaphysical, too much concerned with truth conditions and too little with helping us cope with our social problems. He thought science should be regarded as a tool rather than as Christianity's successor as the deliverer of final truths. For him and I think for Rorty too, the central Western philosophical tradition was not just an irrelevance, but a drag, distracting people from seeking effective ways of coping with modernity's challenges and indeed cultivating a mindset that would make it harder for people to cope with them.

Rorty's rejection of the tradition is reinforced by his belief that altruism and empathy, a widening circle of human sympathies, rather than philosophical notions of justice, are what is needed to bring about the social reforms that he and Nussbaum support. To be motivated to do social reform we need to be able to feel the hopes and sufferings of people very different from ourselves as our own hopes and suffering. We need to expand our sympathies until we feel ourselves to be, in a more than metaphorical sense, members of "the human family," and not just members of our own family, class, sect, or nation. The requisite capacities are emotional and imaginative rather than analytical. "Moral progress is a matter of wider and wider sympathy. It is not a matter of rising above the sentimental to the rational. Nor is it a matter of appealing from lower, possibly corrupt, local courts to a higher court which administers an ahistorical, incorruptible, transcultural moral law" (*Philosophy and Social Hope* 82–83). For aid in developing these capacities Rorty looks to literature—as does Nussbaum, who has sounded even more strongly than Rorty the note that literature is indispensable to

29. Nicholson, note 3 above, at 470.

30. Mill said that what had made "the European family of nations an improving, instead of a stationary portion of mankind" was "not any superior excellence in them . . . but their remarkable diversity of character and culture. Individuals, classes, nations, have been extremely unlike one another: they have struck out a great variety of paths, each leading to something valuable." John Stuart Mill, *On Liberty* 105 (1955 [1859]).

the cultivation of the very sympathies both of them want to enlarge. Only she thinks that philosophy also has an indispensable role to play in this endeavor and he thinks it has no role.

Their takes on literature are interestingly different. Rorty treats it as a compendium of images and narratives designed to widen our sympathies by moving us.[31] To him the significance of *Nineteen Eighty-Four* is that it presents powerfully repulsive images of sadism and cruelty and—in depicting the chief sadist, O'Brien, as an educated and intelligent person, not a brute—warns us that even civilized people can be cruel and sadistic (*Contingency, Irony, and Solidarity*, ch. 8). Nussbaum, we know, sees literature as a compendium of edifying propositions. She emphasizes the message in literature, he literature's psychological impact. She assimilates literature to philosophy, and he philosophy to literature—his academic appointments have for many years been in literature departments, not philosophy departments. Peter Singer's success in advancing the cause of animal welfare by *showing* the suffering of animals suggests that Rorty is on to something, though if my analysis of moralistic criticism in Chapter 6 is correct, Rorty is wrong to assume that the empathic power of literature can make us better people.[32]

A paradoxical difference between Nussbaum and Rorty is that she— the rationalist, the believer in absolute moral truth and the higher law, the conserver of the classical tradition in philosophy—is more empirical and better informed about practical issues of public policy than he, the pragmatist. (In this he resembles his fellow pragmatist philosopher and former student Cornel West.) Nussbaum has traveled extensively in India and consulted with specialists in the problems of development. She has facts and even figures about development at her fingertips. She developed the capabilities approach in collaboration with Amartya Sen,[33] who is an economist first and a philosopher second, and an Indian.

Rorty's forays into public policy are distinctly unworldly. In this, too,

31. Richard Rorty, *Contingency, Irony, and Solidarity* xvi (1989), cited in this chapter as *Contingency, Irony, and Solidarity*.

32. A point made with specific reference to his approach to literature in Nancy Fraser, "Solidarity or Singularity? Richard Rorty between Romanticism and Technocracy," in *Reading Rorty*, note 25 above, at 303, 306.

33. See *Women and Human Development* 11–15. For Sen's approach, see index references to "capabilities" in Amartya Sen, *Development as Freedom* 362 (1999).

he is faithful to John Dewey, an active public intellectual whose public-intellectual writings are in the main nebulous and, where concrete, have not, for the most part, fared well. Dewey was an isolationist (in reaction to his much-criticized support of the United States' entry into World War I) right up to the Japanese attack on Pearl Harbor, a socialist, and a critic of the New Deal as tepid and ineffectual because insufficiently socialistic; his grasp of the nation's foreign and domestic problems was distinctly inferior to Franklin Roosevelt's, although his steadfast anti-communism should be noted—he was a "cold war" intellectual, just like Rorty.

Rorty is nostalgic, pessimistic, almost Spenglerian, cursory, and wholly without practical suggestions. (A strange pragmatist!) He thinks of the United States as a "a country in decline" (*Philosophy and Social Hope* 234).[34] He warns that we are in danger of "Brazilianization," which means "the emergence of an 'overclass' consisting of the top 20 per cent of the population and the steady immiseration of everybody else" (p. 231). The only hope for the United States, in his view, is a revival of the labor movement and a return to the politics of the Old Left, to which class struggle was central.[35] Rorty advocates central planning, fears globalization (in the sense of international capital mobility and multinational corporations), and would like to see the United Nations evolve into a world government that would redistribute wealth from the rich to the poor countries and control substantial military forces. For the diagnosis of the world's ills he turns to the *Communist Manifesto*, and for their cure to the Sermon on the Mount. He is walking backward into the twenty-first century. He has no concrete, realizable projects. He is brilliant but his expertise is in philosophy and literature, not in economics or any other social science, and his career has been entirely an academic one.[36]

Unlike Nussbaum, Rorty is disdainful of the social sciences. He considers psychology and sociology "relatively barren," claims that the

34. And recall the passage I quoted in Chapter 8 from his article "Half a Million Blue Helmets?" *Common Knowledge*, Winter 1995, pp. 10, 13: "America now seems to be having a nervous breakdown: the country is exhausted, dispirited, frightened, irresolute, and utterly unable to contribute to the resolution of international problems."

35. See, for example, Richard Rorty, "Back to Class Politics," *Dissent*, Winter 1997, p. 31.

36. For further criticisms of Rorty and other philosophers as social critics, see Richard A. Posner, *Overcoming Law*, ch. 22 (1995) ("What Are Philosophers Good for?"); Richard A. Posner, *The Problems of Jurisprudence* 383–387 (1990).

"the behavioral sciences never seem to come up with either useful predictions or persuasive advice about what we should do,"[37] and does not even deign to mention economics—while at the same time incautiously making economic points.[38] Suspicious of the natural sciences as well, he denies their relevance even to issues to which they are not only plainly relevant but also helpful to his own positions. An example is gay marriage,[39] which is altogether less threatening if scientists are correct that sexual orientation is innate, rather than acquired and hence possibly the result of persuasion or seduction. Rorty hopes that philosophers might become "all-purpose intellectuals"[40] (which may be another term for public intellectuals), but is insensitive to the limitations of generalist social criticism in an age of science, including social science.

The problem is not that Rorty has no *proposals*. He has many, such as universal health insurance, a prohibition against political candidates' buying time on television, and an end to local financing of public education.[41] They are not *practical* proposals, however, not only because they have no political support but also because Rorty does not expound them in sufficient detail to make them persuasive. They raise complicated issues and invite multitudinous objections, which might or might not be answerable; but to describe and defend each proposal in a few

37. Richard Rorty, "Against Unity," *Wilson Quarterly*, Winter 1998, pp. 28, 35.

38. For example: "Much of the money we in the industrial democracies spend on ourselves is earned by making and selling cluster bombs, white phosphorus, machine pistols, ground-to-air missiles, and other items that make it easier for warlords in places like Burundi and Bosnia to keep control of the people they have terrorized." Rorty, note 34 above, at 10. It is true that the United States exports about $25 billion a year in munitions, but this is a tiny part of our $10 trillion economy and anyway very few of these exports end up in the hands of warlords, as distinct from the legitimate governments of foreign nations. Equally wide of the mark is his claim in the same article that the prosperity of American suburbs "requires keeping a vast reserve army of the unemployed in the inner cities, thereby ensuring that no more than a miserable minimum wage need be paid for any unskilled job." Id. at 11. Most unskilled workers are paid more than the minimum wage; and of all black and Hispanic workers paid by the hour, only 7 percent earn at or below the minimum wage. U.S. Census Bureau, *Statistical Abstract of the United States 1999* 447 (1999) (tab. 706). If the wages of the unskilled were higher, many suburbanites would actually benefit because there would be greater demand for the goods and services that the firms that employ suburbanites produce.

39. Rorty, note 37 above, at 34.

40. Rorty, note 27 above, at xxxix–xl.

41. See Richard Rorty, "First Projects, Then Principles," *Nation*, Dec. 22, 1997, p. 18.

sentences, which is Rorty's approach, is useless. They are armchair proposals, and lack a knowledge base.

As the result of a recent change in the social security law, employed
persons no longer have to wait until they reach the age of seventy to
begin collecting social security retirement benefits. (If not employed,
they would begin collecting full benefits at sixty-five.) Rorty opposed
the change on the ground that it would entitle affluent employed persons like himself (he was sixty-eight when the law was changed) to
additional money that they don't need.[42] This misses the point of the
change in law, which was to alleviate a labor shortage by eliminating a
deterrent to older workers' remaining in the work force. Although
some affluent people benefit from the law, most affluent people are
retired by sixty-five and so do not benefit. The principal beneficiaries are the nonaffluent, who can earn so little more than social security
retirement benefits that before the change in law they had little incentive to work past sixty-five.[43] Not only will these people now have
higher incomes, consisting of modest wages plus social security benefits rather than *either* modest wages *or* social security benefits, but the
nation as a whole will be more prosperous because more people will be
working, generating additional tax revenues available for redistribution.

I mentioned *Nineteen Eighty-Four* in connection with Rorty and I am
about to argue that he gets into trouble in discussing that novel. But it
is no accident that he's drawn to Orwell. There is an affinity between
them, and a comparison can tell us something about the situation of the
public intellectual today. Rorty is our Orwell, in combining an unreflective egalitarianism based on sympathy with human suffering and
hostility to fat cats with a strong dislike of the unpatriotic Left,[44] and in
expressing his views in beautiful prose, at once limpid and passionate.
But apart from having a more limited experience of life than Orwell,
who knew poverty and dreadful health and war and communism and
colonialism all at first hand, Rorty is an academic and most of his writing deals with philosophical issues and texts that hold little interest for

42. Rorty, note 2 above.

43. Before the passage of the law, a person who was entitled to a social security pension of
$10,000 but could earn only $9,000 by working would not work. He probably would not
work even if he could earn somewhat more than $10,000, given costs of work.

44. See, for example, "The Unpatriotic Academy," in *Philosophy and Social Hope* 252.

people who are not professional philosophers and no interest for people who are not academics. What is more, the unpatriotic Left that he attacks is not the intellectual manifestation of a totalitarian world power but a comical sliver of university life, the raw material for academic novels and fevered conservative denunciation, while the unreflective leftism that he defends is, given the advance of economic thinking since Orwell's death in 1950, retrograde and nostalgic. Though almost as skillful a writer as Orwell,[45] better educated, longer-lived, and analytically more acute, Rorty simply does not inhabit the historical circumstances that would enable him to have a comparable career as a public intellectual.

Rorty is well aware that *Nineteen Eighty-Four* is commonly read as the work of "a realist philosopher, a defender of common sense against its cultured, ironist defenders" (*Contingency, Irony, and Solidarity* 172 (footnote omitted); see also p. 173). As an antirealist, an "ironist," Rorty resists an interpretation of the novel that aligns it with his philosophical opponents. He makes the legitimate point that Orwell was not a philosopher and was not trying to write philosophy. But in making this point he overlooks something important—the possible political significance of a *rhetoric* of realism. He says, "the fact that two and two does not make five is not the essence of the matter" (p. 178). But Orwell seems to have believed that insistence on simple, homely truths, however unsophisticated that insistence might seem, *was* the essence of the matter—that it was an essential bulwark against totalitarianism.[46] It is O'Brien who, like Pilate, palters with the concept of truth, plays with it, deconstructs it; and this behavior is depicted in the novel as deeply sinister. Rorty is making the same mistake as the determinist who criticizes the legal system for excluding from evidence confessions that are not the product of the defendant's "free will." Judges are not taking sides in a philosophical debate, but identifying politically unacceptable forms of coercion.

Rorty's insensitivity to the rhetorical function of a realist vocabulary is of a piece with his nostalgia for the early struggles of American labor unions and his fondness for the vocabulary of those struggles,

---

45. And not wholly without a novelist's imagination—see his brilliant rewriting of Heidegger's life in "On Heidegger's Nazism," in id. at 190.

46. See James Conant, "Freedom, Cruelty, and Truth: Rorty versus Orwell," in *Rorty and His Critics* 268 (Robert B. Brandom ed., 2000), esp. pp. 299–300, 310.

with its "masses" and "bosses," its "oligarchs" and "shadowy million-aires." This vocabulary is archaic and jejune. It cannot move anyone under seventy. That Rorty should wish to revive a stale rhetoric is para-doxical in light of his "ironist" belief[47] that we need to forge new vocab-ularies. He hasn't learned from Peter Singer how to communicate ef-fectively with a popular audience. Like the choice of a rhetoric in which to advance political ideas, the issue of truth in *Nineteen Eighty-Four* is political rather than philosophical, and this reinforces one's doubts that philosophy has either positive or negative consequences for social re-form.

The rhetorical contrast between Rorty and Nussbaum is worth a moment's attention because of the centrality of rhetoric to public-intel-lectual work. Rorty does not brandish the illustrious dead as authori-ties, which is to his credit; but having by way of a substitute only the vocabulary of the 1930s, he lacks a voice that can carry weight with the general educated public. Nussbaum uses her authorities to establish her competence to opine on matters that would otherwise seem the province of sociology, economics, and political science. She must make her unquestioned professional competence to interpret Aristotle and other giants of the philosophical tradition appear to equip her to also opine on issues of sociology and economics and political science with-out the usual credentials in those fields. I have expressed my doubt that philosophy has sufficient standing in the eyes of the general public to make this rhetorical move effective either.

The only constructive—and probably the only rhetorically effec-tive—way in which to discuss public policy today is in terms of practical consequences ("practical" to avoid merely relabeling moral concerns in consequentialist language, as by speaking of the consequences of some policy for "human dignity"). That is the pragmatic approach; so if pragmatism is a philosophy rather than, as Rorty and I prefer to think of it, an antiphilosophy, then in saying that the path to social reform lies through the study of consequences I am taking a philosophical stand. On that view philosophy is the pervasive medium in which all students of society swim. But that is either wrong, or empty—and it doesn't matter which.

To do pragmatic analysis of large social, political, and economic is-

47. See id. at 277, quoted in Chapter 1.

sues in a complex society requires combining social scientific knowledge and technique with an empirical understanding of the real-world context of proposed reforms. Of course, an analysis, however rigorous, cannot by itself be a recommendation for action. But that is a concern only when a common normative framework is lacking. Sometimes it is, but often it isn't. It is not true that all policy choices have to be justified by reference to some concept of the social goals that specific policies ought to serve, some notion of "the good" that presumably only a philosopher could elucidate. Only when there is a disagreement about goals that bears upon the particular choice to be made is there any occasion for getting philosophical, though usually with little to show for the attempt. When there is such disagreement, analysis of the consequences of the choices is still important, because even people committed to goals they refuse to defend in terms of costs and benefits are not indifferent to the costs of reaching their goals.

Thus it is useless and even mischievous to advocate equal rights for women in a Third World nation on the basis of general principles without considering the practical entailments of such rights in the specific circumstances of that nation. Consider the question whether to require that girls be guaranteed the same amount of education as boys. Such a guaranty would increase the cost of the educational system unless some of the boys were simply displaced by an equal number of girls. This might or might not be appropriate at the university level, depending on the job market for women. It certainly wouldn't be appropriate at the elementary and secondary school level, where the only realistic proposal would be to enlarge the school system to enable all girls to be educated without having to displace any boys. So the educational system would be more costly, and responsible analysis would have to consider how large the additional cost would be and where the resources would be taken from (from what people, from what programs, and by what methods) to defray the cost and what would be lost by this diversion of resources. The likely impact of additional education on women's lives would also have to be considered.

The net effect of additional education might be wholly good,[48] both for women and for men, if for example it resulted in a lower birth rate

48. As argued in M. Anne Hill and Elizabeth M. King, "Women's Education in Developing Countries: An Overview," in *Women's Education in Developing Countries: Barriers, Benefits, and Policies* 1, 21–29 (Elizabeth M. King and M. Anne Hill eds., 1993).

(by increasing women's earnings and thus the opportunity cost of having a child)[49] and in a diversion of female productivity from the household to the market. But its positive impact would have to be balanced against the cost. In a society in which few occupations are open to women except the bearing and rearing of children, female education is apt to be less productive than male education.[50] And if girls are needed to work in or outside the home, they may not be able to take advantage of the schooling opportunities that are offered to them.[51] Religious and customary obstacles to female education[52] have to be considered, and the costs and benefits of overcoming them assayed too.

One consideration that should be particularly important to an egalitarian is the possible negative impact of a policy of gender equalization on the educational opportunities of the worst-off members of society.[53] Suppose that at present in some poor country only upper middle-class children, mostly male, receive substantial education. Gender equalization might result simply in a relative handful of upper middle-class girls receiving substantial education, whereas the same funds might buy more education,[54] albeit of lower quality, if allocated to poor children of both sexes.

Despite the reservations that I have expressed, my own guess, for what little it is worth, is that a policy of allocating more resources to the education of girls is a sensible policy for a Third World nation. But this is not because of any philosophical arguments in favor of the capabilities approach; it is because of the concrete benefit to a poor country of reducing the birth rate, the most certain consequence of an increase in the female educational level. It is not through philosophy that such a consequence and such a benefit are identified.

49. T. Paul Schultz, "Investments in the Schooling and Health of Women and Men: Quantities and Returns," 28 *Journal of Human Resources* 694, 715–716 (1993); Geoffrey McNicoll, "Changing Fertility Patterns and Policies in the Third World," 18 *Annual Review of Sociology* 85 (1992).

50. See Gary S. Becker, *A Treatise on the Family* 102 (enlarged ed. 1991).

51. Partha Dasgupta, "The Population Problem: Theory and Evidence," 33 *Journal of Economic Literature* 1879, 1888 (1995).

52. Emphasized, with respect to India, in Neera Desai, "Women's Education in India," in *The Politics of Women's Education: Perspectives from Asia, Africa, and Latin America* 23 (Jill Ker Conway and Susan C. Bourque eds., 1993).

53. See John Knodel and Gavin W. Jones, "Post-Cairo Population Policy: Does Promoting Girls' Schooling Miss the Mark?" 22 *Population and Development Review* 683 (1996).

54. Cf. A. K. Sen, *Crisis in Indian Education* 12–13 (1971).

I picked female education in the Third World as my main example of the indispensability of subjecting social proposals to cost–benefit analysis because it seemed to me likely to lie at the core of Nussbaum's philosophical concerns. It is a problem of discrimination against women in the Third World in general and India in particular, and it is a problem of education, on which Nussbaum has written extensively. But in the course of researching the issue I discovered two things. The first is that the studies of the issue by development economists and other social scientists, the studies cited in my footnotes, are not colored by the utilitarian or relativist fallacies that Nussbaum considers serious obstacles to a proper understanding of the problems of the Third World. She may be tilting at philosophical windmills. Second, although *Women and Human Development* and *Sex and Social Justice* contain plenty of criticisms of the economists and the relativists, they contain little in the way of detailed examination of policy or practice. Neither book has an index entry for education, although *Sex and Social Justice* does have a brief discussion of religious obstacles in the Third World to female education.[55]

Nussbaum's book on *American* university education (*Cultivating Humanity)* has considerably more texture, and an especially good chapter on African-American studies (id., ch. 5), though no immediate relevance to educational policy in the Third World. But the book slights the damage that the cultural Left, including radical feminism, has done and is doing to American higher education. The book relies very heavily on a series of short visits that Nussbaum made to a small number of campuses and does not engage adequately with the considerable, though largely anecdotal and often one-sided and intemperate,[56] critical literature on multiculturalism.

There is one Third World practice, however, that Nussbaum has

55. Nussbaum, "Religion and Women's Human Rights," in *Sex and Social Justice* 81, 100–101.

56. Not always, though. For an example of sober and scholarly critique, see *What's Happened to the Humanities?* (Alvin Kernan ed., 1997). What is more, the "left McCarthyism" of the modern American campus, while exaggerated by the Right, is not the myth that Nussbaum thinks it is. See, for a compelling though anecdotal account, Paul Hollander, *Anti-Americanism: Critiques at Home and Abroad 1965–1990*, ch. 3 (1992); and, for a chilling vignette, Lawrence F. Kaplan, "Columbia Blues," *New Republic*, Dec. 4, 2000, p. 58. For criticism of both sides in the "culture wars," see Eugene Goodheart, *Does Literary Studies Have a Future?* (1999).

discussed in great detail, and that is infibulation, which she vigorously opposes. Noting that "it is highly likely that [infibulation] emerged as the functional equivalent to the seclusion of women,"[57] she explains that in Africa, unlike India, women are important agricultural producers, and so it would be too costly to sequester them as a way of ensuring their "purity." By reducing female sexual desire, infibulation provides an alternative form of control over female sexuality. Nussbaum says that "this functional history clearly does not justify the practice."[58] That is true, if it is merely history. But if, as she does not discuss, ensuring women's chastity is functional in the (to us very grim and peculiar) conditions of African society, then we have to consider how important that function is and whether there are feasible alternative means, less harmful to women, of performing it. If it is not functional, the case for abolition is greatly strengthened. But more than assertion is required to show that it is not functional. It may be functional if polygamy, which infibulation supports (by reducing the tendency to female adultery in a culture in which each of the polygamous husband's wives has her own home and is thus not under his surveillance, and in which his sexual contact with each wife is necessarily limited), is functional. Infibulation may even be functional for a reason unrelated to polygamy. It has been conjectured that among Somali herders, a culture in which infibulation is especially widespread, the practice is designed to reduce the emission of female sexual odors, which are disturbing to the herds of sheep and goats for which the women are mainly responsible, and also attract predators.[59]

There is a deeper problem with Nussbaum's analysis of infibulation than her failure to explore its functionality. It is the old problem of underspecialization. Nussbaum is not an anthropologist, nor an expert on Africa. It turns out that there is a rich scholarly literature on infibulation, and it raises serious questions about the accuracy of Nussbaum's premises. In particular, there are doubts about the medical hazards of the procedure, the degree to which it causes sexual dysfunction, and the degree of regret experienced by those who undergo

57. Martha C. Nussbaum, "Judging Other Cultures: The Case of Genital Mutilation," in *Sex and Social Justice* 118, 125.

58. Id.

59. Pia Grassivaro Gallo and Franco Viviani, "The Origin of Infibulation in Somalia: An Ethological Hypothesis," 13 *Ethology and Sociobiology* 253 (1992).

it.[60] So great are these doubts that a very deep immersion in a much more extensive literature than Nussbaum cites would be necessary to still them.[61]

The case of infibulation suggests the inescapability of hard choices in the evaluation of proposals for social reform—hard not in the sense of difficult, though difficulty is also a factor, but in the sense of involving unavoidable loss. This insight is related to Weber's notion of the tragic character of politics (see Chapter 2). The essence of tragedy in the literary sense is the impossibility of reconciling dreams with reality, and thus the unavailability of pat, happy solutions to deep human problems. Tragedy in this sense is ubiquitous in politics for the reasons that Weber explained. The political and literary senses of tragedy join in *Antigone*, which is a political tragedy because there is no way to reconcile the civic interests represented by Cleon with the religious and familial interests represented by Antigone. The tragic sense is alien to both Nussbaum and Rorty.[62] Both believe that the main obstacles to attaining social-democratic heaven are greed, envy, ignorance, the machinations of the bosses, the "selfish indifference" of the middle class which a recession might shock it out of,[63] or, as Nussbaum puts it, "culpable negligence by the powerful."[64] In slighting the systemic, deeply rooted, and functional character of social practices offensive to a modern liberal's sensibility, such a view reveals itself as sociologically and anthopologically naïve. It is likely to induce either pessimism and a sense of helplessness (in Rorty), or a neglect (in Nussbaum) of the economic and political costs of social-democratic reforms.

Utopianism and despair are closely allied. Acutely conscious of the gap between the actual and the conceivable, the utopian despairs when

60. All points emphasized by Nussbaum, note 57 above, at 123–127.

61. See the discussion and extensive bibliography in Richard A. Shweder, "What about FGM? And Why Understanding Culture Matters in the First Place" (forthcoming in *The Free Exercise of Culture: How Free Is It? How Free Ought It to Be?* [Richard A. Shweder, Hazel R. Markus, and Martha Minow eds.]). An especially notable study discussed by Shweder, though in all likelihood published too recently to have come to Nussbaum's attention, is Carla Makhlouf Obermeyer, "Female Genital Surgeries: The Known, the Unknown, and the Unknowable," 13 *Medical Anthropology Quarterly* 79 (1999).

62. See Martha C. Nussbaum, "The Costs of Tragedy: Some Moral Limits of Cost-Benefit Analysis," 29 *Journal of Legal Studies* 1005 (2000); Nussbaum, note 17 above, at 14–21.

63. Richard Rorty, "Intellectuals in Politics: Too Far In? Too Far Out?" *Dissent*, Fall 1991, pp. 483, 484.

64. Nussbaum, note 17 above, at 24.

there is no prospect for bridging it. Intellectuality conduces to utopianism by stimulating the political imagination. The ordinary person has difficulty imagining an ordering of society radically different from the current one. The intellectual does not, and, being inclined by his calling to blame shortcomings on intellectual confusion rather than on practical impediments, thinks that merely pointing to the gap between ideals and achievement is a significant contribution to the cause of social reform.

I do not want to commit the utopian fallacy myself by commending cost–benefit analysis as a panacea for the issues that trouble Rorty and Nussbaum. At some point it will run aground on intractable issues involving religious commitment, cultural values, and the moral significance of expressed or revealed preferences. At that point the moral philosopher may have a role to play. The capabilities approach might then provide a checklist for making sure that, so far as possible, *all* relevant costs and benefits are counted and for smoking out adaptive preferences that seem inauthentic and alterable. Philosophy might even help us understand the importance to social reform of an empathetic awareness of the hopes and fears and sufferings of people who live in the Third World.

In *The Closing of the American Mind*,[65] Allan Bloom argues that the pragmatism of a Dewey or a Rorty is pernicious. This is another way of saying that the central philosophical tradition of the West is indispensable after all; and it has the odd consequence of making Martha Nussbaum and Allan Bloom bedfellows of a sort. Bloom speaks quite seriously of "the German invasion of the United States" (p. 215). By this he means the insidious (because unrecognized) conquest of American social thought by Hegel, Marx, Nietzsche, Freud, Weber, and Heidegger. Pragmatists, such as Dewey, and social scientists of every stripe are our quislings. "Our stars are singing a song they do not understand, translated from a German original . . . Behind it all, the master lyricists are Nietzsche and Heidegger" (p. 152). And there is worse:

---

65. Allan Bloom, *The Closing of the American Mind: How Higher Education Has Failed Democracy and Impoverished the Souls of Today's Students* (1987). Bloom's book may have sold more copies (one-half million in hardback within two years of its publication), and has almost certainly engendered greater controversy, than any other book by a modern American academic public intellectual. See *Essays on* The Closing of the American Mind (Robert L. Stone ed., 1989).

"it was while we were fighting [Hitler] that the thought that had preceded him in Europe conquered here. That thought, which gave him at
least some encouragement and did nothing to prepare us to understand
him, remains dominant" (p. 214). The thought that Bloom is discussing here is that of Max Weber (see pp. 211–214). Like Nussbaum,
Bloom is emphatic in denouncing value relativism, which he considers
the legacy of Nietzsche and Weber and the promise of social science.[66]
He would doubtless share her skepticism about conventional economic
reasoning. And he harks back to Socrates as frequently as she does.

But his celebration of the Western philosophical tradition carries
him in the opposite direction from Nussbaum. Far from thinking that
the tradition underwrites social reform, he thinks that any worldly concerns are utterly destructive of the tradition. A disciple of Leo Strauss,
he holds like his master that philosophy is a dangerous profession to its
practitioners and that beginning with Plato, who wanted to avoid Socrates' fate, philosophers have spoken in riddles.[67] The purpose of universities, the successors to Plato's Grove of Academe, is to provide a
haven for philosophers so that they can speak freely at last. "The university is the place where inquiry and philosophic openness come into
their own. It is intended to encourage the noninstrumental use of reason for its own sake, to provide the atmosphere where the moral and
physical superiority of the dominant will not intimidate philosophic
doubt" (p. 249). Science and the professions don't belong in a university; democracy, with its leveling instinct, its hatred of elites, is hostile
to the proper idea of the university; the pragmatic conception of reason
as a tool rather than as an end in itself is anathema to it. The university
should be a refuge against modernity, with all that modernity implies in
the way of democracy, equality, technology, and instrumental reasoning. The focus of a university education should be on what the Great
Books have to tell us about how to think about life's mysteries, such as
love and death. The deeply emotional content of university education
as Bloom conceives of it suggests an erotic bond between teacher and
student, putting the reader in mind of the *Symposium*.

Bloom is correct that "the noninstrumental use of reason" is an

66. A standard charge against Weber, leveled by, among others, Leo Strauss, Bloom's guru.
See the interesting discussion in John Patrick Diggins, *Max Weber: Politics and the Spirit of
Tragedy* 269–283 (1996).

67. See Leo Strauss, *Persecution and the Art of Writing* (1952).

ivory-tower enterprise and that philosophy is not an adjunct to the social sciences (one possible interpretation of Nussbaum's public-intellectual posture). However, for a philosopher to acknowledge that philosophers speak in riddles, that their writings have an esoteric as well as
an exoteric meaning, the former accessible only to adepts and the two
meanings often opposed to each other, makes it difficult to take *The
Closing of the American Mind* entirely seriously. It is now well known
that Bloom was a homosexual, although the book tries to conceal the
fact by referring to his first college girlfriend. This invites the esoteric
interpretation of his book as being aimed at making universities a haven for homosexuality. It also makes the book's denunciation of the
moral relativism of America's youth seem hypocritical. Its bestsellerdom may have rested on a huge misunderstanding.

The sheer *strangeness* of Bloom's position is a clue to the undiscriminating character of the public-intellectual market. Few nonacademic
readers of the book could have realized where he was coming from intellectually and politically, and most would have been appalled if they
had realized it. "Conservative rhetoricians," as Guyora Binder and
Robert Weisberg insightfully term Strauss and his followers, including
Bloom,

> present themselves as open-minded pluralists, seeking to make
> room for classical ideas in modern debate rather than to replace
> modern ideas. Yet this position may simply reflect an effort to ex-
> ploit the vulnerabilities of liberal ideas like value relativism, value
> neutrality, and tolerance. And it may reflect the awareness of these
> rhetoricians that classical ideas are unlikely to prevail with the
> general public in a modern liberal state. In any case, their teach-
> ings are not primarily directed at the public but at intellectual and
> political elites . . . Conservative rhetoricians place relatively little
> value on candor, which they associate with incontinent self-revela-
> tion and an irresponsible disregard for how information may be
> misused . . . [They] see themselves as a relatively powerless intel-
> lectual elite . . . that must ally with and civilize other sources of po-
> litical power in order to conserve itself and its values. [They] see
> the structure of rhetorical discourse as hierarchical. For those in-
> terlocutors unfit for initiation into wisdom, rhetoric serves to de-
> ceive and mollify. For those fit for instruction . . . a lengthy, sus-

penseful, and eroticized process of initiation serves to confirm the charismatic authority of the teachers and to socialize the pupils to deference and patience.[68]

They start at the same place, Nussbaum and Bloom, with the central philosophical tradition of the West heavily weighted toward the ancient Greek philosophers. Yet they end up at opposite ends of the current political-cultural spectrum. The difference is particularly marked when *The Closing of the American Mind* is juxtaposed with Nussbaum's book on university education, in which the classical philosophers, Socrates in particular, are enlisted in the cause of multicultural education, which is anathema to Bloom. So here is further evidence that philosophy cannot provide direction in practical matters, though it is not conclusive evidence, because Bloom or Nussbaum may have misconceived what is after all a complex tradition, as indeed Nussbaum argues Bloom has done.[69]

They have also, as I have noted, gleaned from the tradition diametrically opposed views of the proper role of the philosopher in relation to practical affairs. For Nussbaum, a natural role for a philosopher to play is that of the public intellectual. For Bloom (paradoxically, given his status as the bestselling American public intellectual of recent times) the role of the philosopher is to eschew the public sphere, to retreat to the university, there to commune with, as Nussbaum derisively puts it, "chosen souls"[70] while, for Rorty, to be a public intellectual requires renunciation of the philosophical tradition to which both Bloom and Nussbaum appeal. What a cacophony!

But that's not the right note on which to end a discussion of the public philosopher. I have mentioned John Stuart Mill a number of times in this book and now it is time to take his measure as a public intellectual, perhaps the greatest of the last two centuries (not the most influential—that dubious honor belongs to Karl Marx). Although it was the

---

68. Guyora Binder and Robert Weisberg, *Literary Criticisms of Law* 329–330 (2000). See also id. at 321–322.

69. *Cultivating Humanity* 33, 132, 298; also Martha Nussbaum, "Undemocratic Vistas," *New York Review of Books*, Nov. 5, 1987, p. 20. Bloom's defenders acknowledge a lack of scholarly rigor in his book. See Peter Shaw, *The War against the Intellect: Episodes in the Decline of Discourse* 173–174 (1989).

70. See Nussbaum, "Undemocratic Vistas," note 69 above.

prestige of Mill's scholarly work in logic and economics that got him a hearing for his public-intellectual work, his is not a case of using scholarly prestige to gain a platform for opining on unrelated matters. The most distinctive arguments made in *On Liberty* concerning the liberties discussed there—freedom of expression and liberty of conduct[71]—derive from Mill's scholarly work in the philosophy of science and in economics. Concerning freedom of expression, it is the fallibilist argument (a precursor of arguments made by such later philosophers of science as Charles Sanders Peirce and Karl Popper, and by Oliver Wendell Holmes, Jr.) that the validity of a hypothesis cannot be determined without making the hypothesis run the gauntlet of hostile challenge.[72] Concerning liberty of conduct, Mill's most distinctive argument is the economist's working assumption that people are better judges of their own self-interest than strangers are; Mill calls this the "strongest" argument against public interference with personal conduct (*On Liberty* 122). Concerning both liberties, there is the idea I mentioned earlier, also derived from observation of scientific practice, that intellectual and social progress is impossible without experimentation, including, in the realm of conduct, "experiments in living" (p. 81), which presuppose diversity of taste and outlook.

There is more, including a version of utilitarianism that can fairly be described as Aristotelian and insists that a happy human life requires the exercise of our highest, most distinctively human powers, and hence liberty, as the mindless contentment of Huxley's brave new worlders does not. The resemblance to Nussbaum's capabilities approach is not accidental; she is an admirer and to an extent a follower of Mill. But the distance between Mill's scholarly work in philosophy (which of course included a treatise on utilitarianism) and economics, and the broad libertarian theses of *On Liberty*, is shorter than that between Nussbaum's professional writing on classical philosophy and the policies, whether related to homosexual rights or economic development, advocated in her public-intellectual work.

What marks *On Liberty* as a public-intellectual work rather than a philosophical treatise is its brevity, concreteness, lucidity, and simple

71. The ideas in *The Subjection of Women* are largely derivative from the thesis on liberty of conduct propounded in *On Liberty*. Gertrude Himmelfarb, *On Liberty and Liberalism: The Case of John Stuart Mill*, ch. 7 (1974).

72. For the clearest statement, see Mill, note 30, at 30, cited hereinafter as *On Liberty*.

eloquence. It is not an academic work. It does not recite the pedigree of its ideas. Mill later acknowledged numerous precursors, but the only one named in the book is Wilhelm von Humboldt. From the standpoint of effective communication with nonscholars, the omission of the others is a strength rather than a weakness. *On Liberty* is not only written for nonspecialists; even today, almost a century and a half after its publication, it is accessible to the educated nonspecialist, something that can be said for few modern works of political philosophy.

My own view is that the liberty (or harm) principle that is at the center of *On Liberty* remains the best starting point for a public philosophy. "The sole end for which mankind are warranted, individually or collectively, in interfering with the liberty of action of any of their number, is self-protection," that is, "to prevent harm to others" (p. 13). Neither law (government regulation) nor morality (condemnation by public opinion) has any business with my "self-regarding" acts, only with my "other-regarding" acts, that is, acts that, like a punch in the nose, inflict temporal harm without consent or justification. (Unfortunately, this terminology has become somewhat obscure as a result of a shift in the connotation of "regarding." We are likely today to think of "self-regarding" as meaning selfish and "other-regarding" as altruistic.) The qualification in *temporal* is key. The harm must be tangible, secular, material—physical or financial, or if emotional focused and direct—rather than moral or spiritual. The line that separates what is the business of others from what is no one's business but one's own runs between slander and giving offense, between dynamiting a competitor's plant and competing with him by means of lower prices or better service or product quality, between rape and engaging in private consensual homosexual activities, between stopping a person from harming another and stopping him from harming himself, and, at its narrowest, between "offences against decency," such as drunkenness, committed in public and the same offenses committed in private (p. 145).

Mill's concept of liberty is thus intended to protect the individual from both well-meaning and hostile interferences with his autonomy. You are not to coerce him because you think you have a superior conception of how he should live (because, for example, you think he has false consciousness or adaptive preferences or fails to worship the true God); and you are not to force him to abandon his opinions or behavior simply because you find them or it offensive. It is the antithesis of Robert Bork's thesis that "no activity that society thinks immoral is victimless. Knowledge that an activity is taking place is a harm to those who find it profoundly immoral."[73] The modern Millian thus combines the antipaternalism and affection for the free market that are components of the ideology of the Republican Party with the tolerance of "deviant" personal behavior that is characteristic of the Democratic Party. The Millian stance offers the public intellectual a chance to stand apart from the current orthodoxies of the Left and the Right. It is a charter of intellectual independence.

Yet even Mill did not avoid the pitfalls of public-intellectual work. Mistaken prophecy, for one. He thought that Europe was being crushed by a spirit of conformity: "The modern *régime* of public opinion is, in an unorganised form, what the Chinese educational and political systems are in an organised" form. Europe was "decidedly advancing towards the Chinese ideal of making all people alike" (pp. 105–106). The spread of education, of communications, and of trade, and above all a trend toward greater social equality, were pushing Europe in that direction, seemingly inexorably (p. 107). Mill was largely unworried about government, however; he thought the days of governmental coercion of the citizenry largely over (wrong again) and that the real danger to be feared was the tyranny of public opinion. "That so few now dare to be eccentric marks the chief danger of the time" (p. 98). An eccentric statement if ever there was one! But the denunciation of conformism is one of the most durable of public-intellectual themes; we should not be surprised, therefore, that a century before David Riesman wrote *The Lonely Crowd*, Mill is telling us: "At present individuals are lost in the crowd" (p. 96).

On Liberty is also, as so much public-intellectual work is, superficial, perhaps owing to its brevity in relation to the breadth of the ground that it covers. To call a work both great and superficial is a paradox easily dispelled. *On Liberty* is great because of the clarity with which it expounds the liberty principle, though the principle itself seems not to have been entirely clear in Mill's mind, as I'm about to point out, and because of the distinctive arguments, sketched above, that *On Liberty* makes in support of the principle. *On Liberty* is superficial in its account of the scope of the principle—though not because, as has often been ar-

73. Robert H. Bork, *The Tempting of America: The Political Seduction of the Law* 123 (1990).

gued,[74] that scope depends on a theory of people's interests that Mill does not supply. If an individual has a legitimate interest in being spared the mental suffering that he experiences when another person ridicules his religious beliefs, that other person is guilty of an other-regarding act and therefore can, notwithstanding the liberty principle, be punished. But Mill fails to explain whether insult is a part of liberty or an infringement of right, although his theory provides the framework for answering the question. The answer should depend on whether privileging some class of insults promotes social and economic progress by encouraging free thinking and experiments in living, whether in other words the long-term benefits of protecting that amount of liberty exceed the costs.

This is fine as theory, but lacks operational content. The most interesting questions about freedom of speech concern its limitations, which Mill does not discuss, apart from the obvious one that it is does not extend to incitements to crime. About libel and slander; about copyright and plagiarism; about sedition; about the theater, parades, picketing, and other demonstrations; about anonymous pamphleting; about obscenity—about all these he is silent. The most interesting questions about liberty of conduct also concern its limitations. Mill makes a number of arguments and proposals that are in tension with his advocacy of liberty of conduct. He says that voluntarily to enslave oneself is inconsistent with liberty of conduct; yet we "enslave" ourselves every time we sign an employment contract. He declares suicide inconsistent with that liberty, even though the decision whether to live or to die would seem to be the ultimate self-regarding act. He says that while it would be improper for the U.S. government or anyone else to interfere with Mormon polygamy in Utah, it would be proper for England to refuse to recognize the validity of a polygamous marriage of Mormons who have come to England, let alone to permit English people to make such marriages, because polygamy is a form of female slavery even when desired by women. He would forbid people to marry unless they could show that they had the financial means to support any children the marriage might produce. He argues that since government has to raise revenue by means of taxation, it might as well tax goods of

74. For example in John Gray, "Introduction," in John Stuart Mill, *On Liberty and Other Essays* vii, xvii–xviii (1991).

which "it deems the use, beyond a very moderate quantity, to be positively injurious" (p. 149), namely liquor. But to the extent that the tax
deters the consumption of the good, it will reduce the revenue raised
by it. Hence the fact that the government must tax does not justify a tax
intended to interfere with people's self-regarding acts, as distinct from a
revenue-maximizing tax that might have an unintended such side-ef-
fect. From the overarching social goal of enabling people to exercise
their rational faculties, Mill derives an argument for universal education at no cost to the poor. But he neglects to note that taxation is a
form of coercion and thus a prima facie infringement of liberty and that
in the case of education the infringement cannot be defended by reference to the harm principle because a person's inability to finance his
children's education is not (not generally, at any rate) the fault of the
well-to-do.

The point is not that these and other interferences with liberty of
conduct cannot be reconciled with Mill's ruling principles; it is that he
makes no, or only perfunctory and unpersuasive, efforts to do so. But
the rough edges in Mill's book can be placed in the proper perspective
by reading the book in the proper way—not as a treatise but as a provocation, in the best tradition of public-intellectual work. Conservatives,
as we saw in the last chapter, are still rising to its bait.

～ *10*

The Public Intellectual
and the Law

$\mathcal{T}$HE DREYFUS AFFAIR marked the public intellectual's twentieth-century début. An auspicious début it was. Zola and other intellectuals were instrumental in rectifying a miscarriage of justice that had grave political overtones. Public intellectuals—some of them lawyers, some not—have continued to interest themselves in law. Two public-intellectual genres are involved. One is "real-time" commentary, that is, commentary on current events, which in the legal setting usually involves commenting on an ongoing trial or other legal proceeding. I illustrated this genre in Chapter 3 with the Clinton impeachment, to which I'll recur briefly in this chapter; it is the *locus classicus* of the difficulty that the modern public intellectual has in contributing constructively to debate on urgent public issues while they are unfolding. The intervention of public intellectuals in the debate over the impeachment, and to an extent in the impeachment proceedings themselves (recall Sean Wilentz's testimony before the House Judiciary Committee), was not an isolated case. It was the culmination of a long series of dubious interventions by public intellectuals on behalf of criminals who enlisted their sympathy—the innocent Dreyfus's guilty successors, such as Sacco and Vanzetti, Alger Hiss, Ezra Pound, Robert Brasillach, the Rosenbergs, and Huey Newton and other Black Panthers.

The other genre in which law and the public intellectual intersect is

359

expert witnessing, and let me start there. Courts allow "experts" to offer their opinions in the form of testimony, whereas the nonexpert witness is permitted to testify only about matters of which he has first-hand knowledge.[1] Most expert testimony is by engineers, physicians, scientists, psychiatrists, and economists and concerns technical matters, though some of these witnesses are public intellectuals and testify about matters with ideological implications, such as Stephen Jay Gould's testimony, given in a First Amendment case involving freedom of religion, that the biblical account of creation is not scientifically respectable.[2] Professors of "softer" subjects, like history, philosophy, literature, art, and music, sometimes testify as experts too. But again it is usually on very narrow issues such as the provenance of a work of art or whether one piece of music was copied from another. Occasionally, however, they testify on nontechnical issues, such as the social worth or the originality of a book or movie or painting, in a case involving obscenity or libel, or historical truth (did the Holocaust really occur?), or the social effects of sexual harassment or racial discrimination. Testimony is not limited to the courtroom. The testimony by Sean Wilentz before the House Judiciary Committee on whether to impeach President Clinton was given under oath in a quasi-judicial proceeding, because the House of Representative corresponds in an impeachment to the grand jury in a criminal proceeding. And the participation of intellectuals in the legal process is not limited to testimony. A court will occasionally permit the views of public intellectuals to be submitted to it in the form of an *amicus curiae* ("friend of the court") brief.

In the case that successfully challenged a provision of the Colorado constitution that forbade the state's municipalities to pass ordinances forbidding discrimination against homosexuals,[3] Martha Nussbaum opined in the form of oral testimony and a subsequent trial affidavit[4] on the attitude of the Greek philosophers toward homosexuality. She was

---

1. See Rules 602 and 701–703 of the Federal Rules of Evidence.

2. See Stephen Jay Gould, *Rocks of Ages: Science and Religion in the Fullness of Life* 139–145 (1999). Cf. Epperson v. Arkansas, 393 U.S. 97 (1968).

3. Romer v. Evans, 517 U.S. 620 (1996). She published an amplified version of her affidavit as an article, "Platonic Love and Colorado Law: The Relevance of Ancient Greek Norms to Modern Sexual Controversies," 80 *Virginia Law Review* 1515 (1994). I cited an abridged version of that article—chapter 11 of Nussbaum, *Sex and Social Justice* (1999)—in discussing her views on the subject in the last chapter.

4. An affidavit is given under oath and is the equivalent of testimony.

rebutting (among others) John Finnis, a law professor, philosopher, and devout Catholic who argued in his testimony that the ancient Greeks disapproved of homosexuality, and Harvey Mansfield, a professor of political science who also testified in favor of the Colorado constitutional provision. The only reference to any of these bodies of testimony in the judicial opinions in the case is a glancing reference in a dissenting opinion to Mansfield's testimony that the provision promoted political stability and respect for the political process by reining in local governments responding to what might be unrepresentative fractions of the state's entire electorate.[5] Similarly, the "philosophers' brief" submitted by Ronald Dworkin, John Rawls, Thomas Nagel, and other philosophers in the Supreme Court's assisted-suicide cases is not mentioned in any of the opinions in those cases.[6]

When one considers the ideological character of the discourse of "public intellectuals" as I am using the term, it is not surprising that courts are reluctant to welcome them as participants in the legal process. An exception that proves (that is, probes) the rule is the remarkable opinion by federal district judge William B. Hand (no relation to Learned) in *Smith v. Board of School Commissioners*.[7] The case had begun as an effort by the father of a schoolchild to enjoin, as an infringement of religious freedom, prayer services in the public schools of Mobile, Alabama, which the child attended. The Supreme Court had long held that school prayer violates the religion clauses of the First Amendment. Although the First Amendment is addressed to the federal government rather than to the states ("Congress shall make no law abridging . . ."), the Court had interpreted the due process clause of the Fourteenth

5. Evans v. Romer, 882 P.2d 1335, 1364 n. 8 (Colo. 1994) (dissenting opinion). The trial judge discussed expert testimony bearing on the causes of homosexuality and the history of discrimination against homosexuals. Evans v. Romer, 1993 WL 518586, at *11 (Denver County, Colorado, District Court, Dec. 14, 1993). The attitudes of the ancient Greeks and Romans toward homosexual conduct may have seemed relevant to the lawyers in *Romer* because of Chief Justice Burger's concurring opinion in Bowers v. Hardwick, 478 U.S. 186, 196 (1986), the case that upheld the constitutionality of state sodomy statutes, in which he stated: "Decisions of individuals relating to homosexual conduct have been subject to state intervention throughout the history of Western civilization." He cited a Roman statute in support of this proposition, but no Greek sources.

6. Washington v. Glucksberg, 521 U.S. 702 (1997); Vacco v. Quill, 521 U.S. 793 (1997). I discuss the brief, which unsuccessfully urged recognition of a constitutional right to assisted suicide, in Richard A. Posner *The Problematics of Moral and Legal Theory* 130–133 (1999).

7. 655 F. Supp. 939 (S.D. Ala.), reversed, 827 F.2d 684 (11th Cir. 1987).

Amendment, which *is* addressed to the states, to incorporate the prohi-
bitions of the First Amendment and thus make them limitations on
state and local government, including public school systems. Judge
Hand, in defiance of the Supreme Court, rejected the incorporation
theory and was duly reversed[8] with instructions that he issue the in-
junction that the plaintiff had asked for. With the case therefore before
him once more, he unexpectedly held that the Mobile public school
system was violating the First Amendment not only by conducting
prayers, as his judicial superiors had insisted, but also by discriminating
in its choice of textbooks in favor of the "religion" of "secular humanism" or "atheistic humanism," a religion whose leaders, the judge explained, included John Dewey and Sidney Hook. The judge enjoined
the school system from teaching from thirty-nine textbooks in home
economics, history, and social studies that he found to be infected by
this religion. He was again reversed.[9] On his view of "religion," virtually no textbook in widespread use in American public schools is free
from taint, since the bland and innocuous books that he enjoined had
betrayed their secular-humanist faith only by emphasizing personal responsibility and omitting a specifically Christian viewpoint on personal
conduct.

Judge Hand's long and superficially erudite opinion relies on testimony by experts in a variety of fields, including psychology and philosophy. The opinion gives particular weight to the testimony of Russell
Kirk, the well-known conservative public intellectual from whom I
quoted a passage of criticism of John Stuart Mill in Chapter 8. Kirk
testified about Dewey and progressive education, about the intimidation of textbook publishers by "well organized pressure groups" hostile
to organized religion, and about the dulling effect of "philosophies fa-
thered by Dewey" on instruction in teachers colleges. Kirk criticized
secular humanists (who he testified should rather be labeled "humani-
tarians") for teaching, erroneously in his view, that man has no soul.[10]
He declared that secular humanism, or humanitarianism, like Marxism,
is a religion.

Kirk was right that the institutional structure and spiritual characteristic of theistic religions can also be found in atheistic bodies of thought

8. Jaffree v. Wallace, 705 F.2d 1526 (11th Cir. 1983), affirmed, 472 U.S. 38 (1985).

9. See note 7 above.

10. My quotations are from the judge's summary of Kirk's testimony. See 655 F. Supp. at
956–957, 959, 961–963, 968–969.

and practice. I pointed out in Chapter 7 the affinities between Soviet communism and Roman Catholicism;[11] they are even closer between, say, Unitarianism (theistic) and Ethical Culture (atheistic). Even the Supreme Court has described "secular humanism" as a religion.[12] But Kirk's testimony—characteristically ignored along with all the other expert testimony by the court of appeals in its opinion reversing Judge Hand—missed both the narrow and the broad point that tells decisively against the judge's result. The narrow point is that none of the offending textbooks advocated "secular humanism"; they merely ignored religion. The broad point is that the First Amendment cannot sensibly be interpreted to forbid public schools to use textbooks that either promote Christianity *or* fail to promote it; it is impossible to write such a textbook.

In expressing skepticism about the role of the public intellectual in the courtroom, I do not mean to deny that the views of public intellectuals may influence judges. Judges read books and magazines, just like other people (in fact a little more so), and so are exposed to writings by public intellectuals that may alter their outlook on issues that may later arise in cases. It would be difficult to trace this influence because judges don't usually cite, or otherwise account for, the nonprofessional sources of their judicial views, especially when those sources are political or otherwise ideological. That is why judges are reluctant to acknowledge the public intellectual as a participant in the judicial process: it would look unprofessional. It is why, perhaps, the "philosophers' brief" was not very philosophical—had in fact been drafted by a law firm and but for the professional affiliations of the *amici* might well have been thought a conventional lawyer's brief.

One place to look for evidence of influence is judicial biographies. There we discover, if we didn't know already, that a number of well-known judges, such as Oliver Wendell Holmes, Louis Brandeis, Benjamin Cardozo, Felix Frankfurter, and Learned Hand, were avid readers of the writings of intellectuals. They did not merely read but also consorted on a personal level with many of the influential intellec-

11. See also Paul Hollander, *Political Will and Personal Belief: The Decline and Fall of Soviet Communism* 294–296 (1999).

12. Torcaso v. Watkins, 367 U.S. 488, 495 n. 11 (1961). Justice Scalia reminded his colleagues of this in his dissenting opinion in Edwards v. Aguillard, 482 U.S. 578, 635 n. 6 (1987), a case involving a Louisiana law that required that any teaching of the theory of evolution in public schools be accompanied by instruction in "creation science."

tuals of their time (including each other!). Traces of the thought of these intellectuals are evident in some of these judges' opinions—for example, the thought of Emerson, James Fitzjames Stephen, Herbert Spencer, and Charles Sanders Peirce in Holmes's opinions. By 1962, however, all these judges had either died or (in the case of Frankfurter) retired from the bench. Their successors have been less intellectual and more narrowly professional. It is one more example of the decline of the independent public intellectual.

This is not to say that judges have become political eunuchs. During the Reagan and Bush administrations, several conservative academics (myself included) were appointed to federal courts of appeals in the hope of correcting a perceived liberal ideological tilt in those courts. One of these academic lawyers made it to the Supreme Court (Scalia) and another (Bork) was tripped up at the threshold. And Clarence Thomas at his confirmation hearing was quizzed on whether he was an adherent to the philosophy of natural law. Recently a number of Reagan and Bush judicial appointees have been criticized for accepting invitations to seminars sponsored by conservative think tanks; it has even been argued that some of their votes in cases have been swayed by the conservative "brainwashing" they received there.[13] Some conservative judges socialize with conservative public intellectuals, moreover—and some liberal judges with liberal public intellectuals.

All that this shows, however, is that at the higher levels of the judiciary, where the conventional materials of decision cannot resolve a case and the judge must fall back on his values, his intuitions, and, on occasion, his ideology, public-intellectual work may have an effect on the judicial process. How large an effect one cannot say. But what is clear is that the work of public intellectuals is only one of the nonlegal influences on judges, others being temperament, life experiences, moral principles, party politics, religious belief or nonbelief, and academic ideas.

◠ THE ONLY AREA of law in which public intellectuals have played a significant *testimonial* role of late (the impeachment of President Clinton to one side) is obscenity. The modern law of obscenity requires the court to decide whether a sexually graphic work has any re-

---

13. Doug Kendall, *Nothing for Free: How Private Judicial Seminars Are Undermining Environmental Protections and Breaking the Public's Trust* (Community Rights Counsel July 2000). I have never attended such a seminar.

deeming social value; if it does, the work is held to be protected by the First Amendment from censorship or punishment. It is common for literary, film, art, dance, or music critics (as the case may be) to be used as expert witnesses on whether the work alleged to be obscene has redeeming social value.[14] The testimony elicited from them tends, however, to be uncritical; they will find socially redeeming value in virtually anything. In one of my own cases, *Piarowski v. Illinois Community College District 515*,[15] the chairman of the University of Chicago's fine-arts department testified to the merit of a stained-glass version of Aubrey Beardsley's pornographic drawings. The charm of the drawings lies in the delicacy and sinuosity of the lines and was completely lost when the drawings were transformed into mosaics, but the witness nevertheless testified that the rendition was interesting and worthwhile. I cannot believe that his private opinion was other than that it was kitsch. But he was standing up for freedom of artistic expression, like the literature professor in *Dillingham v. State*[16] who testified to the redeeming value of a newspaper cartoon depicting a local judge, naked, sitting on a swastika-decorated chair and masturbating.

People professionally involved in the arts, whether as producers or as academic scholars, are for obvious reasons hostile to censorship and dismayed by philistine judges.[17] They know that the best way to defeat censorship is to establish the existence of redeeming social value in all the works that the censors want to suppress, as that will put the censors out of business. So they are led to stretch their normal critical standards to accommodate what typically, in the kind of case brought nowadays, is trash. (Typically, but not always; Robert Mapplethorpe's sexually graphic photographs, the basis of an unsuccessful criminal prosecution of the director of the Cincinnati Art Museum, have undoubted aesthetic merit.)[18] This is another manifestation of academic holiday spirit. The critic who testifies in a courtroom knows that his

14. See Frank Kermode, "'Obscenity' and the 'Public Interest,'" 3 *New American Review* 229 (1968); Al Katz, "Free Discussion v. Final Decision: Moral and Artistic Controversy and the *Tropic of Cancer* Trials," 79 *Yale Law Journal* 209 (1969).

15. 759 F.2d 625 (7th Cir. 1985).

16. 267 A.2d 777, 791 (Md. App. 1970).

17. See, for example, the dissenting opinion in a case that held that William Burroughs's novel *Naked Lunch* was not legally obscene. Attorney General v. A Book Named 'Naked Lunch,' 218 N.E.2d 571, 574–578 (Mass. 1966), referring to "Morman Mailer, novelist." Id. at 575 n. 7.

18. Richard A. Posner, *Sex and Reason* 352–353 (1992).

testimony will never be submitted to a jury of his academic peers—that if they get wind of it at all they will commend him for doing the Lord's work in trying to hamstring the prosecution.

That he may be bending, or even knowingly violating, the oath he swore when he took the witness stand is unlikely to bother him or his academic peers. Oath-taking is not among the rules of the academic game. Academic books and articles do not begin with an oath by the author to tell the truth, the whole truth, and nothing but the truth. This is not to say that academics do not have and comply with norms, including a norm of truth-telling, though some postmodernist academics reject it, regarding their academic work as political work governed by political norms, of which truth-telling, we know, is not one. That spirit is abroad in some of the literature departments of American universities.[19] But my point is only that the academic norm of truth-telling, insofar as it exists, is not expressed in or enforced by oaths. The oath is part of a normative system to which the academic is not native and that he is inclined therefore to scoff at. He is not alone in this; even before President Clinton's collision with the norm of truth-telling in judicial proceedings, many witnesses in such proceedings could not be trusted to take seriously their oath to tell the truth, the whole truth, and nothing but the truth.

I doubt, therefore, that most academics think that testifying under oath as an expert witness in court or before a legislative committee is much different from signing a full-page advertisement urging a particular result upon a court or legislature. Both activities are to their academic careers as making an occasional commercial is to a serious actor. And whatever they think, being questioned in a courtroom is a different experience from the give-and-take of academic debate and is likely to elicit statements that lack the precision and nuance of academic writing.

As Daniel Mendelsohn has put it, "the narrow requirements of legal discourse as it actually proceeds may ultimately be incompatible with the expansive nature of serious humanistic inquiry."[20] He was dis-

19. See, for example, Chris Hedges, "New Activists Are Nurtured by Politicized Curriculums," *New York Times* (national ed.), May 27, 2000, p. A17. Cf. Barbara Epstein, "Postmodernism and the Left," in *The Sokal Hoax: The Sham That Shook the Academy* 214 (edited by the editors of *Lingua Franca*, 2000).

20. Daniel Mendelsohn, "The Stand: Expert Witnesses and Ancient Mysteries in a Colorado Courtroom," *Lingua Franca*, Sept./Oct. 1996, pp. 34, 46.

cussing the accusation that in her affidavit and oral testimony in the *Romer* case Martha Nussbaum had misrepresented the degree to which Greek philosophers approved of homosexuality.[21] Her affidavit and testimony have the feel, the tone, of advocacy. They give short shrift to, and sometimes ignore altogether, the contrary evidence—not mentioning, for example, contrary evidence in one of her own books.[22] These characteristics of her submissions at trial are thrown into relief by a comparison with the subsequent academic versions, which confront many though not all of the criticisms of her principal antagonist, John Finnis.[23] Even the academic versions, however, revealing their origin in the heat of forensic combat, give a one-sided picture of the Greek attitude toward specific homosexual practices, especially anal intercourse, and understate the Greeks' ambivalence toward lesbianism and male homosexuality.[24] After criticizing the partisanship evident in the competing testimony of Nussbaum and Finnis (and Finnis's ally Robert George) concerning Plato's *Laws*, Randall Clark remarks "the

21. See "Rebuttal Affidavit of John Mitchell Finnis," Evans v. Romer, No. 92 CV 7223, Denver County, Colorado, District Court, Oct. 21, 1993; "Addendum to Rebuttal Affidavit of John Mitchell Finnis," id., Oct. 27, 1993; John Finnis, "'Shameless Acts' in Colorado: Abuse of Scholarship in Constitutional Cases," *Academic Questions*, Fall 1994, p. 10; Gerard V. Bradley, "In the Case of Martha Nussbaum," *First Things*, June/July 1994, p. 11. Finnis accuses Nussbaum of "untruths and gross misrepresentations." Finnis, "'Shameless Acts' in Colorado: Abuse of Scholarship in Constitutional Cases," above, at 36. Robert P. George, in his article "'Shameless Acts' Revisited: Some Questions for Martha Nussbaum," *Academic Questions*, Winter 1995–1996, pp. 24, 26, states that "since Professor Nussbaum testified under oath, her misrepresentations, if she knew them to be such, probably constituted perjury"—and he then goes on to argue that undoubtedly she did know them to be such. Nussbaum believes that Finnis and George were trying to provoke her into suing them for libel. She did not rise to the bait.

22. See Martha C. Nussbaum, *The Fragility of Goodness: Luck and Ethics in Greek Tragedy and Philosophy* 143 (1986). Finnis notes, among other things, the implausibility of Nussbaum's testimony that Christianity began to have a big impact on Greek sexual mores in the first century A.D.—a period in which Christianity was still nascent and obscure. Finnis, "'Shameless Acts' in Colorado: Abuse of Scholarship in Constitutional Cases," note 21 above, at 21.

23. Compare Reporter's Transcript, Evans v. Romer, No. 92 CV 7223, Denver County, Colorado, District Court, Oct. 15, 1993, pp. 797, 809, and Affidavit of Martha C. Nussbaum, id., Oct. 21, 1993, with Nussbaum, "Platonic Love and Colorado Law: The Relevance of Ancient Greek Norms to Modern Sexual Controversies," note 4 above, and *Sex and Social Justice*, also note 3 above, at 306.

24. See George, note 21 above; Eva C. Keuls, *The Reign of the Phallus: Sexual Politics in Ancient Athens*, ch. 11 (1985); David Cohen, *Law, Sexuality, and Society: The Enforcement of Morals in Classical Athens*, ch. 7 (1991); Bruce S. Thornton, *Eros: The Myth of Ancient Greek Sexuality* 250 n. 60, 265 n. 206 (1997), and indexed references in his book to "Homosexuality"; Daniel H. Garrison, *Sexual Culture in Ancient Greece* 161 (2000).

persistence of this methodology in the post-trial publications proffered by each of the participants."[25]

An *amicus curiae* brief was submitted in the important post–*Roe v. Wade* abortion case of *Webster v. Reproductive Health Services*[26] on behalf of hundreds of historians (initially 281, but about 120 others joined later).[27] The brief relied heavily on a study of the history of American public policy toward abortion written by James Mohr,[28] one of the signatories, as the brief emphasizes. In fact the brief contradicted his study, as he later backhandedly acknowledged by calling the brief not "history, as I understand that craft" but rather "a political document" that he had signed as a citizen as well as an historian—had signed not because it was consistent with his book, which it was not, but because it "comport[ed] more fully with my understanding of the past than the historical arguments mounted by the other side, some of which also cite my work."[29] The historians' brief cites Mohr's book for the proposition that abortion was not illegal at common law, yet at the very pages cited Mohr states that abortion was legal only before quickening (that is, before the mother could feel the first fetal movements).[30] The brief also cites Mohr for the proposition that physicians' opposition to abortion during the nineteenth century was based primarily on a desire to control reproductive health care. But Mohr's book emphasizes moral and related scientific considerations, primarily that once the scientific significance of quickening was rejected and physicians "decided that human life was present to some extent in a newly fertilized ovum, however limited that extent might be, they became the fierce opponents of

25. Randall Baldwin Clark, "Platonic Love in a Colorado Courtroom: Martha Nussbaum, John Finnis, and Plato's *Laws* in *Evans v. Romer*," 12 *Yale Journal of Law and the Humanities* 1, 5 (2000). See also id. at 6. He was discussing the articles by Finnis and George that I have cited in notes 21 and 24 above.

26. 492 U.S. 490 (1989).

27. Brief of 281 American Historians as Amici Curiae Supporting Appellees, 1988 *U.S. Briefs* 605 (March 30, 1989), in Webster v. Reproductive Health Services, No. 88–605, U.S. Supreme Court, October Term 1988.

28. James C. Mohr, *Abortion in America: The Origins and Evolution of National Policy, 1800–1900* (1978).

29. James C. Mohr, "Historically Based Legal Briefs: Observations of a Participant in the *Webster* Process," 12 *Public Historian*, Summer 1990, pp. 19, 25. The discrepancies between the brief and Mohr's book are reviewed in Finnis, "'Shameless Acts' in Colorado: Abuse of Scholarship in Constitutional Cases," note 21 above, at 12–13, 16–18.

30. Mohr, note 28 above, at 3–19.

any attack upon it."[31] "Most physicians considered abortion a crime because of the inherent difficulties of determining any point at which a steadily developing embryo became somehow more alive than it had been the moment before. Furthermore, they objected strongly to snuffing out life in the making."[32]

Mohr's signing the brief, rather than submitting a truthful statement of his views, was not perjurious, because briefs are not signed under oath. But it was misleading and unprofessional. One recalls from Chapter 3 that another historian signed a political advertisement that contradicted his own contemporaneously published views of the Clinton impeachment controversy, while a third historian, testifying before the House Judiciary Committee that was considering whether to impeach President Clinton, seems not to have been scrupulous about the accuracy of what he was saying, even though he was testifying under oath. We have also noticed that an academic who testifies under oath and then prepares an academic version of his testimony may feel committed to the line taken in the testimony even if his academic research reveals that the testimony was mistaken.

Once the wholly theoretical possibility of being prosecuted for perjury is set to one side, it becomes apparent that a public intellectual is unlikely to pay any price for giving false, exaggerated, or otherwise misleading testimony. The academic standing of Nussbaum, Finnis, and George has not been affected by their squabble, despite its fierceness and covert accusations of perjury. Just as in the case of the public intellectual's erroneous predictions, there is no accountability for inaccuracy (or worse) in testimony by public intellectuals. Indeed, it is even harder to keep track of a public intellectual's testimony than of most other public-intellectual work, because courtroom testimony, although nominally public, is not published and is therefore not readily obtainable by outsiders. Often it will be squirreled away in a warehouse from which an outsider can extract it, if at all, only after a long delay.

This analysis is supported by another forensic venture by a historian, the testimony by Alice Kessler-Harris in a sex discrimination case against Sears Roebuck.[33] Testifying on behalf of the Equal Employ-

31. Id. at 36.
32. Id. at 165.
33. EEOC v. Sears, Roebuck & Co., 628 F. Supp. 1264 (N.D. Ill. 1986), affirmed, 839 F.2d 302 (7th Cir. 1988). The discussion that follows is based on Thomas Haskell and Sanford

ment Opportunity Commission, Professor Kessler-Harris testified that history showed (most improbably) that the allocation of gender roles in the workplace had *nothing* to do with women's interests; only employer discrimination could explain the fact that men preponderate in some types of job and women in other types. As Thomas Haskell and Sanford Levinson point out, "Kessler-Harris's claim is obviously extreme, for it attributes entirely to employers an outcome that is produced by the choices of both employers and female employees."[34] They bolster this claim by noting that, "since the trial, even Kessler-Harris has conceded that the pressure of the adversary system caused her to exaggerate."[35] Echoing Mohr, she has acknowledged that to refute Sears' historian witness, Rosalind Rosenberg, she "found [her]self constructing a rebuttal in which subtlety and nuance were omitted, and in which evidence was marshaled to make a point while complexities and exceptions vanished from sight."[36] She appears to have incurred no adverse consequences from this frank acknowledgement, or from the fact that, again as in Mohr's case (but she was testifying under oath), the statements in her academic writings flatly contradicted her testimony at trial.[37] On the contrary, "in spite of Kessler-Harris's obvious exaggeration, feminist scholars generally have praised her testimony and criticized that of Rosenberg."[38] In fact, as Haskell and Kessler-Harris show, feminist scholars have vilified and ostracized Rosenberg. One interpretation is that academics regard the courtroom as a political forum in which concerns for accuracy should play no part; the oath be damned.

⌒ THE MISMATCH between the courtroom and the intellectual is further shown by the long history of mistaken revisionist challenges to court judgments by public intellectuals, and by the occasional use of

---

Levinson, "Academic Freedom and Expert Witnessing: Historians and the *Sears* Case," 66 *Texas Law Review* 1629 (1988); Haskell and Levinson, "On Academic Freedom and Hypothetical Pools: A Reply to Alice Kessler-Harris," 67 *Texas Law Review* 1591 (1989). See also the brief discussion in Peter Novick, *That Noble Dream: The "Objectivity Question" and the American Historical Profession* 504 (1988).

34. Haskell and Levinson, "Academic Freedom and Expert Witnessing: Historians and the *Sears* Case," note 33 above, at 1635.

35. Id. at 1635.

36. Id., quoting Alice Kessler-Harris, "Equal Employment Opportunity Commission v. Sears, Roebuck and Company: A Personal Account," 35 *Radical History Review* 57, 74 (1986).

37. Haskell and Levinson, "Academic Freedom and Expert Witnessing: Historians and the *Sears* Case," note 33 above, at 1650, 1654.

38. Id. at 1635.

mock trials to answer historical questions, such as whether Richard III killed the little princes or whether Francis Bacon or the Earl of Oxford, rather than William Shakespeare of Stratford, was the real author of Shakespeare's plays. Dignified and prestigious judges, including justices of the U.S. Supreme Court, have presided at such trials. Such trials are a mistake. They convey the false impression that the adversary method is a proper method for determining historical truth. By doing this they play into the hands of Holocaust deniers and other nuts (of whom indeed the people who believe that "that man from Stratford" was not the author of Shakespeare's plays may be some). As Lawrence Douglas has pointed out, the arguments made by the growing corps of Holocaust deniers "powerfully evoke the rhetoric of attorneys practiced in the art of adversarial litigation . . . By casting the trial as a truth-seeking device, the [deniers] are thus able to present the most tendentious and partisan hyperbole as a proper contribution to public debate and historical instruction." Yet criminal justice "has long been dedicated to values such as protecting the dignity and autonomy of the accused that may actually disable the pursuit of truth in a particular case."[39] Supreme Court justices who participate in mock trials of Shakespeare's authorship do not realize that by doing so they are conferring legitimacy on a misuse of trial procedure that undermines standards of historical accuracy, just as academic public intellectuals who give expert testimony in (real) trials may compromise their academic integrity by yielding to the pressures to conform their testimony to the exigencies of trial procedure—a procedure that has additional aims besides determining what is true.[40]

"Additional aims besides determining what is true"—yes, but it doesn't follow, as revisionary public intellectuals are wont to argue, that the courts *typically* get the facts wrong. An example of this revisionary literature is Janet Malcolm's book *The Crime of Sheila McGough* (1999).[41] The author tries to demonstrate the innocence of a woman lawyer who was convicted of having aided and abetted a con man's fraudulent activities. I don't think she succeeds,[42] but that is neither

39. Lawrence Douglas, "The Memory of Judgment: The Law, the Holocaust, and Denial," 7 *History and Memory* 100, 109–110 (1996).

40. This is Mendelsohn's point too. See note 20 above.

41. Which I discuss at greater length in my book *Frontiers of Legal Theory*, ch. 10 (2001).

42. See id.; also Stephan Landsman, "The Perils of Courtroom Stories," 98 *Michigan Law Review* 2154 (2000).

here nor there. What marks Malcolm's book as the work of a public intellectual rather than merely that of a muckraking journalist is its resort to postmodernist skepticism to raise radical questions about the accuracy of the criminal justice system. She says such things as: "The prosecutor prosecuting an innocent person or the defense lawyer defending a guilty client actually have an easier task than their opposite numbers . . . Truth is messy, incoherent, aimless, boring, absurd," and so can prevail at trial only if "laboriously transformed into a kind of travesty of itself" (p. 26). "Trials are won by attorneys whose stories fit, and lost by those whose stories are like the shapeless housecoat that truth, in her disdain for appearances, has chosen as her uniform" (p. 67). "Law stories are empty stories. They take the reader to a world entirely constructed of tendentious argument, and utterly devoid of the truth of the real world, where things are allowed to fall as they may" (pp. 78–79).

All this is greatly exaggerated. Truth is not always "messy, incoherent, aimless, boring, absurd." Often it is clear and riveting, and when it is, as in the case against Sheila McGough which Malcolm insists on mystifying, the law can find it and use it just fine. More troubled than the courtroom's relation to truth is the public intellectual's relation to the courtroom.

⌒ THE EVENTS leading up to Clinton's impeachment, the impeachment proceedings themselves, and the Senate trial were rich in issues of law, public policy, and political and social theory that agitated the nation for more than a year and that continue to generate aftershocks. The media turned to academics for help, many of whom volunteered without having to be drafted by the media. As we saw in Chapter 3, academics signed petitions to Congress and full-page advertisements. They even conducted teach-ins, notably the "Rally against Impeachment" at New York University's law school. The Clinton impeachment showcased the academic lawyer as public intellectual.

Ronald Dworkin is well known for believing that the law in general and constitutional law in particular should be recast as a branch of normative moral philosophy,[43] and for his criticisms of conservative Su-

---

43. See, for example, Ronald Dworkin, *Law's Empire* (1986); Dworkin, "In Praise of Theory," 29 *Arizona State Law Journal* 353 (1997).

preme Court decisions and conservative jurists in the pages of the *New York Review of Books*. He is less well known for his role in the resistance to the impeachment of President Clinton. My book on the impeachment, *An Affair of State*, was sharply critical of that role;[44] and in another book, published at about the same time, I argued, with many critical references to Dworkin, that normative moral philosophy is a weak field in its own right and has nothing to offer law.[45] Dworkin reviewed both books in the *New York Review of Books*.[46]

Dworkin's interventions in the Clinton imbroglio may seem a minor and unrepresentative aspect of his public-intellectual work. They are not. Though distinguishable from his commentary on constitutional cases, they are of a piece with his very public opposition to the appointments of Robert Bork and Clarence Thomas to the Supreme Court, which, as we'll see, mark Dworkin as a *partisan* public intellectual and not just a public philosopher in the style of Nussbaum or Rorty. They also bear on the question of the quality of public-intellectual work disseminated by unfiltered media, such as general-interest magazines and the Internet. "Dworkin's relentless 'spin' and partisanship" and his "reluctance . . . to make and confront the best arguments against [his] own views"[47] have not been confined to the unfiltered media. But they are especially pronounced there, and they illustrate a two-track strategy

44. See Richard A. Posner, *An Affair of State: The Investigation, Impeachment, and Trial of President Clinton* 233–235, 237–241 (1999). I cite this book in this chapter as *"Affair of State."*

45. Posner, *The Problematics of Moral and Legal Theory*, note 6 above, at 130–136, 253–255. I cite this book as *"Problematics."*

46. Ronald Dworkin, "Philosophy and Monica Lewinsky," *New York Review of Books*, March 9, 2000, p. 48. I cite this piece as *"NYRB."* He supplemented his review with two Web postings (available on New York University's Web page), one of which, "The Mistakes Were Posner's Not the Scholars," responds to my criticisms in *An Affair of State* of the public statements made by Dworkin and other public intellectuals concerning the impeachment. The other is entitled "Posner's Charges: What I Actually Said" and responds to what Dworkin claims are mischaracterizations of his views in *Problematics*. I replied to it in Richard A. Posner, "Dworkin, Polemics, and the Clinton Impeachment Controversy," 94 *Northwestern University Law Review* 1023, 1041–1047 (2000).

My response to Dworkin's review of *An Affair of State* provoked a long reply by him. The response and the reply were published together as "'An Affair of State': An Exchange," *New York Review of Books*, April 27, 2000, p. 60. I cite Dworkin's part of the exchange as "Dworkin Replies."

47. Maimon Schwarzschild, Book Review, 108 *Ethics* 597, 599 (1998), reviewing Ronald Dworkin, *Freedom's Law: The Moral Reading of the American Constitution* (1996).

available to academic public intellectuals: careful scholarship in work addressed to peers; reckless abandon in writing for the general public.

Dworkin's style of being a public intellectual is by no means the only one encountered in the legal profession. Alan Dershowitz's (see Chapter 3) is very different. Bruce Ackerman furnishes a particularly instructive contrast to Dworkin, since he too is a prominent law professor who is also both a political theorist and a public intellectual. Dworkin's dominant bent as a public intellectual is to polemicize in favor of a standard menu of left-liberal policies, such as judicial activism, and political positions, such as defense *à outrance* of President Clinton, by attacking the judicial and academic opponents of these policies and positions. Ackerman, though also a left-liberal and Clintonite—Clinton himself, oddly, was not a left-liberal—and an occasional, indeed rather frequent, polemicist,[48] is, in his public-intellectual work, primarily a policy Mr. Fix-It, churning out a stream of ingenious solutions for a variety of policy dilemmas. He has made proposals for a voucher system of financing of political campaigns, for limiting impeachment by lame-duck Congresses, for giving every American $80,000 when he reaches the age of eighteen, and for empowering Congress and the president to amend the Constitution without complying with the procedures for amendment set forth in Article V, heretofore assumed to be the exclusive method of constitutional amendment.[49] To take up each of these proposals would deform this book. And, as we know, the form of public-intellectual work that consists of trying to interest a wider audience

48. But the qualification in "primarily" should not be overlooked. Ackerman was active in the defense of Clinton against impeachment. See, for example, Bruce Ackerman, "This Lame-Duck Impeachment Should Die," *Washington Post*, Dec. 24, 1998, p. A17 (later expanded into the book on impeachment cited in the next footnote), and "What Ken Starr Neglected to Tell Us," *New York Times* (national ed.), Sept. 14, 1998, p. A33. His testimony before the House Judiciary Committee on December 8, 1998, was hyperbolic, as when he said that "if the Committee [not the House of Representatives, but just the House Judiciary Committee] does find President Clinton's conduct impeachable, [it] will be setting a precedent that will haunt this country for generations to come." More recently, Ackerman was active in the 2000 presidential election controversy, as we saw in Chapter 3, and as I discuss at further length in my book *Breaking the Deadlock: The 2000 Election, the Constitution, and the Courts*, ch. 4 (2001).

49. See, for example, Bruce Ackerman, "Reforming Campaign Reform," *Wall Street Journal*, April 26, 1993, p. A12; *The Case against Lameduck Impeachment* (1999); *The Stakeholder Society* (1999) (with Anne Alstott); *We the People*, vol. 1: *Foundations* (1991), vol. 2: *Transformations* (1998).

in specific policy proposals worked out in the academy is less problematic than most forms of public-intellectual work.

Some of Ackerman's public interventions are not public-intellectual work at all, as when he joined with other professors of constitutional law in an open letter to the then Speaker of the House Newt Gingrich on December 23, 1994, opposing on rather technical constitutional grounds a proposal to amend the rules of the House to require a three-fifths vote to enact any law increasing income taxes. This was specialist's work, in contrast to such pronouncements of his as, "in Poland, Czechoslovakia and Russia, the revolutionaries have focused on economics: first create a market economy and worry about constitutionalism later. This is a mistake. It will take decades to create a functioning market system, during which revolutionary leaders inevitably dissipate their popular authority."[50] Here Ackerman becomes a public-intellectual prophet—and, unsurprisingly, makes a bad prediction. Within a few years Poland and the Czech Republic had well-functioning market systems and Russia's market system was at last beginning to function. Ackerman was being unduly alarmist, as he was later to be in commenting on Clinton's impeachment.

⌒ DURING THE RUN up to the impeachment Dworkin had signed a full-page advertisement in the *New York Times* urging that President Clinton not be impeached and describing the impeachment of a president as a "constitutional nuclear weapon" that "should not be used unless it is absolutely necessary to save the Constitution from an even graver injury."[51] The full-page advertisement, I suggested in Chapter 3, is a questionable venue for public-intellectual work and this one was no exception. Although it was a premise of Clinton's defenders that Nixon had committed impeachable offenses—they were not going to defend Clinton if the price was rehabilitating Nixon—it is unclear

50. Bruce A. Ackerman, "1787 and 1993," *New York Times*, April 3, 1993 (late ed.), p. 23. See also his book *The Future of Liberal Revolution* (1992), urging the newly ex-communist nations to adopt written constitutions on the model of the U.S. Constitution. The open letter (of which Ackerman was one of the signatories) to the Florida legislature that I discussed in Chapter 3, although couched in technical legal terms, counts as public-intellectual work because of the haste with which it must have been composed and its failure to discuss the most serious objections to its position.

51. "An Appeal to the U.S. Congress and the Public," *New York Times*, Oct. 7, 1998, p. A13.

that even his offenses had reached the level at which a nuclear strike would have been justified. The advertisement claimed that while Nixon "had unconstitutionally used the pretext of national security to try to cover up criminal acts against political opponents," Clinton had merely "lied in order to hide private consensual sexual acts." But Clinton had lied under oath and engaged in related acts of obstruction of justice, in violation of his constitutional duty to take care that the laws be faithfully executed. Nixon was forced from office not because it was widely believed that, even though his wrongdoing had been exposed and his associates packed off to jail, he could and would still do serious harm to constitutional government, but because people were outraged by his conduct—and he had not been very popular to begin with, and the economy was in trouble.

The advertisement went on to argue that the nation could not afford to allow "the American presidency to twist in the wind, injured and humiliated." By a historical irony, that is an apt description of what might have happened two years later had Dworkin (and no doubt most of the other signatories of the advertisement) gotten his way and the 2000 presidential election remained deadlocked indefinitely, without the saving intervention of the U.S. Supreme Court.[52]

The advertisement recommended that Clinton be censured by Congress "for his actions" and it remarked approvingly on his having "now apologized on several occasions." All he had apologized for, however, was "inappropriate" sexual contact, which in itself was no business of the public, and misleading people, which politicians do all the time— which is a venial sin in them and, as Weber reminds us, sometimes a virtue. Such apologies would not have been a proper foundation for censure. To lay such a foundation Congress would have had to conduct an investigation, accept the Starr Report *in toto*, or censure Clinton for actions not grave enough to warrant censure. As grudging an apology as Clinton was willing to make could, moreover, have been extracted from Nixon, who was left twisting in the wind for a year as the impeachment inquiry proceeded. Not until January 19, 2001, the day before he left office, did Clinton acknowledge having made false statements under oath.

52. See Ronald Dworkin, "A Badly Flawed Election," *New York Review of Books*, Jan. 11, 2001, p. 53.

The advertisement said that censuring Clinton would be "a historic act of punishment." If so, Clinton would be injured and humiliated, which earlier the advertisement had said must not be allowed. So here was another contradiction, and another mistake: censure of President Clinton would not have been an historic act of punishment, since Andrew Jackson had been censured by Congress only to have the censure rescinded a few years later when his party took control of Congress, and it was soon forgotten. The advertisement did not mention the possibility that legislative censure of the president would be a bill of attainder and therefore unconstitutional.

After the House of Representatives impeached Clinton, Dworkin published a short article in which he said: "We must cultivate a long memory."[53] He meant that we must be sure to remember in the election year 2000 the awful thing the House had done, at which time

> we must encourage and support opponents who denounce them [the congressmen who voted to impeach the president] for what they have done, in any way we can, including financially. The zealots will have stained the Constitution [if they succeed in forcing Clinton from office], and we must do everything in our power to make the shame theirs and not the nation's.

The call to arms was rhetorical, since the "we" whom Dworkin was summoning, the readers of the *New York Review of Books,* are for the most part left-liberals who need no encouragement to oppose Republicans. And it was odd to find a campaign-finance solicitation ("including financially") in an intellectual magazine, especially in an article written by someone who wants to limit the private financing of elections,[54] though if pressed on this point Dworkin might respond, fairly enough, that he is not an advocate of unilateral disarmament.

According to the article, the impeachment of Clinton showed that "a partisan group in the House, on a party-line vote, can annihilate the separation of powers." But the power to impeach, a power that can in-

53. Ronald Dworkin, "A Kind of Coup," *New York Review of Books,* Jan. 14, 1999, p. 61. The article is an amplified version of the talk he had given at the "Rally against Impeachment" (see Chapter 3) the month before.
54. See Ronald Dworkin, *Sovereign Virtue: The Theory and Practice of Equality,* ch. 10 (2000).

deed be wielded by the party that controls the House, is part of the separation (more precisely the balance) of powers ordained by the Constitution. And a partisan group, such as the House Democrats, could force the impeachment decision to be made on a party-line basis simply by deciding to vote against impeachment en bloc regardless of the merits. Dworkin said that the House ignored "the most fundamental provisions of due process and fair procedure." He did not explain what additional process the House could have provided that would have altered the outcome without unduly protracting the impeachment inquiry, something the Democrats claimed not to want.

He warned that an impeachment trial in the Senate "would frighten markets." Nothing in Dworkin's previous writings had suggested a concern with stock market fluctuations, and it was also surprising, given his general outlook, that he should defend, as he also did in the article, the cruise-missile attack on Iraq without so much as alluding to the possibility that the timing might have been influenced by the president's desperate desire to head off impeachment. As is so often true of public intellectuals' predictions, Dworkin's prediction that the stock market would be perturbed by impeachment of Clinton was soon falsified. On the day on which the effort to finesse the trial collapsed (January 6, 1999), the stock market reached its all-time high (up to then), and it remained at or near that level throughout Clinton's Senate trial.

Recurring to the theme of the *Times* advertisement, Dworkin argued that because an impeachment trial "is a seismic shock to the separation of powers," it must be reserved for cases in which "there is a constitutional or public danger in leaving a president in office." This principle, consistently applied, might have let Nixon off the hook, since, as I have noted, the exposure of his criminal activities and the prosecution of his principal henchmen may well have eliminated any danger that he would continue these activities in the rump of his term. Dworkin added that the place to deal with Clinton's crimes is in a regular court of law after Clinton leaves office. (That was before the impeachment; after the Senate acquitted Clinton, Dworkin expressed dismay at the prospect that Clinton might be prosecuted in the ordinary way, while at the same time implicitly denying the existence of any exculpatory evidence that the Starr Report might have overlooked ["Dworkin Replies" 62 and n. 4].) He did not discuss the feasibility of such a prosecution or the cloud that the pardon power places over it.

He acknowledged that a president who committed murder could not be allowed to remain in office, but added that "a congressman who thinks that lying to hide a sexual embarrassment, even under oath, is on the same moral scale as murder—that it shows comparable wickedness or depravity—has no moral capacity himself." No one had argued that the president's crimes were as serious as murder. That murder would be sufficient grounds for impeachment and conviction does not imply that no lesser crime would be. Should a president who raped women, or molested children, be permitted to remain in office? If not, how could obstruction of justice be ruled out as a possible ground for removal without an assessment of the full extent of Clinton's criminal conduct?

Dworkin called the impeachment of Clinton a "kind of coup" because the conviction of the president would remove from office "the only official in the nation who has been elected by all the people." That was an illuminating error,[55] as well as a good illustration of the hyperbole that permeated the public debate over the impeachment and indeed that is characteristic of public-intellectual expression generally. The impeachment is the accusation, not the conviction; it does not remove the impeached official from office. And since the vice president is also elected by all the people, a president who is removed from office is succeeded not by any of the putschists but by a nationally elected member of his own party, his designated successor; and in this case the president would have been succeeded by his handpicked successor, his ostentatiously loyal paladin.[56]

Dworkin returned to the fray after the president's acquittal by the Senate.[57] Referring to the fact that the Constitution makes "bribery" an

55. There is further hyperbole in the expression "elected by all the people." President Clinton was elected by a minority of the minority of American adults who bothered to vote in the two elections in which he ran for president. Of course one knows what Dworkin means. But one might have expected more precision and less polemic from a law professor of Dworkin's eminence.

56. Dworkin's point would have had greater force had the office of vice president been vacant (in which event the Republican speaker of the house would have become president if Clinton had been removed from office), had the vice president been appointed rather than elected (like Vice Presidents Ford and Rockefeller), or had the vice president belonged to a different faction of the Democratic Party or, as is not impossible, to a different party. Andrew Johnson was a Democrat running with Republican Abraham Lincoln in 1864 on the "Unionist" ticket.

57. Ronald Dworkin, "The Wounded Constitution," *New York Review of Books*, March 18, 1999, p. 8.

explicit ground for impeachment and that bribery is generally not punished more severely than perjury, he said that "a bribe [unlike Clinton's
conduct] induces an official to act against the national interest." But
this depends on whether the bribe is to do an official act or a purely private act. Dworkin also said that Clinton "can still be indicted and prosecuted when he leaves office," again ignoring the significance of the
presidential pardon power.[58] Dworkin added that "Starr's behavior in
this case would presumably have led to charges being dismissed in an
ordinary criminal case," which is incorrect (*Affair of State*, ch. 2), and
that Judge Susan Webber Wright "had ruled the [president's] deposition [in the Paula Jones case] immaterial," which is also incorrect (id. at
50–51).

Although Dworkin is constantly urging the injection of this or that
moral principle into our public policy and thinks there is too much
pragmatism and too little morality in our law, he had nothing to say
about the lack of moral principle demonstrated by President Clinton in
his struggle to escape from the legal flypaper on which he had landed,
beyond that the president was guilty of "lying to hide a sexual embarrassment."[59] There was no mention of subornation of perjury and witness tampering, or that much of the lying was under oath and continued after the sexual embarrassment could no longer be concealed.[60]

Replying to some of these criticisms in "The Mistakes Were
Posner's,"[61] Dworkin asserts that "congressional censure is not a bill of
attainder if Congress imposes no fine or other punishment beyond a
statement of its opinion." His only support for this too-flat statement is
my description of the question as an open one (*Affair of State* 190–191).
He points out that a practice of impeaching presidents on purely politi-

58. Whether the president can pardon himself has never been authoritatively determined.
Affair of State 107–108 argues that he probably can.

59. Dworkin, note 53 above.

60. The House Democrats were more forthright about Clinton's misconduct. The censure
resolution that they introduced in the House Judiciary Committee as an alternative to impeachment acknowledged that the president had "egregiously failed in th[e] obligation" to
"set an example of high moral standards and conduct himself in a manner that fosters respect
for the truth," had "violated the trust of the American people, lessened their esteem for the
office of President, and dishonored the office which they ha[d] entrusted to him," had "made
false statements concerning his reprehensible conduct with a subordinate," and had taken
"steps to delay discovery of the truth." *Affair of State* 240.

61. Note 46 above.

cal grounds ("political impeachment") would push the nation toward a parliamentary form of government, which is one of concentrated rather than separated powers, but he erroneously conflates impeachment by a party-line vote with political impeachment. The vote of a House controlled by one party to impeach a president from the other party on *nonpolitical* grounds might be made along party lines simply because all the members of the president's party had decided *for purely political reasons* to vote against impeachment. Suppose the Republicans senators had decided in 1974 to vote en bloc against the impeachment of Nixon, not because they thought him innocent of impeachable conduct but because they thought that impeaching him would harm the Republican Party. That would not have made impeaching Nixon, necessarily by a party-line vote, "political impeachment" in the deservedly pejorative sense of that term.

Dworkin deems correction of his oversight to mention that the vice president is an elected official "pedantic," since the vice president is not elected separately and has little power, and since people are not indifferent to whether the person they elected as president or the person they elected as vice president becomes president. All true. But to make the analogy of impeachment to a *coup d'état* more plausible, Dworkin had depicted the vice president as a nonelected official, since it is the rare coup that installs the duly elected successor to the leader deposed in the coup.

"Mistakes" discusses whether prosecutorial leaks of matters before a grand jury might prevent a person indicted by the grand jury from being convicted. They might, though only if they made it impossible to impanel an impartial trial jury. More to the point, when a person commits perjury in testifying before the grand jury itself the secrecy of the grand jury proceedings is necessarily compromised. The transcript of the perjurer's testimony before the grand jury will be the principal evidence at his trial, and with immaterial exceptions trials are public.

Dworkin's review of *An Affair of State* charged me with a violation of judicial ethics in writing about matters that might end up in court, and attributed to me extreme views on such matters as baby selling and infanticide. The charge and the attributions were false, but this is not the place to answer them.[62] They have a twofold significance in the present

---

62. See Posner, "Dworkin, Polemics, and the Clinton Impeachment Controversy," note

context. First, as with the fierce squabble among Nussbaum, Finnis, and George, neither Dworkin nor I have paid any price for our nastly little spat, though a disapproving clucking of tongues is faintly audible in some academic circles. Public intellectuals get away with a lot; that is an aspect of their (of our) striking lack of accountability.

Second, Dworkin's polemic against me recalls his attack on Robert Bork when Bork was nominated for the Supreme Court,[63] an attack Dworkin thought well enough of to republish many years after the threat of Bork's becoming a Supreme Court justice had passed.[64] The attack helped to galvanize the opposition to Bork's confirmation that developed in the academic legal community, though how important that opposition was in his defeat is unclear.

Dworkin accused Bork of having "no constitutional philosophy at all" (p. 267). He said that "Bork's views do not lie within the scope of the longstanding debate between liberals and conservatives about the proper role of the Supreme Court. Bork is a constitutional radical who rejects a requirement of the rule of law that all sides in that debate had previously accepted" and who wishes to replace the constitutional tradition with "some radical political vision that legal argument can never touch" (p. 265). "His principles adjust themselves to the prejudices of the right" (p. 275). Dworkin ended the piece with the following rhetorical question: "Will the Senate allow the Supreme Court to become the fortress of a reactionary antilegal ideology with so meager and shabby an intellectual base?" (id.).

The most arresting item in this litany was the claim that Bork had "no constitutional philosophy at all." Dworkin now says that what he meant was that Bork's "various statements about constitutional adjudication defy generality or abstraction, and are deeply inconsistent."[65] That is the common coin of debate among constitutional theorists— accusing an adversary of having a conception of constitutional law that

---

46 above, at 1030–1035, where they are answered. See also Monroe H. Friedman, "Free Speech for Judges," *Court Review* (forthcoming 2001).

63. Ronald Dworkin, "The Bork Nomination," *New York Review of Books*, Aug. 13, 1987, p. 3.

64. Ronald Dworkin, "Bork: The Senate's Responsibility," in Dworkin, note 47 above, at 265.

65. Dworkin, "Posner's Charges: What I Actually Said," note 46 above.

is deficient in principle, ad hoc, inconsistent, "result oriented." Such charges have been leveled against Dworkin, as against other constitutional theorists. They are not denials that the opponent *has* a theory. In a prefatory note to his republished attacks on Bork, Dworkin says that "it [is] proper to inspect a prospective justice's constitutional philosophy to decide whether his appointment should be confirmed,"[66] implying that Bork does have a constitutional philosophy after all. That philosophy is originalism, and it is perfectly respectable, though neither Dworkin nor I agree with it. It is not a "radical, antilegal position" that seeks to replace the constitutional tradition with "some radical political vision that legal argument can never touch." Indeed, the real objection to Bork's constitutional philosophy is not that it is radical or antilegal, but that it is excessively legalistic and hopelessly old-fashioned.

Dworkin likes to describe his opponents as extremists, and so he describes *An Affair of State* as a partisan attack on Clinton, "drenched in moral indignation" (*NYRB* 48). Yet the book had struck the Clinton haters as tepid and equivocal. And although it "chastises academics and intellectuals who opposed impeachment" (id.), it also chastises the academics and intellectuals (such as Bork, William Bennett, and David Frum) who supported it; indeed, it was a stage in my disillusionment with public intellectuals of both the Left and the Right. Right-wing reviewers considered the book too easy on President Clinton and too hard on his tormenters.[67] They regretted that I was *not* writing for a "conservative claque" (*NYRB* 50) and that I had failed to "back . . . the Republican leadership on several key issues" (*NYRB* 48).

Dworkin quotes the following passage to prove partisanship:

[Clinton] committed repeated and various felonious obstructions of justice over a period of almost a year, which he garnished with gaudy public and private lies, vicious slanders, tactical blunders, gross errors of judgment, hypocritical displays of contrition, affronts to conventional morality and parental authority, and desecrations of revered national symbols. And all this occurred against

66. Dworkin, note 47 above, at 263.

67. David Tell, "Judging Clinton," *Weekly Standard*, Sept. 20, 1999, p. 34; Gary L. McDowell, "Lacking Conviction," *Times Literary Supplement*, Nov. 19, 1999, p. 28.

a background of persistent and troubling questions concerning the ethical tone of the Clinton Administration and Clinton's personal and political ethics. (*Affair of State* 173)

He has cropped the passage by omitting its introductory words, "On the one hand," and the sentence that follows and qualifies the words he did quote: "On the other hand, Clinton acted under considerable provocation—perhaps provocation so considerable that few people in comparable circumstances would not succumb—in stepping over the line that separates the concealment of embarrassing private conduct from obstruction of legal justice" (*Affair of State* 174).[68]

An Affair of State argues that the record compiled by the Independent Counsel fell short in a number of instances of establishing the president's guilt of criminal activity. By not mentioning these instances, Dworkin's review makes the book's treatment of the evidence look one sided, while by failing to discuss the full range of perjurious and otherwise obstructive criminal activity for which there *is* considerable evidence in the Starr Report and elsewhere the review depreciates the scope and gravity of the president's misconduct. This sets the stage for Dworkin's asserting the moral equivalence between that misconduct and the pratfalls and excesses of the president's attackers; he equivocates by calling their misconduct a "moral crime" (*NYRB* 50).

Dworkin dissolves the president's criminality in a cloud of technicalities, beginning with contrived doubt about the materiality of the questions about Lewinsky that President Clinton was asked when he was deposed in the Paula Jones case and ending with confusing the gravity of an offense with whether guilt of the offense is provable beyond a reasonable doubt. (If a person is charged with two felonious acts, and the first is less serious than the second, it doesn't follow that the prosecution would have more difficulty proving his guilt of the first one beyond a reasonable doubt.) A deposition is a search for evidence that

---

68. See also *Affair of State* 92, describing as perfectly legitimate the following characterization of the matter: "the confluence of a stupid law (the independent counsel law), a marginal lawsuit begotten and nursed by political partisanship, a naive and imprudent judicial decision by the Supreme Court in that suit, and the irresistible human impulse to conceal one's sexual improprieties, allow[ed] a trivial sexual escapade (what Clinton and Lewinsky called 'fooling around' or 'messing around') to balloon into a grotesque and gratuitous constitutional drama."

might be usable at trial. If the Jones case had been tried and if at the trial Clinton had denied ever having propositioned or had a sexual encounter with a subordinate, the transcript of *truthful* answers to the questions about Lewinsky at his deposition would have been usable on cross-examination to undermine his trial testimony. The judge presiding at a trial of Paula Jones's case might, it is true, forbid Jones's lawyers to cross-examine the president about other sexual incidents. But she might not and even if she did, the president's own lawyers might on direct examination elicit a denial of any other sexual incidents involving subordinates in order to bolster the credibility of his denial of Jones's charges. Against this possibility her lawyers were entitled to question him about such incidents at his deposition. No more is required to show the materiality of his untruthful answers.[69] If lying in a deposition were permissible unless the prosecution could show that the deponent would *for sure* have been asked the same questions at trial, the utility of depositions would be greatly diminished.

Dworkin says that lying about an extramarital affair would "not become material just because [the liar] would rather have settled the case than risked his marriage by telling the truth" (*NYRB* 49). This is true, but irrelevant, and not only because Clinton did not want to settle the case (he refused to do so until after the scandal broke), as he could have done without lying. He wanted the case dismissed and no doubt thought that telling the truth would reduce the likelihood of a dismissal. A lie that intentionally derails or delays a legal proceeding, sending the other participants on a wild-goose chase, is an obstruction of justice even if it is not material to any issue in the case. Dworkin says that the president's denials could not have derailed or delayed the Jones trial "because her lawyers already knew the truth from Linda Tripp" ("Dworkin Replies" 64). But the president and his defenders were calling Tripp and Lewinsky liars. Given those denials, the lawyers could not have invoked the Lewinsky affair in the Jones litigation without further investigation, which would have taken time.

Dworkin's depreciation of the gravity of the president's lies, which goes so far as to question whether asking someone to lie under oath is a crime unless coercion or deception is used to elicit the lying testi-

---

69. See, for example, United States v. Kross, 14 F.3d 751, 755 (2d Cir. 1994); United States v. Adams, 870 F.2d 1140, 1147 (6th Cir. 1989).

mony,[70] invites comparison to his indignation at attempts to depreciate the gravity of the alleged perjury of Clarence Thomas at Thomas's confirmation hearing.[71] This brings to mind Paul Hollander's point that "intellectuals, like most other people, use double standards and . . . the direction of their moral indignation and compassion is set and guided by their ideologies and partisan commitments."[72] There are valid grounds for refusing to answer questions, such as the privilege against being compelled to incriminate oneself and lack of materiality. In most proceedings a question about a deponent's sex life would be immaterial. But when sexual harassment is charged, such questions often become material. Dworkin has not explained why it was right to quiz Clarence Thomas about sex but not Bill Clinton. Anyway Clinton did not refuse to answer the questions put to him; he answered them falsely.

∼ A SENSITIVE OBSERVER of the contemporary public-intellectual scene has offered the following definition of the public intellectual's proper social role, one that resonates with much of the argument in this book: "it is the public intellectual's job to be the bearer of bad tidings—not cynicism—but difficult truths that cut across lines of political affiliation and enthusiasm, that may put us at odds with those we would much rather be lined up in harmony with, and that may, from time to time, give ammunition to those we would much prefer to see disarmed."[73] What is striking in the present context is how remote this definition is from the lawyer's self-conception—how unfitted therefore most lawyers, even brilliant academic lawyers, are to play well the public-intellectual role.

70. Asking someone to lie under oath *is* the crime of subornation of perjury. Only ignorance of the existence of the federal statute that criminalizes subornation of perjury (18 U.S.C. § 1622, cited in *Affair of State* 43 n. 46) can explain Dworkin's statement that "it is not clear that Clinton would have been guilty of a crime even if Lewinsky's testimony was material and he had explicitly asked her to lie" (*NYRB* 50).

71. See Ronald Dworkin, "Anita Hill and Clarence Thomas," in Dworkin, note 47 above, at 320, 327–328.

72. Paul Hollander, *Political Pilgrims: Travels of Western Intellectuals to the Soviet Union, China, and Cuba 1928–1978* 7 (1981).

73. Jean Bethke Elshtain, "Comments on the Public Intellectual for Celebration of 50th Anniversary of Basic Books" 11–12 (University of Chicago Dept. of Theology, Nov. 2, 2000, unpublished).

Conclusion:
Improving the Market

$\mathcal{T}$HIS BOOK has been critical of the modern academic public intellectual, and it is appropriate therefore that it should end with a stab at making some constructive suggestions. But the critical aspect of the book must not be exaggerated. I have been less interested in criticizing public intellectuals than in showing—through definition and description, the application of social scientific theory, and the use of statistics—that the public intellectual can be studied in a systematic and fruitful fashion. The demographic characteristics of public intellectuals, such as race, political leaning, institutional affiliation, and field, can be analyzed; the genres of public-intellectual work mapped; a market in public-intellectual work demarcated; the constraints and incentives that determine the operation of the market traced; and trends in the market identified, notably the trend toward the ever-increasing domination of the public-intellectual scene by academics.

But the careful study of a market includes alertness to symptoms of "market failure," and these my study has discovered in plenty.[1] I have not proved that the market for public intellectuals is failing to deliver a product of high average quality, and the qualification implicit in "aver-

1. The reader should bear in mind, however, the special, nontechnical sense in which I am using the term "market failure." See Chapter 4.

age" is worth stressing. But I have presented a fair amount of evidence that it is. Anecdotage is not proof. But we have seen that there are good economic reasons for expecting this market to perform badly and statistical evidence that it *is* performing badly compared to other markets in symbolic goods, particularly the academic market. The theory and the statistics buttress the anecdotes; the trio of proofs is convincing. Public-intellectual work, insofar as it seeks to shape public opinion rather than merely to entertain the educated public or to create solidarity among fractions of like-thinking members of that public, is a classic "credence" good, a good the consumer must take largely on faith because he cannot inspect it to determine its quality. The growth in specialization of knowledge has made it extremely difficult for even highly educated people to evaluate the claims made by public intellectuals. The fact that most public intellectuals today are academics, and thus engaged in public-intellectual work on only a part-time basis, enables them to exit the public-intellectual market at low cost and by doing so has reduced to a trivial level the penalty for the public intellectual caught selling a defective product. Absent, then, from this market are the conditions (such as an informed consuming public or expert consumer intermediaries, legally enforceable warranties of product quality, and high costs of exit for sellers detected selling products of poor quality) that discipline other markets in credence goods. The public protects itself against the high variance and low average quality of public-intellectual work mostly by not taking it very seriously.

The chief culprit in the quality problems of the public-intellectual market is the modern university. Its rise has encouraged a professionalization and specialization of knowledge that, together with the comfortable career that the university offers to people of outstanding intellectual ability, have shrunk the ranks of the "independent" intellectual. That is the intellectual who, being unaffiliated with a university (or, today, a think tank)—an outsider to the academic community—can range broadly over matters of public concern unconstrained by the specialist's attitude that a university career breeds. The independent intellectual occupies a distinctive niche as gadfly and counterpuncher. This niche is likely to go unfilled as more and more public intellectuals opt for the safe and secure life of a university professor. At the same time, by fragmenting the educated public into slivers of specialists (people who know a lot, but only about a few subjects) and destroying a common intellectual culture, the university-induced specialization of knowledge has made the audience for public-intellectual work undiscriminating. Neither the public intellectual's academic peers, nor the audience for his public-intellectual work, disciplines his output. The media through which the public intellectual reaches his audience perform virtually no gatekeeping function. The academic whose errors of fact, insight, and prediction in the public-intellectual market are eventually detected can, as I have emphasized, abandon the market, returning to full-time academic work, at slight cost.

There has been no diminution in the *number* of public intellectuals. The demand for and supply of them remain robust. But the demand is now to be filled by academics. The academic who plays the public-intellectual role finds himself in a market that is barren of the ordinary constraints and incentives of the university world, or for that matter of the academically despised, but highly competitive, worlds of popular culture and journalistic reportage. Having slipped his moorings, the cautious academic specialist throws caution to the winds. He is on holiday from the academic grind and all too often displays the irresponsibility of the holiday goer.

What can be done to improve the performance of this market? That question occupies the balance of this Conclusion. The question may seem impertinent, since, as we saw in Chapter 4, the public-intellectual market does not appear to exhibit, at least to any marked degree, "market failure" in the economic sense. But a market can be efficient yet improvable. To think otherwise would be to suppose that every potential profit in a market economy has already been realized. Clearly, though, the shortcomings of the public-intellectual market do not warrant costly methods of correction. (In particular they would not warrant government regulation even if the First Amendment permitted it.) Therefore I discuss only cheap methods. I do not wish to exaggerate their efficacy or express optimism, which would be unwarranted, that any of them is likely to be adopted. In the main we shall have to live with this slightly disreputable market. But what else is new? We *Feinschmeckers* have to live with vulgarity in popular culture, the sight of overweight middle-aged men wearing shorts and baseball caps, weak coffee, and the blare of the television set in every airport waiting lounge. It is doubtful that the public-intellectual market is a more debilitating or less intractable feature of contemporary American culture than these other affronts to the fastidious.

But fatalism is un-American, so I press on. Since the problem with the public-intellectual market is lack of accountability (nobody watching, nobody keeping score), one solution might be for universities to require their faculty members to post annually, on the university's Web page, all the nonacademic writing, in whatever form or medium published, and public speaking that they have done during the preceding year, other than books, articles, and other readily accessible work, which would only have to be cited. The posting would thus include tapes or transcripts of public intellectuals' radio or television appearances and transcripts of any testimony they had given. At the end of the year the contents of the Web page would be downloaded and printed out, and copies deposited in the major university libraries.[2] The ready accessibility of these postings and archived hard copies would make it much easier to monitor the public-intellectual output of academics than is the case at present. Recall the discussion in the last chapter of public-intellectual witnesses in the Colorado homosexuality case: the only publicly available copy of the court record that includes their testimony and affidavits is in a courthouse in Colorado.[3] And try finding all the full-page advertisements, open letters, and congressional testimony in which public intellectuals debated Clinton's impeachment, or all the interviews that Paul Ehrlich gave to popular magazines decades ago predicting imminent Malthusian catastrophes, or all the television appearances of Alan Dershowitz during the investigation and impeachment of President Clinton, or all the *pronunciamentos* of public intellectuals on the 2000 presidential election deadlock.

The existence of easily retrieved and inspected records of public-intellectual activities would be a deterrent to irresponsible interventions by academics in public controversies. It would resemble the mode of control that trial lawyers and judges exert over "professional" expert witnesses, such as engineers, physicians, and economists, who testify repeatedly. Their testimony is a matter of public record, just like other testimony, but it is far more accessible to the trial bar and the judiciary than the testimony of a public intellectual is to someone who merely wants to keep track of what our academic public intellectuals are saying

2. This is essential, because of the instability of the Web, as of electronic data storage generally. One is never sure how long it will remain in cyberspace in accessible, or any, form.

3. The clerk of the court was happy to make a copy for me, but had trouble finding the relevant part of the record. One of my research assistants happened to be in Denver, visited the courthouse, and found it.

in their occasional ventures into the courtroom. Any inconsistency or serious mistake in the testimony of a frequent expert witness is bound to be discovered and thrown at him the next time he testifies. If there are any public intellectuals who testify frequently (I don't know of any), they are subject to the same sort of control, but, at present, only in the courtroom. Their testimony cannot be tracked by their academic colleagues unless it is made available to them in a convenient format, such as a university Web site, which is not done at present.

My proposal may be modest, but it is also bound to be controversial and I hold out no hope that it will be adopted. Academics will denounce it as "McCarthyite" because it could be seen as proposing that academics be made to account for their political activities to their employer. That is not my intention but I do not see how as a practical matter such an interpretation could be prevented. An alternative that would be less objectionable and might be equally effective would be for academics *voluntarily* to post their public-intellectual work on either their university's Web page or their own, readily accessible Web page. One might hope that this practice would emerge as a norm, so that eventually any academic who failed to follow the practice would be subject to the criticism of his peers. Such a practice would go some way toward reining in the more egregious public interventions by academics that I have chronicled in this book, although it is subject to the usual criticisms of Web publication: the medium is unstable, the postings possibly fugitive. That problem would be solved if some university undertook to make its library the depository for public-intellectual Web postings, downloading them periodically and archiving the downloaded materials in hard-copy as well as electronic form.

Such a norm *could* someday emerge, especially since more and more academics are posting more and more of their ephemera, including public-intellectual work, on their Web pages. Suppose a handful of prominent academics adopted the practice of posting their public-intellectual work. This would place pressure on others to do likewise in order to signal their possession of high standards and to avoid suspicion that they had something disreputable to hide. The more academics who adopted the practice, the greater would be the pressure on the others to do likewise to avoid the imputation that they had low standards or had something to hide. Eventually all might comply with the posting norm just as all students authorize their schools to release their transcripts to prospective employers. In game-theoretic terms, there may be no equilibrium in which some academics post their public-intellectual work and others do not, because of the negative inference that would be drawn from the reticence of the latter about their ethical standards.

I realize that full compliance with the suggested norm might be thwarted by the difficulty of delimiting its scope precisely. "Public intellectual," and therefore "public-intellectual work," are not easily defined, as we know from Chapter 1. That is the substantive ambiguity in the suggested norm. But there is also procedural ambiguity. Published work—including interviews, letters to the editors, open letters, full-page advertisements, radio and television appearances that are recorded or transcribed, and testimony before courts, legislatures, and administrative agencies—can readily and appropriately be retrieved and posted, while published books and articles, being easily retrievable, need only be cited, as I have said. But what about a lecture not intended for publication? Must the lecturer make an effort to have it recorded so that it can be posted on his Web site? I think not. Even if it is a public lecture in the technical sense of being delivered in a forum open to the public, it may not be public in the same way that a published work is. The lecturer may be trying out ideas that he is not yet sure he wants to stand by, and may desire a limited circulation of these tentative thoughts. His desire to limit his audience and thus enjoy a measure of creative privacy (see Chapter 7) should be respected. It is when a public intellectual "goes public" in a broader sense, by expressing himself through media of indefinite reach, that he should be willing to preserve his words in a form in which they can be readily retrieved for purposes of critical scrutiny.

Another norm that one would like to see emerge in the public-intellectual arena would be a norm against magazines' commissioning or accepting book reviews written by persons criticized in the book to be reviewed, at least without full disclosure in the review that the reviewer was criticized in the book. Readers bring expectations to a book review that they do not to an openly adversary piece. Still another salutary norm would be disclosure in open letters and full-page advertisements of the relevant expertise of each signer and a certification by the signer that he had acquainted himself with the facts pertinent to the position taken in the letter or advertisement.[4] These disclosures could be made available on a Web site if including them in the letter or advertisement itself would cause excessive clutter.

With trepidation I suggest still a further norm of disclosure: that academic public intellectuals disclose their income from all their public-intellectual work, including their books, articles, and lectures directed to a public audience and all their gigs as consultants and expert witnesses. Public officials are required to disclose both the sources and the amounts of their outside income in order to enable the public to monitor their honesty and application and their compliance with the rules against financial conflicts of interest. As a public official, I don't like this requirement. But it serves a useful purpose. It not only provides information that is pertinent to an evaluation of judicial incentives but also acts as a deterrent to improper and irresponsible moonlighting. It would have these twin effects with regard to academics as well, who sometimes are tempted by money into irresponsible moonlighting as public intellectuals. Revelation of the lucrative character of some of this moonlighting would help the public to evaluate public-intellectual work and would deter some of the most questionable forms of it.

Disclosure of the amount and sources of outside income may be more important in the case of public officials because they are more powerful than academics. (The academic public intellectual has little power, I have argued.) But that is a stronger argument for imposing a *legal* duty of disclosure on public officials and not on academics than it is for discouraging the emergence of a *norm* of disclosure by the latter as well. Another difference—that officials are supported by the taxpayer—is more apparent than real even with regard to faculty at private universities. Their faculty members are direct and indirect recipients of government largesse to private universities in the form of grants, contracts (with generous provision for university "overhead"), tax exemptions, and subsidized student loans. Private universities also receive tax-deductible donations from alumni and foundations and charge tuition. Elite universities are to a considerable extent, moreover, workers' cooperatives because of the dominant role of faculty in the governance of

4. A similar proposal is made independently in Ward Farnsworth, "Talking Out of School: Notes on the Transmission of Intellectual Capital from the Legal Academy to Public Tribunals," 81 *Boston University Law Review* 13, 41–57 (2001).

such universities; so the opportunities for faculty to rip off the university are great.

During the Cold War a number of public intellectuals wrote for the magazine *Encounter*, which unbeknownst to most of them was supported by the CIA. Some left-wing public intellectuals may have been on the payroll of the CIA's Soviet counterpart. Today a number of public intellectuals are either on the payroll of, or supported by research grants by, conservative think tanks that are supported by corporate contributions. One of these think tanks, the Independent Institute, supported research and publication favorable to Microsoft's defense against the government antitrust case while receiving financial support from Microsoft.[5] The institute persuaded 240 academics to sign a full-page advertisement in support of Microsoft's defense without disclosing to them, let alone to the public, that it was receiving financial support from Microsoft. A neat package: academics most of whom could not have been any better informed about the merits of the Microsoft antitrust case than the hundreds of historians and law professors who signed full-page advertisements concerning Clinton's impeachment could have been informed about that case; and an undisclosed financial conflict of interest by the sponsor.

Corporations sometimes offer academics money to write articles that the corporation hopes will advance its interests, and sometimes the article fails to disclose the subvention.[6] That is scandalous. Disclosure of all sources of a public intellectual's earned income would deter this "selling out" by public intellectuals.

Academics are pretty scrupulous about acknowledging in *academic* articles the sources of any financial assistance, but not the amount, even though the amount is relevant to a judgment as to whether the academic's views are likely to have been influenced by the money he received. After being hit with the largest jury award of punitive damages in history as a consequence of the oil spill by its tanker *Valdez*, Exxon funded academic research by law professors and economics professors

5. See Joel Brinkley, "Microsoft Covered Cost of Ads Backing It in Antitrust Suit," *New York Times* (late ed.), Sept. 18, 1999, p. A1.

6. "Nor is the credibility of the [economics] profession helped when, as has recently happened, a scholar's analysis about a public policy dispute is disseminated to the media, and only later disclosed as having been commissioned by a party to the dispute." Michael Weinstein, "Economists and the Media," *Journal of Economic Perspectives*, Summer 1992, pp. 73, 76.

on punitive damages that it then cited in its briefs on appeal without disclosing the fact that it had paid for the research.[7] The articles that the briefs cited disclosed the fact but not the amount of Exxon's payments, and when interviewed the professors declined to reveal the amount. One of them, an economics professor, said that he regarded the amount he had received as akin to a consulting fee. This implies that the amount was large, since academic economists are paid up to $1,000 an hour for their work in big cases and the professor in question, W. Kip Viscusi of the Harvard Law School, is very prominent. Academic work that is commissioned in the hope of influencing litigation is a form of public-intellectual work, and the public should be given the information that will enable it to judge whether the slant of the work is likely to have been influenced by the generosity of the commission.

Faculty who moonlight as public intellectuals—receiving large advances from publishers and large lecture, consulting, or expert-witness fees, traveling hither and yon for book signings and lecturing stints, teaching little and constantly rescheduling their classes to enable them to keep up their busy travel schedules—may be neglecting their university duties, engaging in conflicts of interest, and impairing their university's academic reputation by trading on their academic position to gain an audience for nonacademic utterances that may exceed the limits of their competence or even contradict their considered academic views. As the workers' co-op character of the modern private university discourages university administrations from efforts to discipline their wayward tenured professors, letting the sun shine on academic moonlighting might have salutary effects; at least we'd learn more about the modern public intellectual. Federal judges are now required to disclose not only their outside income but also their non-case-related travel for which they do not pay themselves. I expect that this new requirement will have a salutary effect on judicial globetrotting, which, however, is as nothing compared to the globetrotting of academic public intellectuals.

And while Florida Atlantic University's idea of training graduate students to be public intellectuals (see Chapter 1) strikes me as unpromis-

7. Elizabeth Amon, "Exxon Bankrolls Critics of Punitives," *National Law Journal*, May 17, 1999, p. A1.

ing, the phenomenon of the public intellectual deserves more attention from sociologists, economists, philosophers, and other students of intellectual and expressive activity than it has received. The existing literature on the public intellectual is heavily, to some extent nostalgically, tuned to the past—to the nineteenth-century Russian intelligentsia, the French intellectuals of the Dreyfus era, and the New York intellectuals of the 1920s through the 1960s. The dominant public intellectuals of the present day are the *academic* public intellectuals, and they have received much less scholarly attention. One might hope that as a matter of self-respect the university community could be persuaded to create and support a journal that would monitor the public-intellectual activities of academics and be widely distributed both within and outside the community. Academics who abuse the privileges that the modern academic career confers, by writing or speaking irresponsibly in the public arena, should be hauled before the bar of academic and public opinion.

A norm of retraction is too much to hope for. Alas—for it would be very nice to have a public-intellectual counterpart to the Catholic practice of confession; only it would have to be public rather than private. It would be nice if there were a *Journal of Retractions*, where public intellectuals would periodically review their predictions and other statements and report which ones had turned out to be true and which false.

None of these proposed norms is likely to emerge in the foreseeable future. Public intellectuals will resist them; the irresponsibility of public-intellectual work is one of the rewards of being a public intellectual. Universities are concerned to some extent with *paid* academic moonlighting, but not with unpaid,[8] and most public-intellectual *expressive* work by academics (that is, excluding consulting) is unpaid or meagerly paid or scholarly enough to count as part of the academic's research activity; that is certainly true of a book like Robert Putnam's *Bowling Alone*. There isn't enough public concern with the problem of quality to overcome the resistance of the public intellectuals themselves.

Still, the proposals outlined in this Conclusion may have at least a heuristic value. They underscore the basic problem of the public-intellectual market, which, to repeat one last time, is lack of accountability.

---

8. See, for example, Howard R. Bowen and Jack H. Schuster, *American Professors: A National Resource Imperiled* 254–260 (1986).

Intelligence and scrupulousness are not synonyms. Most academics are well above average in intelligence. But "intelligence" in the academic context means only the ability to perform the intellectual operations required by particular academic specialties. Intelligence is not a synonym for good sense, let alone for character. A talent for mathematics or economics does not imply a talent for government or politics. The brilliant "defense intellectuals," such as Robert McNamara, McGeorge Bundy, William Bundy, Walt Rostow, and Daniel Ellsberg, had less insight into the conduct and prospects of our war in Vietnam than journalists such as Bernard Fall, David Halberstam, and Neil Sheehan, indifferently educated junior army officers such as John Paul Vann, and politicians such as Mike Mansfield and Richard Russell.

When academics operate outside their areas of specialization, and particularly when they write for the general public about issues of or fraught with politics or ideology, they operate without guidance from their training and experience and without the constraints imposed on academic work by the norms of the university community. In the public-intellectual arena, they operate without *any* significant constraints; there is nothing to call them to account. I have sketched some modest possibilities for injecting a modicum of accountability into this market. But my hopes for this book will be amply fulfilled if it merely stimulates a wider recognition of the problematic state of the public intellectual in the United States today and encourages further study of an odd and interesting market.

Acknowledgments

Although most of this book is new, some has been published before in other forms. The last sections of Chapter 3 and 10 are based on my book *An Affair of State: The Investigation, Impeachment, and Trial of President Clinton*, chs. 6 and 7 (1999), and Chapter 10 also draws in part on my share of a debate with Ronald Dworkin, published under the title "'An Affair of State': An Exchange," *New York Review of Books*, April 27, 2000, p. 60, and republished with significant additions as "Dworkin, Polemics, and the Clinton Impeachment Controversy," 94 *Northwestern University Law Review* 1023 (2000). Chapter 6 is based on my article "Against Ethical Criticism: Part Two," 22 *Philosophy and Literature* 394 (1998), and Chapter 7 on my article "Orwell versus Huxley: Economics, Technology, Privacy, and Satire," 24 *Philosophy and Literature* 1 (2000). A few pages of Chapter 8 borrow from "The Moral Minority," *New York Times Book Review*, Dec. 19, 1999, p. 14, my review of Gertrude Himmelfarb, *One Nation, Two Cultures* (1999). The other chapters are completely new; and those that have a provenance in my previously published work I have rewritten, as well as updated and augmented, for inclusion in this book.

I tried out some of my ideas about public intellectuals in a talk that I gave at the Center for the Humanities of City University of New York on May 5, 2000. I thank Lawrence Lessig, Martha Nussbaum, Richard Rorty, and Cass Sunstein for their helpful comments on an early draft of that talk and Vincent Bissonnette, Morris Dickstein, and William Kelly for helpful comments on the talk itself. I thank Paul Choi, Daniel Davis, Schan Duff, Ethan Fenn, Ryan Meyers, Dustin Palmer, and especially Ilisabeth Smith and Bryan Dayton, for their excellent research assistance; the Law and Economics Program of the University of Chicago Law School for generously defraying the expense of my research assistants and of the computer searches required for the empirical analysis reported in Chapter 5; Eric Posner for stimulating discussions of the topic; participants in the Workshop in Rational Models in the Social Sciences of the University of Chicago, where I presented an earlier version of Part One on October 3, 2000, for their helpful criticisms; Gary Becker, Peter Berkowitz, Stephen Breyer, Morris Dickstein, William Domnarski, Eldon Eisenach, Jean Elshtain, Joseph Epstein, Randall Kroszner, William Landes, Edward Laumann, Brian Leiter, Lawrence Lessig, Sanford Levinson, Edward Morrison, Martha Nussbaum, Charlene Posner, Eric Posner, Richard Rorty, Stephen Stigler, Cass Sunstein, and an anonymous reader for the Harvard University Press for many helpful comments; David Bemelmans for his careful copyediting; and Michael Aronson, Michael Boudin, and Stephen Holmes for invaluable criticisms and suggestions at critical stages of the project.

Index

Does not include references to any of the lists of public intellectuals, or other tables, in Chapter 5.

DATE DUE
